First World War
and Army of Occupation
War Diary
France, Belgium and Germany

40 DIVISION
120 Infantry Brigade
Headquarters
1 March 1918 - 28 February 1919

WO95/2610/1

The Naval & Military Press Ltd
www.nmarchive.com
Published in association with The National Archives

Published by

The Naval & Military Press Ltd

Unit 10 Ridgewood Industrial Park,

Uckfield, East Sussex,

TN22 5QE England

Tel: +44 (0) 1825 749494

www.naval-military-press.com

www.nmarchive.com

This diary has been reprinted in facsimile from the original. Any imperfections are inevitably reproduced and the quality may fall short of modern type and cartographic standards.

© Crown Copyright
Images reproduced by permission of The National Archives, London, England, 2015.

Contents

Document type	Place/Title	Date From	Date To
Heading	Bde Headquarters Mar 1918-Feb 1919		
Heading	B.H.Q. 120th Infantry Brigade. March 1918		
War Diary	Pommier In G.H.Q. Reserve.	01/03/1918	11/03/1918
War Diary	Hamelincourt (A.5.b.2.2.) In Close Reserve	12/03/1918	12/03/1918
War Diary	Hamelin-Court (In Close Reserve)	13/03/1918	27/03/1918
War Diary	Walruzel	28/03/1918	28/03/1918
War Diary	Magnicourt-En-Comte	29/03/1918	31/03/1918
War Diary	Fleurbaix	31/03/1918	31/03/1918
Miscellaneous	Minutes Of Conference Held At Brigade H.Qrs. March 1st 1918. Appx I	01/03/1918	01/03/1918
Operation(al) Order(s)	120th (Highland) Infantry Brigade Order No. 174 Appx II	05/03/1918	05/03/1918
Miscellaneous	Table "A" To Accompany 120th (Highland) Infantry Brigade Order No. 174 Dated 5:3:18.	05/03/1918	05/03/1918
Miscellaneous	Table "B" To Accompany 120th (Highland) Infantry Brigade Order No. 174 dated 5:2:18.	05/02/1918	05/02/1918
Miscellaneous	Entraining Instructions to Accompany 120th Infantry Brigade Order No. 174 dated 5th March 1918.	05/03/1918	05/03/1918
Miscellaneous			
Operation(al) Order(s)	120th (Highland) Infantry Brigade Order No. X Appx III	08/03/1918	08/03/1918
Operation(al) Order(s)	120th (Highland) Infantry Brigade Order No. Y	08/03/1918	08/03/1918
Miscellaneous	Instructions For 120th Brigade Scheme		
Map			
Miscellaneous	120th (Highland) Infantry Brigade Instruction No. 1 Appx IV	10/03/1918	10/03/1918
Miscellaneous	Table "A" To Accompany 120th Brigade Instruction Dated 10/3/18.	10/03/1918	10/03/1918
Miscellaneous	To Accompany 120th Bde. Instruction No 1 Table "B" (as for Table "A") Table "C" (i)	10/03/1918	10/03/1918
Miscellaneous	Table "D"		
Miscellaneous	Table "E"		
Miscellaneous	Reference 120th Infantry Brigade Instruction No. 1 dated 10th March 1918.	10/03/1918	10/03/1918
Operation(al) Order(s)	120th (Highland) Infantry Brigade Order No. 175 Appx V	11/03/1918	11/03/1918
Miscellaneous	March Table To Accompany 120th (Highland) Infantry Brigade Order No. 175.		
Miscellaneous	Administrative Instructions to Accompany 120th Infantry Brigade Order No. 175 dated 11th March 1918.	11/03/1918	11/03/1918
Operation(al) Order(s)	120th (Highland) Infantry Brigade Order No. 176. Appx VI	15/03/1918	15/03/1918
Miscellaneous	March Table To Accompany 120th (Highland) Infantry Brigade Order No. 176		
Miscellaneous	Entraining Instructions to Accompany 120th Infantry Brigade Order No. 176 dated 15th March 1918.	15/03/1918	15/03/1918
Miscellaneous	Addendum No. 1 to 120th (Highland) Infantry Brigade Instruction No. 1 Appx VII	10/03/1918	10/03/1918
Miscellaneous	Table "C" (i)		
Miscellaneous	Table "C" (ii)		

Miscellaneous	Table "C" (iii)		
Miscellaneous	Table "C" (iv)		
Miscellaneous	Table "D".		
Miscellaneous	Table "E".		
Operation(al) Order(s)	120th (Highland) Infantry Brigade Order No. 177. Appx VIII	20/03/1918	20/03/1918
Miscellaneous	Table To Accompany 120th (Highland) Infantry Brigade Order No. 177.		
Miscellaneous	120th (Highland) Infantry Brigade. Report On Operation from 21.3.18 to 27.3.18 Appx IX	06/04/1918	06/04/1918
Miscellaneous	120th (Highland) Infantry Brigade Points that came to notice during Operations 21:3:18-27:3:18.	06/04/1918	06/04/1918
Operation(al) Order(s)	120th (Highland) Infantry Brigade Order No. 184 Appx X	28/03/1918	28/03/1918
Miscellaneous	Table To Accompany 120th (Highland) Infantry Brigade Order No. 184		
Miscellaneous	Administrative Instructions to Accompany 120th Infantry Brigade Order No. 184 of 28th March.	28/03/1918	28/03/1918
Miscellaneous	Addendum No. 1 to Administrative Instructions.		
Operation(al) Order(s)	120th (Highland) Infantry Brigade Order No. 185. Appx XI	30/03/1918	30/03/1918
Operation(al) Order(s)	120th (Highland) Infantry Brigade Order No. 186. Appx XII	31/03/1918	31/03/1918
Miscellaneous			
Heading	B.H.Q. 120th Infantry Brigade. April 1918		
Heading	Cover for Documents. Nature of Enclosures. War Diary Hd. Qrs. 120th. (Highland) Infantry Brigade April 1918 Volume XXIII		
War Diary	Fleurbaix	01/04/1918	06/04/1918
War Diary	Le Nouveau Monde	07/04/1918	07/04/1918
War Diary	Le Nouveau Monde G.26.d.9.0.	07/04/1918	12/04/1918
War Diary	Strazeele	13/04/1918	13/04/1918
War Diary	Wemaers-Cappel	13/04/1918	14/04/1918
War Diary	Tatinghem	15/04/1918	21/04/1918
War Diary	Acquin	21/04/1918	30/04/1918
Miscellaneous	A Form. Messages And Signals. Appx Ia	01/04/1918	01/04/1918
Miscellaneous	A Form. Messages And Signals. Appx I	01/04/1918	01/04/1918
Miscellaneous	120th (Highland) Infantry Brigade Intelligence Summary Period from 8 a.m. 31st March to 1st April. Appx I (b)		
Miscellaneous	Messages And Signals. Appx II	02/04/1918	02/04/1918
Miscellaneous	A Form. Messages And Signals. Appx II (a)	02/04/1918	02/04/1918
Miscellaneous	120th (Highland) Infantry Brigade Intelligence Summary Period from 8 a.m. 1st April to 8 a.m. 2nd Appx II (b)		
Operation(al) Order(s)	120th (Highland) Infantry Brigade Order No. 187. Appx III	03/04/1918	03/04/1918
Miscellaneous	To All Recipients Of 120th (Highland) Infantry Brigade Order No. 187	03/04/1918	03/04/1918
Miscellaneous	To All Recipients Of 120th (Highland) Infantry Brigade Order No. 187		
Miscellaneous	A Form. Messages And Signals. Appx IV (a)	03/04/1918	03/04/1918
Miscellaneous	A Form. Messages And Signals. Appx IV	03/04/1918	03/04/1918
Miscellaneous	120th (Highland) Infantry Brigade Intelligence Summary. Period from 8 a.m. 2nd to 8 a.m. 3rd April Appx IV (b)		

Miscellaneous	A Form. Messages And Signals. Appx V	04/04/1918	04/04/1918
Miscellaneous	120th (Highland) Infantry Brigade Intelligence Summary, Period from 8 a.m. 3rd to 8 a.m. 4th April, 1918. Appx V (a)	04/04/1918	04/04/1918
Operation(al) Order(s)	120th (Highland) Infantry Brigade Order No. 188 Appx VI	05/04/1918	05/04/1918
Miscellaneous	Table To Accompany 120th (HD.) Infantry Brigade Order No. 188		
Miscellaneous	A Form. Messages And Signals. Appx VII	05/04/1918	05/04/1918
Miscellaneous	A Form. Messages And Signals. Appx VII (a)	05/04/1918	05/04/1918
Miscellaneous	120th (Highland) Infantry Brigade Intelligence Summary. Period from 8 a.m. 4th to 8 a.m. 5th April. Appx VII (b)		
Miscellaneous	A Form Messages And Signals. Appx VIII	06/04/1918	06/04/1918
Miscellaneous	A Form Messages And Signals. Appx VIII (a)	06/04/1918	06/04/1918
Miscellaneous	120th (Highland) Infantry Brigade Intelligence Summary, Period from 8 a.m. 5th to 8 a.m. 6th April. Appx VIII (b)		
Operation(al) Order(s)	120th (Scottish) Infantry Brigade Order No. 189. Appx IX	07/04/1918	07/04/1918
Miscellaneous	120th Infantry Brigade No. 120/415. Appx X	07/04/1918	07/04/1918
Miscellaneous	Defence Scheme Of Brigade In Divisional Reserve.	07/04/1918	07/04/1918
Miscellaneous	Report On Operations from 9:4:18 to 12:4:18. Appx XI		
Miscellaneous	Report on Operations Appendix No. 11. Precedes War Diary.		
Operation(al) Order(s)	120th (Scottish) Infantry Brigade Order No. 191 Appx XII	13/04/1918	13/04/1918
Operation(al) Order(s)	120th (Scottish) Infantry Brigade Order No. 192. Appx XIII	21/04/1918	21/04/1918
Miscellaneous	March Table To Accompany 120th (Scottish) Infantry Brigade Order No. 192.		
Operation(al) Order(s)	120th (Scottish) Infantry Brigade Order No. 193. Appx XIV	23/04/1918	23/04/1918
Operation(al) Order(s)	120th (Scottish) Infantry Brigade Order No. 194 Appx XV		
Heading	Cover for Documents. Nature of Enclosures. War Diary May 1918 (Volume XXIV) Headquarters, 120th Infantry Brigade.		
War Diary	Lumbres	01/05/1918	03/05/1918
War Diary	Serques	04/05/1918	09/05/1918
War Diary	Esquelbecq	10/05/1918	31/05/1918
Miscellaneous	120th (Highland) Infantry Brigade Order No. 195. Appx I	03/05/1918	03/05/1918
Miscellaneous	March Table To Accompany 120th (Hd) Inf. Bde. Order No. 195		
Operation(al) Order(s)	120th (Highland) Infantry Brigade Order No. 196. Appx II	08/05/1918	08/05/1918
Heading	Cover for Documents. Nature of Enclosures. War Diary Headquarters 120th Infantry Bde. June 1918 Volume XXV		
War Diary	Esquelbecq	01/06/1918	03/06/1918
War Diary	Rubrouck	04/06/1918	08/06/1918
War Diary	Lederzeele	10/06/1918	22/06/1918
War Diary	La Belle Hotesse C.21.d.O.3	23/06/1918	30/06/1918
Operation(al) Order(s)	120th Infantry Brigade Order No. 197 Appx I	15/06/1918	15/06/1918
Operation(al) Order(s)	120th Infantry Brigade Order No. 198. Appx II	18/06/1918	18/06/1918

Operation(al) Order(s)	Appendix "A" To 120th Infantry Brigade Order No. 198.		
Operation(al) Order(s)	Appendix "B" To 120th Infantry Brigade Order No. 198.		
Operation(al) Order(s)	Appendix "C" To 120th Infantry Brigade Order No. 198.		
Miscellaneous	Appendix "A" To 120th Infantry Brigade Order No. 198 Appx III	21/06/1918	21/06/1918
Miscellaneous	Notes For Conference To Be Held at 11.a.m. Tomorrow 21/6/18. Appx IV	21/06/1918	21/06/1918
Miscellaneous	120th Infantry Brigade Order No. 200. Appx V	22/06/1918	22/06/1918
Miscellaneous	Table To Accompany 120th Infantry Brigade Order No. 200		
Miscellaneous	Administrative Instructions-Move 23rd June 1918. To Accompany 120th Brigade Order No. 200.	22/06/1918	22/06/1918
Operation(al) Order(s)	120th Infantry Brigade Order No. 201. Appx VI		
Operation(al) Order(s)	Appendix "A" to 120th Infantry Brigade Order No. 201.		
Miscellaneous	Administrative Instructions-Occupation Of W. Hazebrouck Line.	26/06/1918	26/06/1918
Miscellaneous	Amendment No. 1 to Administrative Instructions-Occupation Of W. Hazebrouck Line.	28/06/1918	28/06/1918
Operation(al) Order(s)	120th Infantry Brigade Order No. 202. app VII	26/06/1918	26/06/1918
Operation(al) Order(s)	120th Infantry Brigade Order No. 203. Appx VIII	26/06/1918	26/06/1918
Heading	Cover for Documents. Nature of Enclosures. War Diary Headquarters 120th Inf. Bde. July 1918. Volume XXVI		
War Diary	La Belle Hotesse. C.21d.O.3.	01/07/1918	18/07/1918
War Diary	Sercus C.3.c.5.3.	19/07/1918	30/07/1918
Miscellaneous	120th Inf. Bde. No. 120/415. 10th Garr. Bn. K.O.S.B. Appx I	01/07/1918	01/07/1918
Miscellaneous	120th Inf. Bde. No. 120/474. 10th K.O.S.Bdrs Appx II	01/07/1918	01/07/1918
Miscellaneous	Brigade Routine Orders by Brigadier General C.J. Hobkirk., C.M.G., D.S.O., Commanding 120th Infantry Brigade. 2nd July 1918.	02/07/1918	02/07/1918
Miscellaneous	120th Infantry Brigade-Training Progress Report. Appx III	05/07/1918	05/07/1918
Miscellaneous	Appendix 'A' to 120th Infantry Brigade Order No. 201 Appx IV	08/07/1918	08/07/1918
Operation(al) Order(s)	120th Infantry Brigade Order No. 204. Appx V	08/07/1918	08/07/1918
Miscellaneous	Amendment To 120th Infantry Brigade Order No. 201 and Revised Appendix "A" Appx VI	10/07/1918	10/07/1918
Miscellaneous	120th Infantry Brigade-Training Progress Report. Appx VII	12/07/1918	12/07/1918
Operation(al) Order(s)	120th Infantry Brigade Order No. 205. Appx VIII	18/07/1918	18/07/1918
Miscellaneous	Appendix 'A' to 120th Infantry Brigade Order No. 205 dated 18-7-18.	18/07/1918	18/07/1918
Miscellaneous	Amendment No. 1 to 120th Infantry Brigade Order No. 205 dated 18-7-18.	18/07/1918	18/07/1918
Miscellaneous	Administrative Instructions-Occupation of W. Hazebrouck Line. To Accompany 120th Brigade Order No. 205.	19/07/1918	19/07/1918
Miscellaneous	Amendment No. 1 to Administrative Instructions issued with 120th Infantry Brigade Order No. 205	20/07/1918	20/07/1918
Miscellaneous	Amendment No. 2 to Administrative Instructions-Occupation Of W. Hazebrouck Line. To Accompany 120th Brigade Order No. 205	23/07/1918	23/07/1918

Operation(al) Order(s)	120th Infantry Brigade Order No. 206. Appx IX	18/07/1918	18/07/1918
Miscellaneous	120th Infantry Brigade-Training Progress Report. Appx X	19/07/1918	19/07/1918
Miscellaneous	120th Infantry Brigade-Training Progress Report. Appx XI	26/07/1918	26/07/1918
Heading	Cover for Documents. Nature of Enclosures. War Diary Headquarters 120th Infantry Brigade. August 1918. Volume XXVII		
War Diary	Sercus	01/08/1918	14/08/1918
War Diary	Fettle Farm. D.24.a.7.1.	15/08/1918	30/08/1918
War Diary	Wallon Cappel	31/08/1918	31/08/1918
Miscellaneous	120th Infantry Brigade-Training Progress Report. Appx I	02/08/1918	02/08/1918
Operation(al) Order(s)	120th Infantry Brigade Order No. 207. Appx II	10/08/1918	10/08/1918
Miscellaneous	March Table To Accompany 120th Inf. Brigade Order No. 207		
Miscellaneous	120th Infantry Brigade Administrative Order No. 207	10/08/1918	10/08/1918
Operation(al) Order(s)	120th Infantry Brigade Order No. 208. Appx III	12/08/1918	12/08/1918
Miscellaneous	Relief Table To Accompany 120th Inf. Bde. Order No. 208		
Miscellaneous	120th Infantry Brigade. Defence Orders. Appx IV	14/08/1918	14/08/1918
Miscellaneous	S.O.S Signal. Appendix I.		
Miscellaneous	Anti-Aircraft Defence. Appendix II.		
Miscellaneous	Anti-Gas Instructions. Appendix III.		
Miscellaneous	120th Infantry Brigade Defence Orders	13/08/1918	13/08/1918
Miscellaneous	A Form. Messages And Signals. Appx V	14/08/1918	14/08/1918
Miscellaneous	A Form. Messages And Signals. Appx V (a)	14/08/1918	14/08/1918
Miscellaneous	120th Infantry Brigade Intelligence Summary. Right Sector 6 a.m. 13:8:18 to 6 a.m. 14:8:18. Appx V (b)	14/08/1918	14/08/1918
Miscellaneous	A Form. Messages And Signals. Appx VI	15/08/1918	15/08/1918
Miscellaneous	A Form. Messages And Signals. Appx VI (a)	15/08/1918	15/08/1918
Miscellaneous	120th Infantry Brigade Intelligence Summary. Right Sector. 6 a.m. 14:8:18 to 6 a.m. 15:8:18. Appx VI (b)	15/08/1918	15/08/1918
Miscellaneous	Administrative Instructions for La Motte Area. Appx VII	15/08/1918	15/08/1918
Miscellaneous	120th Infantry Brigade Defence Orders Appx VIII	13/08/1918	13/08/1918
Operation(al) Order(s)	120th Infantry Brigade Order No. 209. Appx IX	15/08/1918	15/08/1918
Miscellaneous	A Form. Messages And Signals. Appx X	16/08/1918	16/08/1918
Miscellaneous	A Form. Messages And Signals. Appx Xa	16/08/1918	16/08/1918
Miscellaneous	120th Infantry Brigade Intelligence Summary. Right Sector. 6 a.m. 15:8:18 to 6 a.m. 16:8:18. Appx X (b)	16/08/1918	16/08/1918
Miscellaneous	Patrol Report Right Sector	14/08/1918	14/08/1918
Miscellaneous	Shelling Report Right Sector 6 a.m. 15:8:18 to 6 a.m. 16:8:18.	14/08/1918	14/08/1918
Miscellaneous	A Form. Messages And Signals. Appx XI (a)	17/08/1918	17/08/1918
Miscellaneous	A Form. Messages And Signals. Appx XI	17/08/1918	17/08/1918
Miscellaneous	120th Infantry Brigade Intelligence Summary. Right Sector 6 a.m. 16:8:18 to 6 a.m. 17:8:18. Appx XI (b)	17/08/1918	17/08/1918
Miscellaneous	Patrol Report Right Sector Right Secton 6 a.m. 16:8:18 to 17:8:18 6 a.m.	17/08/1918	17/08/1918
Miscellaneous	A Form. Messages And Signals. Appx XII (a)	18/08/1918	18/08/1918
Miscellaneous	A Form. Messages And Signals. Appx XII	18/08/1918	18/08/1918
Miscellaneous	120th Infantry Brigade Intelligence Summary. Right Sector 6 a.m. 17:8:18 to 6 a.m. 18:8:18. Appx XII (b)	18/08/1918	18/08/1918
Miscellaneous	A Form. Messages And Signals. Appx XIII (a)	19/08/1918	19/08/1918

Miscellaneous	Patrol Report Right Sector. 6 a.m. 17:8:18 to 6 a.m. 18:8:18.	18/08/1918	18/08/1918
Miscellaneous	Hostile Shelling Report 6 a.m. 17:8:18 to 6 a.m. 18:8:18. Right Sector	18/08/1918	18/08/1918
Miscellaneous	A Form. Messages And Signals. Appx XIII	19/08/1918	19/08/1918
Miscellaneous	120th Infantry Brigade Intelligence Summary. Right Sector. 6 a.m. 18:8:18 to 6 a.m. 19:8:18. Appx XIII (b)	19/08/1918	19/08/1918
Miscellaneous	Patrol Reports Right Sector. Right Sector. From 6 a.m. 18:8:18 to 6 a.m. 19:8:18.	19/08/1918	19/08/1918
Miscellaneous	A Form. Messages And Signals. Appx XIV	20/08/1918	20/08/1918
Miscellaneous	A Form. Messages And Signals. Appx XIV (a)	20/08/1918	20/08/1918
Miscellaneous	120th Infantry Brigade Intelligence Summary. Right Sector. 6 a.m. 19:8:18 to 6 a.m. 20:8:18. Appx XIV (b)	20/08/1918	20/08/1918
Operation(al) Order(s)	120th Infantry Brigade Order No. 210. Appx XV	20/08/1918	20/08/1918
Miscellaneous	A Form. Messages And Signals. Appx XVI	21/08/1918	21/08/1918
Miscellaneous	120th Infantry Brigade Intelligence Summary. Right Sector. 6 a.m. 20:8:18 to 6 a.m. 21:8:18. Appx XVI (a)	21/08/1918	21/08/1918
Operation(al) Order(s)	120th Infantry Brigade Order No. 211. Appx XVII	21/08/1918	21/08/1918
Operation(al) Order(s)	120th Infantry Brigade Order No. 212. Appx XVIII	21/08/1918	21/08/1918
Miscellaneous	A Form Messages And Signals. Appx XIX	22/08/1918	22/08/1918
Miscellaneous	A Form Messages And Signals. Appx XIX (a)	22/08/1918	22/08/1918
Miscellaneous	120th Infantry Brigade Intelligence Summary. Right Sector. 6 a.m. 21:8:18 to 6 a.m. 22:8:18. Appx XIX (b)	22/08/1918	22/08/1918
Miscellaneous	120th Infantry Brigade Order No. 213. Appx XX	22/08/1918	22/08/1918
Miscellaneous	Administrative Instructions No. 213. Right Brigade.	23/08/1918	23/08/1918
Operation(al) Order(s)	120th Infantry Brigade Order No. 214. Appx XXI	22/08/1918	22/08/1918
Miscellaneous	A Form Messages And Signals. Appx XXII (a)	23/08/1918	23/08/1918
Miscellaneous	A Form Messages And Signals. Appx XXII	23/08/1918	23/08/1918
Miscellaneous	A Form Messages And Signals.		
Miscellaneous	A Form Messages And Signals.	23/08/1918	23/08/1918
Miscellaneous	120th Infantry Brigade Intelligence Summary. Right Sector. 6 a.m. 22:8:18 to 6 a.m. 23:8:18. Appx XXII (b)	23/08/1918	23/08/1918
Operation(al) Order(s)	120th Infantry Brigade Order No. 215 Appx XXIII	23/08/1918	23/08/1918
Miscellaneous	Appx "A"		
Miscellaneous	Messages And Signals. Appx XXIV	24/08/1918	24/08/1918
Miscellaneous	120th Infantry Brigade Intelligence Summary. Right Sector. 6 a.m. 23:8:18 to 6 a.m. 24:8:18. Appx XXIV (a)	24/08/1918	24/08/1918
Miscellaneous	120th Infantry Brigade Intelligence Summary. Right Sector. 6 a.m. 24:8:18 to 6 a.m. 25:8:18. Appx XXV	25/08/1918	25/08/1918
Miscellaneous	A Form. Messages And Signals. Appx XXVI	26/08/1918	26/08/1918
Miscellaneous			
Miscellaneous		26/08/1918	26/08/1918
Operation(al) Order(s)	120th Infantry Brigade Order No. 216. Appx XXVII	26/08/1918	26/08/1918
Map			
Miscellaneous	A Form. Messages And Signals. Right Sector 6 a.m. 26:8:18 to 6 a.m. 27:8:18. Appx XXVIII	27/08/1918	27/08/1918
Miscellaneous	120th Infantry Brigade Intelligence Summary. Right Sector. 6 a.m. 26:8:18 to 6 a.m. 27:8:18. Appx XXVIII (a)	27/08/1918	27/08/1918
Miscellaneous	120th Infantry Brigade No. 120/426. 15th K.O.Y.L.I. Appx XXIX	27/08/1918	27/08/1918
Miscellaneous	A Form. Messages And Signals. Appx XXX	28/08/1918	28/08/1918
Miscellaneous	A Form. Messages And Signals. Appx XXX (a)	28/08/1918	28/08/1918
Miscellaneous	K.W.M.		

Miscellaneous	120th Infantry Brigade Intelligence Summary. Right Sector. 6 a.m. 27:8:18 to 6 a.m. 28/8/18. Appx XXX (b)	28/08/1918	28/08/1918
Operation(al) Order(s)	120th Infantry Brigade Order No. 217. Appx XXXI	28/08/1918	28/08/1918
Operation(al) Order(s)	120th Infantry Brigade Order No. 218. Appx XXXII	28/08/1918	28/08/1918
Miscellaneous	A Form. Messages And Signals. Appx XXXIII	29/08/1918	29/08/1918
Miscellaneous	120th Infantry Brigade Intelligence Summary. Right Sector. 6 a.m. 28:8:18 to 6 a.m. 29:8:18. Appx XXXII (a)	29/08/1918	29/08/1918
Miscellaneous	120th Infantry Brigade Intelligence Summary. Right Sector. 6 a.m. 29th Augt. to 6 a.m. 30th Aug. Appx XXIV	30/08/1918	30/08/1918
Miscellaneous	120th Infantry Brigade Administrative Instructions. Appx XXXV	29/08/1918	29/08/1918
Heading	Cover for Documents. Nature of Enclosures. War Diary Headquarters 120th Infantry Brigade. September 1918		
War Diary	Wallon Cappel	01/09/1918	11/09/1918
War Diary	Wink Cottage A.20.b.3.3.	12/09/1918	14/09/1918
War Diary	Lower FM. A.24.c.6.8.	14/09/1918	23/09/1918
War Diary	Wink Cottage A.20.b.3.3.	23/09/1918	30/09/1918
Miscellaneous	120th Brigade Sports 'Sept 7th 1918. Appx III		
Operation(al) Order(s)	120th Infantry Brigade Order No. 219. Appx IV	10/09/1918	10/09/1918
Miscellaneous	Move Of 120th Infantry Brigade-Embussing Table Appendix 'A'		
Miscellaneous	March Table For Transport Of 120th Infantry Brigade. Appendix "B"		
Operation(al) Order(s)	120th Infantry Brigade Order No. 220. Appx V	11/09/1918	11/09/1918
Miscellaneous	Relief Table To Accompany 120th Infantry Brigade Order No. 220. Night 13/14th Septr. 1918.		
Miscellaneous	A Form. Messages And Signals. Appx V (b)	15/09/1918	15/09/1918
Miscellaneous	A Form. Messages And Signals. Appx 5 (c)	15/09/1918	15/09/1918
Miscellaneous	120th Infantry Brigade Intelligence Summary. Right Sector. From 6 a.m. 14:9:18 to 6 a.m. 15:9:18. Appx V (a)	15/09/1918	15/09/1918
Operation(al) Order(s)	120th Infantry Brigade Order No. 221. Appx VI	15/09/1918	15/09/1918
Miscellaneous	A Form. Messages And Signals. Appx VII (a)	14/09/1918	14/09/1918
Miscellaneous	120th Infantry Brigade Intelligence Summary. Right Sector. From 6 a.m. 15:9:18 to 6 a.m. 14:9:18. Appx VII		
Miscellaneous	A Form. Messages And Signals. Appx VIII (a)	16/09/1918	16/09/1918
Miscellaneous	A Form. Messages And Signals. Appx VIII (b)	16/09/1918	16/09/1918
Miscellaneous	120th Infantry Brigade Intelligence Summary. Right Sector. From 6 a.m. 15:9:18 to 6 a.m. 16:9:18. Appx VIII	16/09/1918	16/09/1918
Miscellaneous	A Form. Messages And Signals. Appx X (a)	17/09/1918	17/09/1918
Miscellaneous	A Form. Messages And Signals. Appx X (b)	17/09/1918	17/09/1918
Miscellaneous	120th Infantry Brigade Intelligence Summary. Right Sector. 6 a.m. 16:9:18 to 6 a.m. 17:9:18. Appx X	17/09/1918	17/09/1918
Miscellaneous	Hostile Shelling Report From 6 a.m. 16:9:18 to 6 a.m. 17:9:18.	17/09/1918	17/09/1918
Operation(al) Order(s)	120th Infantry Brigade Order No. 222. Appx XI	18/09/1918	18/09/1918
Miscellaneous	A Form. Messages And Signals. Appx XII (a)	18/09/1918	18/09/1918
Miscellaneous	A Form. Messages And Signals. Appx XII (b)	18/09/1918	18/09/1918
Miscellaneous	120th Infantry Brigade Intelligence Summary. Right Sector. 6 a.m. 17:9:18 to 6 a.m. 18:8:18. Appx XII	18/09/1918	18/09/1918
Miscellaneous	A Form. Messages And Signals. Appx XIII (a)	19/09/1918	19/09/1918
Miscellaneous	A Form. Messages And Signals. Appx XIII (b)	19/09/1918	19/09/1918

Miscellaneous	120th Infantry Brigade Intelligence Summary. Right Sector. 6 a.m. 18:9:18 to 6 a.m. 19:8:18 Appx XIII	19/09/1918	19/09/1918
Miscellaneous	A Form. Messages And Signals. Appx XIV (a)	20/09/1918	20/09/1918
Miscellaneous	A Form. Messages And Signals. Appx XIV (b)	20/09/1918	20/09/1918
Miscellaneous	120th Infantry Brigade Intelligence Summary. Right Sector. 6 a.m. 19:9:18 to 6 a.m. 20:9:18. Appx XIV	20/09/1918	20/09/1918
Operation(al) Order(s)	120th Infantry Brigade Order No. 223. Appx XV	21/09/1918	21/09/1918
Miscellaneous	Relief Table To Accompany 120th Infantry Brigade Order No. 223.		
Miscellaneous	A Form. Messages And Signals. Appx XVI (b)	21/09/1918	21/09/1918
Miscellaneous	A Form. Messages And Signals. Appx XVI (a)	21/09/1918	21/09/1918
Miscellaneous	120th Infantry Brigade Intelligence Summary. Right Sector. 6 a.m. 20:9:18 to 6 a.m. 21:9:18. Appx XVI	21/09/1918	21/09/1918
Miscellaneous	A Form Messages And Signals. Appx XVII (a)	22/09/1918	22/09/1918
Miscellaneous	A Form Messages And Signals. Appx XVIII (b)	22/09/1918	22/09/1918
Miscellaneous	120th Infantry Brigade Intelligence Summary. Right Sector. 6 a.m. 21:9:18 to 6 a.m. 22:9:18. Appx XVII	22/09/1918	22/09/1918
Miscellaneous	A Form. Messages And Signals. Appx XVIII	23/09/1918	23/09/1918
Operation(al) Order(s)	120th Infantry Brigade Order No. 224. Appx XIX	30/09/1918	30/09/1918
Miscellaneous	Relief Table To Accompany 120th Infantry Brigade Order No. 224.		
Heading	Cover for Documents. Nature of Enclosures. War Diary Headquarters 120th Inf. Bde. October 1918		
War Diary	Wink Cottage A.20.b.3.3.	01/10/1918	02/10/1918
War Diary	Touquet Permentier B.21.a.9.5.	02/10/1918	07/10/1918
War Diary	H.11.b.4.6.	07/10/1918	14/10/1918
War Diary	Touquet Parmentier B.21.a.9.5.	14/10/1918	16/10/1918
War Diary	H.11.b.4.6.	16/10/1918	18/10/1918
War Diary	Wambrechies	18/10/1918	18/10/1918
War Diary	St Andre	19/10/1918	28/10/1918
War Diary	Lannoy	28/10/1918	31/10/1918
War Diary	Wink Cottage A.20.b.3.3.	01/10/1918	02/10/1918
War Diary	Touquet Permentier B.21.a.9.5.	02/10/1918	07/10/1918
War Diary	H.11.b.4.6.	07/10/1918	14/10/1918
War Diary	Touquet Parmentier B.21.a.9.5.	14/10/1918	16/10/1918
War Diary	H.11.b.4.6.	16/10/1918	18/10/1918
War Diary	Wambrechies	18/10/1918	18/10/1918
War Diary	St Andre	19/10/1918	28/10/1918
War Diary	Lannoy	28/10/1918	31/10/1918
Miscellaneous	A Form Messages And Signals. Appx I (a)	02/10/1918	02/10/1918
Miscellaneous	Intelligence Report-120th Infantry Brigade. Right Sector. 6 a.m. 1-10-18 to 6 a.m. 2-10-18. Appendix I		
Miscellaneous	Shelling Report. Right Sector.	02/10/1918	02/10/1918
Miscellaneous	A Form. Messages And Signals. Appx II (a)	03/10/1918	03/10/1918
Miscellaneous	A Form. Messages And Signals. Appx II (b)	03/10/1918	03/10/1918
Miscellaneous	Intelligence Report-120th Infantry Brigade. Right Sector. 06.00 2-10-18 to 06.00 3-10-18 Appendix II	03/10/1918	03/10/1918
Miscellaneous	Hostile Shelling Report. Right Sector	03/10/1918	03/10/1918
Miscellaneous	A Form Messages And Signals. Appx III (a)	04/10/1918	04/10/1918
Miscellaneous	A Form Messages And Signals. Appx III (b)	04/10/1918	04/10/1918
Miscellaneous	Intelligence Report-120th Infantry Brigade. Right-Secton. Appendix III		
Miscellaneous	Hostile Shelling Report. Right Sector.	04/10/1918	04/10/1918
Operation(al) Order(s)	120th Infantry Brigade Order No. 225. Appendix IV	05/10/1918	05/10/1918
Miscellaneous	Relief Table To Accompany 120th Infantry Brigade Order No. 225 dated 5-10-18.	05/10/1918	05/10/1918

Miscellaneous	120th Infantry Brigade Instructions No. 1. Appendix V	05/10/1918	05/10/1918
Miscellaneous	A Form Messages And Signals. Appx VI (a)	05/10/1918	05/10/1918
Miscellaneous	A Form Messages And Signals. Appx VI (b)	05/10/1918	05/10/1918
Miscellaneous	Intelligence Report-120th Infantry Brigade. Right-Sector. 0600 4-10-18 to 0600 5-10-18. Appendix VI		
Miscellaneous	Hostile Shelling Report. Right Sector.	05/10/1918	05/10/1918
Miscellaneous	A Form Messages And Signals. Appx VII (a)	06/10/1918	06/10/1918
Miscellaneous	A Form Messages And Signals. Appx VII (b)	06/10/1918	06/10/1918
Miscellaneous	Intelligence Report-120th Infantry Brigade. Right Sector. 06.00 5-10-18 to 0600 6-10-18. Appendix VII	06/10/1918	06/10/1918
Miscellaneous	Hostile Shelling Report. Right Sector.	06/10/1918	06/10/1918
Miscellaneous	A Form. Messages And Signals. Appx VIII (b)	07/10/1918	07/10/1918
Miscellaneous	A Form. Messages And Signals. Appx VIII (a)	07/10/1918	07/10/1918
Operation(al) Order(s)	120th Infantry Brigade Order No. 226. Appendix IX	08/10/1918	08/10/1918
Miscellaneous	A Form. Messages And Signals. Appx X (a)	08/10/1918	08/10/1918
Miscellaneous	Appx X (b)	08/10/1918	08/10/1918
Miscellaneous	Intelligence Report-120th Infantry Brigade. Right Sector. 06.00 7-10-18 to 06.00 8-10-18. Appendix X	08/10/1918	08/10/1918
Miscellaneous	Hostile Shelling Report. Right Sector	08/10/1918	08/10/1918
Miscellaneous	Messages And Signals. Appx XI (a)	09/10/1918	09/10/1918
Miscellaneous	A Form. Messages And Signals. Appx XI (b)	09/10/1918	09/10/1918
Miscellaneous	Intelligence Report-120th Infantry Brigade. Right Sector. 06.00 8-10-18 to 06.00 9-10-18. Appendix XI	09/10/1918	09/10/1918
Miscellaneous	Hostile Shelling Report. Right Sector.	09/10/1918	09/10/1918
Miscellaneous	A Form. Messages And Signals. Appx XII (a)	10/10/1918	10/10/1918
Miscellaneous	A Form. Messages And Signals. Appx XII (b)	10/10/1918	10/10/1918
Miscellaneous	Intelligence Report-120th Infantry Brigade. Right Sector. 06.00 9-10-18 to 06.00 10-10-18 Appendix XII	10/10/1918	10/10/1918
Miscellaneous	120th Infantry Brigade Shelling Report.		
Miscellaneous	120th Infantry Brigade Order No. 227. Appendix XIII	11/10/1918	11/10/1918
Miscellaneous	A Form. Messages And Signals. Appx XIV (a)	11/10/1918	11/10/1918
Miscellaneous	Appx XIV (b)	11/10/1918	11/10/1918
Miscellaneous	Intelligence Report-120th Infantry Brigade. Right Sector. 06.00 10-10-18 to 06.00 11-10-18. Appendix XIV	11/10/1918	11/10/1918
Miscellaneous	120th Infantry Brigade Shelling Report. Right Sector. 06.00 10-10-18 to 06.00 11-10-18.	11/10/1918	11/10/1918
Operation(al) Order(s)	120th Infantry Brigade Order No. 228. Appendix XV	12/10/1918	12/10/1918
Miscellaneous	Relief Table To Accompany 120th Infantry Brigade Order No. 228 dated 12-10-18.	12/10/1918	12/10/1918
Miscellaneous	A Form. Messages And Signals. Appx XVI (a)	12/10/1918	12/10/1918
Miscellaneous	Appx XVI (b)	12/10/1918	12/10/1918
Miscellaneous	Intelligence Report-120th Infantry Brigade. Right Sector. 06.00 11-10-18 to 06.00 12-10-18. Appendix XVI	12/10/1918	12/10/1918
Miscellaneous	Appx XVII (a)	13/10/1918	13/10/1918
Miscellaneous	Appx XVII (b)	13/10/1918	13/10/1918
Miscellaneous	Intelligence Report-120th Infantry Brigade. Right Sector. 06.00 12-10-18 to 06.00 13-10-18. Appendix XVII	13/10/1918	13/10/1918
Miscellaneous	120th Infantry Brigade Shelling Report. Right Sector.		
Miscellaneous	Defence Instructions For Nieppe System. Appendix XVIII	14/10/1918	14/10/1918
Operation(al) Order(s)	120th Infantry Brigade Warning Order No. 229. Appendix XIX	16/10/1918	16/10/1918
Miscellaneous	120th Infantry Brigade Instructions No. 2.	07/10/1918	07/10/1918

Miscellaneous	120th Infantry Brigade Instructions No. 3. Appendix XX	16/10/1918	16/10/1918
Operation(al) Order(s)	120th Infantry Brigade Order No. 230. Appendix XXI	18/10/1918	18/10/1918
Miscellaneous	March Table To Accompany 120th Infantry Brigade Order No. 230		
Operation(al) Order(s)	120th Infantry Brigade Order No. 231. Appendix XXII	27/10/1918	27/10/1918
Heading	Cover for Documents. Nature of Enclosures. War Diary Headquarters 120th Infantry Brigade. November 1918 Volume XXX		
War Diary	Lannoy	01/11/1918	07/11/1918
War Diary	Leers-Nord.	08/11/1918	09/11/1918
War Diary	Herinnes	10/11/1918	12/11/1918
War Diary	Toufflers	12/11/1918	25/11/1918
War Diary	Lannoy	26/11/1918	29/11/1918
Miscellaneous	March Table To Accompany 120th Infantry Brigade Order No. 232 dated 5-11-18.	05/11/1918	05/11/1918
Operation(al) Order(s)	120th Infantry Brigade Order No. 232. Appendix I.	05/11/1918	05/11/1918
Miscellaneous	Administrative Instructions. Move Of 120th Infantry Brigade-6th November, 1918.	05/11/1918	05/11/1918
Operation(al) Order(s)	120th Infantry Brigade Order No. 233. Appendix II		
Miscellaneous	March Table To Accompany 120th Infantry Brigade Order No. 234 dated 11-11-18.	11/11/1918	11/11/1918
Operation(al) Order(s)	120th Infantry Brigade Order No. 234. Appendix III	11/11/1918	11/11/1918
Operation(al) Order(s)	120th Infantry Brigade Order No. 235. Appendix IV	25/11/1918	25/11/1918
War Diary	Lannoy	03/12/1918	31/12/1918
Miscellaneous	Notes on Conference. Held at 40th Divisional Head Quarters. 19th December, 1918. Appendix I	19/12/1918	19/12/1918
War Diary	Lannoy	01/01/1919	29/01/1919
Miscellaneous	Ceremonial To Be Adopted At Reception And Consecration Of New Colours By Battalions Of 120th Infantry Brigade. Appendix I		
Diagram etc	Plan I.		
Diagram etc	Plan II		
Diagram etc	Plan III		
Diagram etc	Plan IV		
Heading	War Diary For The Month Of February 1919. Of Hqrs 120th Infantry Brigade Volume XXXIII		
War Diary	Lannoy	04/02/1919	28/02/1919

40TH DIVISION
120TH INFY BDE

BDE HEADQUARTERS

~~JAN~~ 1918 - FEB 1919
MAR

40th Division.

WAR DIARY

B. H. Q.

120th INFANTRY BRIGADE.

MARCH 1 9 1 8

Army Form C. 2118.

Instructions regarding War Diaries and Intelligence Summaries are contained in F. S. Regs., Part II. and the Staff Manual respectively. Title pages will be prepared in manuscript.

1.

WAR DIARY
or
INTELLIGENCE SUMMARY.
(Erase heading not required.)

MARCH 1918.

VOLUME XXII.

Hd.Qrs. 120th (Hd.) Inf.Bde.

Place	Date	Hour	Summary of Events and Information	Remarks and references to Appendices
POMMIER In G.H.Q. Reserve.	1918 March 1st.		Disposition of Units :- Brigade Hd. Qrs.) 14th H. L. I.) ... ... POMMIER. 120th T. M. Bty.) 10/11th H. L. I.) 14th A. & S. Hrs.) ... ... BERLES-AU-BOIS. Units engaged in cleaning up generally.	
		3 pm.	Conference held at Brigade Hd. Qrs., Battalion Commanders and O.C., 120th T. M. Battery attending.	App. I.
	2nd		Units engaged in Company and Battalion Training - Tactical Schemes, etc.	
	3rd		-Do- -do- -do- -do-	
	4th		-Do- -do- -do- -do-	
	5th	3 pm.	Brigadier-General Commanding met Commanding Officers, Company Commanders and Junior Officers on BERLES-POMMIER Road, for short staff tour.	
		7.30 pm.	120th Inf. Bde. Order No. 174 issued, detailing entraining, etc. arrangements of 120th Brigade Group in the event of an enemy attack taking place on any front other than the VI Corps front or those parts of the neighbouring Corps fronts adjoining.	App. II.
	6th	11.35 a.m.	Special Attack Scheme carried out by 14th H. L. I. between BIENVILLERS and MONCHY-AU-BOIS, assisted by smoke barrage and contact aeroplanes. Other units engaged in Company and Battalion Training.	
		3 pm.	Conference held at 40th Divnl. Hd. Qrs., G.O.C. and Brigade Major 120th Bde. attending. Subjects discussed:- "The co-operation of Infantry and Tanks" and "Anti-Tank Defence."	
		4 pm.	Elementary Class at Brigade Signal School re-assembled with the same personnel as had already started the course, i.e. - 4 O.R. per Battalion.	

D. D. & L., London, E.C. (A8093) Wt. W1771/M2031 750,000 5/17 Sch. 52 Forms/C2118/14

Instructions regarding War Diaries and Intelligence Summaries are contained in F. S. Regs., Part II. and the Staff Manual respectively. Title pages will be prepared in manuscript.

Army Form C. 2118.

WAR DIARY or INTELLIGENCE SUMMARY.

MARCH 1918. VOLUME XXII.

(Erase heading not required.)

Hd.Qrs. 120th (Hd.) Inf. Bde.

Place	Date	Hour	Summary of Events and Information	Remarks and references to Appendices
	1918			
POMMIER In G.H.Q. Reserve.	March 7th		Reconnaissances of the Forward Area - North and South of VI Corps, carried out by G.O.C., 120th Bde., Bn. & Coy. Commanders and O.C. T.M. Battery. Units engaged in Battalion & Company Training - Tactical Schemes, Musketry, etc.	
	8th	3 pm.	Lieut.-General Sir AYLMER HALDANE, K.C.B., D.S.O., Commanding VIth Corps, inspected the 120th (Hd.) Infantry Brigade between POMMIER and BIENVILLERS.	
		5 pm.	Brigade Commander conferred with Battalion Commanders at Brigade Hd. Qrs.	
	9th		Brigade Attack Scheme carried out between ESSARTS and MONCHY-AU-BOIS, all units of 120th Bde. participating.	App. III
	10th		Units engaged in Battalion and Company Training - Tactical Schemes, etc.	
		8 pm.	120th Infantry Brigade Instruction No. 1 issued, detailing positions of Assembly in the event of an enemy attack taking place on VI Corps Front, or on the front of Left Division of the IV Corps, Or the Right Division of XVII Corps.	App. IV.
	11th	8 pm.	120th Brigade Order No. 175 issued. The 40th Division will move from the BASSEUX Area to the BOISLEUX Area on 12th March. The 120th Brigade Group will move on this date to HAMELINCOURT-ERVILLERS Area.	App. V.
HAMELINCOURT (A.5.b.2.2.) In Close Reserve.	12th		120th Brigade Group moved from POMMIER Area to HAMELINCOURT-ERVILLERS Area, in accordance with 120th Inf. Bde. Order No. 175 dated 11/3/18.	
		6 pm.	120th Inf. Bde. Hd.Qrs. closed at POMMIER and re-opened at same hour at HAMELINCOURT. Dispositions of Brigade :- 10/11th H. L. I. ... ... Belfast Camp, ERVILLERS. 14th H. L. I. ... ... Enniskillen Camp, ERVILLERS. 14th A. & S. Hrs. ... ... Clonmel Camp, HAMELINCOURT. 120th T. M. Bty. ... ... Belfast Camp, ERVILLERS.	
		10.30 p.m.	Order received that while in Close Reserve, the Division will be prepared to move at 3 hours notice from 8 a.m. to 8 p.m. and at 1½ hours notice from 8 p.m. to 8 a.m.	

D. D. & L., London, E.C. (A8001) Wt. W1771/M2031 750,000 5/17 Sch. 52 Forms/C2118/14

Instructions regarding War Diaries and Intelligence Summaries are contained in F. S. Regs., Part II. and the Staff Manual respectively. Title pages will be prepared in manuscript.

Army Form C. 2118.

WAR DIARY or INTELLIGENCE SUMMARY.

(Erase heading not required.)

MARCH 1918. VOLUME XXII.

Hd.Qrs., 120th (Hd.) Inf. Bde.

Place	Date	Hour	Summary of Events and Information	Remarks and references to Appendices
	1918 March			
HAMELIN-COURT (In close Reserve)	13th 14th		Units training in vicinity of camps. -Do- -do- -do-	
	15th		120th Infantry Brigade Order No. 176 issued, detailing action of units of 120th Brigade Group in the event of a move by rail from the HAMELINCOURT Area. Lieut.-Colonel R.F.FORBES, D.S.O., Commanding 10/11th H.L.I., assumed Command of 120th Infantry Brigade on the departure to ENGLAND of Brig.-General The Honble. C.S.H.D.WILLOUGHBY, C.B., C.M.G.	App.VI.
	16th) 17th) 18th)		Units training in vicinity of camps.	
	19th	12.30 pm.	Addendum No. 1 to 120th Infantry Brigade Instruction No. 1 of 10/3/18 issued.	App.VII.
		9.30 pm.	120th Infantry Brigade Order No. 177 issued. 120th Bde. will relieve 9th Infantry Brigade (3rd Division) in the line on 22nd March should present situation remain unchanged.	App.VIII.
	20th		Demonstration of the Co-operation between Infantry and Tanks, at WAILLY, attended by 42 Officers and 110 O.R. of 120th Bde.	
	21st) 22nd) 23rd) 24th) 25th) 26th)		120th Infantry Brigade in action. 23rd: Brig. General C.J. HOBKIRK D.S.O. assumes Command of 120th Infantry Brigade. (For detailed report of operations, see Appendix IX). 26th: Brigade Major (Captain H. J. Eady, M.C.) admitted to Hospital - sick Casualties: Killed Offrs. 8, O.R. 68; Wounded Offrs. 13, O.R. 344; Missing Offrs. 11, O.R. 466.	App.IX.
	27th	4.30 pm.	120th Bde. arrived in billets at WALRUZEL (XIII Corps Area).	
WALRUZEL	28th	11.30 pm.	120th Bde. Order No. 184 issued. 40th Division will be transferred from Third to First Army, and 120th Bde. Group will march and buss to MONCHY BRETON area on 29th March.	App. X.

Army Form C. 2118.

Instructions regarding War Diaries and Intelligence Summaries are contained in F. S. Regs., Part II. and the Staff Manual respectively. Title pages will be prepared in manuscript.

-4-

MARCH 1918.

WAR DIARY
or
INTELLIGENCE SUMMARY.
(Erase heading not required.)

VOLUME XXII.

Hd. Qrs., 120th Inf. Bde.

Place	Date	Hour	Summary of Events and Information	Remarks and references to Appendices
	1918 March			
MAGNICOURT-EN-COMTE.	29th	7.30 am.	Brigade Headquarters closed at WALRUZEL and re-opened at MAGNICOURT-EN-COMTE on arrival. Move of Brigade Group to MONCHY BRETON Area completed, in accordance with 120th Bde. Order No. 184 dated 28/3/18.	
		12 m'nt.	40th Division Warning Order No. 141 received. 40th Division, less Artillery, will be transferred from the XIIIth Corps to XVth Corps, with a view to relieving 57th Division, less Artillery.	
	30th		120th Inf. Bde. Order No. 185 issued. 120th Bde. Group will move by bus on 30th inst. to SAILLY-SUR-LA-LYS - MONDE Area.	App.XI.
		5 pm.	Move completed in accordance with above order.	
	31st	1.40 pm.	120th Inf. Bde. Order No. 186 issued. 120th Inf. Bde. will relieve the 172nd Inf. Bde. in the FLEURBAIX SECTOR on night 31st March/1st April.	App.XII.
FLEURBAIX.		7 pm.	Brigade Headquarters closed at SAILLY-SUR-LA-LYS, and re-opened at MARE'S NEST, FLEURBAIX at same hour.	
	Night 31/1st.		Relief of 172nd Inf. Bde. by 120th Inf. Bde. in FLEURBAIX SECTOR (Right Brigade) completed, in accordance with 120th Bde. Order No. 186 of 31/3/18. Dispositions :- RIGHT SUBSECTOR ... 14th A. & S. Hrs. LEFT SUBSECTOR ... 14th H. L. I. IN THE LINE ... 120th T. M. Bty. BRIGADE RESERVE ... 10/11th H.L.I.	

[signature]

Brigadier-General,
Commanding 120th (Highland) Infantry Bde.

31:3:18.

D. D. & L., London, E.C.
(A8004) Wt. W1771/M2 31 750,000 5/17 Sch. 52 Forms/C2118/14

Appx I

MINUTES OF CONFERENCE HELD AT BRIGADE H.QRS.

MARCH 1st 1918.

1. (a) The actual marching of units into this area and the numbers of men who fell out were satisfactory.

(b) 200 yards between companies always to be maintained and transport to move closed up.

(c) Orderlies and small bodies of men not to move about the column on their own.
Cyclist Orderlies to be sent on in advance as advanced party.
Spare horses to be led and not ridden.

(d) Each company to have its own Lewis gun limber moving behind it, and someone responsible for the guns always to march with the limber.

(e) Wagons only to be loaded according to road table. Other stores to wait for lorries.
It was considered advisable for a battalion officer always to accompany the battalion lorries.

(f) Clock hour halts always to be observed.
Brigade time to be obtained before moving off.

(g) Attention was drawn to the necessity of making men wear belts when out of billets, and of making officers check any man seen improperly dressed on the road.

2. (a) Training Grounds were allotted :-

10/11th H.L.I. Ground East of BERLES - MONCHY Road.
14th A. & S.H. " West " " " "
14th High.L.I. " South of BIENVILLERS-MONCHY Rd.

(b) Battalions to Practice Attack through MONCHY-AU-BOIS, which is allotted to Bns. as follows for this purpose:-

4th March ... 10/11th H. L. I.
5th " ... 14th H. L. I.
6th " ... 14th A. & S. Hrs.

(c) At least two companies a day to be practiced in the Attack in the Open by each Battalion, and companies to be complete with all specialists when carrying out this training.

(d) Range of 200 yards at W.13.c.8.2., with 4 targets, allotted as follows :-

4th March ... 14th H. L. I.
5th " ... 14th A. & S.H.
6th " ... 10/11th H.L.I.
etc. etc.
As much advantage as possible to be taken of this.

3. Counter Stroke.

(a) Decided that normally 2 battalions would attack, each on two-company front, with 1 battalion in reserve.

Possibility of putting 1 attacking battalion on 3-company front, providing depth for it from the Reserve Battalion, and the other attacking battalion on a 1-company front, providing its own depth, was discussed.

It was decided that the battalions that took over the line would carry out the attack.

It was also decided that one platoon per company would have to be detailed as carrying and ration parties.

The possibility of using the Works Platoon for this was also mentioned.

(b) First Line Transport.

During a march Lewis gun limbers will normally follow their respective companies.

During the move of the Brigade to an assembly position with a view to counter-attack, Echelon A of first line transport (as laid down in this Office No. 120/443 dated 19:11:17) will accompany the troops to the assembly position if circumstances permit. If not, this Echelon will be parked, together with Echelon B, some distance to the rear. The Lewis gun limbers will be taken forward in rear of Companies as far as possible.

(c) S.A.A. and Bombs

Each man will be issued with 50 additional rounds S.A.A. at the assembly position (if this has not already been done). Lewis gun limbered G.S. wagons are to be off-loaded at once and returned to Brigade Ammunition Officer, who will be responsible for refilling from D.A.C., or S.A.A. Dump.

1 G.S. limbered wagon of S.A.A. per battalion will be retained as Brigade Reserve. Remainder will be at disposal of O.C. Battalion.

It is to be noted that the mobile Reserve of Grenades is carried unfuzed. These grenades should be fuzed before the Battalion moves to the assembly position.

4. Schools.

It was decided to maintain the Lewis Gun, Bombing and Signalling Schools, also the Demonstration Platoon. C.Os. were asked to try and find a suitable officer for the latter.

5. The necessity of trying to avoid changes in Commands of Platoons and Companies, was emphasised.

6. Attention was called to the necessity of sending good men to the Trench Mortar Battery.

--*-*-*-*-*-*-*-*-*-*-*-*

Appx II

SECRET

COPY NO. 4.

120TH (HIGHLAND) INFANTRY BRIGADE ORDER NO. 174.

Ref. LENS 11.
1/100,000.

5 : 3 : 18.

120th (Highland) Infantry Brigade Order No. 173 dated 3:3:18, with attached March Table, is cancelled and the following substituted :-

1. The 40th Division is at present in G.H.Q. Reserve and may be ordered to move by strategical or tactical trains at 24 hours notice.

2. The 120th Brigade Group, consisting of the troops mentioned in para. 3, will be prepared to entrain at FREVENT or at TINQUES at 24 hours notice.

3. For purposes of entrainment, the 120th Brigade Group will consist of :-

   120th (Highland) Infantry Brigade.
   231st Field Company, R.E.
   Hd. Qrs. 40th Battn. M.G. Corps.
   "B" Coy. -------do------
   "D" Coy. -------do------
   No.3 Coy. 40th Divnl.Train.
   135th Field Ambulance.
   Divisional Employment Company.

4. All troops and transport will arrive at the entraining station 3 hours before the time of departure of the train.

5. Details regarding composition and allotment of trains, and of entraining, are given in attached Administrative Instructions.

6. Movement of troops and transport to the Staging Area and to the entraining stations are given in attached tables "A" and "B"

7. Battalions will move with 200 yards between Companies, and clock hour halts will be observed by all troops.

8. ACKNOWLEDGE.

[signature]
Captain,
Brigade Major,
120th (Highland) Infantry Brigade.

Issued through
Signals
at 7.30 p.m.

Distribution :-

Copy No.		
1	...	G.O.C.
2	...	Brigade Major.
3	...	Staff Captain.
4	...	War Diary.
5	...	File.
6	...	10/11th H. L. I.
7	...	14th H. L. I.
8	...	14th A. & S. Hrs.
9	...	120th T. M. Bty.
10	...	231st Field Coy. R.E.
11	...	40th Bn. M.G. Corps.
12	...	"B" Coy. -do-
13	...	"D" Coy. -do-
14	...	No. 3 Coy. 40th Div. Train.
15	...	135th Field Ambulance.
16	...	Divisional Employment Coy.
17	...	40th Division "G"
18	...	40th Division "Q"
19	...	119th Inf. Bde.
20	...	121st Inf. Bde.
21	...	C.R.E.
22	...	40th Divnl. Train.
23	...	A.D.M.S.
24	...	T.O., 17th Welsh Regt.
25	...	A.P.M., 40th Division.
26	...	Brigade Supply Officer.
27	...	Brigade Signals.
28	...	R.T.O., FREVENT.
29	...	R.T.O., TINQUES.
30	...	Area Comdt. HAPARCQ.
31	...	" " FOSSEUX.
32	...	" " AVESNES-LE-COMTE.
33	...	" " VILLERS SUR SIMON.

****

TABLE "A"

TO ACCOMPANY 120TH (HIGHLAND) INFANTRY BRIGADE ORDER NO. 174 DATED 5:3:18.

Entraining Station - FREVENT. Staging Area - LIENCOURT.

Serial No.	Unit	Date	From	To	Starting Point	Hour of Departure.	Route	Serial No. of Train	Hour of Departure of Train	Remarks.
1.	No.3 Coy.40th Divl.Train.	A day	POMMIER	BERLENCOURT	POMMIER Church.	-	LA CAUCHIE-LAHERLIERE -SAULTY - SOMBRIN - GRAND RULLECOURT.			Time of departure to depend upon refilling. Instructions will be issued by Bde.H.Q. on receipt of details of refilling.
2.	14th H.L.I.	-do-	POMMIER	LIENCOURT	POMMIER Church	Z	-do-			
3.	120th Bde. H.Qrs.and Sig.Sect-	-do-	-do-	-do-	-do-	Z plus 25 mins.	-do-			
4	120th T.M. Battery.	-do-	-do-	-do-	-do-		-do-			To follow directly behind Serial No.2
5.	14th A. & S.H.	-do-	BERLES-AU-BOIS	LIGNEREUIL.	Road Junctn. on BERLES-AU-BOIS - POMMIER Rd. ½ mile S.W. of BERLES-AU-BOIS.	Z plus 15.	POMMIER-LA CAUCHIE-LAHERLIERE- SAULTY-SOMBRIN- GRAND RULLECOURT.			

Serial No.	Unit	Date	From	To	Starting Point	Hour of Departure	Route	Serial No. of Train	Hour of Departure of Train	Remarks
6.	10/11th H.L.I.	A day	BERLES-AU-BOIS	GRAND RULLECOURT	Rd. Junctn. on BERLES-AU-BOIS - POMMIER Rd. ½ mile S.W. of BERLES-AU-BOIS	Z plus 40	POMMIER-LA CAUCHIE-LAHERLIERE-SAULTY-SOMBRIN- GRAND RULLECOURT			
7.	231st Field Coy. R.E.	-do-	BIENVILLERS	BEAUFORT	BIENVILLERS Church	Z plus 1¼ hrs.	LA CAUCHIE-LAHERLIERE-SAULTY-SOMBRIN- GRAND RULLECOURT			
8.	135th Field Ambulance.	-do-	BIENVILLERS	GRAND RULLECOURT	-do-	-	-do-			To follow 200 yds. behind Serial No. 7.
9	237th Divnl. Empt. Coy.	-do-	BEAUMETZ	LE CAUROY		Any hour	GOUY - FOSSEUX-BARLY- SOMBRIN-GRAND RULLECOURT			
10	H.Qrs. and "B" and "D" Coys. 40th M.G. Battn.	-do-	HENDECOURT	DENIER		Z				
11.	Bde. H.Q. and Sig. Section	E day	LIENCOURT	FREVENT	Cross Roads due West of L in LIENCOURT	X-6½	Main Road	3	X	
12.	120th T.M. Bty.	-do-	-do-	-do-	-do-		-do-	3	X	To move immediately behind Serial No. 11.
13.	1 Coy., 1 Cooker & team 14 H.L.I.	-do-	-do-	-do-	-do-	X-6¼	-do-	3	X	
14.	"D" Coy. 40th M.G. Battn.	-do-	DENIER	-do-	Junction of 4 roads just S.W. of D in DENIER.	X-6	BERLENCOURT-WAMIN	3	X	

Serial No.	Unit	Date	From	To	Starting Point	Hour of Departure	Route	Serial No. of Train	Hr. of dep. of train.	Remarks
15.	14th H.L.I. less 1 Coy., 1 Cooker and team.	B day	LIENCOURT	FREMENT	Cross Roads due West of L in LIENCOURT	X-3½	Main Road	6	X plus 3	
16	10/11th H.L.I. less 1 Coy., 1 Cooker & team	-do-	GRAND RULLECOURT	-do-	Road Junction of GRAND RULLECOURT -LIENCOURT Road and GRAND RULLECOURT- LE CAUROY Roads.	X-1	LIENCOURT thence Main Road	9	X plus 6	
17.	14th A. & S.H. less 1 Coy., 1 Cooker and team.	-do-	LIGUEREUIL	-do-	Western edge of LIGUEREUIL Village on road to DENIER.	X plus 2¼	DENIER-BERLENCOURT-WAMIN.	12	X plus 9	
18.	237th Divnl. Empt.Coy.	-do-	LE CAUROY	-do-	Road junction due North of R in LE CAUROY	X plus 5	Main Road.	15	X plus 12	
19.	1 Coy., 1 Cooker & team 10/11th H.L.I.	-do-	GRAND RULLECOURT	-do-	Junction of GRAND RULLECOURT - LE CAUROY and GRAND RULLECOURT - LIENCOURT Rds.	X plus 4½	LIENCOURT thence Main Road.	15	X plus 12	
20.	"D" Coy. 40th Bn. M.G.Corps	-do-	DENIER	-do-	Junction of 4 roads just S.W. of D in DENIER	X plus 5	BERLENCOURT-WAMIN.	15	X plus 12.	
21	135th Field Ambulance.	-do-	GRAND RULLECOURT	-do-	Junction of GRAND R'COURT LE CAUROY and GRAND R'COURT-LIENCOURT Rds.	X plus 7½	LIENCOURT thence Main Road.	18	X plus 15.	

Serial No.	Unit	Date	From	To	Starting Point	Hour of Dept[r]	Route	Serial No. Train	Hour of Dep. Train	Remarks.
22	H.Qrs. M.G. Battn.	B day	DENIER	FREVENT	Junction of 4 roads just S.W. of of D. in DENIER	X plus $8\frac{1}{2}$	BERLENCOURT-WAMIN	18	X plus 15	If there is insufficient accommodation in train 18 for Serials Nos. 21, 22 & 23, part of H.Qrs. M.G Battn. will travel in train No.21 which leaves at X plus 18
23	1 Coy., 1 Cooker & team 14th A. & S.H.	-do-	LIGNEREUIL	-do-	Western edge of LIGNEREUIL Village on road to DENIER.	X plus $8\frac{1}{4}$	DENIER - BERLENCOURT - WAMIN.	18	X plus 15.	
24	No. 3 Coy. 40th Divnl. Train	-do-	BERLENCOURT	-do-	Cross Roads at IGNOCOURT.	X plus 12	WAMIN thence Main Road.	21	X plus 18	
25	231st Field Coy. R.E.	-do-	BEAUFORT	-do-	Cross roads just N.E. of last E in APPEGRENEE	X plus 11	Main Road	21	X plus 18.	

TABLE "B"

TO ACCOMPANY 120TH (HIGHLAND) INFANTRY BRIGADE ORDER NO. 174 dated 5:2:18.

Entraining Station - TINQUES. Staging Area - AVESNES-LE-COMTE.

Serial No.	Date	Unit	From	To	Starting Point	Hour of Starting	Route	Train No. of	Train Hour of depr	Remarks
1.	A day	No.3 Coy. 40th Div. Train	POMMIER	AVESNES-LE-COMTE.	POMMIER Church		LA CAUCHIE - BAVINCOURT - BARLY.			Hr.of departure to depend upon time of refilling Hour will be detailed by Bde.H.Q.on receipt of information as to refilling
2.	-do-	14th H.L.I.	-do-	-do-	-do-	Z	-do-			
3.	-do-	H.Qrs.120th Bde.& Sig.Secn	-do-	-do-	-do-	Z plus 25 minutes	-do-			
4.	-do-	120th T.M.Bty.	-do-	-do-	-do-		-do-			To follow 200 yards behind Serial No.3.
5.	-do-	231st Field Coy. R.E.	BIENVILLERS	LATTRE ST QUENTIN.	BIENVILLERS Church.	Z plus 20	POMMIER - LA CAUCHIE - BAVINCOURT - BARLY-AVESNES -LE-COMTE- LATTRE ST QUENTIN.			
6.	-do-	135th Field Ambulance.	-do-	AVESNES-LE-COMTE	-do-	Z plus 35	POMMIER - LA CAUCHIE - BAVINCOURT - BARLY			

Serial No.	Date	Unit	From	To	Starting Point	Hour of Starting	Route	Train No. of	Train Hour of dep.	Remarks.
7.	A day	10/11th H.L.I.	BERLES-AU-BOIS	LATTRE ST QUENTIN	Road junctn on BERLES-POMMIER roads & ½ mile from BERLES.	Z plus 1 hour	POMMIER-LA CAUCHIE-BAVINCOURT-BARLY-AVESNES-LE-COMTE.			
8.	-do-	14th A. & S.H.	-do-	-do-	-do-	Z plus 1½	-do-			
9.	-do-	237th Divnl. Empt. Coy.	BEAUMETZ	HERMAVILLE	-do-	-do-	SIMENCOURT-WANQUENTIN-HAUTEVILLE-LATTRE-ST-QUENTIN.			To move any time.
10	-do-	Hd.Qrs. and "B" & "D" Coys. 40th M.G.Battn.	HENDECOURT	HAUTEVILLE	-do-	Z	BLAIRVILLE-BRETENCOURT-BEAUMETZ-SIMENCOURT-WANQUENTIN-HAUTEVILLE.			To give way to troops of any other Brigade on the road.
11.	- - B day	1 Coy., 1 Cooker and team 14th H.L.I.	AVESNES-LE-COMTE.	TINQUES Station	Level Xng. just South of C in AVESNES-LE-COMTE, on road to GIVENCHY-LE-NOBLE.	X-6	GIVENCHY-LE-NOBLE- PENIN.	3	X	
12.	-do-	120th T.M.Bty.	-do-	-do-	-do-		-do-	3	X	To follow 200 yards behind Serial No 11.
13.	-do-	120th Bde.H.Q. & Sig.Sectn	-do-	-do-	-do-		-do-	3	X	To follow 200 yards behind Serial No.12.

Serial No.	Date	Unit	From	To	Starting Point	Hour of Starting	Route	Train No. of	Train Hour of dep.	Remarks.
14.	B day	"B" Coy. 40th M.G. Battn.	HAUTEVILLE	TINQUES Station	Junction of HAUTEVILLE-LATTRE ST QUENTIN and HAUTEVILLE-AVESNES Roads	X-6½	AVESNES-GIVENCHY-LE-NOBLE- PENIN.	5	X	
15	-do-	14th H.L.I. less 1 Coy. 1 Cooker and team.	AVESNES-LE-COMTE	-do-	Level Crossing just South of C in AVESNES-LE-COMTE on road to GIVENCHY-LE-NOBLE.	X-2¾	GIVENCHY-LE NOBLE- PENIN	6	X plus 3.	
16.	-do-	10/11th H.L.I. less 1 Coy., 1 Cooker and team.	LATTRE ST QUENTIN.	-do-	Road junct[n] immediately West of L in LATTRE ST QUENTIN.	X	NOYELLE-VION - MANIN- GIVENCHY-LE-NOBLE-PENIN	9	X plus 6	
17.	-do-	14th A. & S.H. less 1 Coy., 1 Cooker and team.	-do-	-do-	-do-	X plus 3	-do-	12	X plus 9	
18.	-do-	1 Coy., 1 Cooker and team 10/11th H.L.I.	-do-	-do-	-do-	X plus 5¾	-do-	15	X plus 12	
19.	-do-	"D" Coy. 40th Bn. M.G.Corps.	HAUTEVILLE	-do-	Junction of HAUTEVILLE-LATTRE ST QUENTIN & HAUTEVILLE-AVESNES Roads	X plus 5½	AVESNES - GIVENCHY-PENIN.	15	X plus 12.	

Serial No	Date	Unit	From	To	Starting Point	Hour of Starting	Route	Train No. of	Train Hour of dep.	Remarks
20.	B day	237th Divnl. Empt.Coy.	HERMAVILLE	TINQUES	Junction of 6 roads North of second E in HERMAVILLE	X plus 6	Cross Roads ½ mile N.E. of TILLOY - on to ARRAS-ST POL Road.	15	X plus 12	
21.	-do-	135th Field Ambulance.	AVESNES-LE-COMTE.	TINQUES	Level Crossing just South of C in AVESNES-LE-COMTE., on road to GIVENCHY-LE-NOBLE.	X plus 8½	GIVENCHY-LE-NOBLE- PENIN.	18	X plus 15	
22	-do-	1 Coy., 1 Cooker and team 14th A. & S. H.	LATTRE-ST QUENTIN.	-do-	Road Junction & immediately West of L in LATTRE.	X plus 8½	NOYELLE-VION -GIVENCHY-LE-NOBLE- PENIN.	18	X plus 15	
23.	-do-	Hd.Qrs. 40th M.G.Battn.	HAUTEVILLE	-do-	Junction of HAUTEVILLE-LATTRE and HAUTEVILLE-AVESNES Rds.	X plus 8½	AVESNES-GIVENCHY-PENIN.	18	X plus 15	If there is insufficient accommodation for Serial Nos.21,22,& 23 in train No.18, some of 40th M.G.Bn.will travel by Train 21 which leaves at X plus ~~15~~. 18.
24.	-do-	No.3 Coy. 40th Div. Train	AVESNES-LE-COMTE	-do-	Level Crossing just South of C in AVESNES-LE-COMTE on Rd.to GIVENCHY	X plus 12¼	GIVENCHY-PENIN.	21	X plus 18	

Serial No.	Date	Unit	From	To	Starting Point	Hour of Starting	Route	Train No. of	Train Hr. of dep.	Remarks.
25	B day	231st Field Coy. R.E.	LATTRE ST QUENTIN	TINQUES	Road Junction immediately West of L in LATTRE ST QUENTIN.	X plus 12¼	NOYELLE-VION-GIVENCHY-LE-NOBLE.-PENIN.	21	X plus 18.	

Entraining Instructions to accompany 120th Infantry Brigade Order No. 174 dated 5th March 1918.

****

Re M O V E.

1. Reference 120th Infantry Brigade Order No. 174 the Brigade will be prepared to entrain in accordance with attached Time Table. Zero hour (hour of departure of first train from TINCQUES or RREVENT according to Staging Area used) will be notified by wire.

2. Accommodation in Staging Areas is allotted in attached Table. Billetting parties will be sent on in advance under Regimental Arrangements. No lorries will be available. These parties will report to Area Commandant or Sub-Area Commandant concerned (See 40th Divn. C/128/Q of 4.3.1918 ~~attached~~).

3. Entraining Officers. 10/11th High.L.I. and 14th A.&.S. Highlanders will each detail an officer not below the rank of Captain to assist units entraining and will remain at the Station until the last unit ofthe Brigade Entraining Group has entrained. They will travel by the last train. These officers will report to R.T.O. ~~4~~ 4 hours before ZERO hour.

4. Entraining Parties. An entraining party of 2 Officers and 100 O.Rs. will be detailed as in attached time table. One officer will report to R.T.O. on arrival for instructions. Remainder of party will remain with unit outside station yard until instructions are received.

5. Detraining Parties. A party of 2 Officers and 100 O.Rs will be detailed from company of 14th High.L.I. travelling by train No. 3 for detraining duties. They will report on arrival to R.T.O. at Detraining Station and will work under his orders.

6. Hour of Arrival at Station. Troops and transport will be at entraining station 3 hours before the scheduled time of departure of train. Loading of all trains must be completed ½ hour before train is due to depart.

7. Entraining States. A completestate shewing number of Officers, O.Rs., horses, limbered G.S.Wagons, bicycles and technical vehicles will be forwarded to this office as soon as possible after instructions to move are received. Duplicate will be handed to R.T.O. at Entraining Station and no troopswill enter the station yard until the O.C. the unit has reported to the R.T.O. and handed in the state.

8. Breast ropes will be provided by units themselves.

9. Water carts to entrain full. Water bottles to be filled before entrainment. Horses should be watered before entrainment.

10. Rations will be taken on the train for consumption on day following detrainment. Units entrain with their Baggage and Supply wagons. Detailed instructions later.

11. Senior Officer present will be responsible for discipline of the troops in his train. Pickets will be detailed for duty at halts during the journey to prevent the troops leaving the compartments without orders.

12. Lorries will be provided to move blankets and heavy baggage.

A.B. [illegible] Captain,
Staff Captain,
120th Infantry Brigade.

Unit.	Present Location.	Location in HERMAVILLE Area. Entraining Station TINCQUES.	Location in LE CAUROY Area. Entraining Station FREVENT.	Train No.	Time of Departure.	Entraining parties to be detailed by (see para 4).
Bde.Hd.Qrs. including Signals.	POMMIER.	AVESNES-LE-COMTE.	LIENCOURT.	No.3.	X.	
'B' Coy. 40th Bn.M.G.Corps.	HENDECOURT.	HAUTEVILLE.	DENIER.	No.3.	X.	Coy. of 14th H.L.I.
120th T.M.Batty.	POMMIER.	AVESNES-LE-COMTE.	LIENCOURT.	No.3.	X.	
1 Coy. 1 Cooker & Team of 14th High.L.I.	POMMIER.	AVESNES-LE-COMTE.	LIENCOURT.	No.3.	X.	
14th H.L.I. (less 1 Coy., 1 cooker & team).	POMMIER.	AVESNES- LE-COMTE.	LIENCOURT.	No. 6.	X plus 3	14th H.L.I.
10/11th H.L.I. (less 1 Coy., 1 cooker & team.)	BERLES-AU- BOIS	LATTRE.ST.QUENTIN	GRAND RULLECOURT	No. 9.	X plus 6	10/11th H.L.I
14th A.&.S.Hdrs (less 1 Coy., 1 cooker & team).	BERLES-AU-BOIS	LATTRE.ST.QUENTIN.	LIGNEREUIL.	No.12.	X plus 9.	14th A.&.S.H
'D' Coy. 40th Bn.M.G.Corps.	HENDECOURT.	HAUTEVILLE.	DENIER.	No.15.	X plus 12	
237th Div. Emplovt. Coy.	BEAUMETZ.	HERMAVILLE.	LE CAUROY.	No.15.	X plus 12.	Coy of 10/11 H.L.I.
1 Coy., 1 cooker & team of 10/11th H.L.I.	BERLES-AU-BOIS	LATTRE.ST.QUENTIN.	GRAND RULLECOURT.	No.15	X plus 12.	H.L.I.
1 Coy., 1 cooker & team of 14th A.&.S.Hdrs.	BERLES-AU-BOIS	LATTRE.ST.QUENTIN.	LIGNEREUIL.	No.18.	X plus 15	Coy. of 14th A.&.S.Hrs.
135th Fd. Ambulance.	BIENVILLERS.	AVESNES-LE-COMTE.	GRAND RULLECOURT.	No.18.	X plus 15	
Part Hd.Qrs. 40th Bn.M.G.C.	HENDECOURT.	HAUTEVILLE.	DENIER.	No.18.	X plus 15.	
Remdr. of Hd.Qrs. 40th Bn. M.G.Corps.	HENDECOURT.	HAUTEVILLE.	DENIER.	No.21.	X plus 18	231st Fd.Coy R.E.
No.3 Coy. 40th Div. Train.	POMMIER.	AVESNES-LE-COMTE.	BERLENCOURT.	No.21.	X plus 18.	
231st Fd.Coy. R.E.	BIENVILLERS.	LATTRE.ST.QUENTIN.	BEAUFORT.	No.21.	X plus 18.	

SECRET

Appx III COPY NO.....

120TH (HIGHLAND) INFANTRY BRIGADE ORDERNO. X.

Ref. 57D. N.E.
Trench Map (Hatched). 8: 3: 18.

1. At 3 p.m. to-day the enemy heavily attacked the British line running from Eastern outskirts of ESSARTS through F.14 central to Eastern edge of ADINFER WOOD. Opposite ESSARTS and ADINFER WOOD the attack was repulsed, but the enemy is reported to have broken through the line between these two points.

2. The 40th Division has been ordered to move forward preparatory to a counter-attack.

3. The 120th Brigade will move forward to a position of assembly in the valley about E.10.c. Advanced parties will meet the Staff Captain at 9.15 a.m. at the cross roads in HANNESCAMPS, E.16.a.5.9. Units will be in position by 9.45 a.m.

4. Brigade Headquarters will open at 9.15 a.m. at the road junction at E.3.c.0.0. in BIENVILLERS, where there will be a conference at 9.30 a.m. C.Os. and representatives from the Tank Corps will attend.

--------oOo--------

S E C R E T　　　　　　　　　　　　　　　　COPY NO.....

120TH (HIGHLAND) INFANTRY BRIGADE ORDER NO. Y.

8: 3: 18.

1. The enemy has broken through the British line between ESSARTS and ADINFER WOOD, and his and the British present lines are shown on attached map.

2. The 120th Brigade has been ordered to counter-attack to regain the original line.

3. The capture of the first objective, shown on attached map, will be carried out by the 14th H.L.I. on the right and the 10/11th H.L.I. on the left. The 14th A. & S. H. will be in reserve.
Boundaries of attacking battalions are shown on attached map.
14th H.L.I. will be directing battalion.

4. The 10/11th and 14th Battns. H.L.I. will remain on the first objective and consolidate it, and the 14th A. & S.H. will pass through them to capture the second objective.

5. On completion of the capture of the second objective, the 10/11th and 14th H.L.I. will extend the flanks of the 14th A. & S.H. to join up with Brigades on either flank.

6. O.C., T.M.Battery will place two Stokes Mortars at the disposal of the A. & S.H. to assist in the capture of the second objective.

7. Details of artillery barrages, time table of attack, and co-operation of Tanks will be issued later.

8. ZERO hour will be 10.22 a.m. This will be the hour at which the two attacking battalions move off from the assembly positions.

--------oOo--------

INSTRUCTIONS FOR 120TH BRIGADE SCHEME

--*-*-*-*-*-*-*-*-*-*-*-*-*-*-*-*-*

1. The enemy will be represented by men of the T.M.Battery, who will wear caps, and 3 drummers from each battalion. They will all report to Captain OMAN and Lieut. CUTHBERTSON at 9 a.m. at E.24.b.8.3. on HANNESCAMPS - ESSARTS Road.

2. The enemy is supposed to have organised several strong points, in which the drummers will be placed. Rolls on their drums will represent hostile M.G. fire from these strong points.

3. Smoke candles will be lit at various points to simulate enemy barrages, and units may be told by one of the umpires that they are being shelled with gas shell and must move forward with box respirators.

4. Tanks will be represented by a stretcher and two bearers accompanied by 3 other men, one carrying a white signal flag and the other two wire cutters to cut lanes for the tanks where necessary. Each battalion will provide 4 of these parties. They will be at the Cross Roads at HANNESCAMPS, E.10.c.2.3. at 9.15 a.m. Detailed instructions will be given to them later by officers of the Tank Corps.

5. Lieut.-Colonel BENZIE, D.S.O. will be chief umpire, and the 10/11th and 14th H.L.I. will each detail a senior officer to act as umpires under Colonel BENZIE. Umpires will wear a white band on their arms. Brigade Staff Officers will also assist. Battalions will send 2 runners with each umpire, each with 2 blue signal flags. If any units are put out of action by an umpire, they will be given one of these blue flags to put up.
All units will comply strictly with umpire's decision.
Umpires will report to Lieut.-Colonel BENZIE at ESSARTS at

6. As the attack may last a considerable time, units should make arrangements to provide men with food.

7. Lewis gun limbers, S.A.A. limbers and pack animals will be taken, and will be parked under the T.O. of the 10/11th H.L.I., who will report for instructions to the Staff Captain with the advanced parties of battalions.
Pack animals should actually be sent up after the attack.

8. Scouting aeroplanes, representing hostile harassing 'planes and British planes looking for anti-tank guns, will probably be flying over the heads of the troops.

****

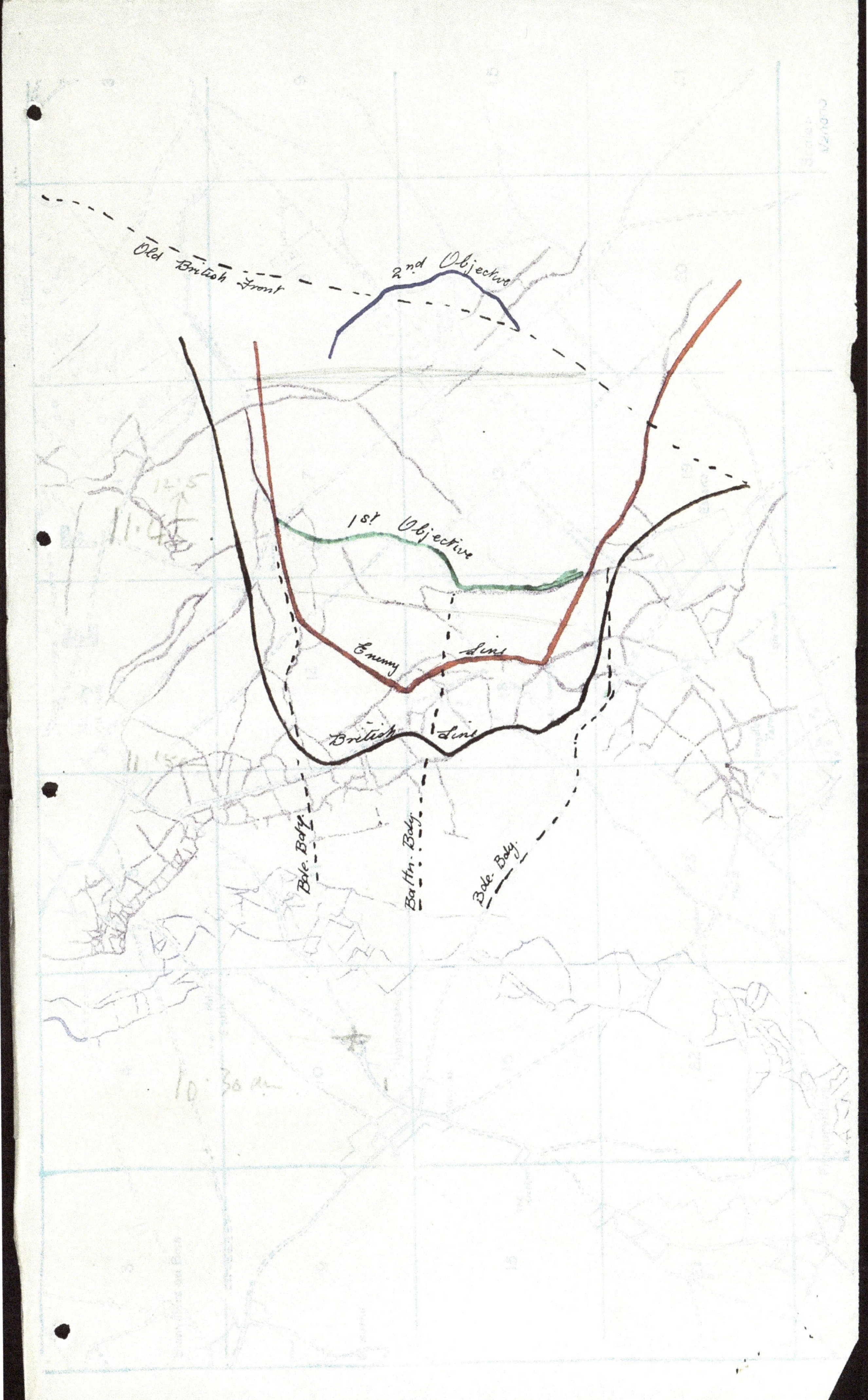

Old British Front
2nd Objective
1st Objective
Enemy Line
British Line
Bde. Bdy.
Battn. Bdy.
Bde. Bdy.

War Diary.

Appx IV

SECRET.

COPY NO. 4

120TH (HIGHLAND) INFANTRY BRIGADE INSTRUCTION No.1.

-

Ref. Maps.
LENS 11 1/100,000
Sht. 51b 1/40,000
57c 1/40,000

10 : 3 : 18.

1. The 40th Division is in G.H.Q. Reserve and quartered in the BASSEUX Area.

2. (a) In the event of an enemy attack taking place on any front other than the VI Corps front or those parts of the neighbouring Corps fronts adjoining, the 120th Brigade Group, comprising the units mentioned in 120th (Highland) Infantry Brigade Order No. 174, will move by rail and road in accordance with 120th (Highland) Infantry Brigade Order No. 174.

(b) If the attack is on the VI Corps front or on the front of the left Division of the IV Corps or the right Division of the XVII Corps, the 40th Division will be placed at the disposal of the G.O.C. VI Corps.

3. In the event of para 2 (b), the 120th Brigade Group will be prepared to move forward to positions of assembly in accordance with Tables A and B attached.
The routes laid down will be reconnoitred by units as early as possible.

4. From the Positions of Assembly, Brigade may be ordered forward to any of the places of Deployment (Rendezvous) shown on map E, forwarded to Battalions on 24/3/18 in accordance with attached table C.

5. From these places of Deployment the 120th Brigade may be ordered :-

(a) To occupy a portion of the 3rd System on the threatened front.
(b) To carry out an immediate counter-attack (i.e. within 24 hours of the original attack) to regain any portion of the Second System in which the enemy may have gained footing.

For this purpose Battalion Commanders will carry out reconnaissances so as to be able to counter-attack to regain and hold any portion of :-

(I) The front line of the Second System between MOREUIL and LONGATTE (both inclusive)
(II) Any portion of the front line of the Second System between ECOUST and CROISILLES (both inclusive)
(III) Any portion of the front line of the Second System immediately North of CROISILLES.
(IV) HENIN HILL
(V) WANCOURT TOWER RIDGE.
(VI) The front line of the second system North of the River COJEUL probably in co-operation with the Reserve Division of the XVII Corps.

6. For the immediate counter-attack ordered in para 5, the following additional artillery will be placed under the command of the C.R.A. :-

One Brigade of Heavy Artillery (already in position).

In addition, the attack would be supported by such other artillery, in position, on the Corps front, which can be brought to bear, under arrangements to be made by the G.O.C. R.A. V1 Corps.

7. Tanks may be available for the immediate counter-attack, but Battalions must not rely on their assistance owing to the short time available before this attack is launched.

8. Battalions will carry out tactical exercises based on the tasks allotted to them vide para 5.

9. Position of Dumps of Ammunitién, Bombs and R.E. material is shown on Appendix 11 attached.

10. The 120th Brigadewill also be prepared in combination with other Brigades to carry out a deliberate Counter-attack (i.e. after the lapse of 24 hours) to regain any larger portion of the Battle Zone which may have been lost. The arrangements for this attack would be in greater detail (in accordance with S.S.135)

11. For a deliberate counter-attack the following artillery, in addition to that already in the line, would probably be available for the Division :-

(a) Within 48 hours.
Our own Divisional Artillery.
2 A.F.A. Brigades.
2 H.A. Brigades.

(b) Within 96 hours.
As in (a) plus 2 A.F.A.Brigades and 3 H.A. Brigades and possibly the Divisional Artillery of co-operating Divisions.

12. One Battalion Tank Corps (36 Tanks) would be available to co-operate in any deliberate counter-attack carried out by the Division.

13. In the event of an attack limited to the front of either the 1V Corps or XV11 Corps, the 120th Brigade will be prepared to co-operate as follows :-

(1) Attack limited to 1V Corps front.

(a) The Brigade will march to rendezvous in the 1V Corps area in accordance with table D attached.
(b) The Battalions of the Brigade will be prepared to move from these rendezvous to occupy the portion of Third System in the Left Sector of the 1V Corps Area (from I.6.a.0.8. 400 yds North of MORCHIES Northwards to the boundary between 1V and V1 Corps)

(c) .....

(c) From the Third System the Brigade may be required to counter- attack to regain either of the spurs North and South of LAGNICOURT.

(d) In carrying out the operations b and c above, the Division would be supported by our own Divisional Artillery.

(2) <u>Attack limited to XVII Corps front.</u>

(w) The 120th Brigade will march to the NEUVILLE VITASSE Area in accordance with attached table E.

(x) The Battalions will be prepared to move from those rendezvous to occupy [illegible] part of the Third Trench System from the River Scarpe Southwards to the boundary between VI and XVII Corps.

(y) From the Third System the Brigade may be required to counter-attack to regain the Second System South of MONCHY-LE-PREUX.

(z) In carrying out the operations X,Y, above, the Division will be supported by our own Divisional Artillery.

(3) Battalion Commanders will carry out the necessary reconnaissances of those portions of the Third System mentioned in (1) and (2) of the covered routes leading to them and also the ground between the Third and Second Systems over which they may have to counter-attack.

14. Contact aeroplanes will act in conjunction with battalions in any counter-attacks undertaken by the Brigade.

15. Dress will be as laid down in Sec. XXXI, S.S.135, except that -

(a) Leather jerkins will be carried.

(b) Only Bombs and Rifle Grenades carried as mobile Reserve will be taken as far as the places of Deployment where additional ammunition etc. can be distributed.

(c) Aeroplane flares, if available.

(d) S.O.S. Signals ,,

(e) Artillery flags if issued.

(f) P. or K.J. Bombs ,,

(g) The tools to be taken will be those carried on the Transport. They will only be issued to the troops when ordered by Brigade Commander.

16. The minimum numbers which must be left behind when units move to the Assembly positions are laid down in Sec. XXX S.S.135. These Officers and other ranks will remain in their present billeting area and will take charge of all stores etc. left behind when the units move.

(1).

17\. The maps to be carried by all in possession of the same are those quotes at the top of these Instructions.

In addition, a special map showing Battle Zone and trench systems will be taken by units to whom they have been issued.

18\. Units will report by wire the completion of all moves laid down in these Instructions.

19\. A C K N O W L E D G E.

[signature]

Captain,
Brigade Major,
120th (Highland) Infantry Brigade.

Issued through
Signals
at 8 p.m.

Distribution :-

Copy No. 1. ... G.O.C.
2 ... Brigade Major.
3 ... Staff Captain.
4 ... File.
5 ... War Diary.
6 ... 10/11th High. L. I.
7 ... 14th High. L. I.
8 ... 14th Arg. & Suth'd Highrs.
9 ... 120th T. M. Battery.
10 ... 231st Field Coy. R.E.
11 ... 40th Battn. M. G. Corps
12 ... No. 3 Coy., 40th Divn. Train.
13 ... 135th Field Ambulance.
14 ... 237th (Divn) Employment Coy.
15 ... 40th Division (G)
16 ... 40th Division (Q)
17 ... 119th Infantry Brigade.
18 ... 121st Infantry Brigade.
19 ... C.R.E., 40th Division.
20 ... 40th Divnl. Train.
21 ... A.D.M.S., 40th Division.
22 ... T.O., 17th Welsh Regt.
23 ... A.P.M., 40th Division.
24 ... Bde. Supply Officer.
25 ... Bde. Signals.
26 ... Area Commandant ERVILLERS.
27 ... Area Commandant MERCATEL.
28 ... [illegible]
29

****

TABLE "A" TO ACCOMPANY 120TH BRIGADE INSTRUCTION DATED 10/3/18.

Serial No.	Unit	From	To	Starting Point	Hour of Starting	Route	Remarks.
1.	Hd.Qrs., B & D Coys.40th Bn. M.G.Corps.	HENDECOURT	ERVILLERS	HENDECOURT Church.	Z hour	ADINFER-COURCELLES-LE-COMTE.	Details of billeting accommodation will be issued later.
2.	231st Field Coy. R.E.	BIENVILLERS	-do-	BIENVILLERS Church	Z hour	MONCHY-ADINFER-COURCELLES.	-do-
3.	135th Field Ambulance.	-do-	-do-	-do-	Z plus 15.	-do-	-do-
4.	Transport 17th Welsh.	-do-	-do-	-do-	Z plus 25	-do-	-do-
5.	Hd. Qrs. 120th Bde. & Signal Section.	POMMIER	-do-	Junction of POMMIER-BIENVILLERS & POMMIER ST AMAND Roads.	Z plus 30	BIENVILLERS- MONCHY ADINFER-COURCELLES.	-do-
6.	120th T.M.Bty.	-do-	-do-	-do-	Z plus 35	-do-	-do-
7.	14th H. L. I.	-do-	-do-	-do-	Z plus 45	-do-	-do-
8.	No. 3 Coy. Div. Train.	-do-	-do-	-do-	-	-do-	Hour of starting to depend upon time of refilling.
9.	10/11th H.L.I.	BERLES-AU-BOIS	-do-	Junction of BERLES-POMMIER & BERLES-BIENVILLERS Rds.	Z plus 60	-do-	Details of billeting accommodation will be issued later.

Serial No.	Unit	From	To	Starting Point	Hr. of Starting	Route	Remarks.
10.	14th A. & S. H.	BERLES-AU-BOIS.	ERVILLERS	Junction of BERLES-POMMIER & BERLES-BIENVILLERS Rds.	Z plus 85	BIENVILLERS-MONCHY-ADINFER-COURCELLES.	Details of billeting accommodation will be issued later.
11.	237th Employment Company	BEAUMETZ	-do-				Route and time - any.

TO ACCOMPANY 120TH BDE. INSTRUCTION NO. 1 DATED 10:3:18.

TABLE "B" (as for TABLE "A")

TABLE "C" (1) :-

Serial No.	Unit	From	To	Starting Point	Hour of Starting	Route	Remarks.
1.	HdQrs.120th Bde. & Signal Section	ERVILLERS Area	M.36.c.8.0.	Junction of ERVILLERS-ARRAS & ERVILLERS-HAMELINCOURT Rds.	Z	Main BAPAUME-ARRAS Road.	Details of billeting to be issued later.
2.	120th T.M.Battery.	-do-	MERCATEL Area.	-do-	Z plus 5	-do-	-do-
3.	10/11th H. L. I.	-do-	-do-	-do-	Z plus 15	-do-	-do-
4.	14th H. L. I.	-do-	-do-	-do-	Z plus 35	-do-	-do-
5.	14th A. & S. Hrs.	-do-	-do-	-do-	Z plus 55	-do-	-do-
6.	B & D Coys. 40th Bn. M.G. Corps.	-do-	-do-	-do-	Z plus 75	-do-	-do-
7.	H.Qrs.40th M.G.Bn.	-do-	BOISLEUX-AU-MONT	-do-		-do- then BOISLEUX ST MARC.	-do- As convenient.
8.	231st Field Coy.R.E.	-do-	BOISLEUX ST MARC.	-do-	Z plus 90	-do-	Details of billeting issued later
9.	135th Fd.Ambulance.	-do-	-do-	-do-	Z plus 100	-do-	-do-
10	No. 3 Coy. 40th Div. Train.	-do-	-do-	-do-	-	-do-	Hr. of start to depend upon time of refilling.
11.	Divl. Employment Coy.	-do-	DURHAM "B" LINES	-do-		HAMELINCOURT	As convenient.

TABLE C (ii).

Serial No.	Unit	From	To	Starting Point.	Hour of Starting	Route	Remarks.
1.	Hd.Qrs.120th Bde. & Signal Section.	ERVILLERS Area	"F" Deployment Position - T.1.c. & d. HQ. M.36.c.8.0.	Junction of ERVILLERS-ARRAS & ERVILLERS-HAMELINCOURT Rds.	Z	Main BAPAUME-ARRAS Road.	
2.	120th T.M.Battery.	-do-	-do- "F" Deployment Position T.1.c.&d.	-do-	Z plus 5	-do-	
3.	10/11th H. L. I.	-do-	-do-	-do-	Z plus 15.	-do-	
4.	14th H. L. I.	-do-	-do-	-do-	Z plus 35	-do-	
5.	14th A. & S. Hrs.	-do-	-do-	-do-	Z plus 55	-do-	
6.	B Coy.40th M.G.Bn.	-do-	-do-	-do-	Z plus 75	-do-	
7.	D Coy.40th M.G.Bn.	-do-	MERCATEL	-do-	Z plus 90	-do-	Hd.Qrs.at H.Q.119th Bde.
8.	H.Qrs.40th M.G.Bn.	-do-	BOISLEUX-AU-MONT	-do-	As convenient	HAMELINCOURT -BOISLEUX- -AU-MONT.	To give way to any troops of 121st Bde. when moving through HAMELINCOURT.
9.	231st Field Coy.R.E.	-do-	BOISLEUX ST MARC	-do-	Z plus 100	As for Serial No. 8.	
10.	135th Field Ambce.	-do-	-do-	-do-	Z plus 110	---------ditto-----------	
11.	No.3 Coy.Div.Train.	-do-	-do-	-do-	-	---------ditto---	Hr.of departure to depend upon time of refilling.
12.	Div. Employment Coy.	-do-	DURHAM "B" LINES.	-do-		--------ditto------	

TABLE " C" (iii)

Serial No.	Unit	From	To	Starting Point	Hour of Starting.	Route	Remarks.
1.	Hd.Qrs.120th Bde and Signal Section.	ERVILLERS Area	YORK EXCHANGE B.2.b.8.4.	Junction of ERVILLERS-ARRAS & ERVILLERS-HAMELINCOURT Rds.	Z hour.	B.8.a. and B.2.c.	
2.	120th T. M. Bty.	-do-	"C" Position of Deployment B.3.c.	-do-	Z plus 5	-do-	
3.	10/11th H. L. I.	-do-	-do-	-do-	Z plus 10	-do-	
4.	14th H. L. I.	-do-	-do-	-do-	Z plus 30	-do-	
5.	14th A. & S. Hrs.	-do-	-do-	-do-	Z plus 50	-do-	
6.	B Coy. 40th M.G. Battalion.	-do-	-do-	-do-	Z plus 70	-do-	
7.	H.Qrs. 40th M.G.Bn.	-do-	GOMIECOURT			direct	Hr. as convenient.
8.	D Coy. 40th M.G.Bn.	-do-	HAMELINCOURT Area	-do-	Z plus 80	direct.	Can move earlier if not on ERVILLERS-ARRAS Road.
9.	231st Field Coy.R.E.	Remain in ERVILLERS Area.					
10.	135th Fd.Ambulance.						
11.	No.3 Coy.Div.Train.						
12.	Divl.Employment Coy.						

TABLE " C" (iii)

Serial No.	Unit	From	To	Starting Point	Hour of Starting.	Route	Remarks.
1.	Hd.Qrs.120th Bde and Signal Section.	ERVILLERS Area	YORK EXCHANGE B.2.b.8.4.	Junction of ERVILLERS-ARRAS & ERVILLERS-HAMELINCOURT Rds.	Z hour.	B.8.a. and B.2.c.	
2.	120th T. M. Bty.	-do-	"C" Position of Deployment B.3.c.	-do-	Z plus 5	-do-	
3.	10/11th H. L. I.	-do-	-do-	-do-	Z plus 10	-do-	
4.	14th H. L. I.	-do-	-do-	-do-	Z plus 30	-do-	
5.	14th A. & S. Hrs.	-do-	-do-	-do-	Z plus 50	-do-	
6.	B Coy. 40th M.G. Battalion.	-do-	-do-	-do-	Z plus 70	-do-	
7.	H.Qrs. 40th M.G.Bn.	-do-	GOMIECOURT			direct	Hr. as convenient.
8.	D Coy. 40th M.G.Bn.	-do-	HAMELINCOURT Area	-do-	Z plus 80	direct.	Can move earlier if not on ERVILLERS-ARRAS Road.
9.	231st Field Coy.R.E.	Remain in ERVILLERS Area.					
10.	135th Fd.Ambulance.						
11.	No.3 Coy.Div.Train.						
12.	Divl.Employment Coy.						

TABLE C (iv).

Serial No.	Unit	From	To	Starting Point	Hour of Starting	Route	Remarks.
1.	120th Bde.H.Qrs & Signal Section.	ERVILLERS Area	C.19.c.5.3.	Cross Roads B.13.d.8.5.	Z	MORY - B.22 & 23.	
2.	120th T. . Bty.	-do-	"A" Deployment Position - B.24.	-do-	Z plus 5.	-do-	
3.	10/11th H. L. I.	-do-	-do-	-do-	Z plus 10	-do-	
4.	14th H. L. I.	-do-	-do-	-do-	Z plus 30	-do-	
5.	14th A & S. Hrs.	-do-	-do-	-do-	Z plus 50	-do-	
6.	B Coy 40th M.G.Bn.	-do-	-do-	-do-	Z plus 70	-do-	
7.	H.Qrs.40th M.G.Bn.	-do-	GOMIECOURT	.......As	convenient.............		
8.	231st Field Coy.R.E.	Remain in ERVILLERS Area.					
9.	135th Fd.Ambulance.						
10.	No. 3 Coy. Div. Train.						
11.	D Coy. 40th M.G.Battn.						
12.	Divnl. Employment Coy.						

TABLE "D".

Serial No.	Unit	From	To	Starting Point	Hour of Starting	Route	Remarks.
1.	231st Field Coy.R.E.	BIENVILLERS	FAVREUIL	BIENVILLERS Church	Z	BIENVILLERS-HANNESCAMPS-BUCQUOY-ACHIET-LE-GRAND-MONUMENT-FAVREUIL.	
2.	135th Field Ambulance	-do-	H.12.a. & c.	-do-	Z plus 10	-do-	
3.	120th Bde. Hd. Qrs. & Signal Section.	POMMIER	H.12.c.2.3. near BEUGNATRE	POMMIER Church	Z plus 5	-do-	
4.	120th T.M. Battery.	-do-	H.12.a. & c. near BEUGNATRE.	-do-	Z plus 10	-do-	
5.	14th H. L. I.	-do-	-do-	-do-	Z plus 15	-do-	
6.	10/11th H.L.I.	BERLES-AU-BOIS	-do-	Junction of BERLES-POMMIER and BERLES-BIENVILLERS Rds.	Z plus 45	-do-	
7.	14th A & S. H.	-do-	-do-	-do-	Z plus 65	-do-	
8.	40th Bn.M.G.Corps.	Under 119th Brigade Group Orders.					
9.	No.3 Coy. Div.Train.)	Under arrangements to be issued later.					
10.	Divnl.Employment Coy.)						

TABLE "E"

Serial No.	Unit	From	To	Starting Point	Hour of Starting	Route	Remarks.
1.	231st Field Coy. R.E.	BIENVILLERS	NEUVILLE Mill M.24.d.	BIENVILLERS Church	Z hour	MONCHY-ADINFER-BOIRY ST RICTRUDE-BOISLEUX-AU-MONT-BOIRY BECQUERELLE.	
2.	135th Field Ambce.	-do-	MERCATEL	-do-	Z plus 10	-do-	
3.	Hd.Qrs.120th Bde. and Signal Section	POMMIER	M.36.8.0.	POMMIER Church	Z plus 5	-do-	
4.	120th T. M. Battery.	-do-	MERCATEL Area	-do-	Z plus 10	-do-	
5.	14th H. L. I.	-do-	-do-	-do-	Z plus 30	-do-	
6.	10/11th H.L.I.	BERLES-AU-BOIS	-do-	Junction of BERLES-POMMIER and BERLES-BIENVILLERS Rds.	Z plus 50	BIENVILLERS thence as for Serial No.1	
7.	14th A. & S. H.	-do-	-do-	-do-	Z plus 70	-do-	
8.	40th M.G.Battn.	Under arrangements of 119th Brigade Group.					
9.	No. 3 Coy. Div.Train.	Under arrangements to be issued later.					
10.	Divnl. Employment Coy.						

Reference 120th Infantry Brigade Instruction No. 1

dated 10th March 1918.

A. Surplus Personnel.

1. Reference para. 16 all surplus personnel will be billetted in BERLES-AU-BOIS. In calculating numbers to be left behind in accordance with Sect. XXX of S.S.135 allowance will be made for Officers and O.R. on Courses, leave, etc.

2. Major SEAGRIM, 14th High.L.I., will be in charge of all Details.

3. All units of Brigade Group will wire to this office, as soon as possible, number of personnel being left behind (and names of officers) so that arrangements may be made with VI Corps Troops Supply Column for rations.

B. Surplus Transport.

1. 12th Welsh Transport will remainin the area and will move to BERLES-AU-BOIS underarrangements with Area Commandant.

2. Transport Officer, 17th Welsh will detail 2 G.S.Limber Wagons to report, on orders for move being received, to 120th T.M.Battery to carry 8-3" Stokes Guns.

3. Brigade Supply Officer will arrange to ration through Brigade Headquarters 120th T.M.Battery, when move is ordered. Rations will also be required for two drivers and 4 horses detached from 17th Welsh Regt.

C. Surplus Baggage.

1. Only baggage wagons of units will be available for conveyance of baggage. These will be lightly loaded and will probably move with the No.3 Coy. Train.

2. All surplus officers' kits, mens' blankets and greatcoats, and quartermasters' Stores of units in the Brigade Group as detailed in 120th Brigade Order No. 174 will be collected as soon as possible after the move by 17th Welsh Transport under orders of O.C., Details and stored in accommodation at BERLES-AU-BOIS allotted by Area Commandant.

D. Dress.

Reference para. 15. Jerkins and packs not haversacks will be carried. Otherwise dress will be as in Section XXXl of S.S. 135.

E. Reinforcements.

All reinforcements and men returning from leave will be sent under Divisional arrangements from Railhead to report to Officer i/c Details at BERLES-AU-BOIS.

F. Moves.

Reference Tables 'D' and 'E' of 120th Brigade Instruction No.1. Instructions are being issued to units concerned (40th Divn. Train and Divnl. Employment Coy) by Divisional Headquarters as early as possible.

Accommodation/

Contd.

G. Accommodation.

Accommodation in Assembly Areas is limited and troops will require to bivouac.

Instructions as to time and place for Advanced parties to meet Staff Captain will be notified as soon as the order to move is issued.

H. Ammunition.

Lieut.R.A.Cuthbertson, 10/11th Highland Light Infy., will act as Brigade Ammunition Officer and will report to Brigade Headquarters on arrival at Assembly Area.

Location of dumps is as follows :-

Deployment Positions.	S.A.A., Grenades and 3" Stokes Dumps.
'A' and 'B'.	MORY. B.22.b.3.6.
'C') 'D')	34th Divn. Main Dump. T.25.c.9.3. 800 yards. South of MAISON ROUGE, main ARRAS - BAPAUME Road. ST. LEGER T.28.c.5.4.
'E') 'F')	NEUVILLE VITASSE, N.19.c.1.9. 34th Divn. Main Dump, T.25.c.9.5.
'G') 'H')	NEUVILLE VITASSE. N.19.c.1.9.

I. Brigade Transport Officer.

1. Captain J.A.CAMPBELL, M.C., 10/11th High.L.I., will act as Brigade Transport Officer and will take command where Transport is Brigaded.

2. Transport will move to assembly areas with units.

K. Medical Arrangements.

135th Field Ambulance is moving with Brigade Group to Assembly Areas. Thereafter Bearer Sections will accompany Brigade to positions of Deployment.

L. Transport Lines and Quartermasters' Stores.

Normally Echelon 'B' of 1st Line Transport will remain with Quartermasters' Stores and Echelon 'A' will accompany units to positions of Deployment, if circumstances permit.

Locations when battalions move to Deployment areas will be:-

Contd.

Deployment Area.	QM. Stores and Echelon 'B' of 1st line Transport.
'A'.	ERVILLERS.
'C'.	ERVILLERS.
'F'.	BOISLEUX-ST.-MARC.
MERCATEL Area.	Transport Lines YORK CAMP.

M. **Positions of Deployment and Positions of Assembly.**

Reference para. 4 of 120th Brigade Instructions No. 1. The alteration in the use of the term " Position of Assembly" is to be noted.

H.B. Kerr
Captain,
Staff Captain,
120th Infantry Brigade.

10.3.1918.

War Diary

Appx V

S E C R E T

COPY NO.....4

120TH (HIGHLAND) INFANTRY BRIGADE ORDER No. 175

Ref Maps
LENS 11. 1/100,000.
51B. 1/100,000.
57C. 1/40,000

11: 3 : 18.

1. The 40th Division is moving from the BASSEUX Area to the BOISLEUX Area on 12th March.

2. The 120th (Highland) Brigade Group, comprising the troops mentioned in para. 3, will move to the HAMELINCOURT-ERVILLERS Area on the 12th inst., in accordance with the attached march table.

3. The 120th Brigade Group will consist of :-

120th Bde.H. Qrs. & Signal Section.
10/11th H. L. I.
14th H. L. I.
14th A. & S. Hrs.
120th T. M. Battery.
231st Field Coy. R.E.
135th Field Ambulance.
"B" and "D" Coys., 40th M.G.Battn.

4. Details of lorries for advanced billeting parties and blankets, and of disposal of surplus baggage, etc., are given in attached Administrative Instructions.
Advanced parties will proceed to the respective camps shown in attached march table, and will wait there till the accommodation has been allotted by the Staff Captain, who will visit each camp in turn.

5. The greatest care will be taken by all units to ensure that no lights or fires which might be seen by the enemy are lit by troops arriving in the new area.

6. The strictest attention will be paid to the hour of start ordered in attached march table, and to the clock hour halts, as other troops will be moving immediately in rear of the Brigade Group.

7. Completion of all moves will be wired to Brigade H.Qrs.

8. Brigade Hd. Qrs. will close at POMMIER at 6 p.m. and re-open at the same hour at HAMELINCOURT.

9. A C K N O W L E D G E.

Issued through
Signals
at 7.30 p.m.

H. C. Emery
Captain,
Brigade Major.
120th (Highland) Infantry Brigade.

Distribution :-

Copy No.	1	...	G.O.C.
	2	...	Brigade Major.
	3	...	Staff Captain.
	4	...	War Diary.
	5	...	File.
	6	...	10/11th H.L.I.
	7	...	14th H.L.I.
	8	...	14th A. & S. H.
	9	...	120th T. M. Bty.
	10	...	231st Field Coy.R.E.
	11	...	135th Field Ambulance.
	12	...	40th Bn. M.G. Corps.
	13	...	B Coy. -do-
	14	...	D Coy. -do-
	15	...	No. 3 Coy. Div. Train.
	16	...	40th Division "G".
	17	...	40th Division "Q".
	18	...	119th Inf. Bde.
	19	...	121st Inf. Bde.
	20	...	C.R.E. 40th Division.
	21	...	A.D.M.S., 40th Divn.
	22	...	C.R.A., 40th Divn.
	23	...	A.P.M., 40th Divn.
	24	...	T.O., 17th Welsh Regt.
	25	...	Bde. Supply Officer.
	26	...	Bde. Signals.
	27	...	Area Commandant, ERVILLERS.
	28	...	Area Commandant, BERLES.

****

MARCH TABLE TO ACCOMPANY 120TH (HIGHLAND) INFANTRY BRIGADE ORDER NO. 175.

Serial No.	Unit	From	To	Starting Point	Hr. of starting	Route	Remarks.
1.	231st Field Coy.R.E.	BIENVILLERS	ARMAGH CAMP at HAMELINCOURT.	BIENVILLERS Church	6.30 p.m.	MONCHY-ADINFER-AYETTE-MOYENNEVILLE-HAMELINCOURT.	Not to halt at 6.50 p.m. First halt to be 7.50 p.m.
2.	135th Field Ambce.	---do---	---do---	---do---	6.35 p.m.	---do---	---do---
3.	120th Bde. Hd. Qrs. and Signal Section	POMMIER	HAMELINCOURT	Junction of POMMIER-ST AMAND & POMMIER-BIENVILLERS Rds.	6.20 p.m.	BIENVILLERS, thence as for Serials Nos. 1 & 2.	---do---
4.	120th T. M. Battery.	---do---	BELFAST CAMP B.13.a.5.7. (57c.)	---do---	6.25 p.m.	BIENVILLERS-MONCHY-ADINFER-AYETTE-COURCELLES-LE-COMTE-ERVILLERS.	---do---
5.	14th H. L. I.	---do---	ENNISKILLING CAMP B.13.b.F.5. (57c.)	---do---	6.30 p.m.	---do---	---do---
6.	10/11th H. L. I.	BERLES-AU-BOIS	BELFAST CAMP B.13.a.5.7. (57c.)	Junction of BERLES-POMMIER & BERLES-BIENVILLERS Roads.	6.45 p.m.	---do---	---do---
7.	14th A. & S. Hrs.	---do---	CLONMEL CAMP (HAMELINCOURT)	---do---	6.55 p.m.	BIENVILLERS-MONCHY-ADINFER-AYETTE-MOYENNEVILLE	---do---
8.	B. Coy. 40th M.G.Bn.	HENDECOURT	ENNISKILLEN CAMP B.13.b.7.5.(57c)	HENDECOURT Church	6.15 p.m.	Any	To give way to any troops of 119 Bde.on move
9	D Coy. -do-	-do-	CLONMEL CAMP (HEMELINCOURT)	-do-	6.20 p.m.	Any	---do---

N.B. Battalions will move closed up. 100 yards interval will be maintained between units.

Administrative Instructions to accompany 120th Infantry Brigade Order No. 175 dated 11th March 1918.

1. **Accommodation.**

Units should be prepared to find in all camps details of Battalions which have previously occupied them. 250 Other ranks of Corps Heavy Artillery are now in ARMAGH CAMP and will remain there. Actual accommodation in each camp will be allotted at the camps by Staff Captain during the day.

2. **Lorries.**

Four lorries will report at 8 am. on 12th instant to carry Advance Parties to new area, these are allotted as follows :-

1 lorry ... Bde.Hd.Qrs., 135th Fd.Amb., and 231st Fd. Coy. R.E.
1 lorry ... 14th H.L.I., 'B' Coy., M.G.Battn.
1 lorry ... 14th A.&.S.Hdrs., 'D' Coy., M.G.Battn.
1 lorry ... T.M.Bty., 10/11th H.L.I.

The first mentioned unit in each case will send a guide to Brigade Hd.Quarters and this unit will also be responsible that the lorry picks up advance parties of other units as mentioned above.

3. **Transport.**

As a general rule no Transport Lines will be available and suitable sites will be selected in the open.

4. **Details.**

Surplus personnel, surplus baggage, surplus transport 17th Welsh Rgt. will be dealt with as in 120th Inf. Bde. Instruction No. 1 dated 10th instant - paras (a), (b) and (c) - except that great-coats will be carried on the man and one blanket per man will be carried by lorry. Lorries for this purpose will report at 2 pm. on 12th instant to Brigade Hd.Qrs. and will be detailed as follows :-

1 lorry ... Bde.Hd.Qrs & T.M.Batty.
1 lorry ... 10/11th High. L.I.
1 lorry ... 14th H.L.I.
1 lorry ... 14th A.&.S.Hdrs.
1 lorry ... 'B' and 'D' Coys. M.G.Battn.

Cyclist guide will be sent to Brigade Hd.Qrs. to take these lorries to units.

5. **Arrivals.**

All personnel arriving at Railhead on and after 12th March will be disposed of in accordance with 120th Inf. Bde. Inst. No.1 para. (E).

6. **D.A.D.O.S.**

Is moving to S.14.a (North of BOIRY.ST.RICTRUDE) on 13th March.

7. **Railhead.**

From 13th March inclusive railhead will be at BOISLEUX-AU-MONT.

H.B. Kemp [signature]
Captain,
Staff Captain,
120th Infantry Brigade.

11.3.1918.

War Diary Appx VI

S E C R E T COPY NO. 4

120TH (HIGHLAND) INFANTRY BRIGADE ORDER NO. 176.

Ref. Maps
57c. 1/40,000.
LENS 11. 1/100,000.

15 : 3 : 18

1. While the 120th (Highland) Infantry Brigade Group is in the HAVRINCOURT Area it will be prepared to entrain at BAPAUME MAIN. 120th (Highland) Infantry Brigade Order No. 174 dated 5:3:18 is therefore cancelled under the present circumstances, but will still hold good in the event of the Brigade Group moving back into the POMMIER Area again.

2. For the purposes of entrainment at BAPAUME, the 120th Brigade Group will consist of :-

   120th (Highland) Infantry Brigade
   231st Field Coy. R.E.
   40th Bn. M.G. Corps less 2 companies.
   No. 3 Coy. Divnl. Train.
   135th Field Ambulance.
   Divisional Employment Coy.

3. All troops and transport will arrive at the entraining station 3 hours before the time of departure of the train.

4. Details regarding composition and allotment of trains, and entrainment are given in attached administrative instructions.

5. Movement of troops and transport to the entraining station are given in attached March Table.

6. Battalions will move with 200 yards between companies, and clock hour halts will be observed by all troops.

7. A C K N O W L E D G E.

Issued through
Signals
at 10 a.m.

H. E. Enoch
Captain.
Brigade Major.
120th (Highland) Infantry Brigade

Distribution:-

Copy No. 1 ... G.O.C.
2 ... Brigade Major.
3 ... Staff Captain.
4 ... War Diary.
5 ... File.
6 ... 10/11th H.L.I.
7 ... 14th H.L.I.
8 ... 14th A. & S.H.
9 ... 120th T.M.Bty.
10 ... 231st Field Coy.R.E.
11 ... 40th Bn. M.G.Corps.
12 ... "B" Coy. ---do---
13 ... "D" Coy. ---do---
14 ... No.3 Coy.40th Div.Train.
15 ... 135th Field Ambulance.
16 ... Divnl.Employment Coy.
17 ... 40th Division "G".
18 ... 40th Division "Q".
19 ... 119th Inf. Bde.
20 ... 121st Inf. Bde.
21 ... C.R.E. 40th Division.
22 ... 40th Divnl. Train.
23 ... A.D.M.S. 40th Divn.
24 ... O.C., 120th Bde.Details.
25 ... A.P.M., 40th Division.
26 ... Bde. Supply Officer.
27 ... Bde. Signals.
28 ... R.T.O., BAPAUME.
29 ... Area Commandant, ERVILLERS.
30 ... Area Commandant, BERLES-AU-BOIS.

****

MARCH TABLE TO ACCOMPANY 120TH (HIGHLAND) INFANTRY BRIGADE ORDER NO. 176.

Serial No	Unit	From	To	Starting Pt.	Hour of Start	Route	TRAIN Serial No. of	TRAIN Hr. of Depture	Remarks.
1.	1 Coy., 1 Cooker & Team 14th H.L.I.	ENNISKILLEN CAMP	BAPAUME MAIN	Road Junction B.13.b.3.2.	X - 5¼	Main ARRAS-BAPAUME Road.	3	X hr.	
2.	"B" Coy. 40th Bn. M.G.Corps.	--do--	--do--	--do--		--do--	3	X hr.	To follow 200 yds behind Serial No. 1. Details of B Coy. will rejoin the Coy before latter moves, under Coy. arrangements.
3.	120th T.M.Bty.	BELFAST CAMP	--do--	Road Junction B.13.b.3.0.	X - 5	--do--	3	X hr.	
4.	Bde. Hd.Qrs. and Signal Section.	HAMELINCOURT	--do--	Road Junction A.6.c.0.7.	X - 5¼	ERVILLERS then Main BAPAUME road.	3	X hr.	
5.	Details of Bde.H.Q., Signals, 14th H.L.I., 120th T.M.Bty., and Demonstration Platoon at BERLES.	BERLES-AU-BOIS.	--do--	Junction of BERLES-POMMIER and BERLES-BIENVILLERS Rds.	X - 9	BIENVILLERS-HANNES-CAMPS-BUCQUOY-ACHIET-LE-PETIT-ACHIET-LE-GRAND-BIEFVILLERS.	3	X hr.	To move as one column under orders of senior officer. Those for whom there is insufficient accommodation on train 3 will travel on train 6.
6.	14th H.L.I., less 1 Coy., 1 Cooker and Team.	ENNISKILLEN CAMP	--do--	Road Junction B.13.b.3.2.	X - 2	Main Road	6	X plus 3	Surplus os train 3 will also travel on this train if possible
7.	10/11th H.L.I., less 1 Coy., 1 Cooker and Team.	BELFAST CAMP	--do--	Road Junction B.13.b.3.0.	X plus 1	--do--	9	X plus 6	
8.	Details of 10/11th H.L.I. at BERLES.	BERLES-AU-BOIS	--do--	Junction of BERLES-POMMIER and BERLES-BIENVILLERS Rds.	X - 3	BIENVILLERS-HANNES-CAMPS-BUCQUOY-ACHIET-LE-PETIT-ACHIET-LE-GRAND-BIEFVILLERS.	9	X plus 6	Those for whom there is insufficient accommodation on this train will travel on train 15

Serial No.	Unit	From	To	Starting Pt.	Hr. of Start	Route	TRAIN Serial No. of	Hr. of Dep.	Remarks.
9.	14th A. & S.H. less 1 Coy., 1 Cooker & Team.	CLONMEL CAMP	BAPAUME MAIN.	Road Junction ?. A.6.c.0.7.	X plus $3\frac{3}{4}$	ERVILLERS thence Main Rd.	12	X plus 9	
10.	Details of 14th A. & S.H. at BERLES.	BERLES-AU-BOIS.	--do--	Junction of BERLES-POMMIER & BERLES-BIENVILLERS Roads.	x hr	BIENVILLERS-HANNESCAMPS-BUCQUOY-ACHIET-LE-PETIT-ACHIET-LE-GRAND-BIEFVILLERS	12	X plus 9	Those for whom there is insufficient accm on this train will travel on train 18.
11.	"D" Coy. 40th M.G. Bn.	CLONMEL CAMP	--do--	Road Junction A.6.c.0.7.	X plus $6\frac{3}{4}$	ERVILLERS thence Main Road.	15	X plus 12	Details will join the Coy. before it moves under Coy. arrangements.
12.	1 Coy., 1 Cooker & 1 team 10/11th H.L.I.	BELFAST CAMP.	--do--	Road Junction B.13.b.3.0.	X plus 7	Main Road	15	X plus 12	Surplus of train 9 will also travel by this train.
13.	237th Empl[t] Coy.	BASSEUX	--do--	------------Any convenient------------			15	X plus 12	
14.	1 Coy., 1 Cooker & Team 14th A.S.H.	CLONMEL CAMP	--do--	Road Junction A.6.c.0.7.	X plus $9\frac{1}{4}$	ERVILLERS thence Main Rd.	18	X plus 15	Surplus of train 12 will also travel by this train.
15	135th Fd.Amboe.	ARMAGH CAMP	--do--	--do--	X plus $9\frac{3}{4}$	--do--	18	X plus 15	
16.	Part of H.Qrs. 40th M.G.Battn.	BASSEUX	--do--				18	X plus 15	Route. etc. as convenient.
17.	Remainder of H.Q. 40th M.G. Battn.	--do--	--do--				21	X plus 18	Route, etc. as convenient
18.	231st Field Coy. R.E.	ARMAGH CAMP	--do--	Road Junction A.6.c.0.7.	X plus $12\frac{1}{2}$	ERVILLERS thence Main Rd.	21	X plus 18	

Serial No.	Unit	From	to	Starting Pt.	Hr. of start	Route	TRAIN Serial No. of	Hr. of Dep	Remarks.
19.	No.3 Coy. 10th Divnl. Train	HENDECOURT	BAPAUME Main		~~X plus 11~~	ADINFER-AYETTE-ALLAINZEVILLE-ACHIET-LE-GRAND-BIEFVILLERS.	21	X plus 18	To enter ADINFER at X+11 hrs.
20.	Details of 231st Field Coy. R.E.	BIENVILLERS	--do--	BIENVILLERS Church	X plus 10½	HANNESCAMPS- BUCQUOY ACHIET-LE-PETIT - ACHIET-LE-GRAND-BIEFVILLERS	21	X plus 18	

N.B. In all cases, sufficient men of the details will remain to load lorries and will then proceed to BAPAUME on the lorries. -

Entraining Instructions to accompany 120th Infantry Brigade Order No. 176 dated 15th March 1918.

1. Reference 120th Infantry Brigade Order No. 176 the Brigade Group will be prepared to entrain in accordance with attached Time Table. Zero hour i.e. hour of departure of first train of Brigade Group (No.3 Train) from BAPAUME MAIN will be notified by wire.

2. ENTRAINING STATION :- BAPAUME MAIN.

UNIT.	Train No.	Time of Departure.	Entraining parties to be detailed by (see para. 4).
Bde.Hd.qrs. including Signals and Demonstration Platoon.	No.3.	X.	
'B'Coy.40thBn.M.G.Corps.	No.3.	X.	Coy. of
120th T.M.Batty.	No.3.	X.	14th H. L. I.
1 Coy., 1 cooker & team of 14th High.L.I..	No.3.	X.	
14th H.L.I. (less 1 Coy., 1 cooker & team).	No 6.	X plus 3.	14th H.L.I.
10/11th H.L.I. (less 1 Coy., 1 cooker & team).	No.9.	X plus 6.	10/11th H.L.I
14th A.&.S.Hrs (less 1 Coy., 1 cooker & team).	No.12.	X plus 9.	14th A.&.S.H
'D' Coy.40thBn.M.G.Corps.	No.15.	X plus 12.	
237th Div. Employt. Coy.	No.15.	X plus 12.	Coy. of
1 Coy., 1 cooker & team of 10/11th H.L.I.	No.15.	X plus 12.	10/11 H.L.I.
H.Q. 40th Divnl. Arty.	No.15.	X plus 12.	
1 Coy., 1 cooker & team of 14th A.&.S.Hdrs.	No.18.	X plus 15.	Coy. of 14th
135th Fd. Ambulance.	No.18.	X plus 15.	
Part Hd.qrs. 40th Bn.M.G.C.	No.18.	X plus 15.	A.&.S.Hdrs.
Remdr. of Hd.qrs. 40th Bn. M.G. Corps.	No.21.	X plus 18.	231st Field
No.3 Coy.40th Div. Train.	No.21.	X plus 18.	
231st Fd. Coy., R.E.	No.21.	X plus 18.	Coy. R.E.

3. See Entraining Instructions issued with 120th Brigade Order No. 174 dated 5.3.1918. Instructions contained in paras. 3 to 12 remain in force.

4. Lorries detailed for conveyance of surplus stores in BERLES-AU-BOIS area will be despatched by O.C. Brigade Details in time to reach BAPAUME MAIN Station 3 hours before train for unit concerned is due to leave.

5. O.C. Brigade Details will travel by last train of Brigade Entraining Group (No.21) and will be responsible that all troops are despatched from BERLES-AU-BOIS.

H.B. Kerr
Captain,
Staff Captain,
120th Infantry Brigade.

ADDENDUM NO. 1 Appx VII

to

120TH (HIGHLAND) INFANTRY BRIGADE INSTRUCTION NO. 1

Dated 10:3:18.

1. The moves referred to in Table "A" issued with 120th (Highland) Infantry Brigade Instruction No.1 have been completed.

2. The attached Tables "C" (i), "C" (ii), "C" (iii), "C" (iv), "D" and "E" are substituted for those issued with 120th (Highland) Infantry Brigade Instruction No.1.

3. The 120th Brigade Group now consists of :-

120th (Highland) Infantry Brigade.
231st Field Company, R.E.
"B" and "D" Coys., 40th Bn., M.G.Corps.
135th Field Ambulance.

4. A C K N O W L E D G E.

Captain,
Brigade Major,
120th (Highland) Infantry Brigade.

Issued through
Signals
at 12.30 p.m.
to
All Recipients
of
120th (Hd.) Inf.
Bde.Instruction
No.1 dated 10:3:18.

****

TABLE "C" (i).

Serial No.	Unit	From	To	Starting Point	Hour of Start.	Route	Remarks.
1.	120th Bde. Hd.Qrs. and Signal Section.	HAMELINCOURT	N.19.c.2.8.	Cross Roads T.25.c.7.7.	Z	ARRAS-BAPAUME Rd. thence by covered route through N.30.c., N.25.a.	
2.	14th A. & S. Hrs.	--do--	"G" Deployment Position.	--do--	Z plus 5	---do---	
3.	"D" Coy. 40th Bn. M.G. Corps.	--do--	MERCATEL Area.	--do--	Z plus 20	---do---	
4.	10/11th H. L. I.	ERVILLERS	~~[illegible]~~ "G" Deployment Position	Rd. Junction B.13.b.3.1.	Z	---do---	
5.	"B" Coy. 40th Bn. M. G. Corps.	--do--	--do--	--do--	Z plus 15	---do---	
6.	14th H. L. I.	--do--	--do--	--do--	Z plus 25	---do---	
7.	120th T. M. Bty.	--do--	--do--	--do--		---do--	To follow 200 yds. behind Serial 6.
8.	231st Fd.Coy.R.E.	HAMELINCOURT	BOISLEUX ST MARC			Via BOISLEUX-AU-MONT	To clear ARMAGH Camp when convenient, but to give way to movements of other troops in the Bde. Group.
9.	135th Fd.Ambulance.	--do--	--do--			--do--	------do------

TABLE "C" (ii).

Serial No.	Unit	From	To	Starting Point	Hour of Starting	Route	Remarks.
1.	120th Bde. Hd.Qrs. and Signal Section	HAMELINCOURT	R.F.C.Directing Station BOIRY-BECQUERELLE.	Cross Rds. T.25.c.7 7.	Z	ARRAS - BAPAUME Road	
2.	14th A. & S. Hrs	--do--	Deployment Position "E". T.7 d.	--do--	Z plus 5	ARRAS-BAPAUME Rd.thence by covered route to "E" position through T.13.a.	
3.	"D" Coy 40th Bn. M.G. Corps.	--do--	MERCATEL	--do--	Z plus 20	ARRAS-BAPAUME Road.	
4.	231st Fd.Coy.R.E.	--do--	BOISLEUX ST MARC			Via BOISLEUX-AU-MONT	To move when convenient, but to give way to all other troops in the Bde. Group.
5.	135th Fd.Ambulance	--do--	--do--	--do--		--do--	------do------
6	10/11th H. L. I.	ERVILLERS	Deployment Position "E".	Rd. Junction B.13.b.3 1.	Z	ARRAS-BAPAUME Rd.thence by covered route to "E" position through T.13.a.	
7.	"B" Coy. 40th Bn. M.G.Corps.	--do--	--do--	--do--		----do----	To follow 200 yds. behind Serial 6.
8.	14th H. L. I.	--do--	--do--	--do--	Z plus 20	----do----	
9.	120th T. M. Bty.	--do--	--do--	--do--		----do----	To follow 200 yds. behind Serial 8.

TABLE "C" (iii)

Serial No.	Unit	From	To	Starting Point	Hour of Starting	Route	Remarks
1.	120th Bde. Hd.Qrs and Signal Section	HAVRINCOURT	YORK EXCHANGE B.2.b.8.4.	Cross Rds. T.25.c.7.7.	Z	ARRAS-BAPAUME Road thence by covered route through B.7.b., B.8.a.	
2.	14th A. & S. Hrs.	--do--	Deployment Position "C" B.3.c.	--do--	Z plus 5	--do--	
3.	10/11th H. L. I.	ERVILLERS	--do--	Rd.Junction B.13.b.3.1.	Z plus 20	--do--	
4.	"B" Coy. 40th Bn. M.G. Corps.	--do--	--do--	--do--	"	--do--	To follow 200 yds. behind Serial 3.
5.	14th H. L. I.	--do--	--do--	--do--	Z plus 45	--do--	
6.	120th T.M.Bty.	--do--	--do--	--do--	-	--do--	To follow 200 yds. behind Serial 5.
7.	"D" Coy. 40th Bn. M.G.Corps.	HAVRINCOURT	ERVILLERS	HAVRINCOURT Cemetery.	Z plus 25	Direct	To give way to any other troops of the Brigade Group.
8.	231st Fd.Coy.R.E.	--do--	--do--	--do--	Z plus 35	Direct	------do------
9.	135th Fd.Ambulance	--do--	--do--	--do--	Z plus 45	Direct	------do------

TABLE "J" (iv).

Serial No.	Unit	From	To	Starting Point	Hour of Starting	Route	Remarks.
1.	120th Bde. H.Q. & Signal Section.	HAMELINCOURT	C.19.c.5.3.	HAMELINCOURT Cemetery	Z plus 10	ERVILLERS-MORY	
2.	14th A. & S. H.	--do--	Deployment Position "A"	--do--	Z plus 15	--do--	
3.	"D" Coy. 40th Bn. M.G.Corps.	--do--	ERVILLERS	--do--	Z plus 30	Direct	
4.	10/11th H. L. I.	ERVILLERS	Deployment Position "A"	Road Junction B.13.b.3.1.	Z hour	Via MORY	
5.	"B" Coy. 40th Bn. M.G. Corps.	--do--	--do--	--do--		--do--	To follow 200 yds. behind Serial 4.
6.	14th H. L. I.	--do--	--do--	--do--	Z plus 20	--do--	
7.	120th T.M.Bty.	--do--	--do--	--do--		--do--	To follow 200 yds. behind Serial 6.
8.	231st Field Co.R.E.	------------- Remain at HAMELINCOURT -------------					
9.	135th Fd.Ambulance.						

TABLE "D".

Serial No	Unit	From	To	Starting Point	Hour of Starting	Route	Remarks.
1.	120th Bde. Hd.Qrs. and Signal Section.	HAMELINCOURT	H.18.c.2.3.	HAMELINCOURT Cemetery	Z plus 10	ERVILLERS-MONUMENT-FAVREUIL-BEUGNATRE	
2.	14th A. & S.Hrs.	--do--	Area H.12.a. & c.	--do--	Z plus 15	--do--	
3.	"D" Coy.40th Battn. M.G.Corps.	--do--	H.17.d.	--do--	Z plus 30	--do--	
4.	135th Fd.Ambulance.	--do--	H.12.a. & c.	--do--	Z plus 40	--do--	
5.	231st Fd.Coy.R.E.	--do--	FAVREUIL	--do--	Z plus 50	--do--	
6.	10/11th H. L. I.	ERVILLERS	H.12.a. & c. area.	Road Junctn B.13.b.3.1.	Z hour	--do--	
7.	"B" Coy.40th Battn M.G.Corps.	--do--	H.17.d.	--do--	-	--do--	To follow 200 yds behind Serial 6
8.	14th H. L. I.	--do--	H.12.a.& c.	--do--	Z plus 20	--do--	
9.	120th T.M.Bty.	--do--	--do--	--do--	-	--do--	To follow 200 yds. behind Serial 8.

TABLE "E"

Serial No.	Unit	From	To	Starting Point	Hr. of Start	Route	Remarks
1.	120th Bde. Hd. Qrs & Signal Section.	HAMELINCOURT	N.19.c.2.8.	Cross Roads T.25.c. 7.7.	Z	ARRAS-BAPAUME Rd., thence covered route through N.30.c., N.25.a	
2.	14th A. & S. Hrs.	--do--	Deployment Position "G"	--do--	Z plus 5	----do----	
3.	"D" Coy. 40th Bn. M.G. Corps.	--do--	Deployment Position "H"	--do--	Z plus 20	Main Road thence covered route to "H"	
4.	231st Fd. Coy. R.E	--do--	NEUVILLE MILL N.24.d	--do--	Z plus 30	Main road.	
5.	135th Fd. Ambulance	--do--	MERCATEL	--do--	Z plus 40	Main road	
6.	10/11th H. L. I.	ERVILLERS	Deployment Position "G"	Road Junction B.13.b.3.1.	Z plus 20	Main road, thence by covered route.	
7.	"B" Coy 40th Bn. M.G. Corps.	--do--	--do--	--do--		---do---	To follow 200 yds. behind Serial 6.
8.	14th H. L. I	--do--	--do--	--do--	Z plus 40	---do---	
9.	120th T. M. Bty.	--do--	--do--	--do--		---do---	To follow 200 yds. behind Serial 8

SECRET   COPY NO. 4

Appx VIII

120TH (HIGHLAND) INFANTRY BRIGADE ORDER NO. 177

Ref. Map
51b. 1/40,000.

20 : 3 : 18.

1. The 120th (Highland) Infantry Brigade will relieve the 9th Infantry Brigade (3rd Division) in the line on the 22nd instant, in accordance with attached table

2. All details of reliefs, guides, etc, will be arranged direct between C.Os. concerned.
All troops will be moved by bus to BOIRY BECQUERELLE and will then move forward by march route

3. In movements of troops East of the ARRAS - BAPAUME Road, 300 yards distance will be maintained between platoons.

4. All maps, defence schemes, details of proposed work, etc. will be taken over from units relieved and receipts given.

5 All camps and horse lines vacated by units in the ERVILLERS-HAMELINCOURT Area will be left in a perfectly clean condition and certificates obtained from Town Majors or Area Commandants, and will be forwarded to Brigade Head Quarters.

6. A rough sketch showing detailed dispositions will be forwarded by units to Brigade Hd.Qrs. as soon after completion of relief as possible.

7. In the event of there being any hostile attack during the relief, units will place themselves at the disposal of the units they are relieving.

8. The completion of reliefs will be wired to Brigade Hd.Qrs. using the following code words :-

10/11th H. L. I.	...	ALPHA
14th H. L. I.	...	BETA
14th A. & S.Hrs.	...	GAMMA
120th T. M. Bty.	...	DELTA

9. The Command of the Brigade Front will pass to the 120th Brigade on completion of relief, at which time 120th Bde. Hd.Qrs. will re-open at N.34.b.5.3. in SHAFT SWITCH.

10. ACKNOWLEDGE.

[signature]

Captain,
Brigade Major,
120th (Highland) Infantry Brigade.

Issued through Signals at 9.30 p.m.

Distribution:-

Copy No.1 ... G.O.C.
2 ... Bde.Major.
3 ... Staff Capt.
4 ... War Diary.
5 ... File.
6 ... 10/11th H.L.I.
7 ... 14th H.L.I.
8 ... 14th A. & S.H.
9 ... 120th T.M.Bty.
10 ... 231st Fd.Coy.R.E.
11 ... 135th Fd.Ambce.
12 ... 40th Bn.M.G.Corps
13 ... "B" Coy. -do-
14 ... "D" Coy. -do-
15 ... 40th Divn. "G"
16 ... 40th Divn. "Q"
17 ... 119th Inf.Bde.
18 ... 121st Inf.Bde.
18a ... A P.M. 40th Div.
19 ... A.D.M.S.
20 ... C.R.A.
21 ... C.R.E.
22 ... 40th Div.Trn.
23 ... 9th Inf.Bde.
24 ... Bde.Supply Off
25 ... Bde.Signals.
26 ... Town Major, HAMELINC'T.
27 ... Area Comdt. ERVILLERS

TABLE TO ACCOMPANY 120TH (HIGHLAND) INFANTRY BRIGADE ORDER NO. 177.

Serial No.	Unit	From	To	Embussing Point	Hr. of Embussing	Debussing Point	Route	Unit being relieved	Remarks
1.	10/11th H. L. I.) 120th T. M. Bty.)	ERVILLERS	Line	BELFAST CAMP	1 p.m.	BOIRY BECQUERELLS	Via HENIN - ST MARTIN - sur-COJEUL.	1st Northumberland Fusiliers.	Rendezvous for meeting guides will be arranged direct between C.Os. Battns. will embuss by Coys. and 10 minutes interval will be maintained between groups of busses containing Coys.
2.	14th A. & S. Hrs	HAMELINCOURT	Support in SHAFT	CLONMEL CAMP	2.30 p.m.	--do--	--do--	4th Battn. Royal Fusiliers	
3.	14th H. L. I.	ERVILLERS	Reserve in SHAFT	ENNISKILLEN CAMP	3.30 p.m.	--do--	--do--	15th King's Liverpools.	

NOTE :- Battalions will arrange to take over the Transport Lines and Q.M. Stores of the units they are relieving.

--*-*-*-*-*-*-*-*

War Diary

APPX IX

120th (Highland) Infantry Brigade.

Report on Operations from 21:3:18 to 27:3:18.
****

21/3/18.

On the morning of the 21st, the 120th (Highland) Brigade was in the ERVILLERS-HAMELINCOURT Area, disposed as follows:-

Brigade Hd. Qrs.	HAMELINCOURT.
10/11th H. L. I.	BELFAST CAMP, ERVILLERS.
14th H. L. I.	ENNISKILLEN CAMP -do-
14th A. & S. Hrs	CLONMEL CAMP, HAMELINCOURT.

About 12.45 p.m. verbal orders were received that the Brigade was to move up as soon as possible to take over the portion of the Third System between the MORY-ECOUST Road and the VAULX-LONGATTE Road. Verbal orders were then issued by the Brigade to Os.C.Battalions, and the Brigade, with "D" Coy. 40th Bn. M.G.Corps, moved off at 2.15 p.m., with strong patrols in advance and on the flanks, to take over the Third System, with the 14th A. & S. Hrs. on the right, 10/11th H.L.I. on the left, and 14th H.L.I. in Reserve behind the high ground in B.29 central.

Brigade Hd. Qrs. was opened in the sunken road S.E. of MORY about 3.30 p.m.

Elements of the 59th Division were still holding the front line of the Third System, and the 14th A. & S. Hrs. and 10/11th H.L.I. went into the line with them, but they were not in touch with the 6th Division on the right, as there was a pocket of the enemy holding out in the front trench of the Third System.

The 14th A. & S. Hrs. were ordered to push strong patrols down and gain touch with the 6th Division. At 10.5 p.m. the 14th A. & S. H. and 10/11th H.L.I. were ordered to push out strong patrols towards the Second System and try and clear any pockets of enemy digging in between the 2nd and 3rd Systems. At 10.45 p.m. reports were received that battalions were in position and that the 14th H.L.I. were in touch with the 6th Division on the right on the line of the Army Line.

?A.&S.H.

22/3/18.

The night of 21st/22nd was generally reported quiet, and at 3.30 a.m. on 22nd, the 14th A. & S. Hrs. had cleared the enemy from the Third System and were in touch with the Division on the right.

At 9 a.m. on the 22nd, on receipt of instructions from 40th Division, the 14th A. & S. Hrs. and 10/11th H.L.I. were ordered to send out strong patrols again and try and drive in the enemy who were reported to be digging-in in small numbers between the 2nd and 3rd Systems. At the same time the 14th A. & S. Hrs. reported that the enemy had again effected a lodgement in the front line of the 3rd System between them and the 6th Division, and that they were preparing to drive this pocket out again.

The 14th H.L.I., in Reserve, were at once ordered to push strong patrols through VRAUCOURT to assist the 14th A. & S. Hrs. and to ensure touch with the 6th Division.

At 10.55 a.m. the 14th A. & S. H. reported the enemy driven out and touch regained with the 6th Division.

About 12.30 p.m. very heavy enemy attacks were launched on the 14th A. & S. Hrs. and 10/11th H.L.I., and the left of the Argyll's and the right of the 10/11th H.L.I. was for a time driven back, but the line was re-established about 1 p.m.

About 1.30 p.m. information was received that the enemy had forced back the left of the 6th Division, and that the right flank of the Brigade was in the air. The 10/11th H.L.I. refused their flank towards VRAUCOURT SUCRERIE, and the 14th H.L.I. were ordered to extend this defensive flank along the VRAUCOURT-BEUGNATRE Road to the Army Line. The right of the Argyll's was in the air and they were instructed to withdraw to this defensive flank, but as information was then received that the IV Corps were about to counter-attack to re-establish the position about VAULX-VRAUCOURT, O.C. 14th A. & S.H. agreed that he could hang on the line in front of VRAUCOURT.

About 2.30 p.m. Brigade Hd.Qrs. moved to BEHAGNIES.

About 6 p.m. the counter-attack on the right apparently not having matured, the 14th A. & S.H. were forced to withdraw to the defensive flank along the BEUGNATRE Road.

About 6.30 p.m. heavy attacks were made on this flank, which was also strongly enfiladed by rifle and M.G. fire, and battalions were forced back to the Army Line, which was finally occupied about 7 p.m. with the 14th A. & S. Hrs. on the right, the 10/11th H.L.I. (who had lost very heavily in the 3rd System) in the centre, and the 14th H.L.I. on the left, and the Brigade was in touch with the 6th Division on the right.

At 11.10 p.m. orders were given for the 10/11th H.L.I. to come out into Reserve, and for the other two battalions to hold the Army Line.

The situation on the left was very obscure, and the 14th H.L.I. were therefore ordered to send strong patrols to try and gain touch with the battalion on the left in front of MORY.

The night of the 22nd/23rd was fairly quiet. Touch, however, could not be gained by the 14th H.L.I. with the battalion on the left, though patrols had been as far as HALLY COPSE during the night.

23/3/18. About 6 a.m. on the morning of the 23rd, the enemy were seen massing on the high ground N.E. of MORY, and continuous strong attacks were made on the left of the 14th H.L.I. and on MORY, and the H.L.I. formed a defensive flank facing N.W. on a line running through B.22.c and d. Continual efforts were made by the enemy during the day to mass for attacks on MORY, but the concentrations were broken up by Artillery, M.G. and L.G. fire.

At about 8 a.m. on 23rd, Brigade Hd.Qrs. moved to GOMIECOURT.

Following instructions received from 40th Division, orders were issued to the Battalions about 11 p.m. to take over the line from the remnants of the 59th Division, which were still with them, and for the latter to withdraw.

24/3/18 By about 3 a.m. the re-organisation of the line was complete and touch gained on the left with the 20th Middlesex Regt. South of MORY. No touch could be gained in or East of MORY.

From daylight on the 24th, incessant attacks were made by the enemy to gain the whole of MORY and to debouch down the Valley in B.28.a., but all attacks were held up.

Repeated attacks were also made on the Division on the right, and about 7.15 p.m. the Durham Light Infantry on the right of the 14th A. & S. Hrs. were forced to withdraw to a line in front of FAVREUIL towards H.3 central, and the 14th A. & S. H. refused their flank to conform to this movement.

In accordance with instructions received from 40th Division, the Brigade was ordered to withdraw from the Army Line about 9.45 p.m. and occupy the line of trenches South of MORY. On completion of this withdrawal, the Brigade was to be relieved by the 125th Infantry Brigade.

The situation on the right of the 14th A. & S.H. had meanwhile become serious, as a gap had been formed where the D.L.I. withdrew, and the 12th East Surrey Regt., who were about B.27.d., were instructed to move to fill up this gap.

The situation on the left was also very obscure, as touch could not be gained with Bde. on the left, and after the withdrawal to the trenches South of MORY had been completed, the left of the 14th H.L.I. was in the air, and they were forced back to a line East of BEHAGNIES-ERVILLERS Road. The 125th Infantry Brigade had meanwhile been sent to restore the situation on the right, and the relief of the 120th Bde. became impossible.

25/3/18 At 5 a.m. on the 25th, the Brigade was holding a line roughly East of BEHAGNIES, through DERMY COPSE and thence along a line about 500 yards East of the BEHAGNIES-ERVILLERS road, and was in touch with other units on both flanks.

Heavy attacks by the enemy were started at dawn from BEUGNATRE and FAVREUIL and continued throughout the day, especially on the Brigade on our right, threatening the right flank of the 120th Bde.

All ranks had now been fighting incessantly for 3½ days, and, in order to raise morale and to relieve the situation on the right, a local counter-attack on the right of the Brigade was asked for. Instructions were received from the 40th Division to arrange this direct with the 127th Infantry Brigade, which was in Reserve, and a counter-attack was pushed home.

About 3 p.m. information was received that the enemy had broken through by BIHUCOURT and ACHIET-LE-GRAND, and communications with the Division were then broken. As the right flank was being so hard pressed, it was decided, after consultation with the Brigades of 42nd and 59th Divisions, to withdraw the line to the high ground S.E. of GOMIECOURT, and about 4 p.m. this withdrawal was carried out, under intense machine gun fire.

About 4.30 p.m. Brigade Hd.Qrs.moved back to ABLAINZEVILLE, and arrangements were made with the 125th Infantry Brigade for the carrying out of the relief ordered for the previous night. Battalions of the 120th Brigade moved out during the night to AYETTE and DOUCHY-LES-AYETTE, but were kept as a Reserve to the 125th Brigade, in accordance with instructions received from the 42nd Division.

26/3/18 At 5 a.m. on the 26th, Brigade Hd.Qrs. opened at MONCHY-AU-BOIS.

About 11 a.m. on the 26th, information was received that the enemy had broken through in the vicinity of HEBUTERNE, and that a defensive line was to be taken up South of ADINFER WOOD. A line was taken up with the 14th H.L.I. on the right, the 14th A. & S. Hrs. on the left, and the 10/11th H.L.I. in Reserve on the right.

Brigade Hd.Qrs. were established at ADINFER WOOD.

No enemy attack materialised, and about 9.30 p.m. orders were issued for the Battalions to withdraw at 1.30 a.m. on the 27th to a Brigade rendezvous at RANSART, prior to moving to WALRUZEL.

Brig.-General,
6/4/18. Commanding 120th (Highland) Inf.Bde.

120TH (HIGHLAND) INFANTRY BRIGADE

Points that came to notice during Operations 21:3:18 - 27:3:18.

(a) One of the first and most important points was the lack of liaison between this Brigade and that of the 6th Division on our right.
Patrols were sent out on our right to try to find our neighbouring battalion (the Durham Light Infantry) of the 6th Division and get touch with them, but no sign of it or its patrols could be seen.
This was a source of great trouble at one period on our right flank.
This lack of liaison is due to an insufficiency of inter-Brigade communication between Brigades on the flanks of Corps.

(b) Deep dugouts, intended as Brigade Hd.Qrs., should no longer be constructed in villages, as at GOMIECOURT, where the vicinity of HdQrs.was at one period so heavily bombarded that runners could neither be got into them or away from them.
This will always be the case with villages in the battle zone.

(c) During training, far more attention should be paid to fire control and fire discipline, and their importance emphasised.
An enormous amount of ammunition was expended uselessly on many occasions, and the best results were not obtained owing to lack of proper fire control and discipline.

(d) I would strongly advocate a mobile reserve of Machine Guns being placed at the disposal of Brigadiers, even a small one. This would have been invaluable on several occasions and more especially when the right flank of this Brigade was for so long in danger.

(e) Each battalion on going into action should leave a carrying party for rations, ammunition, etc., with Bde. H.Q., or in some suitable place in rear - strength about a platoon.
Once the battalion is engaged, it is difficult to send parties back, and frequently casualties result in so doing.

(f) A great deal of shelling of our troops by our own guns took place, consequent on the indiscriminate calls for fire on supposed German targets by people in front who were not in touch with the situation, and gave these targets direct to F.O.Os.
Carelessness or excitement would also appear to have been responsible for such shooting on occasions, as for instance when one of our own batteries was shelled from in rear (and not from enfilade).
The demoralising effect of such shooting is a serious consideration.

Brig.-General,
6/4/18. Commanding 120th (Highland) Inf.Bde.

A pp'x X

S E C R E T

COPY NO. 4

120TH (HIGHLAND) INFANTRY BRIGADE ORDER NO. 184

Ref.
LENS 1/100,000.

28: 3: 18.

1. The Brigade Group composed as under will march in accordance with attached time table to MONCHY BRETON Area to-morrow, 29th inst.

Brigade Headquarters.
10/11th H. L. I.
14th H. L. I.
14th A. & S. Hrs.
120th T. M. Bty.
135th Field Ambulance.
231st Field Coy. R.E.
No. 3 Coy. 40th Div. Train.

2. Battalion Field Cookers and Mess Carts will move with units, so that a hot meal may be given at mid-day halt. One cooker will be detailed by 10/11th H.L.I. to report to O.C., 231st Field Coy. R.E., SOMBRIN to-morrow, 29th inst. at 7 a.m. for use during the march. It will be returned on completion of move to-morrow. Remainder of battalion transport will be Brigaded under Brigade Transport Officer. Transport of 135th Field Ambulance and 231st Field Coy. R.E. will march with respective units.

3. Blankets will be carried by lorry. Surplus kits. etc. will be stored in a Brigade Dump to be formed at WARLUZEL.

4. Arrangements as to Advanced Billetting Parties will be notified by Staff Captain.

5. Brigade H.Q. will march at the head of the column.

6. A C K N O W L E D G E.

H B Kerr
Captain,
A/Brigade Major,
120th (Highland) Infantry Brigade.

Issued through
Signals
at 11.30 p.m.

Distribution :-

Copy No.					
1	...	G.O.C.	11	...	135th Fd.Ambce
2	...	Brigade Major.	12	...	231st Fd.Coy.
3	...	Staff Captain.	13	...	No. 3 Coy.Train.
4	...	War Diary.	14	...	40th Div. "G".
6	...	File.	15	...	40th Div. "Q"
7	...	10/11th H. L. I.	16	...	40th Div. Train.
8	...	14th H. L. I.	17	...	A.P.M.
9	...	14th A. & S. Hrs.	18	...	Bde.Supply Officer
10	...	120th T. M. Bty.	19	...	Bde. Signals.

****

TABLE TO ACCOMPANY 120TH (HIGHLAND) INFANTRY BRIGADE ORDER NO. 184

Serial No.	Unit	From	Starting Point	Time of passing Starting Point	Route	Remarks.
1.	Brigade H.Q.	WARLUZEL	Road Junction 800 yds. EAST of D in GRAND RULLECOURT	8.30 a.m.	GRAND RULLECOURT - AMBRINES - AVERDOINGT.	
2.	10/11 H.L.I.	-do-	-do-	8.35 a.m.	-do-	To follow Serial No. 1 at 200^x interval
3.	14th A. & S.H.	-do-	-do-	8.40 a.m.	-do-	" " " No.2 -do-
4.	14th H.L.I.	-do-	-do-	8.45 a.m.	-do-	" " " No.3) -do-
5.	120th T.M.Bty.	-do-	-do-	8.50 a.m.	-do-	" " " No.4)
6.	Transport of Battns. less Cookers and Mess Carts.	-do-	-do-	9.5 a.m.	-do-	" " " No.5 -do-
7.	135th Fd.Amb.	-do-	-do-	9.15 a.m.	-do-	" " " No.6 -do-
8.	231st Fd. Coy. R.E.	SOMBRIN	-do-	9.20 a.m.	-do-	" " " No.7 -do-
9.	No.3 Coy. 40th Div.Train	HUMBERCOURT		9.25 a.m.	-do-	" " " No.8 -do-

<u>NOTE</u> :- 30 lorries will be available for conveyance of troops recently engaged in fighting. Details will be issued verbally.

Administrative Instructions to accompany 120th Infantry Brigade Order No. 184 of 28th March.

****

1. Lorries.

3 Lorries will report at WARLUZEL (Brigade Hd.qrs) to-morrow at 6 am. for the carriage of blankets only. These are allotted as under :-

10/11th High.L.I.	...	1 - To be shared with 14th High.L.I. on 2nd journey.
14th High. L.I.	...	1 - To be at disposal of 135th Fd. Amb & 120th T.M.Bty. on 2nd journey.
14th A.&.S.Hdrs.	...	1 - ½ allotted to take any surplus kit not capable of being carried by other units on 2nd journey.
135th Fd.Amb.) 120th T.M.Bty.)	...	1 - share 14th H.L.I. lorry on 2nd journey.

Not more than 4 men to travel with each lorry.

2. Billotting.

The Staff Captain will meet billotting parties at 9 am. at a place to be notified later. Advance parties will proceed on bicycles if available.

3. Dumps for surplus kits.

All surplus kit may be dumped at Billot No. 13 (Brigade Hd.qrs. Mess) by 7 am. to-morrow, 29th March. One O.R. must be left by each unit dumping any kit as a guard: with three days rations He should be instructed to apply to the Area Commandant, MONDICOURT for rations if not relieved before the expiration of 3 days.

4. The accummulation of mail at HENU will be disposed of under Divisional arrangements.

[signature]
Captain,
A/Staff Captain,
120th Infantry Brigade.

28.3.1918.

Addendum No. 1 to Administrative Instructions.

****

Reference para. 2 the Staff Captain will meet billotting ~~parties~~ officers at Brigade Headquarters at 7.30 am. to give particulars of rendezvous.

*****

APPx XI

SECRET   COPY NO .4.

120TH (HIGHLAND) INFANTRY BRIGADE ORDER NO. 185.

30:7:18.

1. 120th Brigade Group, composed as under will move to-day 30th inst. to SAILLY Sur-la-Lys - MONUE Area by bus :-

Brigade Headquarters.
10/11th H. L. I.
14th H. L. I.
14th A. & S. Hrs.
120th T. M. Bty.
138th Field Ambulance.
231st Field Company, R.E.
"A" Coy. 40th Bn. M.G. Corps.

2. Embussing Point on ST POL - BRUAY Road with head of column at Road Junction DIEVAL facing North East.

3. Lorry Route.

DIEVAL - BETHUNE - HINGTON - MERVILLE - ESTAIRES - NEUF BERQUIN

4. Debussing Point.

On ESTAIRES - NEUF BERQUIN road, tail of column just clear of ESTAIRES

5. Units will embuss in following order :-

Unit	From	Time to reach embussing point.
138th Fd. Ambulance.	LA THIEULOYE	10 a.m.
"A" Coy. M.G.Battn.	-do-	
14th A. & S. Hrs.	MONCHY BRETO	10.10 a.m.
14th H. L. I.	-do-	10.20 a.m.
231st Fd. Coy.R.E.	ROCOURT	10.30 a.m.
10/11th H. L. I.	MAGNICOURT -EN-COMTE	10.40 a.m.
Brigade Hd. Qrs.	-do-	10.50 a.m.

Route to embussing point to be reconnoitred on receipt of this Order.

6. First line transport will be Brigaded and will move under Captain CAMPBELL, M.C., 10/11th H.L.I. They will march to-day to LILLERS. Route :- HOUDAIN - MARLES-les-MINES- LOZINGHEM - LILLERS. Accommodation to be obtained for the night 30/31st from Town Majors, LILLERS and ECQUEDECQUES.
March to be resumed on morning of 31st to new area. Any route to be used.

7. 120th Trench Mortar Battery will march with the transport.

8. Rations will be taken in accordance with 120th Bde. Warning Order.

Issued to All Units of Bde. Group at 8.35 a.m.

Captain,
A/Brigade Major.
120th (Highland) Infantry Bde.

SECRET

APPx XII

120th [illegible] Infantry Brigade Order 186.

Ref. Trench Map 1/20,000. [illegible]

31-3-18.

1. 120th Infantry Brigade will relieve the [illegible] Infantry Brigade in [illegible] Sector tonight 31st March/1st April in accordance with attached table.

2. [illegible]

3. 40th Bn. M.G. Coys. [illegible] on 31st March and 1st April under arrangements made by the [illegible] commanders.

4. Details of [illegible] will be arranged between the commanders.

5. Advance parties of 1 officer [illegible] as soon as possible. These should report at [illegible]

6

7

8

1.40 pm

	Unit.	From.	To	In Relief of	Time & Rendezvous for Guides.	Remarks
1.	10/11th H.L.I.	NOUVEAU MONDE	RESERVE	2/4 S. Lancs. Regt.	G. 29. d. 65. 85 2 Coys. 5 pm. 2 Coys. 7 pm.	
2.	14th H.L.I.	SAILLY	LEFT Subsector	2/10th Kings Liverpool Regt.	Road Junction H. 26. a. 15. 15 7. 30 pm.	SAILLY SUR LA LYS – ROUGE de BOUT road. not to be used
3.	14th A. & S. Hrs.	NOUVEAU MONDE	RIGHT Subsector	9th Kings Liverpool Regt.	ROUGE de BOUT G. 36. d. 7. 7 7. 30 pm	To follow Serial 1
4.	120th T.M. Bty.	SAILLY	LINE	172nd T.M. BTY.	Road Junction H. 26. a. 15. 15. 8 pm.	
5.	120th Bde. H.Q.	SAILLY	MARES NEST	172nd Bde. H.Q.		

1. Routes to Rendezvous for Guides to be reconnoitred.
2. Units to move with an interval of 200 yds. between platoons.

40th Division.

WAR
DIARY

B. H. Q.

120th INFANTRY BRIGADE.

APRIL 1918.

Appendices attached :- Report on Operations
9th-12th April

Operation Orders etc.

(6339) Wt. W160/M3016 1,500,000 10/17 McA & W Ltd (E 1898) Forms W3091. Army Form W.3091.

WO 95/2623

120/28

Cover for Documents.

Nature of Enclosures.

War Diary

Hd. Qrs. 120th (Highland) Infantry Brigade

April 1918

VOLUME XXIII

Notes, or Letters written.

21

Original

Instructions regarding War Diaries and Intelligence Summaries are contained in F. S. Regs., Part II. and the Staff Manual respectively. Title pages will be prepared in manuscript.

I

WAR DIARY
~~or~~
~~INTELLIGENCE SUMMARY.~~
(Erase heading not required.)

VOLUME XXIII

Headquarters,
120th Infantry Brigade

Army Form C. 2118.

APRIL 1918.

Place	1918 Date APRIL	Hour	Summary of Events and Information	Remarks and references to Appendices
FLEURBAIX	1st		Under command of 57th Division.	
			Disposition of Brigade:-	
			Brigade Headquarters - - - MARES NEST	
			14th Arg. & Suth'd Hrs - - - Right Subsector.	
			14th High. L. I. - - - Left Subsector.	
			10/11th High. L. I. - - - Brigade Reserve.	
			120th T. M. Battery - - - In the line	
			For events see Morning & Evening wires and Daily Intelligence Summary.	Appx I (a & b)
			Casualties: 1 OR Killed 1 OR wounded	
	2nd	10 AM	Command of FLEURBAIX Sector passed from 57th to 40th Divisional Commander	
		3.30 pm	Conference held at 40th Divnl. Hd. Qrs. G.O.C. Bde and Bde Major attended.	
			For events see Morning and Evening wires and Daily Int. Summary	Appx II (a & b)
			Casualties 3 OR wounded (includes 1 S.I.W)	

A6945 Wt. W11422/M1160 350,000, 12/16 D. D. & L. Forms/C.2118/14.

Instructions regarding War Diaries and Intelligence Summaries are contained in F. S. Regs., Part II. and the Staff Manual respectively. Title pages will be prepared in manuscript.

II

WAR DIARY
or
~~INTELLIGENCE SUMMARY.~~

(Erase heading not required.)

VOLUME XXIII

Army Form C. 2118.

~~Headquarters~~ 120th Infantry Brigade

APRIL 1918.

Place	1918 Date APRIL	Hour	Summary of Events and Information	Remarks and references to Appendices
FLEURBAIX	3rd	10.30 AM.	Brigade Commander met Battalion Commanders and O.C. 120th T.M. Battery in Conference at Left Battalion Headquarters N. 3. b. 35. 27.	[initials]
		2.15 pm	120th Infantry Brigade Order No 187 issued. The 10/11th High. L.I. in Reserve Positions of FLEURBAIX Sector will be relieved on night 3rd/4th inst. by 21st Middx Regt (121st Inf Bde), which Battalion will be attached to 120th Inf Bde. for tactical purposes from 6 pm. 3rd April. 10/11th High. L.I. will then relieve 14th Arg. & Suth. Highrs. in Right Subsector on night 3rd/4th inst.	Appx III. [initials]
		7.30 pm	Recipients of above order notified that moves detailed will not take place till further notice.	[initials]
		11 pm	Bde. Major returned to duty from Hospital.	[initials]
			For events see Morning & Evening Wires & Daily Int. Summary	Appx IV (a & b)
			Casualties. Nil.	
	4th	10 AM	Recipients of 120th Inf. Bde. Order No 187 of 3-4-18 notified that moves detailed in above order will take place on night 3rd/4th April.	[initials]

A6945 Wt. W11422/M1160 350,000 12/16 D. D. & L. Forms/C./2118/14.

Instructions regarding War Diaries and Intelligence Summaries are contained in F. S. Regs., Par. II. and the Staff Manual respectively. Title pages will be prepared in manuscript.

111

WAR DIARY
~~or~~
~~INTELLIGENCE SUMMARY.~~
(Erase heading not required.)

VOLUME XXIII

Army Form C. 2118.

Headquarters, 120th Infantry Brigade APRIL 1918.

Place	1918 Date APRIL	Hour	Summary of Events and Information	Remarks and references to Appendices
FLEURBAIX	4th		Reliefs carried out in accordance with 120th Inf. Bde. Order No. 187 of 3.4.18	
			Dispositions :-	
			Right Subsector ... 10/11th High. L. I.	
			Left Subsector ... 14th High. L. I.	
			Brigade Reserve ... 21st Middx. Regt.	
			In the Line ... 120th T. M. Battery	
			LE NOUVEAU MONDE (In billets ... 14th Arg. & Suthd. Highrs.	
			For events see Morning & Evening Wires & Daily Int. Summary	Appx V (a ~~+b~~)
			Casualties :- 4 O.R. wounded	
	5th	7.30pm	120th Inf. Bde. Order No. 188 issued. 120th Inf. Bde. will be relieved in FLEURBAIX Sector by 119th Inf. Bde. on night 6/7th April	Appx VI
			For events see Morning & Evening Wires & Daily Int. Summary.	Appx VII (a+b).
			Casualties :- 1 OR Killed 6 OR wounded.	

A6945 Wt. W11422/M1160 350,000 12/16 D. D. & L. Forms/C./2118/14.

Instructions regarding War Diaries and Intelligence Summaries are contained in F. S. Regs., Part II. and the Staff Manual respectively. Title pages will be prepared in manuscript.

IV

WAR DIARY or ~~INTELLIGENCE SUMMARY.~~

(Erase heading not required.)

VOLUME XXIII

Headquarters, 120th Infantry Brigade APRIL 1918.

Army Form C. 2118.

Place	Date 1918 APRIL	Hour	Summary of Events and Information	Remarks and references to Appendices
FLEURBAIX	6th		Reliefs carried out in accordance with 120th Inf Bde Order No 188 dated 5.4.18.	WR
			Dispositions:	
			Brigade Headquarters, 14th High. L. I., 120th T. M. Battery ... LE NOUVEAU MONDE.	
			10/11th High. L. I. ... ESTAIRES.	
			14th Arg. & Suth'd Highrs ... SAILLY	
		7.30 pm.	Brigade Headquarters closed at MARES NEST - FLEURBAIX and re-opened at same hour at LE NOUVEAU MONDE - G. 26. d. 9. 0. (CROIX-DU-BAC Sheet 1/20,000)	WR
			For events see Morning & Evening Wires & Daily Int. Summary.	Appx VIII (a & b)
			Casualties: 2 O.R. wounded.	
LE NOUVEAU MONDE	7th		In Divisional Reserve.	WR
		3.15 pm.	2nd Bn. Royal Scots Fusiliers disposed 14th Bn. Arg. & Suth'd Highrs. in 120th Inf. Bde. on disbandment of latter.	

A6945 Wt. W11422/M1160 350,000 12/16 D. D. & L. Forms/C./2118/14.

Instructions regarding War Diaries and Intelligence Summaries are contained in F. S. Regs., Part II. and the Staff Manual respectively. Title pages will be prepared in manuscript.

V

WAR DIARY
or
~~INTELLIGENCE SUMMARY.~~
(Erase heading not required.)

VOLUME XXIII

Army Form C. 2118.

Headquarters 120th Infantry Brigade APRIL 1918.

Place	Date 1918 APRIL	Hour	Summary of Events and Information	Remarks and references to Appendices
LE NOUVEAU MONDE G 26 d. 9.0	7th	8 pm	120th Inf. Bde Order No 189 issued. 10/11th High. L.I. will be relieved by a battalion of the 151st Inf. Bde. at 10 AM on 8th inst. After 4 AM 8th inst. 10/11th High L.I. will be tactically at the disposal of the 120th Inf. Bde. and will be prepared to move in accordance with the new Reserve Brigade Defence Scheme issued to-day.	Appx IX
		9.30 pm	Defence Scheme of Brigade in Divisional Reserve issued, detailing action of Brigade in the event of a serious attack developing upon the 2nd Portuguese Division.	Appx X
	8th		NIL	
	9th to 12th		Brigade in action. For events see attached report on operations.	Appx XI
STRAZEELE.	13th		120th Inf. Bde concentrated at STRAZEELE and then marched to WEMAERS-CAPPEL with transport.	

A6945 Wt. W11422/M1160 350,000 12/16 D. D. & L. Forms/C.2118/14.

Instructions regarding War Diaries and Intelligence Summaries are contained in F. S. Regs., Par. II. and the Staff Manual respectively. Title pages will be prepared in manuscript.

VI

WAR DIARY or ~~INTELLIGENCE SUMMARY.~~

(Erase heading not required.)

VOLUME XXIII

Army Form C. 2118.

Headquarters. 120th Infantry Brigade

APRIL 1918

Place	Date 1918 APRIL	Hour	Summary of Events and Information	Remarks and references to Appendices
WEMAERS-CAPPEL	13th		120th Inf Bde order No 191 issued. Brigade will march on 14th inst to an Area West of St OMER.	Appx XII
	14th	8.15 Am	120th Bde Hd Qrs closed at WEMAERS-CAPPEL and re-opened at TATINGHEM on arrival.	
		5 pm	Move of 120th Bde to West of St OMER completed in accordance with 120th Bde Order No 191 of 13-4-18. Bde settling in Billets at TATINGHEM.	
TATINGHEM	15th		Brigade in Corps Reserve. G.O.C. 40th Division met Brigade Commanders in Conference at Divisional Hd Qrs at LONGUENESSE.	
	16th		Units training in vicinity of billets.	
	17th		40th Division (less Artillery) transferred from XV Corps to VIII Corps in accordance with 40th Div. Order No 152 of 16-4-18.	

A6945 Wt. W11422/M1160 350,000 12/16 D. D. & L. Forms/C.2118/14.

Instructions regarding War Diaries and Intelligence Summaries are contained in F. S. Regs., Part II. and the Staff Manual respectively. Title pages will be prepared in manuscript.

VII

WAR DIARY
or
~~INTELLIGENCE SUMMARY.~~
(Erase heading not required.)

VOLUME XXIII

Army Form C. 2118.

Headquarters 120th Infantry Brigade. APRIL 1918.

Place	Date 1918 APRIL	Hour	Summary of Events and Information	Remarks and references to Appendices
TATINGHEM	17th		Units engaged in training.	[initials]
		4.30 pm	Conference of Battalion Commanders held at Brigade Headquarters.	[initials]
	18th		Training carried out by Units in vicinity of billets	
	19th		– do – – do – – do –	[initials]
		3.30 pm	Conference at Divnl. Hd.Qrs., Bde. Comdr. & Bde. Major attending.	
	20th	9 AM	Brigade Signal School formed for men with no knowledge of signalling, 8 OR per Battn. attending for instruction.	[initials]
			200 men from 10/11th High. L.I. and	
			100 men from 14th High. L.I.	
			despatched to 15th High. L.I. 3rd Division.	
			100 men from 14th High. L.I.	
			despatched to 9th High. L.I. 33rd Division.	
	21st	10 Am	120th Inf. Bde. Order No 192 issued. 120th Bde. Group will move to the ACQUIN Area on afternoon of 21-4-18.	[initials] Appx XIII
		2 pm	Bde. Hd.Qrs. closed at TATINGHEM and re-opened at ACQUIN on arrival.	

A6945 Wt. W11422/M1160 350,000 12/16 D. D. & L. Forms/C.2118/14.

Instructions regarding War Diaries and Intelligence Summaries are contained in F. S. Regs., Part II. and the Staff Manual respectively. Title pages will be prepared in manuscript.

VIII

WAR DIARY
or
~~INTELLIGENCE~~ SUMMARY.
(Erase heading not required.)

VOLUME XXIII

Army Form C. 2118.

Headquarters, 120th Infantry Brigade

APRIL 1918

Place	1918 Date APRIL	Hour	Summary of Events and Information	Remarks and references to Appendices
ACQUIN	21st	8.30pm	Move of 120th Bde Group to ACQUIN area completed.	WB
			Dispositions:-	
			Bde Hd Qrs. --- ACQUIN.	
			2nd R. Ir. Fusrs. --- QUERCAMP & LA WATTINE.	
			10/11th High. L. I. --- VAL D'ACQUIN.	
			14th High. L. I. --- ACQUIN	
			120th Tm. Bty. --- LE NOOVRE.	
	22nd "	10.15 AM	Brigade Commander met O.C. Battalions in conference at Bde H.Qrs.	WB
			Training carried out by Units.	
	23rd "	3.20pm	40th Divn. Warning Order No. 157 received intimating that the whole personnel of the Division, less Divn. Bde & Battn. Hd Qrs. and a small staff of Instructors are to be sent to the Base. 120th Bde. to form a composite Battn. under one of their Battn. Staffs and to be prepared to move on afternoon of 24th April.	WB

A6945 Wt. W11422/M1160 350,000 12/16 D. D. & L. Forms/C.2118/14.

Instructions regarding War Diaries and Intelligence Summaries are contained in F. S. Regs., Part II. and the Staff Manual respectively. Title pages will be prepared in manuscript.

IX

WAR DIARY
or
INTELLIGENCE SUMMARY.
(Erase heading not required.)

VOLUME XXIII

Army Form C. 2118.

Headquarters, 120th Infantry Brigade APRIL 1918

Place	1918 Date APRIL	Hour	Summary of Events and Information	Remarks and references to Appendices
ACQUIN	23rd	8 pm.	120th Inf. Bde. Order No 193 issued. One composite battalion from the 10/11th High. L.I. and 14th High. L.I. will be formed at once and be prepared to move on 24th inst. to the CASSEL Area for work on a defensive line. Battalion to be formed as follows:– Batt. Hd. Qrs. Staff ... 14th High. L.I. 2 Companies (each 100 Strong) ... 14th High. L.I. 2 Companies (– do –) ... 10/11th High. L.I.	XIV.
	24th	12.30 pm.	Divn. notified cancellation of paras 3 & 4 of Warning Order No. 157 of 23.4.18, excepting in so far as Field Coy. R.E. are concerned. In consequence 120th Bde. Composite Batt. did not move as ordered and transport (which had already moved) was recalled.	
	25th	6 AM	2nd Bn. Royal Scots Fusiliers left 120th Bde., being despatched as a complete battalion to 9th Division (South African Brigade) in accordance with instructions from Army H.Q. conveyed by 40th Divn. No. 8181/1/A dated 24th April 1918.	

A6945 Wt. W11422/M1160 350,000 12/16 D. D. & L. Forms/C.2118/14.

Instructions regarding War Diaries and Intelligence Summaries are contained in F. S. Regs., Part II. and the Staff Manual respectively. Title pages will be prepared in manuscript.

X

WAR DIARY
or
~~INTELLIGENCE~~ SUMMARY.
(Erase heading not required.)

VOLUME XXIII
Headquarters,
120th Infantry Brigade

Army Form C. 2118.

APRIL 1918

Place	Date 1918 APRIL	Hour	Summary of Events and Information	Remarks and references to Appendices
ACQUIN	26		NIL	
	27			[initials]
	28th		Brig. General C. J. Hobkirk, D.S.O. Commanding, 120th Infantry Brigade assumed command of No. 1 Composite Brigade	
	29th		NIL	[initials]
	30th		Composite Battalion consisting of Hd. Qrs. & 2 Companies 14th High. L. I. 2 Companies 10/11th High. L. I. left 120th Bde. to join No. 2 Composite Brigade at BONNEGHEM	[initials]
		12 noon	120th Inf. Bde. Order No. 194 issued. Brigade Group consisting of:- 120th Inf. Bge. Headquarters 10/11th High. L. I. — do — 21st Middx. R. — do — 120th T. M. Btg. 135th Field Ambulance. No. 3 Coy. Div. Train. 51st M. Vet. S. 40th Divn. Wing 14th High. L. I. details will move to the LUMBRES Area forthwith.	Appx XV

A6945 Wt. W11422/M1160 350,000 12/16 D. D. & L. Forms/C./2118/14.

Instructions regarding War Diaries and Intelligence Summaries are contained in F. S. Regs., Part II. and the Staff Manual respectively. Title pages will be prepared in manuscript.

XI

WAR DIARY
or
INTELLIGENCE SUMMARY.
(Erase heading not required.)

VOLUME XXIII

Headquarters, 120th Infantry Brigade

APRIL 1918

Army Form C. 2118.

Place	Date	Hour	Summary of Events and Information	Remarks and references to Appendices
[illegible]	25th	1 pm	Move of 120th Bde Group completed in accordance with 120th Bde Order No 136 of 24/4/18	
			Dispositions:	
			Bde H.Q. [illegible]	
			Remainder of Group [illegible]	

[illegible] Capt.
Brigade Major
Comdg 120th Infantry Brigade

Form.

Army Form C. 2121.
(In pads of 100.)

MESSAGES AND SIGNALS.

No. of Message..........

Prefix..........Code..........m.	Words.	Charge.	This message is on a/c of:	Recd. at..........m.
Office of Origin and Service Instructions.	Sent		App I a ....Service.	Date..........
	At..........m.			From..........
	To..........			
	By..........		(Signature of "Franking Officer.")	By..........

TO	YEG	YDZ	MEADOW	INA

* Sender's Number.	Day of Month.	In reply to Number.	
G219	1		AAA

Situation	normal	AAA	Weather
fine	AAA	Wind	NE

Addsd YEG repeated YDZ MEADOW INA

Priority

From PZA

Place

Time 3.35 pm

The above may be forwarded as now corrected. (Z)

..........Censor.

Signature of Addressor or person authorised to telegraph in his name.

Capt.

* This line should be erased if not required.

(3796.) Wt. W492/M1647. 650,000 Pads. 5/17. H.W. & V., Ld. (E. 1187.)

"A" Form.
MESSAGES AND SIGNALS.

Army Form C. 2121.
(In pads of 100.)

Prefix......... Code.............. m. | Words. | Charge. | This message is on a/c of | Recd. at .... m.
No. of Message..............

Office of Origin and Service Instructions.

Sent
At.............. m.
To...............
By...............

Appy I .... Service.

(Signature of "Franking Officer.")

Date...............
From...............
By.................

TO { YDZ
YEG } MEADOW INA

Sender's Number.	Day of Month.	In reply to Number.	
* MW 1	1		AAA

Morning wire AAA Situation quiet weather fine AAA

Addressed YEG YDZ repeated MEADOW INA

Priority

From PZA
Place
Time

The above may be forwarded as now corrected. (Z)

Censor. Signature of Addressor or person authorised to telegraph in his name

[signature] Capt
Brigade Major

* This line should be erased if not required.

(3796.) Wt. W 492/M1647. 650,000 Pads. 5/17. H.W. & V., Ld. (E. 1187.)

War Diary

App I (b)

CONFIDENTIAL.

120TH (HIGHLAND) INFANTRY BRIGADE INTELLIGENCE SUMMARY
Period from 8 a.m. 31st March to 1st April.

---

1. OPERATIONS.

PATROLS. Covering patrols saw no signs of the enemy.

ARTILLERY. Slight shelling of back areas during day. Opened in retaliation for hostile fire at 4-30 a.m.

SNIPING. Hit claimed at N.10.d.35.75.

AIRCRAFT. Normal.

11. HOSTILE ACTIVITY.

ARTILLERY. Quiet during day. At 5-30 p.m. hostile artillery shelled CROIX BLANCHE and vicinity, about 300 shells being fired, mainly 7.7 cm and 10.5 cm.

MOVEMENT. Individual movement during day on roads and tracks at N.27.a., 0.13.c., 0.19.b., 0.20.a., and at LONG BARN.
Man seen standing outside dugout at N.16.a.9.6.
6 men seen on road N.16.b. at 12-20 p.m. Men seen here at various times.
3 men seen in NEGATINE DRIVE at 8-5 a.m.

AVIATION. Nil.

111. HOSTILE DEFENCES.

M. G. Active against our aeroplanes.

T. M. 3 M.T.Ms. fell near CELLAR FARM AVE. at 3 p.m. L.T.M. fired from N.16.b.40.65.

1V. HOSTILE ORGANISATION.

H.Q. Smoke seen at 0.15.a.95.55. and at N.15.d.02.45

V. MISCELLANEOUS.

LIGHTS. At 4-30 a.m. when hostile shelling opened on our right the enemy sent up red lights all along his line. Several green lights were also fired. Shelling ceased at 5-15 a.m.

D McL Oman

Captain,
Intelligence Officer,
120th (Highland) Infantry Brigade.

Prefix........ Code........m	Words. 20	Charge. text	This message is on a/c of: Appx IV ....Service. (Signature of "Franking Officer.")	Recd. at ....m.
Office of Origin and Service Instructions.	Sent			Date............
	At............m.			From ....
	To............			
	By............			By............

TO YEG YDZ ~~MEADOW~~ WVA INA

Sender's Number.	Day of Month.	In reply to Number.	AAA
* MW 2	2		

Morning wire AAA Situation normal weather fine wind light SW

Addsd YEG repeated YDZ MEADOW INA

Priority

From PZA
Place
Time

The above may be forwarded as now corrected. (Z)

Censor. Signature of Addressor or person authorised to telegraph in his name.

* This line should be erased if not required.

(3796.) Wt. W 492/M1647. 650,000 Pads. 5/17. H.W. & V., Ld. (E. 1187.)

"C" Form.
Army Form C. 2121.
(In pads of 100.)

MESSAGES AND SIGNALS.

No. of Message............

Prefix......Code......m	Words.	Charge.	This message is on a/c of:	Recd. at......m.
Office of Origin and Service Instructions.	Sent		......Service.	Date......
	At......m.		Appd [illegible]	From......
	To......			
	By......		(Signature of "Franking Officer.")	By......

TO { BBA WVA INA

Sender's Number.	Day of Month.	In reply to Number.	AAA
* G221	2		

Evening	wire	AAA	Situation
normal	AAA	weather	fine
AAA	wind	SW	
Added BBA	repeated	WVA	INA

From TDV
Place
Time

[illegible]

The above may be forwarded as now corrected. (Z)

Censor. Signature of Addresser or person authorised to telegraph in his name.

* This line should be erased if not required.

(3796.) Wt. W 492/M1647. 650,000 Pads. 5/17. H.W. & V., Ld. (E. 1187.)

War Diary

Appx II (6)

ONFIDENTIAL.

120TH (HIGHLAND) INFANTRY BRIGADE INTELLIGENCE SUMMARY
Period from 8 a.m. 1st April to 8 a.m. 2nd

"A" OUR OPERATIONS.

1. PATROLS. Fighting patrol reconnoitred NO MAN'S LAND in N.7.c. and d but saw no signs of enemy. The going was difficult owing to water filled shell holes and to trip wire being stretched between trees. A great number of Very Lights were sent up from enemy lines.
Fighting and reconnoitring patrols on the left encountered no enemy parties. There was a considerable amount of fire from light M.Gs. and numerous lights were sent up. Sounds of shouting heard in enemy lines.

2 ARTILLERY. quiet during period, activity being confined to back areas.

9. AIRCRAFT. Very active during the day. An enemy O. B. is reported to have been brought down by one of our machines about 10 miles S. of our front.

"B" ENEMY OPERATIONS

1. ARTILLERY. RUE DES LOMBARDS shelled during afternoon by six gun battery.
ELBOW FARM shelled intermittently between 9-30 a.m. and 4 p.m.
Counter battery work carried out on G.30.a. area.
Area round H.34.b.7.9. received attention during the day with 10.5 cm and 15 cm. Gas shells were used betwenn 6-30 p.m. and 7-30 p.m.
CROIX BLANCHE received about 20 shells at 7 p.m.
During the night RUE DES BASSIERES from LE CROIX LESCORNEX [illegible] to H.33.d.4.1. was shelled also RUE DES LOMBARDS between 11 p.m. and midnight. DEAD DOG DUMP was shelled between 4 a.m. and 5 a.m. with 10.5 cm.
At 5-45 a.m. enemy fired tear shells into [illegible].12.b. a[illegible] apparently searching for our batteries.

2. T. Ms. Several aerial darts fell short opposite right sub-sector during the day.

3. M. Gs. Active against our aeroplanes.

7. SIGNALS. At evening "Stand to" enemy sent up several lights consisting of rows of green stars. One of our aeroplanes was up at the time.

11. GENERAL. From the number of lights sent up during the night enemy appears to be veru nervous.

D.McL. Duncan
Captain,
Intelligence Officer,
120th (Highland) Infantry Brigade.

S E C R E T

COPY NO. 4. Appx III

120TH (HIGHLAND) INFANTRY BRIGADE ORDER NO. 187.

Ref. 1/20,000 CROIX DU BAC.

3: 4: 18.

1. The 10/11th H.L.I. in Reserve positions of FLEURBAIX SECTOR, will be relieved to-night, 3rd/4th inst. by 21st Middlesex Regiment, and the 21st Middlesex Regt. will be attached to 120th Infantry Brigade for tactical purposes from 6 p.m. to-night.

2. The 10/11th H.L.I. will then relieve the 14th A. & S. Hrs. in the right subsector to-night 3rd/4th instant.

3. On completion of relief the 14th A. & S. Hrs. will move to LE NOUVEAU MONDE area, and will take over the billets of 21st Middlesex Regt. at SAILLY.

4. Details of Reliefs will be arranged between C.O.'s concerned.

5. Completion of Relief will be wired to Brigade Hd.Qrs. using following code word :-

HIGHLAND.

6. Trench Stores, etc. and Defence Schemes will be handed over and receipts given.

7. A C K N O W L E D G E.

H.B. Kerr
Captain,
A/Brigade Major
120th (Highland) Infantry Brigade.

Issued through Signals at 2.15 p.m.

Distribution :-

Copy No. 1 ... G.O.C.
2 ... Brigade Major.
3 ... Staff Captain.
4 ... War Diary.
5 ... File.
6 ... 10/11th H.L.I.
7 ... 14th H.L.I.
8 ... 14th A. & S. H.
9 ... 120th T.M.Bty.
10 ... 4th Portuguese Brigade.
11 ... 21st Middx. Regt.
12 ... 119th Inf. Bde.
13 ... 121st Inf. Bde.
14 ... 40th Division "G".
15 ... 40th Division "Q".
16 ... No. 3 Coy. Div. Train.
17 ... 137th Field Ambulance.
18 ... "B" Coy. M.G. Bn.
19 ... Bde. Supply Officer.
20 ... Town Major, NOUVEAU MONDE.
21 ... Bde. Signals.

****

TO ALL RECIPIENTS OF

120TH (HIGHLAND) INFANTRY BRIGADE ORDER NO. 187.

Moves ordered in above will not take place until further notice.

Authority -

40th Div. G.F.104 dated 3:4:18.

H.B. Kerr

Captain,
A/Brigade Major,
120th (Highland) Infantry Brigade.

Issued
through Signals
at 7.30 p.m.

TO ALL RECIPIENTS OF

120TH (HIGHLAND) INFANTRY BRIGADE ORDER NO. 187.

Moves ordered in above will take place to-night 4/5th April.

[signature]

Issued through
Signals
at 10 a.m.

Captain,
Brigade Major,
120th (Highland) Infantry Brigade

m.

Army Form C. 2121.
(In pads of 100.)

MESSAGES AND SIGNALS.

No. of Message...........

Prefix.......... Code.......... m. | Words. | Charge.

Office of Origin and Service Instructions.

Sent
At..........m.
To..........
By..........

This message is on a/c of:
..........Service.
(Signature of "Franking Officer.")

Recd. at..........m.
Date..........
From..........
By..........

TO	BBA	TDJ	INA

Sender's Number.	Day of Month.	In reply to Number.	AAA
* G 224	3		

Evening wire AAA Situation normal AAA Weather dull AAA Wind S

Added BBA repeated TDJ INA

Priority

From TDV
Place
Time

The above may be forwarded as now corrected. (Z)

Censor. Signature of Addressor or person authorised to telegraph in his name

* This line should be erased if not required.

(3796.) Wt. W492/M1647. 650,000 Pads. 5/17. H.W. & V., Ld. (E. 1187.)

"A" Form.

Army Form C. 2121.
(In pads of 100.)

MESSAGES AND SIGNALS.

No. of Message............

Prefix........ Code........ m. | Words. | Charge.

Office of Origin and Service Instructions.

Sent
At........m.
To........
By........

This message is on a/c of: .... Service.
(Signature of "Franking Officer.")

Recd. at........m.
Date........
From........
By........

TO BBA TDJ INA

Sender's Number.	Day of Month.	In reply to Number.	AAA
* MW 3	3		

Morning wire AAA Situation Normal aaa Weather fine Wind SW

Addsd BBA repeated TDJ INA

Priority

From TDV
Place
Time

The above may be forwarded as now corrected. (Z)

Censor. Signature of Addressor or person authorised to telegraph in his name.

Capt.

* This line should be erased if not required.

(3796.) Wt. W 492/M1647. 650,000 Pads. 5/17. H.W. & V., Ld. (E. 1187.)

Appx IV (6)

CONFIDENTIAL.

120TH (HIGHLAND) INFANTRY BRIGADE - INTELLIGENCE SUMMARY.

Period from 8 a.m. 2nd to 8 a.m. 3rd April

"A" OPERATIONS.

10. PATROLS. Fighting patrol left from "C" Post N.[illegible].c.[illegible].[illegible]. and reconnoitred to N.8.d. central. No signs of enemy were seen and patrol returned to our lines along the RIVIERE des LAIES. Sounds of digging heard from N.15.c. and transport heard apparently close behind enemy lines.

Patrol reconnoitred NO MAN'S LAND between "B" and "C" Posts. No signs of enemy seen.

1. ARTILLERY. Normal.

2. T. Ms. Heavy T.M. fired between 10-30 a.m. and noon on targets at N.5.d.40.19. and N.11.b.30.67.

3. AIRCRAFT. Active. Engaged by hostile A. A. fire, and M. G. fire when nearing line.

"B" ENEMY OPERATIONS.

1. ARTILLERY. More active than usual.

Support line in Left Sub-sector and DEAD DOG AVENUE shelled steadily between 10-30 a.m. and 5 p.m. with 7.7 cm and 10.5 cm from the direction of DURET WOOD.

Heavies fired intermittently on our back areas.

CROIX PLANCHE vicinity shelled during afternoon.

Front System at N.8.central shelled between 1-30 p.m. and 1-15 p.m. with 7.7 cm.

Hostile artillery becomes more active between noon and 5 p.m. Chief targets appear to be vicinity of CROIX PLANCHE and our supports generally, N.[illegible].d. coming in for special attention.

2. T. Ms. T.M. seen to fire on a T.B. 169° from Hill O.P. N.[illegible].a.90.05. Firing on vicinity of "B" Post.

3. M. Gs. Suspected emplacement in ruined house at N.[illegible].d. [illegible]0.75.

5. DEFENCES.

O. P. Suspected in tree at N.[illegible].d.[illegible].[illegible].

H. Q. Smoke seen rising from dugout at N.16.c.10.10. and also from N.15.b.30.35. There appears to be a Post built up in trench at latter point. May be an O. P.

BATTERY. Two gun battery active on a T. B. 138° from N.2[illegible].d.03.25. Firing into copse near ROUGE DE BOUT.

~~Three gun battery appeared to fire from direction~~ of convent O.14.a.

8. AIRCRAFT. Single E.A. reported at 8 a.m., [illegible]-55 p.m. and 5-35 p.m.

9. MOVEMENT. 4-30 p.m. Two men seen on road N.16.d.35.[illegible].

5-50 p.m. Three men carrying tins at N.[illegible].c.30.30. proceeded towards HOYON FARM.

6-20 p.m. Five men in C.T. N.15.d.05.50.

Individual movement seen during day round HOYON FARM.

[signature]

Captain,
Intelligence Officer,
120th (HIGHLAND) Infantry Brigade.

****

Army Form C. 2121.
(In pads of 100.)

"A" Form.

MESSAGES AND SIGNALS.

No. of Message..............

Prefix.......... Code.......... m	Words.	Charge.	This message is on a/c of:	Recd. at .... m.
Office of Origin and Service Instructions.	Sent		Service.	Date..........
	At.......... m.			From ....
	To..........			By..........
	By..........		(Signature of "Franking Officer.")	

TO { BBA TDJ INA

Sender's Number.	Day of Month.	In reply to Number.	AAA
* G 229	4		

Evening	Line	AAA	Situation
normal	AAA	Weather	dull
AAA	Wind	W	
AAA	BBA	repeats TDJ	INA
			Division

From TDV
Place
Time

The above may be forwarded as now corrected. (Z)

Censor. Signature of Addressor or person authorised to telegraph in his name.

* This line should be erased if not required.

(3796.) Wt. W 492/M1647. 650,000 Pads. 5/17. H.W. & V., Ld. (E. 1187.)

Appx V(a)

CONFIDENTIAL.

120TH (HIGHLAND) INFANTRY BRIGADE - INTELLIGENCE SUMMARY,
Period from 8 a.m. 3rd to 8 a.m. 4th April, 1918.

"A" OPERATIONS.

1. ARTILLERY. Quiet during day. Fired according to programme during the night. Between 6-30 and 8 a.m. 76 rounds 18 pdrs and 25 rounds heavies were fired on enemy transport routes.

6. WIRE. Wiring on RIVER LAINS continued.

7. WORK. Pumping work carried out in [illegible] AVENUE. Improvement of Posts and Coy. H.Q. in right sub-sector. Draining of dugouts and relaying of duck-boards.

8. AIRCRAFT. Very active all day. Hostile A.A. and M.G. fire was very heavy. All M.G. fire came from well behind the enemy front line trenches.

10. PATROLS. Patrol left "C" post and reconnoitred road through N.9.c. to about N.9.d.30.20. The mine craters in N.9.d. were examined and no signs of occupation found. Talking could be heard from enemy front line posts. Very Lights were fired from rear defences and not from front line. There appeared to be a considerable amount of transport moving behind enemy lines.
Patrols on left encountered no enemy. The enemy were very active with M.Gs. and flares one man being wounded.

"B" ENEMY OPERATIONS.

1. ARTILLERY.

Time	Target.	Calibre.	Rounds.
8-15 to 8-30 a.m. / 3 p.m. to 3-30 p.m.	Cross roads N.25.d.10.20.	7.7 cm	-
1 p.m. to 4 p.m.	CELLAR FARM AVENUE	7.7 cm	-
1-30 p.m.	"F" Track and DEAD DOG DUMP	10.5 cm	60.
3 p.m. to 6 p.m.	HORNETS NEST.	7.7 cm	300

2. T.Ms. 50 L.T.Ms. fell on left sub-sector. Direction of fire unknown.

5. DEFENCES. Suspected hostile battery - 4 guns - firing from N.17.d. N.E. corner of DUBEN WOOD. Artillery informed.

8. AIRCRAFT. Nil.

9. MOVEMENT.
8-50 a.m. Two men seen near Water Tower N.22.d.60.70.
10-45 am. Four men walking E. behind NATTY TRENCH.
11-20 am. Six men working behind trench at N.16.c.05.05.
Individual movement on road from N.22.c.80.90. to MOYON FARM during morning also along NATTY TRENCH in N.15.d.
Movement at LONG BARN.
2-45 pm. Three men left house at N.22.d.90.70. and went off in a S.W. direction.

11. GENERAL. Smoke visible at following points :-

N.16.c.10.10.
N.15.d.95.55. - dugout.
N.22.b.40.10.
N.22.d.05.90. - short chimney at earthworks.
N.16.a.90.60. - Pillbox.
N.10.d.20.80. - dugout.
N.28.a.10.90. - shelters in FROMELLES AUBERS ROAD.

[signature]
for Intelligence Officer.
120th (Highland) Infantry Brigade.

ANNX VI   4

S E C R E T   COPY NO. 25

120TH (HIGHLAND) INFANTRY BRIGADE ORDER NO. 188.

Ref. CROIX DU BAC Sheet
1/20,000.   5:4:18.

-----

1. The 120th Brigade will be relieved in the FLEURBAIX SECTOR by 119th Brigade on night 6/7th instant, in accordance with attached table

2. Guides will be provided at the rate of one per platoon.

3. Details of Reliefs will be arranged between Commanding Officers concerned.

4. Defence Schemes, Trench Stores, etc. will be handed over and receipts forwarded to this office by noon 8th instant.
Special attention to be paid to the handing over of Reserve Rations and water in keeps, etc.

5. Transport Lines and Quartermasters' Stores will not move.

6. 14th A. & S.H. in Corps Reserve will come under command of G.O.C., 120th Infantry Brigade after 7.30 p.m. on 6th instant.

7. Completion of Reliefs will be wired to Bde. HdQrs. using following code words :-

10/11th H.L.I.	...	TRENCH
14th H.L.I.	...	MORTAR.
120th T.M.Bty.	...	BATTERY.

8. Brigade Headquarters at MARE'S NEST will close at 7.30 p.m. on 6th inst. and will re-open at the same hour at LE NOUVEAU MONDE - G.26.d.9.0.

9. A C K N O W L E D G E.

H. B. Kerr
Captain,
for Brigade Major,
120th (Highland) Infantry Brigade.

Issued through
Signals
at 7.30 p.m.

Distribution:-

Copy No.					
1	...	G.O.C.	11	...	5th Portuguese Bde.
2	...	Brigade Major.	12	...	119th Inf. Bde.
3	...	Staff Captain.	13	...	121st Inf. Bde.
4	...	War Diary.	14	...	40th Divn. "G".
5	...	File.	15	...	40th Divn. "Q".
6	...	10/11th H.L.I.	16	...	No. 3 Coy. Div.Trn.
7	...	14th H.L.I.	17	...	137th Fd.Ambce.
8	...	14th A. & S.H.	18	...	"B" Coy.M.G.Bn.
9	...	120th T.M.Bty.	19	...	Bde.Supply Officer.
10	...	21st Middx.R.	20	...	Town Major, N.MONDE.
21	...	Bde. Signals.			
22-24		2?th Bde H.Q.			

****

25. ... 4th Portuguese Bde.

TABLE TO ACCOMPANY 120TH (HD.) INFANTRY BRIGADE ORDER NO. 188.

Unit	From	To	Relieved by		Remarks
14th H.L.I.	LEFT SECTOR	LE NOUVEAU MONDE	13th E. Surrey Regt.	(1)	Rendezvous and time for meeting guides to be arranged by Os.C. concerned.
10/11th H.L.I.	RT.SECTOR	ESTAIRES	18th Welsh Regt.		
120th T.M.Bty.	LINE	LE NOUVEAU MONDE	119th T. M. Bty.	(2)	Relieving units not to cross RUE du QUESNOY before 7.15 p.m.
120th Bde.H.Q.	MARES NEST	LE NOUVEAU MONDE	119th Bde.H.Qrs.		

"A" Form

MESSAGES AND SIGNALS.

Army Form C. 2121
(in pads of 100).

Prefix........ Code........ m. | Words | Charge. | No. of Message........

Office of Origin and Service Instructions.
TDV

Sent
At........ m.
To........ BBA
By........

This message is on a/c of:
.... Service.
(Signature of "Franking Officer.")

Recd. at........ m.
Date........
From........
By........

TO	BBA	TDJ	INA	

* Sender's Number.	Day of Month.	In reply to Number.	AAA
MW5	5		

Morning wire AAA

[illegible]

Addsd BBA repeated TDJ INA

From TDV
Place
Time

priority

The above may be forwarded as now corrected. (Z)

Censor.

Signature of Addressor or person authorised to telegraph in his name.

*This line should be erased if not required.

(18965.) Wt. W12952/M1294. 187,500 Pads. 1/17 McC. & Co., Ltd. (E. 818.)

Lieut.

"A" Form
MESSAGES AND SIGNALS.

Army Form C. 2121 (in pads of 100).

Prefix.............Code...............m. | Words. | Charge. | No. of Message...............

Office of Origin and Service Instructions.

Sent At...............m. To............... By...............

This message is on a/c of: ....Service. (Signature of "Franking Officer.")

Recd. at...............m. Date............... From............... By...............

TO BBA TDJ 5th PORTUGUESE Bd

Sender's Number.	Day of Month.	In reply to Number.	AAA
EW5	5		

Evening wire AAA Situation normal AAA Weather dull AAA Wind northerly

Added BBA repeated TDJ 5th Portuguese Bde

From TDV
Place
Time

The above may be forwarded as now corrected. (Z)

Censor. Signature of Addressor or person authorised to telegraph in his name.

* This line should be erased if not required.

(18965.) Wt. W12952/M1294. 187,500 Pads. 1/17 McC. & Co., Ltd. (E. 818.)

CONFIDENTIAL.

120TH (HIGHLAND) INFANTRY BRIGADE - INTELLIGENCE SUMMARY.
Period from 8 a.m. 4th to 8 a.m. 5th April.

"A" OPERATIONS.

ARTILLERY. Fairly quiet. Our heavies retaliated during the afternoon for hostile shelling.

WORK. Improvement work carried on. Pumping water out of dugouts Clearing damaged trenches.

AIRCRAFT. Nil.

PATROLS. Fighting patrols were out along our front but saw no signs of the enemy. Much shouting was heard from enemy lines and usual sounds of transport.

"B" ENEMY OPERATIONS.

ARTILLERY. Hostile artillery much more active than usual.

Time.	Target.	Calibre	Rounds.	Remarks.
1-[illegible]0 to 2-30 pm	RUE DES LOMBARDS	Medium	-	-
1-30 to [illegible]-30 pm	FORAY HOUSE and TIN BARN TRAMWAY	7.7 cm	200	Salvoes of [illegible].
2-[illegible] to 2-25 pm	Front & Support Lines between "A" and "C" Posts.	10.5 cm	150	About 50% duds.
2-30 to 6 p.m.	HORNETS NEST	7.7 and 10.5cm	250	Bursts of 50.
[illegible]-50 to 5-10 pm	Vicinity of V.C. House.	10.5 cm	12	
5-0 to 5-10 pm	CROIX BLANCHE	10.5 cm	40	
5-20 to 5-40 pm	CROIX BLANCHE	10.5 cm	40	
[illegible]-0 to 6-30 pm	CELLAR FARM AVE.	15 cm	50	
[illegible]-0 to 7-30 p.m.	TIN BARN and DEAD DOG TRAMWAY	Gas and Medium H.E.	-	
6-20 to 6-25 pm	DOG TRENCH	15 cm	40	
[illegible]-10 to 6-30 pm	Vicinity of "B" & "C" Posts	7.7 and 10.5 cm	190	

From 7-30 to 8 p.m. and systematic bombardment of CROIX MARECHAL POST was carried out the enemy using medium and heavy H.E.

The C.Ts. between Support and Front Lines were damaged in places. Hostile artillery quiet during the night.

T.Ms. Quiet. About 20 L.T.M. shells fell in vicinity of "B" Post.

ENEMY WORKS. Sounds of work heard about N.10.d.30.90.

AIRCRAFT. Nil.

MOVEMENT. "B" Post reports a party of about 50 men moving along [illegible] AVENUE towards front line between 7-30 and 7-40 p.m. They were in full kit and carried rifles.

Visibility during day was poor and no movement was seen

GENERAL. No signs of sentry posts can be seen in enemy front line by day.

[signature]

Captain,
Intelligence Officer.
120th (Highland) Infantry Brigade.

"A" Form
MESSAGES AND SIGNALS.

Army Form C. 2121 (in pads of 100).

No. of Message ....

Prefix..........Code..........m. Words. Charge.

Office of Origin and Service Instructions.

Sent At..........m. To.......... By..........

This message is on a/c of: ....Service.

(Signature of "Franking Officer.")

Recd. at..........m. Date.......... From.......... By..........

TO	BBA	TDJ	INA

Sender's Number.	Day of Month.	In reply to Number.	AAA
MW 6	6		

Morning wire AAA
[illegible]

Addsd BBA repeated TDJ INA

[illegible]

From TDV
Place
Time

The above may be forwarded as now corrected. (Z)

Censor. Signature of Addressor or person authorised to telegraph in his name.

* This line should be erased if not required.

(18965.) Wt. W12952/M1294. 187,500 Pads. 1/17 McC. & Co., Ltd. (E. 818.)

"A" Form
MESSAGES AND SIGNALS.

Army Form C. 2121 (in pads of 100).

No. of Message..............

Prefix.........Code.........m. Office of Origin and Service Instructions.	Words.	Charge.	This message is on a/c of: ....Service. (Signature of "Franking Officer.")	Recd. at.........m. Date........ From........ By........
	Sent At.........m. To......... By.........			

TO BBA 'G' TDF   INA

Sender's Number.	Day of Month.	In reply to Number.	AAA
* EW6	6		

Enemy	wire	AAA	Situation
normal	AAA	Weather	fine
AAA	Wind	Westerly	

Addsd BBA 'G' repeated   INA

From	TDF		
Place			
Time			

The above may be forwarded as now corrected. (Z)

Censor. Signature of Addressor or person authorised to telegraph in his name

*This line should be erased if not required.

(18965.) Wt. W12952/M1294. 187,500 Pads. 1/17 McC. & Co., Ltd. (E. 818.)

CONFIDENTIAL.

120TH (HIGHLAND) INFANTRY BRIGADE - INTELLIGENCE SUMMARY.
Period from 8 a.m. 5th to 8 a.m. 6th April.

"A" OPERATIONS.

PATROLS. Fighting and reconnoitring patrols were out from each Company front. NO MAN'S LAND was patrolled up to the enemy's wire but no signs of hostile patrols were seen. Sounds of voices could be heard. New wire appeared to be in course ofconstruction in front of NEPHEW TRENCH.

ARTILLERY. Quiet.

"B" ENEMY OPERATIONS.

ARTILLERY. Fairly quiet.
A few short bursts of 10 rounds were fired at HORNETS NEST.
25 rounds 10.5 cm and gas shells fell 150 yards short of CHARREL [illegible] POST.
Slight shelling of back areas during the morning.
CROIX MARECHAL POST shelled intermittently.

AERIAL. At 3-15 p.m., 6-10 p.m. and 7 p.m. a fast E.A. flew low along our lines and was fired on by rifles and M.Gs.

MOVEMENT. At evening "Stand to" two men were observed about N.10.b.70.30. Suspected M.G. position for night firing at this point.
Individual movement on road between N.22.c.80.90. and HOYON FARM.
Slight movement during day in N.[illegible]2.a.

MISCELLANEOUS.

Red signalling lamp seen flashing for 10 minutes from direction of FROMELLES CHURCH.

Captain,
Intelligence Officer,
120th Infantry Brigade.

War Diary
Appx IX

SECRET

COPY NO. 4

120TH (SCOTTISH) INFANTRY BRIGADE ORDER NO. 189.

7:4:18.

1. The 10/11th H.L.I. at ESTAIRES will be relieved by a battalion of the 151st Infantry Brigade at 10 a.m. on 8th instant.

2. After 4 a.m., 8th instant, the 10/11th H.L.I. will be tactically at the disposal of the 120th Brigade, and will be prepared to move in accordance with the new Reserve Brigade Defence Scheme issued to-day.

3. On completion of relief, the 10/11th H.L.I. will move to NOUVEAU MONDE.

4. Details of billets have already been issued to the 10/11th H.L.I.

5. ACKNOWLEDGE.

Issued through
Signals
at 8 p.m.

Captain,
Brigade Major,
120th (Scottish) Infantry Brigade.

Distribution :-

Copy No.		
1	...	G.O.C.
2	...	Brigade Major.
3	...	Staff Captain.
4	...	War Diary.
5	...	File.
6	...	10/11th H.L.I.
7	...	14th H.L.I.
8	...	2nd Royal Scots Fusrs.
9	...	120th T.M.Bty.
10	...	151st Inf. Bde.
11	...	119th Inf. Bde.
12	...	121st Inf. Bde.
13	...	40th Division "G".
14	...	40th Division "Q".
15	...	No. 3 Coy.Div.Train.
16	...	136th Field Ambce.
17	...	"B" Coy. 40th M.G.Bn.
18	...	231st Field Coy.R.E.
19	...	Bde. Supply Officer.
20	...	Town Major, NOUVEAU MONDE.
21	...	57th D.A.
22	...	40th M.G. Bn
23	...	Bde. Signals.

****

B.Le. W.D.

Appx X

SECRET

120th Infantry Brigade No. 120/415.

2nd Royal Scots Fusiliers.
10/11th H. L. I.
14th H. L. I.
120th T. M. Bty.
40th Bn. M.G.Corps.
****

Reference attached Brigade Defence Scheme.

Units will arrange to carry out the necessary reconnaissances to-morrow morning, 8th instant, and will report to Brigade Head quarters when this has been done, and notification of the sites selected for Hd.Qrs. sent.

While the 120th (Scottish) Brigade is in Divisional Reserve,

"A"	Battalion will be the	10/11th H.L.I.
"B"	" " " "	14th H.L.I.
"C"	" " " "	2nd Royal Scots Fusrs.

Details of M.G. and T.M. positions will be issued to units as soon as they have been decided upon.

[signature]

Captain,
Brigade Major,
120th (Scottish) Infantry Brigade.

7/4/18.

DEFENCE SCHEME

OF

BRIGADE IN DIVISIONAL RESERVE.

Reference Maps :-
XV Corps Secret Map.
Sheets 36 N.W., 36.a.N.E.
36.a.S.E., 36 S.W.
All 1/20,000.

7: 4: 18.

1. After 4 a.m., 8th instant, the Brigade will be released from Corps Reserve and will become Divisional Reserve; the Defence Scheme taken over from the Previous Brigade is therefore cancelled and the following substituted.

2. In the event of a serious attack developing upon the 2nd Portuguese Division, the Brigade in Divisional Reserve will have at its disposal 1 section of Machine Guns of 40th Division and will be responsible

   (a) For occupying the crossings over the LYS from NOUVEAU MONDE (inclusive) to SAILLY (inclusive).

   (b) For taking over the defence of the line COCKSHY HOUSE POST (exclusive) where touch will be gained with the 151st Infantry Brigade, to CHARRED POST (exclusive), where touch will be gained with the Right Brigade of the Division in the line.

3. To effect this, units will be prepared to move as follows, at 30 minutes notice :-

   (a) "A" Battalion from NOUVEAU MONDE will move via the road from NOUVEAU MONDE Church through G.33.b., or by emergency tracks S.W. of this road and take up the line from COCKSHY HOUSE POST (exclusive) - in front of LAVENTIE - to LAVENTIE EAST POST inclusive, the battalion being disposed in depth, and touch being gained with the 151st Infantry Brigade, whose left flank will rest in COCKSHY POST.
   Battalion Hd.Qrs.will be at a site to be detailed later.

   (b) "B" Battalion from NOUVEAU MONDE will move via the road through G.27.d. and 34.b. or by emergency tracks N.E. of the road from NOUVEAU MONDE Church through G.33.b., and take up the line from LAVENTIE EAST POST (exclusive) to CHARRED POST (exclusive), the battalion being disposed in depth, and touch being gained at LAVENTIE EAST POST with "A" Battalion, and at CHARRED POST with the Right Brigade in the Line.
   Battn. Hd.Qrs. will be at a site to be detailed later.

(c) "C" Battalion will be in Reserve, but will be responsible for occupying the crossings over the LYS from NOUVEAU MONDE (inclusive) to SAILLY (inclusive). For this purpose, small guards will be sent from "C" Battalion to hold the Bridgeheads. The remainder of the battalion will rendezvous in an assembly area to be reconnoitred about G.28.b. and G.29.a. Battalion Hd.Qrs. will be at a site to be detailed later.

(d) The section M.G.Coy., 40th Division and the 120th T. M. Battery will move to an assembly position about G.34.a., and will reconnoitre positions in defence of the COCKSHY HOUSE POST - CHARRED POST LINE.

4. Brigade Hd. Qrs. will be at NOUVEAU MONDE - G.26.d.9.0.

[signature]

Captain,
Brigade Major,
120th (Scottish) Infantry Brigade.

Issued through
Signals
at 9.30 p.m.

Distribution :-

Copy No. 1	...	G.O.C.
2	...	Brigade Major.
3	...	Staff Captain
4	...	War Diary.
5	...	File.
6	...	2nd Royal Scots Fusrs.
7	...	10/11th H.L.I.
8	...	14th H.L.I.
9	...	120th T. M. Bty.
10	...	40th Division.
11	...	40th Bn. M.G.Corps.
12	...	119th Infantry Bde.
13	...	121st Infantry Bde.
14	...	151st Infantry Bde.
15	...	57th D.A.
16	...	Bde. Signals.

Appx XV. Copy.

REPORT ON OPERATIONS from 9:4:18 to 12:4:18.

On the morning of the 9th, the 120th (Scottish) Infantry Brigade was in Reserve about the SAILLY - NOUVEAU MONDE Area, disposed as follows :-

Brigade Hd.Qrs. ...	NOUVEAU MONDE.
2nd R.S.Fsrs. ...	SAILLY.
10/11th H.L.I. ...	NOUVEAU MONDE.
14th H.L.I. ...	NOUVEAU MONDE.
Trench Mortar Bty..	SAILLY.
1 Section "D" Coy.. 40th Bn.M.G.C.	SAILLY, was at the disposal of the Brigade.

11 Lewis guns and teams were on anti-aircraft defence, and were not at the disposal of the Brigade.

The role of the Brigade in the event of an attack on the Portuguese Front had been laid down in the Defence Scheme of the Brigade in Divisional Reserve, issued on the 7th instant.

This entailed holding a front of 3,000 yards with about 1,500 men, which was the eventual fighting strength of the Brigade.

At 4.20 a.m. on the 9th, a very heavy bombardment was opened on both front and back areas, and battalions and transport were ordered to "stand-to".

About 6.15 a.m., in accordance with instructions received from the Division, the battalions were ordered to move forward to Assembly Positions, and, by soon after 7 a.m., battalions were in these positions, disposed as follows :-

10/11th H.L.I. ...	At about G.33.b.
14th HL.I. ...	" " G.29.c.
Trench Mortar Bty...	" " G.28.d.
Section of M.G.Coy..	" " G.28.d.
2nd R.S.F. (In Reserve)	" " G.28.b.

120 O.R. from the 2nd R. S.F. meanwhile had to be detailed to act as Traffic Control Posts at the various bridges of the LYS, thus leaving the Reserve Battalion about 250 strong.

The fighting strength of battalions was as follows:-

2nd R.S.F. ...	300 (approximately).
10/11th H.L.I. ...	600 (-do-).
14th H.L.I. ...	600 (-do-).

All the back areas were being shelled, and some casualties were inflicted on battalions in their assembly positions.

No information could be obtained from the Portuguese, and a liaison officer was sent on a motor bicycle to the Portuguese Divisional Head q uarters to try and find out the situation.

About 8.30 a.m., in accordance with instructions from the Division, battalions were ordered forward to occupy the line of LAVENTIE EAST POST - CHARRED POST, in accordance with the Defence Scheme. From this time, the movements of the forward Companies of the 10/11th and 14th H.L.I. became very obscure. The greatest difficulty was experienced in distinguishing in the mist between the Portuguese withdrawing and the enemy advancing, and after parties of Portuguese had, on two or three occasions, been mistaken for the enemy, men began to withhold fire, and there appears little doubt that the enemy in several cases dribbled small parties with machine guns round the right flank of these companies by mingling them with the Portuguese as they withdrew. By the time the forward companies got in touch with the enemy, the latter were, apparently, in possession of the line from COCKSHY HOUSE POST to CHARRED POST, and no trace could be found of any British troops on the right of the 120th Brigade.

By 10.40 a.m., as no information had been received from forward companies, and it was evident that the enemy was moving round the right flank of this Brigade and of the 119th Brigade, the 10/11th H.L.I. prepared to hold the line of MUDDY LANE POST - LAVENTIE NORTH, with the 14th H.L.I. prolonging their left flank towards CHARRED POST.

The situation on the left had meanwhile, apparently, become very serious, as the enemy had turned the right flank of the 119th Brigade and heavily attacked the 14th H.L.I., with the result that their left flank was in danger. The 2nd R.S.F., with a Section of M.Gs., were ordered to move in support of the 14th H.L.I. and protect their left, gaining touch with the Reserve Battalion of the 121st Bde., who were reported to be holding the FLEURBAIX Defences.

The whole of the line was then being very heavily attacked and a gap existed between the right of the 10/11th H.L.I. and the troops on their right. Attempts were made to protect their flank with what reserves were still available, but the enemy pressure became so great that the right flank remained endangered and the enemy continued his pressure along the whole line.

By this time the Brigade only numbered about 400 rifles, with 4 machine guns, and, for about 4 hours, they delayed the advance of the enemy on a front of 2,500 yards on the South East of the LYS, fighting a rearguard action to cover the bridgeheads, the 10/11th H.L.I. covering the bridge at NOUVEAU MONDE, the 14th H.L.I. and 2nd R.S.Fs. holding the ground about G.28.b. and c., to cover the bridges at PT DE LA JUSTICE and MAISON ROUGE FARM. Later, the 2nd R.S.Fs. found that apparently the SAILLY Bridge was not being covered, and their dispositions were altered so as to cover that bridge, holding out on the Eastern outskirts as long as possible.

By about 4 p.m. the remnants of the Brigade, numbering some 200 rifles, with only 2 Lewis guns, were across the river and holding the Western bank in conjunction with troops of the 150th Brigade, who had moved up to cover the bridges.
The NOUVEAU MONDE - PT DE LA JUSTICE and MAISON ROUGE FARM Bridges had been destroyed, but the SAILLY Bridge had only been partially so, and the enemy made repeated attempts to cross there, all of which were driven back by the 2nd R.S.Fs., who inflicted considerable casualties on the enemy, and nowhere on the Brigade front did any of the enemy succeed in crossing the river.

About 7 p.m., orders were received from the Division to withdraw the elements of the Brigade and concentrate them at LE MORTIER, but as no other troops but the 2nd R.S.Fs. were covering the SAILLY Bridge, they were left in position, and the other two battalions concentrated at LE MORTIER, together with some drafts which had arrived, and elements of carrying parties. About 300 rifles were collected in all at LE MORTIER and were formed into a composite battalion.

On arrival at LE MORTIER, information was received that the enemy had crossed the river at BAC ST MAUR, had taken CROIX DU BAC, and was moving against the left flank, but that the 74th Brigade were moving to counter-attack them. An outpost position round LE MORTIER had been taken up by a composite battalion of the 119th Brigade, and the 120th Brigade battalion was held in Reserve to them. Battalions were instructed to get as much rest as possible.

About 4 a.m. on the 10th, the 119th Bde. battalion moved forward to occupy the line of the STEENWERCK SWITCH, and the 120th Bde. battalion moved into a position in Reserve, about A.27.c. and d., and dug a line about FROID NID FARM, facing S.E. The counter-attack of the 74th Brigade was apparently temporarily successful, but later a heavy hostile counter-attack developed, they were driven back and a heavy enemy attack developed on the STEENWERCK SWITCH. As the left flank of the 119th Bde. was in the air, in consultation with G.O.C. 119th Bde., it was decided to send the 120th Bde. battalion to prolong the left flank along the line of the STEENWERCK SWITCH, and by about 12 noon, this battalion was in position.

Meanwhile considerable enemy activity was developing about PT DE LA BOUDRETTE, and the troops on both flanks of the 2nd R.S.Fs., opposite the SAILLY Bridge, withdrew. For a considerable time the 2nd R.S.Fs. were left entirely alone, hanging on to this position, but later the troops on either flank were again brought on to a line some 200 yards to the rear of the original one. As the situation at this point looked rather serious, 1 Company of the Pioneer Battalion was moved round to about G.10.c., to be at the disposal of O.C. R.S.Fs.

At about 2 p.m. the enemy were reported to have apparently crossed the STILBECQUE by G.10.b. and d., and were maintaining heavy pressure all along the line of the SWITCH. The 74th Brigade had meanwhile apparently been pressed back towards STEENWERCK, and at one time had formed a defensive flank about 29.a. and 24.c., facing West, which fired for some time at the 120th Bde. battalion.

Continual and heavy pressure was maintained all along the line of the STEENWERCK SWITCH, and the situation remained obscure. Gaps were known to exist at several places, but battalions were ordered to hold on at all costs, as information was received that the 29th Division were going to counter-attack.

About 6.30 p.m., the 120th Bde. battalion reported that the enemy advance had been temporarily checked, that they had counter-attacked and advanced, in conjunction with the 119th Bde., some 500 yards from A.27.b. in the direction of the SWITCH. They were in touch with the 119th Bde. on the right, but no touc h could be gained with troops on the left.

About 9 p.m., as far as could be ascertained, the situation was as follows :-

The 88th Brigade were holding a line facing S. and S. E., from A.12.central to A.10 central to A.15 central.

The left of the 120th Bde. battalion rested about the B of BEAUMART, and there was a complete gap between this and the 88th Brigade. The battalion was in touch on the right on a line running, roughly, 300 yds. E. of the road running North and South through 27.b. The 2 nd R.S.Fs. were holding the ground about G.9.b. and d., having been forced back by heavy attacks which drove the troops on their right back to G.8.b. Another Brigade of the 29th Division was dug in about CRUSEOBEAU, facing, roughly, South and South-East.

About 200 Sappers and Pioneers, and stragglers from the 74th and 150th Brigades were formed up and sent to prolong the left of the 120th Brigade battalion, and t ry and get into touch with the 88th Brigade.

The night of the 10/11th remained, on the whole, uneventful.

At dawn on the 11th, the enemy started a heavy bombardment of the Southern portion of the line, and massing about BOUDRELLES and South of it, made heavy attacks. About 10 a.m., the troops on the right of the 2nd R.S.Fs. began to withdraw rapidly, and the enemy worked round the right flank of this bat talion, causing them very heavy casualties, and even tually forcing them back on to the line of the 29th Division, which was slowly falling back on DOULIE U. Meanwhile strong attacks were being made on the line North of this, especially N. of the STEENWERCK - LEVERRIER Road, where t ouch had never been gained with the 88th Brigade, and by 12 noon, the line roughly ran from the direction of CRUSEOBEAU, where the situation was obscure, FROID NID FARM, to CHIEN BLANC. Thence the flank was thrown back in the direction of FME. DU BOIS to A.13.d., w here the flank was apparently in the air.

The li ne by CRUSEOBEAU was steadily driven back towards DOULIEU, and the situation about FROID NID FARM became serious, as the li ne was very thin and strong attacks were being made. One battalion of the 29 th Division was ordered to move in support in the direction of G.27. a., but apparently became involved before its arrival, and the line was forced back to the DECAUVILLE line about LEVERRIER, round the East of LEVERRIER through FME. DU BOIS. Only about 3 Officers and 20 O. R. of the R.S.Fs. were now together and they had been withdrawn behind the line of the 29th Division about DOULIEU. Owing to the serious situation on the left flank, O.C., 2nd R.S.F. was ordered to move the rem ains of his battalion, with stragglers of the battalions of several Divisions which had been collected, to the support of the left flank.

This line was then held intact until the 31st Division had counter-attacked and re-taken LA B ECQUE and had relived the 119th and 120th Bde. battali ons about 6 a.m. on the 12th.

On the morning of the 12th, the Brigade concentrated about STRAZEELE.

CASUALTIES.

Unit.	Killed.		Wounded.		Missing.	
	Off.	O.R.	Off.	O.R.	Off.	O.R.
2nd R.S.F.	1	10	3	72	-	81
10/11th H.L.I.	1	4	5	58	8	341
14th H.L.I.	-	23	3	128	11	317
120th T.M.Bty.	-	-	-	1	-	2

Total 32 Officers 1037 O.R.

(Sgd). C. J. Hobkirk

Brigadi er - General,
Commanding 120th (Scottish) Inf.Bde.

Report on Operations

Appendix No. 11.

precedes War Diary.

SECRET

Appx XII

Copy No. 8

120th (Scottish) Infantry Brigade Order No. 191

13-4-18

1. The 120th Brigade and 135th Field Ambulance will continue its march tomorrow to an area West of St OMER.

2. The Brigade units will move in following order:.

Brigade Headquarters
T M Battery.
2nd R. S. Fusrs.
10/11th H. L. I.
14th H. L. I.
135th Field Ambulance.

The starting point will be the cross roads in N. 12. d. 4. 1.
Hour at which the head of the Column will pass this point will be 9.15 am.

3. Route to be followed will be COIN - PERDU CLAIRMARAIS - ST OMER

4. When the head of the column reaches the C of CLAIRMARAIS the column will halt for 2 hours for dinner. after which time the march will be resumed.

5. Clock-hour halts will be observed.

6. 200 yds distance will be maintained between battalions and field ambulances.

7. Transport will move with battalions

8. Mounted billeting parties and guides from all Brigade units and from 135th Field Ambulance will meet the Staff Captain at 11 a.m. tomorrow at the Town Hall in the main square at ST OMER. The guides will then be sent by the Staff Captain to the Eastern outskirts of ST OMER to inform their respective units of the villages in which they are to be billeted.

9. Completion of all moves will be notified to Brigade Headquarters

10. ACKNOWLEDGE

Distribution

Copy No 1 ... 203 RE ...
2 ... 10th [illegible] HLI
3 ... 11th HLI
4 ... 120th [illegible] Bde
5 ... 135th Fd Ambce
6 ... GOC
7 ... Staff Captain
8 ... [illegible]

[illegible] Captain
Brigade Major
[illegible] Infantry Bde

appx XIII

SECRET

COPY NO. 4

120TH (SCOTTISH) INFANTRY BRIGADE ORDER NO. 192.

Ref. Maps
HAZEBROUCK 5A.
27A. S.E.
1/20,000.

21:4:18.

1. The 40th Division, less Divisional Headquarters, Divisional R.A., Composite Brigade and 40th Divnl. M.T. Company, will move to the BOISDINGHEM Area to-day.

2. 120th (Scottish) Brigade Group, consisting of the troops mentioned in para. 3, will move to the ACQUIN Area in accordance with the attached March Table.

3. For the purposes of the move, the 120th (Scottish) Brigade will consist of :-

120th (Scottish) Infantry Bde.
No. 3 Coy. 40th Div. Train.
12th Yorks Rcgt. (Pioneers)
135th Field Ambulance.
231st Field Coy. R.E.

4. Billeting parties will meet the Staff Captain at 11.30 a.m. at the Area Commandant's Office, BOISDINGHEM.

5. Transport will move with its own unit.

6. On the march, 100 yds. distance will be maintained between companies, and between units and transport, and 500 yds. between battalions.

7. Brigade Headquarters will close at TATINGHEM at 2 p.m. and re-open at ACQUIN on arrival.

8. ACKNOWLEDGE.

[signature]
Captain,
Brigade Major,
120th (Scottish) Infantry Brigade.

Issued through
Signals
at 10 a.m.

Distribution :-

Copy No.			Copy No.		
1	...	G.O.C.	11	...	12th Yorks (Pioneers)
2	...	Brigade Major.	12	...	135th Fd.Ambulance
3	...	Staff Captain.	13	...	40th Div. "G".
4	...	War Diary.	14	...	40th Div. "Q".
5	...	File.	15	...	119th Inf. Bde.
6	...	2nd R.S.Fsrs.	16	...	121st Inf.Bde.
7	...	10/11th H.L.I.	17	...	Bde. Supply Offr.
8	...	14th H.L.I.	18	...	A.P.M.
9	...	120th T.M.Bty.	19	...	Area Comdt. ST MARTIN AU-LAERT.
10	...	No. 3 Coy. Train.			
20	...	Area Comdt. BOISDINGHEM.			
21	...	Bde. Signals			
22	...	231st Fd. Coy. R.E.			

****

MARCH TABLE TO ACCOMPANY 120TH (SCOTTISH) INFANTRY BRIGADE ORDER NO. 192.

Serial No.	Unit	From	To	Starting Point	Hr. of Start	Route	Remarks.
1.	120th (Scottish) Bde. Hd.Qrs	TATINGHEM	ACQUIN	Pt. W.12.c.5.5 on TATINGHEM-QUELMES Road	2.30 p.m.	via QUELMES	
2.	2nd R.S.Frs.	-do-	QUER CAMP & LA WATTINE.			QUELMES-ACQUIN -NORDAL.	To follow 100 yds. behind Serial 1.
3.	10/11th H. L. I.	-do-	VAL D'ACQUIN			QUELMES-ACQUIN	To follow 500 yds. behind Serial 2.
4.	14th H. L. I.	-do-	ACQUIN			QUELMES.	To follow 500 yds. behind Serial 3.
5.	No. 3 Coy. 40th Div. Train.	-do-	NORDAL			QUELMES-ACQUIN	To follow 500 yds. behind Serial 4.
6.	120th T.M.Bty.	LONGUENESSE	LE NOOVRE	TATINGHEM Church.	2.30 p.m.	QUELMES-ACQUIN	To follow 100 yds. behind Serial 5.
7.	135th Fd.Ambulance	-do-	LE POOVRE	-do-		-do-	To follow 100 yds. behind Serial 6.
8.	231st Fd. Coy. R.E	CORMETTE	ZUTOVE			ZUDAUSQUES.	To clear CORMETTE by 2.30 p.m.
9.	12th Yorks (Pnrs).	SALDERWICK	WESTBECOURT & MERZUIL.			TATINGHEM-QUELMES- ACQUIN	Not to enter TATINGHEM before 3.15 p.m.

appx XIV

SECRET COPY NO. 4

120TH (SCOTTISH) INFANTRY BRIGADE ORDER NO. 193.

23:4:18.

1. One composite battalion from the 10/11th and 14th H.L.I. will be formed at once and be prepared to move to-morrow to the CASSEL Area for work on a defensive line.

2. The Battalion will be formed as follows :-

Battalion Hd.Qrs. Staff	...	14th H.L.I.
2 Companies	... ...	14th H.L.I.
2 Companies	... ...	10/11th H.L.I.

Each of these companies will be made up to 100 strong, leaving out specialists as far as possible.

3. Transport will be provided by 14th H.L.I.

4. The Battalion Hd.Qrs.Staff and details of the 10/11th H.L.I., and details of the 14th H.L.I. will remain in their present billets and will continue training.

5. Details as to the actual move will be issued later.

H. Clark[?]

Captain,
Brigade Major,
120th (Scottish) Infantry Brigade.

Issued through
Signals
at 8 p.m.

Distribution:-

Copy No.					
1	...	G.O.C.	11	...	231st Fd.Coy.R.E.
2	...	Bde.Major.	12	...	No. 3 Coy.Div.Train.
3	...	Staff Capt.	13	...	119th Inf. Bde.
4	...	War Diary.	14	...	121st Inf. Bde.
5	...	File.	15	...	40th Divn. "G".
6	...	2nd R.S.F.	16	...	40th Divn. "Q"
7	...	10/11th H.L.I.	17	...	Bde. Supply Officer.
8	...	14th H.L.I.	18	...	A.P.M.
9	...	120th T.M.Bty.	19	...	Area Comdt.BOISDINGHEM.
10	...	135th Fd.Ambce.	20	...	Bde. Signals.

****

Bar Diary

Secret

Appx XV

Copy No 4

120th (Highland) Infantry Bde. Order No 14

The Brigade Group consisting of 120th Bde. Headquarters, 10/11th H.L.I., [illegible] [illegible] [illegible], 120th T.M. Bty., 133rd Field Ambulance, No 3 Coy. Train, [illegible] M.V.S. [illegible] [illegible] [illegible] H.L.I. [illegible] will move to the LUMBRES area today.

Brigade H.Q. will move to LUMBRES and all units of Bde. Group to SENINGHEM.

Billeting parties will meet Staff Captain at 2 pm at SENINGHEM Church.

Units will march independently as soon after billeting parties as possible.

Bde. H.Q. Qrs will close at ACQUIN and re-open at LUMBRES CHATEAU on arrival.

Completion of move will be reported to Bde. H.Q. Qrs. 120th Bde.

30/[illegible]

Bde. [illegible]

(6339) Wt. W160/M3016 1,500,000 10/17 McA & W Ltd (E 1898) Forms W3091. Army Form W.3091.

WL 24

Cover for Documents.

Nature of Enclosures.

War Diary

May 1918

(VOLUME XXIV)

Headquarters, 120th Infantry Brigade

Notes, or Letters written.

Instructions regarding War Diaries and Intelligence Summaries are contained in F. S. Regs., Part II. and the Staff Manual respectively. Title pages will be prepared in manuscript.

1.

WAR DIARY
or
INTELLIGENCE SUMMARY.
(Erase heading not required.)

MAY 1918.

VOLUME XXIV.
Headquarters,
120th Infantry Brigade.

Army Form C. 2118.

Place	Date	Hour	Summary of Events and Information	Remarks and references to Appendices
LUMBRES	1918 May 1st		Disposition of Brigade Group :- Brigade Headquarters ... ... LUMBRES. 10/11th H. L. I.) 14th H. L. I.) 21st Midd'x. Regt.) ... ... SENINGHEM. 120th T. M. Bty.) 135th Field Ambulance)	
	2nd		40th Division (less Artillery) transferred from VIIIth to VIIth Corps (vide 40th Division Order No. 161 dated 5:5:18.)	
	3rd	3.30 p.m.	120th Bde. Order No. 195 issued, ordering move of 120th Brigade Group to WATTEN area on 4th instant.	App.I.
SERQUES.	4th	4 pm.	Move of 120th Bde. Group to WATTEN area completed, in accordance with 120th Brigade Order No. 195 of 3:5:18. Dispositions :- Brigade Headquarters ... ... SERQUES. H.Q. & Details 10/11th H.L.I ...) -Do- 14th H.L.I ...) WATTEN. 120th T. M. Battery ... ...) 21st Midd'x. Regt. ... ... NIEURLET. Brigadier-General C.J.HOBKIRK, D.S.O. resumed Command of 120th Inf. Bde.	
	5th	3 pm.	At a Ceremonial Parade held at WATTEN, Major-General J. PONSONBY, C.B., C.M.G., D.S.O., distributed to N.C.Os. and men of 120th Bde. Military Medal ribbands won during operations 21st - 26th March 1918.	
	6th		Personnel of 10/11th H.L.I., 14th H.L.I. and 120th T.M.Battery (less Training Staffs and Transport) proceeded to CALAIS, in accordance with 40th Division No. 818 (Q) dated 4:5:18.	

D. D. & L., London, E.C. (A8001) Wt. W1771/M2031 750,000 5/17 Sch. 52 Forms/C2118/14

Army Form C. 2118.

Instructions regarding War Diaries and Intelligence Summaries are contained in F. S. Regs., Part II. and the Staff Manual respectively. Title pages will be prepared in manuscript.

2.

WAR DIARY or INTELLIGENCE SUMMARY.

(Erase heading not required.)

MAY 1918.

VOLUME XXIV.

Headquarters, 120th Inf. Bde.

Place	Date 1918	Hour	Summary of Events and Information	Remarks and references to Appendices
SERQUES.	May. 7th		Nil.	
	8th		Battalion Training Staff and Transport of 12th Yorks Regt. (Pioneers) came under administration of H.Q. 120th Bde.	
			120th Bde. Order No. 196 issued. 120th Brigade, 12th Yorks Rgt. (P.) and No. 3 Coy. Div. Train will move to ESQUELBECQ area on 9th and 10th May.	App. II.
	9th		120th Bde. Headquarters closed at SERQUES and re-opened at ANNEUX FARM, ESQUELBECQ (C.2.b.2.7.) on arrival.	
ESQUELBECQ	10th	5 pm.	Move to ESQUELBECQ Area of 120th Bde. Group completed, in accordance with 120th Brigade Order No. 196 of 8:5:18.	
	11th		Nil.	
	12th	6 pm.	G.O.C. met Os.C. units and Adjutants in conference at Brigade Headquarters.	
	14th		Brigade 1st Line Transport proceeded to concentration camp at CUCQ COMMON (3 miles South of ETAPLES) in accordance with 40th Division No. 818/3 (Q) dated 9:5:18.	
	12th to 31st		Reconnaissances and organization of Northern Sector of WINNEZEELE Defence Line carried out.	
	31st		Brig.-General C.J.HOBKIRK, D.S.O. presented to N.C.Os. and men of 10/11th and 14th H.L.I., at the H.Q. of the former, Military Medal ribbands won during operations 9th to 12th April 1918.	

C.J. Hobkirk

Brig.-General,
Commanding 120th (Highland) Infantry Bde.

D. D. & L., London, E.C. (A8001) Wt. W1771/M2031 750,000 5/17 Sch. 52 Forms/C2118/14

APPX I

SECRET

Copy No 7

120th (Highland) Infantry Brigade Order 195

3-5-18

1. The 120th Brigade Group will move to the WATTEN Area to-morrow, 4th inst. in accordance with attached march table.

2. Billeting Officers from all Units, 120th Brigade will report to the Area Commandant, WATTEN at 10.30 AM.

3. The Composite Battn. H.L.I. will move to a tented Camp in the WATTEN area under orders being issued by the 119th Brigade.

4. Clock hour halts, and a midday halt of one hour in the TATINGHEM Area for dinners, will be observed. During the one hours halt, all troops and transport will be taken off the main road.

5. OC 10/11th High. L.I. will be in charge of the column.

6. Completion of moves will be notified to Brigade Headquarters.

[signature]

Captain
Brigade Major
120th (Hd) Inf. Bde.

3/5/18

Copy No

1. ... 10/11th High. L.I.
2. ... 120th T.M. Bty
3. ... No 3 Coy. Train
4. ... 21st Middx. Regt
5. ... 119th T.M. Bty
6. ... 40th Divn. "G"
7. ... [illegible]
8. ... File

March Table to accompany 120th (Hd) Inf. Bde. Order No 195

Serial No	Unit	From	To	Starting Point	Hour of Start	Route	Remarks
1	Bde. Hd. Qrs.	LUMBRES	ZUDROVE	Cross Rds. due E of E in LUMBRES	10.15 am	LUMBRES - SETQUES - TATINGHEM - ST MARTIN-AU-LAERT - TILQUES - SERQUES - WATTEN.	To await the rest of the Column.
2	Hd. Qrs. & Details 10/11th H.L.I.	SENINGHEM	WATTEN	SENINGHEM church. N. of M in SENINGHEM	9 a.m.	— Do —	
3.	120th T.M. Bty.	- Do -	- Do -	- Do -		— Do —	To follow 50 yds. behind Serial 2.
4.	No 3 Coy. Div. Train.	- Do -	BLEUE MAISON	- Do -		— Do -	To follow 50 yds behind Serial 3.
5.	21st Middx. & 119th T.M. Bty.	- Do -	NIEURLET (N.E. of ST OMER)	- Do -		LUMBRES - SETQUES - TATINGHEM - ST MARTIN-AU-LAERT - ST OMER - ST MOMELIN.	To follow 50 yds. behind Serial 4 as far as ST MARTIN-AU-LAERT, thence to move independently, reporting to 119 Bde. H.Qrs at NIEURLET on arrival.

SECRET [illegible]

APPX II

120th [illegible] Infantry Brigade [illegible]

[illegible] HAZEBROUCK 5 A

[illegible] 18

1. 120th Brigade [illegible] [illegible] [illegible] following [illegible]

9th [illegible] — [illegible] [illegible] [illegible]

10th [illegible] — [illegible] [illegible]

2. The [illegible] [illegible] by 3 pm at [illegible] Church

3. [illegible] [illegible] [illegible] [illegible] [illegible] Church

4. Bde [illegible] [illegible] North [illegible] [illegible] E [illegible]

5. [illegible] [illegible] probably [illegible] [illegible]

[illegible] at 8 pm

[illegible]
Brigade Major
120th Infantry Brigade

Distribution

Copy No 1 ... 10/11th H.L.I.

" " 2 ... 14th H.L.I.

" " 3 ... 12th Yorks Regt

" " 4 ... 1st Coy 40th Div Train

" " 5 ... 40th Divl Train

" " 6 ... 40th Division G

" " 7 ... 40th Division Q

" " 8 ... Area Commandant WATTEN

(6392) Wt. W6192/P875 1,500,000 4/18 McA & W Ltd (E 2815) Forms W3091/4.

Army Form W.3091.

WO 95/2605

Cover for Documents.

Nature of Enclosures.

– War Diary –

Headquarters 120th Infantry Bde.

June 1918

VOLUME XXV

Notes, or Letters written.

ORIGINAL

JUNE, 1918.
VOLUME XXV.

Army Form C. 2118.

Instructions regarding War Diaries and Intelligence Summaries are contained in F. S. Regs., Part II. and the Staff Manual respectively. Title pages will be prepared in manuscript.

1.

WAR DIARY
or
INTELLIGENCE SUMMARY.
(Erase heading not required.)

Headquarters,
120th Infantry Brigade.

Place	JUNE Date 1918.	Hour	Summary of Events and Information	Remarks and references to Appendices
ESQUELBECQ	1st		Reconnaissances and Organization of BALEMBERG LINE (NORTHERN SECTOR) carried out 1st to 20th June, 1918.	MBK.
	3rd		Training Cadres of 10/11th Highland Light Infantry and 14th Highland Light Infantry proceeded to RINXENT (near CALAIS) and transferred to 34th Division, in accordance with 40th Division No. 818/10/Q dated 2nd June.	MBK
RUBROUCK.	4th	10 am	120th Infantry Brigade Headquarters closed at AMMEUX FME. ESQUELBECQ (C.2.b.2.7.) and re-opened at Farm H.3.a.2.5. (Sheet 27) RUBROUCK, on arrival.	MBK
	5th) 6th) 7th)		Reconnaissances and Organization of BALEMBERG LINE (NORTHERN SECTOR) carried out.	MBK
	8th		Notification received from 40th Division (No. 75/G) of the raising of Infantry Garrison Guard Battalions composed of men of category lower than 'A'. These Units to be posted in first instance to the cadres of 40th and 59th Divisions as a temporary measure.	MBK
LEDERZEELE.	10th	10 am	120th Infantry Brigade Headquarters closed at RUBROUCK and re-opened at LEDERZEELE on arrival.	
			Headquarters of Garrison Guard Battalions Nos. 6 to 11 inclusive, joined 120th Infantry Brigade in accordance with 40th Division No. 835 "Q" dated 9-6-18.	MBK
	12th	9 am	Permanent designations allotted to Garrison Battalions, as under, came into force (vide 40th Division No. 835 (A) dated 11-6-18)	MBK

OLD DESIGNATION.		NEW DESIGNATION.
No. 6 Garrison Battalion	... ...	11th Garr. Bn. Cameron Highlanders.
7 " "	... ...	13th Garr. Bn. R. Innis. Fusrs.
8 " "	... ...	13th Garr. Bn. E. Lancs. Regt.
9 " "	... ...	10th Garr. Bn. K. O. S. B.
10 " "	... ...	15th Garr. Bn. K. O. Y. L. I.
11 " "	... ..	12th Garr. Bn. N. Staffs. Regt.

D. D. & L., London, E.C.
(A8001) Wt. W1771/M2031 750,000 5/17 Sch. 52 Forms/C2118/14

Army Form C. 2118.

Instructions regarding War Diaries and Intelligence Summaries are contained in F. S. Regs., Part II. and the Staff Manual respectively. Title pages will be prepared in manuscript.

WAR DIARY
or
INTELLIGENCE SUMMARY.
(Erase heading not required.)

JUNE, 1918.
VOLUME XXV.
Headquarters,
120th Infantry Brigade.

Place	Date JUNE 1918.	Hour	Summary of Events and Information	Remarks and references to Appendices
LEDERZEELE.	13th) 14th)		Reconnaissances and Organization of BALEMBERG LINE (NORTHERN SECTOR) carried out.	HBR
	15th		Formation of Garrison Battalions completed and three Battalions, as under, transferred to the 119th Infantry Brigade :- 13th Garr. Bn. R. Innis. Fusrs. 13th Garr. Bn. E. Lancs. Regt. 12th Garr. Bn. N. Staffs Regt. leaving in the 120th Infantry Brigade :- 10th Garr. Bn. K. O. S. B. 15th Garr. Bn. K.O.Y.L.I. 11th Garr. Bn. Cameron Highrs.	HBR
		9 am	G.O.C., 40th Division inspected Battalions of 120th Infantry Brigade.	
		8 pm	120th Infantry Brigade Order No. 197 issued. In the event of an enemy attack on the Second Army front, the 40th Division and attached troops, will man the WEST HAZEBROUCK LINE, the 120th Infantry Brigade, with attached troops, manning the Southern Section.	Appx I.
	16th		G.O.C., 120th Infantry Brigade reconnoitred that portion of the WEST HAZEBROUCK LINE assigned to 120th Infantry Brigade in the event of an attack on Second Army front.	HBR
	18th	2-35am	120th Infantry Brigade Order No. 198 issued, cancelling Order No. 197 and laying down alternative instructions in the event of an enemy attack on Second Army front (a) before 19th June and (b) on or after 19th June, with appendices showing location of attached troops in either eventuality.	Appx II HBR
		3 pm	Brigade Major (Captain H.G.EADY,M.C., R.E.) proceeded to England on one months leave.	
	19th	7 am	Amendments issued to 120th Infantry Brigade Order No. 198 dated 18-6-18. Alterations in composition of attached troops.	Appx III HBR
		3-15pm	D.A.G., G.H.Q. inspected Garrison Battalions of 120th Infantry Brigade.	

D. D. & L., London, E.C. (A8001) Wt. W1771/M2031 750,000 5/17 Sch. 52 Forms/C2118/14

Instructions regarding War Diaries and Intelligence Summaries are contained in F. S. Regs., Part II. and the Staff Manual respectively. Title pages will be prepared in manuscript.

3.

WAR DIARY
or
INTELLIGENCE SUMMARY.
(Erase heading not required.)

JUNE, 1918.
VOLUME XXV.

Army Form C. 2118.

Headquarters,
120th Infantry Brigade.

Place	JUNE. Date 1918.	Hour	Summary of Events and Information	Remarks and references to Appendices
LEDERZEELE	20th		Organization of BALEMBERG LINE (NORTHERN SECTION) completed and Report and Maps forwarded to 40th Divisional Headquarters in accordance with their No. 51/97/G dated 6-6-18.	HBR
	21st	11am	G.O.C., Brigade Major and Battalion Commanders attended Conference at 40th Divisional Headquarters.	HBR Appx IV
		10-30pm	40th Division Warning Order No. 173 received, re move of 40th Division (less Artillery) to RENESCURE Area on the 23rd instant.	
	22nd	10-30am	120th Infantry Brigade Warning Order No. 199 issued, notifying Units that the 120th Infantry Brigade, less transport, will move by busses or lorries to LA BELLE HOTESSE Area on 23rd instant. Transport to move by march route.	HBR
		5-30pm	40th Division Order No. 174 received, detailing move of 40th Division when transferred from V11 Corps to the XV Corps on the 23rd instant.	
		10pm	120th Infantry Brigade Order 200 issued. 120th Infantry Brigade Group will move by Bus from LEDERZEELE Area to Area West of LA BELLE HOTESSE on 23rd instant. 1st Line Transport to move by march route.	Appx V
LA BELLE HOTESSE. C.21.d.0.3.	23rd		Move carried out in accordance with 120th Infantry Brigade Order No. 200 dated 22-6-18. Dispositions :- 120th Infantry Brigade H.Q. ... 36A. C.21.d.0.3. 10th Garr. Bn. K.O.S.B. ... C.21.a.2.5. 15th Garr. Bn. K.O.Y.L.I. ... C.14.d.6.2. 11th Garr. Bn. Cam. Highrs ... C.14.c.7.7. 12th Yorks Rgt. (P) Training Staff C.14.c.7.2.	HBR
	24th		Field Marshal Commanding-in-Chief visited the Division and inspected one battalion from each Brigade at their work; 10th Garr. Bn. K.O.S.B. representing 120th Infantry Brigade carried out Squad Drill.	HBR

D. D. & L., London, E.C.
(A8001) Wt. W1771/M2031 750,000 5/17 Sch. 52 Forms/C2118/14

Instructions regarding War Diaries and Intelligence Summaries are contained in F. S. Regs., Part II. and the Staff Manual respectively. Title pages will be prepared in manuscript.

4.

WAR DIARY
or
INTELLIGENCE SUMMARY.
(Erase heading not required.)

JUNE, 1918.
VOLUME XXV

Headquarters,
120th Infantry Brigade.

Army Form C. 2118.

Place	JUNE Date 1918.	Hour	Summary of Events and Information	Remarks and references to Appendices
LA BELLE HOTESSE. C.21.d.0.3.	25th	7 am	40th Division Order No. 175 received, cancelling 40th Division Order Nos. 170, 171 and Appendix 'A'. In the event of an enemy attack on the Second Army front the 40th Division and attached troops will man the WEST HAZEBROUCK LINE from D.25.c. in the South to the road (inclusive) running through V.6.central, a distance of about 13,000 yds.	WHR
		9 am	Elementary Class at Brigade Signal School assembled - 8 men per battalion attending for instruction.	
		9-15 pm	120th Infantry Brigade Order No. 201 issued, cancelling 120th Infantry Brigade Order No. 198 and Appendices, and laying down instructions in the event of an enemy attack on the Second Army front with Appendix 'A' showing location of attached troops which would be at disposal of Brigade. 120th Infantry Brigade will man the Southern Section of Divisional Sector.	Appx VI.
		9-30 pm	40th Division Order No. 176 received, giving routes by which attached troops will move to the assembly positions.	
	26th	7-30 am	40th Division Order No. 177 received ordering a practice concentration of Labour and R.E. Units on 27th instant.	WHR.
		5-45 p.m.	120th Infantry Brigade Order No. 202 issued detailing routes to be taken by Battalions and attached troops when moving to their positions in the WEST HAZEBROUCK LINE.	Appx VII
		5-45 p.m.	120th Infantry Brigade Order No. 203 issued. With reference to 120th Infantry Brigade Orders No. 201 and 202, a practice concentration of Labour and R.E. Units will be carried out on 27th instant.	Appx VIII
	27th		Training carried out by battalions, special attention being given to rapid loading which has been greatly facilitated by the issue of dummy cartridges. Rifle range practice has also been carried out daily. Concentration of Labour and R.E. Units ordered in 120th Infantry Brigade Order No. 203 carried out successfully.	WHR.

D. D. & L., London, E.C. (A8001) Wt. W1771/M2031 750,000 5/17 Sch. 52 Forms/C2118/14

Instructions regarding War Diaries and Intelligence Summaries are contained in F. S. Regs., Part II. and the Staff Manual respectively. Title pages will be prepared in manuscript.

5.

WAR DIARY
or
INTELLIGENCE SUMMARY.
(*Erase heading not required.*)

JUNE, 1918.
VOLUME, XXV.

Army Form C. 2118.

Headquarters,
120th Infantry Brigade.

Place	Date JUNE 1918.	Hour	Summary of Events and Information	Remarks and references to Appendices
LA BELLE HOTESSE. C.21.d.0.3.	28th		Training generally carried out by Battalions of Brigade.	HBK.
		6 pm	G.O.C. and Brigade Major attended a Conference at Divisional Headquarters.	HBK
	29th) 30th)		Training generally carried out by Battalions of Brigade.	HBK.

G. Hobbs [signature]

Brigadier General,
Commanding, 120th Infantry Brigade.

D. D. & L., London, E.C.
(A8001) Wt. W1771/M2031 750,000 5/17 Sch. 52 Forms/C2118/14

appx I

S E C R E T   COPY NO...4..

120TH INFANTRY BRIGADE ORDER NO. 197.

15.6.18.

Ref.
Map Attached.

36A. N.W.
36A. N.E.
1/20,000.

---

1. In the event of an enemy attack on the Second Army front, the 40th Division and attached troops will man the WEST HAZEBROUCK Line from D.25.c. in the South to V.6.d. in the North.

2. The 120th Brigade and attached troops, shown in para. 3, will man the Southern Section of this line, as shown on attached map.

3. The following troops will be attached to 120th Brigade in the event of this line being manned, and will be placed at the disposal of battalions as shown :-

   236 A.T.Coy.R.E. attached 10th K.O.S.B.
   94 Labour Coy. attached 15th K.O.Y.L.I.
   12 Labour Coy. attached 11th Camerons.

   Each of these Labour Coys. has one officer per 100 men, and the men are at present untrained. Approx.strength of each Coy. is 350 men. Their present locations are :-

   236 A.T.Coy. ... C.9. SERCUS.
   94 Labour Coy... C.22.d.6.5.
   12 -Do- ... C.5.d.9.5.

4. The 120th Brigade Sector will be divided up into 3 sections, as shown on attached map, of which the Southern one will be held by the 10th K.O.S.B., the centre by 15th K.O.Y.L.I., and the Northern by the 11th Cameron Highlanders, each with the attached troops shown in para. 3.

5. The Battalions of 120th Brigade will proceed from billets to the vicinity of the trench system by busses, details of which will be issued later.

6. Brigade Headquarters will be established at C.9.d.90.35. Sites for Battalion H. Qrs. will be decided upon by respective battalions, and their location reported to Bde. Hd. Qrs.

7. The defence of the line will be organised in depth, and troops disposed so as to hold both the Outpost Line &the Main Line of Resistance. In making their dispositions, C.Os. must realise the comparative lack of mobility of the troops at their disposal.

It/

It must be impressed upon all ranks that they are to hold the line in which they are posted, whether it be the Outpost Line or the Main Line of Resistance, to the last man and the last round of ammunition. No withdrawal of troops will take place even from the Line of Observation, unless orders are received from Brigade Headquarters.

8. 120 rounds of S.A.A. will be carried by each man to the trenches, and 2000 rounds per Lewis Gun.

9. Rations for the day and one iron ration per man will be carried.

10. Battalions will prepare a scheme for the occupation of their section with the troops attached to them. This will be forwarded to these Headquarters as early as possible.

11. ACKNOWLEDGE.

Issued through Signals at 8 p.m.

Captain,
Brigade Major,
120th Infantry Brigade.

Distribution :-

Copy No.		
1	...	G.O.C.
2	...	Brigade Major.
3	...	Staff Captain.
4	...	War Diary.
5	...	File.
6	...	10th K.O.S.B.
7	...	15th K.O.Y.L.I.
8	...	11th Cameron Hdrs.
9	...	119th Inf. Bde.
10	...	121st Inf. Bde.
11	...	40th Division "G".
12	...	40th Division "Q".
13	...	40th Div. Train.
14	...	236 A.T.Coy.R.E.
15	...	No. 3 Labour Group.
16	...	No. 3 Labour Group.
17	...	No. 3 Labour Group.
18	...	Labour Comdt.VIIth Corps.
19	...	Bde. Supply Officer.
20	...	Bde. Signals.

****

appx II
4

S E C R E T   COPY NO......

120TH INFANTRY BRIGADE ORDER NO. 19[illegible].

Ref. maps

36 A N.W.
36 A N.E.
1/20,000

18:6:1[illegible].

1. 120th Infantry Brigade Order No. 197 is cancelled and the following substituted.

2. In the event of an enemy attack on the Second Army front, the 40th Division and attached troops, will man the WEST HAZEBROUCK line from D.25.c. in the South to V.6.d. in the North

3. The 120th Brigade, and attached troops, shown in Appendix "A", will man the Southern section of this line, i.e.- from D.25.c. in the South to C.6.d.5.2.

4. (a) In the event of an attack taking place before the 19th instant, the 15th K.O.Y.L.I. will be attached to the 121st Infantry Brigade, and will not be available for manning the Southern section.

(b) In the event of an attack taking place on or after the 19th instant, the whole of the 120th Infantry Brigade and attached troops will be available.

The methods of holding the line in each of the above eventualities are shown in attached Appendices "B" and "C".

5. The following troops will be conveyed by bus from billets to their assembly positions, under arrangements which have already been issued :-

120th Infantry Brigade.
229th Coy. R.E. (in lorries under arrangements made by Major-General Kenyon).
25[illegible]th Tunnelling Coy.
26th Labour Group

6. In the event of lorries not being available, units must be prepared to move by march route.
C.R.Es. and Labour Group Commanders will be responsible for the embussing and debussing of troops under their command.

7. The assembly position for the Southern section will be at C.17.c. & 23.a.
On the alarm being given, all Field Coys., Tunnelling, Army Troops and Labour Companies will be concentrated by their C.R.Es. and Labour Group Commanders at the assembly positions, and will then be taken over by the infantry battalions to which they are allotted. Each battalion will send an officer to the assembly position to take over its attached troops and to give them the necessary orders.

8/

8. Brigade Headquarters will be established at O.9.d.90.35.

Sites for Battalion Headquarters for both eventualities mentioned in para. 4 will be chosen by Battalions, and their locations reported to these Headquarters.

Labour Group Commanders will establish a Head-:quarters in the vicinity of Brigade Headquarters.

9. The defence of the line will be organised in depth, and in accordance with S.S.210 - "The Division in Defence", as far as troops are available, but in any case troops will be disposed so as to hold both the Observation and the Main Line of Resistance. Where no Observation Line exists already dug, Battalions will push out advanced posts in front of the existing line of resistance.

In making their dispositions, C.Os. must realise the comparative lack of mobility of the troops at their disposal, and the small number of Lewis guns which can be manned. It must be impressed upon all ranks that they are to hold the line in which they are posted, whether it be the Observation or Main Line, to the last man. No withdrawal of troops will take place, even from the Line of Observation, unless orders to that effect are received from Brigade Headquarters.

10. 120 rounds S.A.A. will be carried by each man to the trenches, and 2000 rounds per Lewis gun.

11. Rations for the day and 1 iron ration per man will be carried on the man.

12. All administrative details have been dealt with in "Administrative Instructions for occupation of WEST HAZEBROUCK Line".

13. Battalions will draw up schemes for the occupation of the line in either of the eventualities mentioned in para. 4. Copies of these schemes will be forwarded to these Headquarters.

14. ACKNOWLEDGE.

Captain,
Brigade Major,
120th Infantry Brigade.

Issued through
Signals
at 2.35 a.m.

Distribution :-

Copy No. 1 ... G.O.C.
2 ... Bde.Major.
3 ... Staff Capt.
4 ... War Diary.
5 ... File.
6 ... 10th K.O.S.B.
7 ... 15th K.O.Y.L.I.
8 ... 11th Cameron Hrs.
9 ... 119th Inf. Bde.
10 ... 121st Inf. Bde.
11 ... 40th Div. "G".
12 ... 40th Div. "Q".
13 ... 40th Div.Train.
14 ... 236 A.T.Coy.R.E.
15 to.18 No.5 Labour Gp.
19 .. Labour Comdt.VIIth Corps
20 .. 236th Coy. R.E.
21 .. 229th Field Coy.R.E.
22 .. 258th Tunnelling Coy.
23 .. 64th Labour Group.
24 .. 26th Labour Group.
25 .. C.R.E. 40th Divn.
26 .. Lt.-Col. Hoysted,R.E.
27 .. Lt.-Col.White, R.E.
28 .. Lab.Comdt.ST OMER Defences.
29 .. Bde. Supply Off.
30 .. Bde. Signals.

<u>APPENDIX "A"</u>

<u>TO 120TH INFANTRY BRIGADE ORDER NO. 198.</u>

Troops attached to 120th Brigade

Unit	Location		Approximate rifle strength
<u>R.E.</u>			
236 Army Troops Coy.	C.9. SERCUS.	...	130
229 Field Company.	B.28.b.5.2.	...	100
258 Tunnelling Coy. (less 1 Section)	M.39.a.0.0.	...	170
<u>Labour Coys.</u>			
64th Labour Group consisting of :-	BLARINGHEM.		
No. 3 Labour Coy.	C.23.b.	...	140
No. 4 Labour Coy.	C.4.c.7.8.	...	210
No.35 Labour Coy.	C.3.central	...	380
No.48 Labour Coy.	C.8.d.5.3.	...	280
No.136 Labour Coy.	U.28.b.5.2.	...	200
No.174 Labour Coy.	36A/I.3.a.8.5.	...	1[illegible]
26th Labour Group consisting of :-	EBLINGHEM		
No. 6 Labour Coy.	N.35.b.2.6.)		
No. 84 Labour Coy.	S.6.a.5.5.)		
No. 92 Labour Coy.	T.11.d.6.7.)	...	3[illegible]
No.110 Labour Coy.	N.27.c.6.6.)		
No.138 Labour Coy.	N.35.b.6.3.)		
	<u>Total No. of Rifles</u>	...	1610

APPENDIX "B"

TO 120TH INFANTRY BRIGADE ORDER NO. 198.

Method of holding the line in the event of the 15th

K.O.Y.L.I. being attached to the 121st Infantry Bde.

---

1. The 120th Brigade Sector will be divided into two sections, of which the Southern will be held by the K.O.S.Bs., and the Northern by the Cameron Highlanders, each with the attached troops as shown in para. 3.

2. The inter-battalion boundary will be :-

D.13.d.4.6 (road inclusive to Southern Battalion) - D.13.c.5.5. - cross roads C.17.d.8.1. - thence along road to C.16.d.3.7.

3. The Battalions will have the following troops attached to them :-

K.O.S.B.
258 Tunnelling Coy. R.E.
No. 4 Labour Coy.) of 64th
No.136 -Do-) Labour Group.
No. 49 Labour Coy.

Cameron H'rs.
236 A.T. Coy. R.E.
229 Field Coy. R.E.
No. 30 Labour Coy. R.E.
No. 3 -Do-
No.174 -Do-

4. The 26th Labour Group will remain in reserve in the vicinity of Brigade Headquarters.

****

APPENDIX "C"

TO 120TH INFANTRY BRIGADE ORDER NO. 198.

Method of holding the line in the event of the whole of the 120th Inf.Bde. being available.

---

1. The 120th Brigade Sector will be divided into 3 sections of which the Southern will be held by the K.O.S.B., the centre by the K.O.Y.L.I., and the left by the Cameron Highlanders, each with the attached troops shown in para. 3.

2. The boundaries of sections are as follow :-

   <u>Between K.O.S.B. and K.O.Y.L.I.</u>

   D.19.a.3.2 (road inclusive to K.O.S.B.) - along road to C.24.a.9.4. - cross roads C.23.b.2.3.

   <u>Between K.O.Y.L.I. and Cameron H'rs.</u>

   C.18.b.8.8. - C.11.c.9.1.

3. Battalions will have the following troops attached to them :-

   <u>K.O.S.B.</u> 258 Tunnelling Coy. R.E.
   No. 4 Labour Coy. R.E.
   No. 136 Labour Coy.R.E.

   <u>K.O.Y.L.I.</u> No. 3 Labour Coy.
   No.48 Labour Coy.
   No.174 LabourCoy.

   <u>Cameron Hrs.</u>
   No. 236 A.T.Coy. R.E.
   No. 229 Field Coy. R.E.
   No. 35 Labour Coy.

4. The 26th Labour Group will remain in Reserve in the vicinity of Brigade Headquarters.

****

Appx III

APPENDIX "A"
to
120TH INFANTRY BRIGADE ORDER NO. 193.

Appendix "A" issued 19-8-18 is cancelled and the following substituted :-

1. The 120th Brigade Sector will be divided into 3 sections of which the Southern will be held by the K.O.S.Bs., the centre by the K.O.Y.L.I., and the left by the Cameron Highrs., each with the attached troops shown in para 3.

2. The boundaries of sections are as follows :-

Between K.O.S.B. and K.O.Y.L.I.

D.19.a.2.2. (road inclusive to K.O.S.B.) - along road to C.24.a.9.4.- Cross Roads C.23.b.3.3.

Between K.O.Y.L.I. and Cameron Highlanders.

D.7.c.5.2 .- C.18.b.3.8. - C.11.c.9.1.

3. Battalions will have the following troops attached to them :-

K.O.S.B.	Approximate strength. Rifle	L.G.
258th Tunnelling Coy. (less 1 section)	169	1.
No. 3 Labour Coy.	250	1.
No. 4 - do -	232	-
No. 6 - do -	336	-
No.21 - do -	235	1.
K.O.Y.L.I.		
229th Field Coy.	98	1.
No.25 Labour Coy.	330	-
No.63 - do -	307	1.
No.156 - do -	331	1.
Cameron Highlanders.		
238 Army Troops Coy.	127	1.
No.174Labour Coy.	292	1.
No.84 - do -	334	-
No.92 - do -	372	-

4. Nos. 110, 121, 128 and 131 Labour Coys. will remain in Reserve in the vicinity of Brigade Headquarters.

Captain,
A/Brigade Major,
120th Infantry Brigade.

21-8-18.

Issued to :-
40th Divn. "G". 13th E.Bn. K.O.S.Bs. 13th G.Bn. K.O.Y.L.I.
11th G.Bn.Cam.Hrs. 28th Labour Group. 64th Labour Group.
Bde. Supply Officer.

Appx IV

NOTES FOR CONFERENCE TO BE HELD AT 11.a.m. TOMORROW 21/6/18.

1. Redistribution of men either in accordance with the regiment to which they formerly belonged and according to nationality or ?

2. Nomenclature of Battalions. Should the word "Garrison" be omitted, etc.

3. Is it advisable for Commanding Officers to explain to the men the probable role of the Division in future as regards their duty in active operations.

4. Lectures on Military Subjects to be arranged for. Ask for names of officers able to lecture and the subjects.

5. Route Marching by progressive stages.

6. Musketry. Competitions and Prizes.

7. Recreational Training.

8. Attention to personal cleanliness, and cleanliness in camps, bivouacs, and billets.

9. Any other training subjects which anyone desires to bring forward.

10. Provision of Officers and N. C. O's.

Suggested names of Battalions :-

Scotch:-

"Duke of Buccleuch's Regiment of Highlanders". Known as "The Buccleuch Highlanders".

"Duke of Montrose's Regiment of Highlanders". Known as "The Montrose Highlanders".

"General Campbell's Regiment of Scottish Foot."

Irish:-

"The Earl of Athlone's Regiment of Irish Foot".

English:-

"General Ruggles-Brise's Regiment of Foot."

"General Willoughby's Regiment of Foot."

"General Byng's Regiment of Foot".

"General Pulteney's Regiment of Foot".

"General Haldane's Regiment of Foot.

Appx V

SECRET.

COPY NO. 4.

120TH INFANTRY BRIGADE ORDER NO. 200.
**************** ***********************

Maps. HAZEBROUCK.

22-6-18.

Sheet 27 1/40,000
" 36A 1/40,000

1. 120th Infantry Brigade Group will move by Bus in accordance with attached table from LEDERZEELE AREA to Area WEST of LA BELLE HOTESSE to-morrow, 23rd inst.

2. 1st Line Transport will be Brigaded under Captain TRITTON, Transport Officer, 10th Garr. Bn. K.O.S.Bs., and will move to new area in following order :-

120th Brigade Headquarters (including Signal Section)
10th Garr. Bn. K.O.S.Bs.
15th Garr. Bn. K.O.Y.L.I.
11th Garr. Bn. Cameron Highlanders.
12th Yorks Regt. (Pnrs).

ROUTE. OOST HOUCK - M.12. -CRIN BERGU - Cross Roads N.33.b. - T.11.a. - EBBLINGHAM - LYNDE.
Roads to be reconnoitred by Brigade Transport Officer Head of column to pass starting point (OOST HOUCK CHURCH) at 9-30 a.m. Battalions will arrange to have guides for transport at LYNDE CHURCH.

3. No. 3 Coy. 40th Divnl. Train will move by march route to new Area under their own arrangements.

4. Brigade Headquarters will close at LEDERZEELE at 9-30 a.m. and will re-open at LA BELLE HOTESSE, C.22.c.5.4. on arrival.

5. ACKNOWLEDGE.

H B Kerr
Captain,
A/Brigade Major,
120th Infantry Brigade.

Issued through Signals
at 10 p.m.

Copy No. 1. ... G.O.C.
2 ... Brigade Major,
3 ... Staff Captain,
4 ... War Diary.
5 ... File.
6 ... 10th Garr. Bn. K.O.S.Bs.
7. ... 15th Garr. Bn. K.O.Y.L.I.
8. ... 11th Garr. Bn. Cam. Highrs.
9. ... 12th Yorks Rgt. (Pnrs)
10 ... 120th T. M. Bty.
11 ... No. 3 Coy. Div. Train.
12 ... Bde. Supply Officer
13 ... 40th Divn. "G"
14 ... 40th Divn. "Q"
15 ... 119th Inf.Bde.
16 ... 121st Inf. Bde.
17 ... A.P.M., 40th Divn.
18 ... Bde. Signals.
19 ... Captn. TRITTON, K.O.S.Bs.

TABLE TO ACCOMPANY 120TH INFANTRY BRIGADE ORDER No.200.

Serial No.	UNIT.	LOCATION.	ROUTE TO EMBUSSING POINT.	BUSSES ALLOTTED	REMARKS.
1.	120th Bde. Hd.Qrs.	LEDERZEELE.	LEDERZEELE - ST MOMELIN ROAD.	Two Busses of First Group.	
2.	10th G.Bn. K.O.S.Bs.	BUSSYCHEURE.	G.35. G.34. G.33.	CENTRAL Group.	
3.	15th G.Bn. K.O.Y.L.I.	- do -	- - do - -	FIRST Group less 4 Busses.	To follow Serial No. 2 from BUSSYCHEURE.
4.	120th T. M. Battery.	- do -	- - do - -	Two Busses of FIRST Group.	To follow serial No. 3 from BUSSYCHEURE.
5.	11th G.Bn. Cam. Highrs.	CROME STRAETE - LERERZEELE ROAD.	CROME STRAETE - LERERZEELE CROSS ROADS.	LAST Group less two Busses.	
6.	12th Yorks Rgt. (Pnrs)	LES CINQ RUES (B.25.c.)	LEDERZEELE - ERKELSBRUGGE ROAD.	Two Busses of LAST Group.	

A. EMBUSSING POINT. ... ST MOMELIN - LEDERZEELE ROAD, head of Column facing S.W. at G.33.c.

B. TIME OF EMBUSSING. ... 8 a.m.

C. ROUTE FOR LORRIES. ... ST MOMELIN - OWERSTEL - SERQUES - TILQUES - X.4. - X.10. - ARQUES - CAMPAGNE - B.28.d. - BLARINGHEM.

D. DEBUSSING POINT. ... EAST of BLARINGHEM from B.23.b. to C.13.d.

E. One Officer per Unit will report to Brigade Headquarters at 7-30 a.m. to-morrow for instructions regarding the embussing of his Unit. Units will not enter main LEDERZEELE - ST MOMELIN ROAD until Embussing Officer has reported to Commanding Officers concerned.

<u>Administrative Instructions - Move 23rd June 1918.</u>

To accompany 120th Brigade Order No. ~~129~~ 200.

1. <u>Accommodation.</u> Units of the Brigade will be accommodated in tented camps and available billets as follows :-

Brigade Headquarters	.....	Billet No.5. C.22.c.4.4.
10th K.O. Sco. Bordrs.	.....	C.21.a.2.6.
15th K.O.Y.L.I.	.....	C.14.d.5.0.
11th Cam. Highrs.	.....	C.14.d.0.8.
12th Yorks (P) Regt.	.....	(With Cam. Highrs) C.14.d.0.8.
120th T.M.Batty. (With 15th K.O.Y.L.I).	..	C.14.d.5.0.
No.5 Coy., A.S.C. Train.	.....	C.14.c.4.7.

A number of tents and shelters will be dumped at C.13.b.6.2 at 11 am. on 23rd June 1918.

Units will arrange to have a representative at the dump at 11 am. to meet the Staff Captain and take over the canvas which will be pitched under unit arrangements. Lorries conveying baggage will be used to take canvas from dumps to camp sites.

The exact map reference of all fields in which camps are pitched will be forwarded to Brigade Headquarters as early as possible so that notification may be sent to the Rents Officer concerned. Claims for damages will thus be diminished.

2. Lorries are reporting to Brigade Headquarters at 7 am. on 23rd June and will be allotted to units as under. A guide from each unit will report to Staff Captain by 7 am.

<u>Unit.</u>	<u>No. of lorries.</u>	<u>To be used for</u>
10th K.O.Sco. Bordrs.	3.	To carry stores, blankets, packs and S.A.A.
15th K.O.Y.L.I.	3.	
11th Cam. Highrs.	3.	
12th Yorks (P) Regt.	1.	
Bde. Hd. Quarters.	2.	

120th T.M.Batty. half lorry from Brigade Headquarters will be detailed to carry stores, baggage, etc. of Battery.

<u>N O T E</u> :- Packs to be carried on the man in motor omnibus.

3. All tents now in possession will be handed in to Area Commandant and receipts obtained. Receipts to be forwarded to Brigade Headquarters by 24th instant.

4. Advance parties will proceed on the lorries allowed for stores etc. Such parties to be cut down to a minimum.

5. Baggage wagons should be used for Officers kits, etc. L.G.S. Wagons for Lewis Guns and ammunition. Remainder of ammunition on lorries.

6. <u>Surplus Kit.</u> Any surplus kit which is not likely to be required in the HAZEBROUCK Area will be dumped by Battalions in Battalion Stores and a guard of 1 N.C.O. and 3 o.rs. left in charge. The guard to have two days rations and instructions to report at once to Area Commandant so that he may arrange for their rations in the future. Site of any dumps so formed to be reported to Area Commandant and these Headquarters as early as possible.

7. D.A.D.O.S., 40th Division will remain at EBBLINGHEM.

8/-

8. Supply Railhead will be EBBLINGHEM from and including 23rd June, 1918.

9. Personnel Railhead remains at WATTEN for the present.

10. 51st Mobile Veterinary Section will be located near LYNDE.

11. Medical. 137th Field Ambulance will be located at SERCUS.

12. Water Supply. The BORRE BECQUE from U.21.d. to the HAZEBROUCK - ST.SYLVESTRE CAPPEL Road is an important source of water supply and must be protected from pollution. The following precautions will be taken:-

(a) No washing or bathing will be allowed in the stream.
(b) No camp or horse lines will be permitted within 200 yards of the stream.
(c) No baths or ablution places are to be allowed to drain into the stream.

A.P.M., 40th Division, will arrange for Military Police to assist Regimental Police in enforcing this order.

13. Full advantage will be taken of the cover from view afforded by hedges and trees when pitching camps.

Tents and shelters must be coloured. If kutch is not obtainable mud is to be used.

Lieut.,
A/Staff Captain,
120th Infantry Brigade.

22nd June 1918.

appx VI

S E C R E T. COPY NO...4..

120th INFANTRY BRIGADE ORDER NO. 201.

Ref. Maps: 36.a. N.W. 36.a. N.E. 1/20,000.

1.

1. 120th Infantry Brigade Order No. 198 and appendices are cancelled and the following substituted.

2. In the event of an enemy attack on the Second Army Front the 40th Division and attached troops will man the W.HAZEBROUCK Line from D.25.c. in the South to V.6 central in the North.

3. The 120th Infantry Brigade with attached troops shown in Appendix 'A' will man the Southern Section of this line.
Boundaries of Brigade Section are as follows :-
Southern Boundary - a line drawn from D.26.c.4.3 - D.25.d.3.5 - C.29.d.5.8 to C.26.a.5.7.
Northern Boundary - C.6.d.0.2 - C.6.c.0.6 - C.5.d. 0.3 - C.4.d.5.2. - C.3.d.2.0 - C.2.d.0.7.

4. For the purpose of defence the Brigade Section will be divided into 3 Battalion Sub-sections, and will be held by units as follows :-
Southern Sub-section.
10th K.O. Sco. Bordrs and attached troops with Headquarters at C.23.a.
Centre Sub-section.
15th K.O.Y.L.I. and attached troops with Headquarters at C.18.c.3.9.
Northern Sub-section.
11th Cam. Highrs. and attached troops with Headquarters at C.11.d.4.8.

5. Boundaries of Sub-sections will be as follows :-
Between 10th K.O. Sco. Bordrs. & 15th K.O.Y.L.I.
D.19.a.3.2 (road inclusive to K.O.S.Bs.) - along road to C.24.a.9.4 - Cross Roads C.23.b.2.3.
Between 15th K.O.Y.L.I. & 11th Cam. Highrs.
D.7.c.5.2 - C.18.b.8.8 - C.11.c.9.1.

6. The following troops will be conveyed by Bus from their billets to the Assembly position under arrangements which have been made by "Q", 40th Division :-
26th Labour Group.
258th Tunnelling Coy., R.E.
These units will enbus at LE NIEPPE: head of Column facing South at T.11.a.5.7 and will proceed via RENESCURE - WARDRECQUES and BLARINGHEM, debussing at LE CROQUET.
In the event of busses or lorries not being available units will be prepared to move by march route.
C.R.Es. and Labour Group Commanders will be responsible for the embus ing and debussing of troops under their command.

7. On the alarm being given Tunnelling and Labour Companies whether proceeding by bus or by march route will report as stated on Appendix "A".

8/ The

8. The defence of the line will be organised in depth, and in accordance with S.S.210 - "The Division in Defence" - as far as troops are available but in any case troops will be disposed so as to hold both the Observation and the Main Line of Resistance. Where no Observation Line exists, already dug, battalions will push out Advance Posts in front of the existing Line of Resistance.

In making their dispositions, Commanding Officers must realize the comparative lack of mobility of the troops at their disposal, and the small number of Lewis Guns which can be manned. It must be impressed upon all ranks that they are to hold the line in which they are posted, whether it be the Observation or Main Line, to the last man. No withdrawal of troops will take place, even from the lin. of observation, unless orders to that effect are received from Brigade Headquarters.

9. Brigade Headquarters will be established at C.21.d.0.3.

10. 120 Rounds S.A.A. will be carried by each man to the trenches and 2,000 rounds per Lewis Gun.

Three Reserve Ammunition Dumps are being established at:-

Sheet 36.a. C.10.a.3.7.
C.17.c.5.4.
C.22.d.7.7.

11. Rations for the day and one Iron Ration per man will be carried on the man.

12. Battalions will draw up schemes of the Occupation of the Line with the troops allotted in Appendix "A". Copy of this Scheme will be forwarded to these Headquarters as soon as possible.

13. A C K N O W L E D G E.

H.B. Kerr
Captain,
A/Brigade Major,
120th Infantry Brigade.

Issued through Signals at 9.15 pm.

Distribution :-

Copy No.					
1.	...	G.O.C.	12.	...	40th Divn "G".
2.	...	Bde.Major.	13.	...	40th Divn "Q".
3.	...	Staff Capt.	14.	...	40th Div.Train.
4.	...	War Dairy.	15 to 23.		64th Labour Group.
5.	...	File.	24 to 27.		26th Labour Group.
6.	...	10th R.O.S.B.	28.	...	Lab.Comdt., ST.OMER.
7.	....	15th K.O.Y.L.I.	29.	...	258th Tun.Coy.R.E.
8.	...	11th Cam. Hrs.	30.	...	C.R.E., 40th Divn.
9.	...	120th T.M.Bty.	31.	...	Lt.Col.WHITE, R.E.
10.	...	119th Inf. Bde.	32.	...	Bde. Supply Officer.
11.	...	121st Inf. Bde.	33.	...	Bde. Signals.

APPENDIX "A"

to

120TH INFANTRY BRIGADE ORDER NO. 201.

Unit.	Location.	Approx. Strength.		On Alarm. To report	
		Rifles.	L.Guns.	To.	At.
Southern Sub-section.					
10th K.O.S.Bdrs.		655	16	O.C., 10th K.O.S.Bdrs.	Batn.H&Qrs. C.23.a.
258 ~~178~~th Tunn. Coy., R.E.	M.29.a.0.0.	171	1		
No.3 Labour Coy.	C.23.b.	230	1		
6 Labour Coy.	C.22.d.2.0.	386	-		
174 Labour Coy.	C.22.d.2.0.	292	1		
Centre Sub-section.					
15th K.O.Y.L.I.		750	16	Officer & Guides detailed by 15 KOYLI.	X Roads. C.14.d.5.2.
84th Labour Coy.	S.6.a.5.5.	364	-		
92nd Labour Coy.	T.11.d.6.7.	372	-		
110th Labour Coy. (All from 26th Labour Group).	N.27.c.6.6.	332	-		
Northern Sub-section.					
11th Cam. Highrs.		638	16	Officer & Guides detailed by 11 Cam.Hrs.	X Roads. C.10.a.8.8.
4th Labour Coy.	C.4.c.7.6.	230	1		
48th Labour Coy.	C.5.d.5.8.	307	1		
136th Labour Coy.	U.22.b.5.2.	331	1		
31st Labour Coy.	T.18.c.2.7.	285	-		
Brigade Reserve.					
35th Labour Coy. and will report to Bde.Hd.Qrs at C.21.d.0.3.	n0.8 central	380	-		

ADMINISTRATIVE INSTRUCTIONS - OCCUPATION OF W. HAZEBROUCK LINE.

Ref. Map:
1/40,000.
Sheets 27.
36a.

28th June 1918.

Reference 120th Infantry Brigade Order No. 201 dated 25.6.1918.

The Administrative Instructions issued with 120th Brigade Order No. 197 - dated 15.6.1918 - are cancelled.

1. Surplus Kit.

(a) Units will arrange to form a dump in present quarters of all kit, blankets, stores, etc. not absolutely essential for fighting.

(b) Guard of one N.C.O., 3 O.Rs. will be left with each Battalion Dump and will be provided with two days rations. Units will arrange for these men to be rationed.

(c) Dress will be fighting order with greatcoats.

2. Transport.

(a) Battalion transport lines and Quartermasters' Stores will be situated at approximately B.10.d. and B.11.a. (Sheet 36.a.) to which place transport will move under orders to be issued from these Headquarters.

(b) Captain L.J.TRITTON, 10th Battn. K.O. Sco. Bordrs. will be in charge of all transport on arrival at assembly position named.

(c) On the Alarm being given all available transport of attached Royal Engineer and Labour Companies will proceed to approximately B.10.d. and report to Officer i/c Brigade Transport.

3. Water tins.

100 water tins which have been issued to battalions and any others which may be available will be filled and carried forward to the line by the battalion.

4. Rations.

(a) Rations for the day and one iron ration per man will be carried forward on the men.

(b) A supply of sandbags has already been issued to battalions. These are for carrying rations to the line after it has ~~xxxx~~ been manned. They should be used very sparingly as it may be impossible to get a further supply.

(c) The attention of Quartermasters is to be drawn to the comparative uselessness of sending forward fresh meat. The Brigade Supply Officer will arrange for preserved meat to be issued as far as possible but for the first two days a large percentage of fresh meat must be expected. Quartermasters will therefore cook as much of this meat as possible at the stores.

5. Ammunition.

(a) 120 rounds S.A.A. per man and 2,000 rounds per

Lewis/

Lewis gun will be taken forward byall units.

(b) Three Reserve Small Arm Ammunition Dumps of 50 Boxes S.A.A. are being established as follows :-

Sheet 36.a. ... C.11.b.2.1.
C.18.b.8.2.
C.30.b.4.0.

The map references given in 120th Infantry Brigade Order No. 201 para. 10 are cancelled.

(c) Officers Commanding Battalions will arrange for personnel to take charge of the dumps situate in their sectors. When it is necessary to draw on these dumps units will notify Brigade Headquarters.

(d) Brigade Reserve Ammunition Dump will be established at C.21.a.6.5. 10th K.O. Sco. Bordrs. will detail one N.C.O. and one O.R. to take charge of this dump. They will report to Brigade Headquarters as soon as possible after the alarm has been given.

6. Medical Arrangements.

(a) An Advanced Dressing Station for the Southern Sector will be established by Captain W.L.JOHNSON, R.A.M.C. at B.18.c.5.6.

(b) O.C., 64th Labour Group will detail 100 men from unarmed personnel for duty as stretcher bearers. They will report to the Advanced Dressing Station as soon as possible. Care is to be taken that the men selected are of good physique and able to perform the duties which will be required of them.

[signature]

Lieut.,
A/Staff Captain,
120th Infantry Brigade.

Amendment No. 1 to

ADMINISTRATIVE INSTRUCTIONS - OCCUPATION OF W. HAZEBROUCK LINE.

Para. 6 of Administrative Instruction dated 26th June is cancelled.

Medical Arrangements.

1. The 135th Field Ambulance will be responsible for the evacuation of all casualties from this Brigade Sector.

2. The Advanced Dressing Station will be established at C.14.a.1.0 (Sheet 36a).

3. The Main dressing Station will be established at B.18.c.0.0. (Sheet 36.a.).

4. O.C., 64th Labour Group will detail 100 men from unarmed personnel for duty as stretcher bearers and they will report as early as possible to 135th Field Ambulance B.18.c.0.0. (Sheet 36.a). Care is to be taken that the men selected are of good physique and able to perform the duties which will be required of them.

Lieut.,
A/Staff Captain,
120th Infantry Brigade.

28th June 1918.

SECRET. COPY NO. 4

App VII

120TH INFANTRY BRIGADE ORDER NO. 202.

Ref. Maps:
36.a. N.W.
36.a. N.E.
1/20,000.

26-6-18.

------

1. With reference to 120th Infantry Brigade Order No. 201, Battalions will use following roads when moving to their positions in W. HAZEBROUCK LINE :-

UNIT.	ROAD.
10th K.O.S.Bs.	Through LA BELLE HOTESSE.
15th K.O.Y.L.I.	C.21.a.3.5. - C.22.a.2.9. - C.16.d.3.3. - across country to C.16.d.8.7. - C.17.d.8.1.
11th Cam. Highrs.	C.14.d.2.5. - C.16.a.4.4. - C.16.c.3.8. - C.16.d.3.8. - C.11.d.0.1.

2. Labour Companies will use following roads to meeting places allotted in Appendix "A" to 120th Infantry Brigade Order No. 201 :-

UNIT	ROAD
258th Tunnelling Coy. 84th Labour Company. 92nd Labour Company. 110th Labour Company.	LE CROQUET - LA BELLE HOTESSE ROAD.
3rd Labour Company. 4th Labour Company. 6th Labour Company. 174th Labour Company. 48th Labour Company. 136th Labour Company.	MOST DIRECT ROUTE.
31st Labour Company	U.19.a. - ST LEGER.

35th Labour Company in Brigade Reserve will move across country and occupy Reserve Line in C.15.d. and C.21.b. An Officer will report at Brigade Headquarters when this Company is in position.

3. 300 yards distance will be maintained between Companies on the march.

4. In the event of a Block on the roads, troops will march off the road until clear of theobstruction.

5. Should troops of 29th Division be met on the Line of March, they are to have priority of road.

6. In the event of locations of Companies being altered before amendment is notified, the Group Commander will detail the route to the assembly position.

7. Routes will be reconnoitred and if necessary marked.

8. ACKNOWLEDGE.

A.B. Kerr
Captain,
A/Brigade Major,
120th Infantry Brigade.

Issued through Signals
at ..5.45. p.m.
to all recipients of 120th
Infantry Brigade Order No. 201.

Appx VIII

SECRET.

COPY NO. 4

120TH INFANTRY BRIGADE ORDER NO. 203.

Ref. Maps:
36.a. N.E.
36.a. N.W.
1/20,000

26-6-18.

1. With reference to 120th Infantry Brigade Orders Nos. 201 and 202 a practice concentration of Labour and R.E. Units will be carried out to-morrow, 27th instant.

2. O.C., 64th Labour Group will arrange for his Companies to report as ordered in Appendix "A" of 120th Infantry Brigade Order No.201 at 11 a.m.

3. Companies of 26th Labour Group and 258th Tunnelling Company are marching as complete units only as far as the Bus concentration point at LE NIEPPE, arriving there at 9-30 a.m.
   One bus will take selected Officers and N.C.Os. to meeting point, C.14.d.5.2. Remainder of Companies are marching back to billets.

4. Battalion Commanders with required number of guides will meet Companies at meeting points at 11 a.m. and issue orders as to disposition of labour companies in the line.
   These orders will be actually carried out on the ground as far as possible.

5. Reports on the concentration will be submitted by Labour Group Commanders and O.C., 258th Tunnelling Company to Brigade Headquarters.

6. ACKNOWLEDGE.

H B Kerr
Captain,
A/Brigade Major,
120th Infantry Brigade.

Issued through Signals
at 5.45 p.m.

Distribution:-

Copy No.			Copy No.		
1	...	G.O.C.	12 to 20		64th Lab. Group.
2	...	Brigade Major,	21 to 24		26th Lab. Group.
3	...	Staff Captain.	25	...	Lab. Comdt. St. OMER.
4	...	War Diary.			
5	...	File	26	...	258th T. Coy. R.E.
6	...	10th K.O.S.B.	27	...	Lt.-Col. WHITE, R.E.
7	...	15th K.O.Y.L.I.	28	...	Bde. Signals.
8	...	11th Cam. Hrs.			
9	..	120th T. M. Bty.			
10	...	40th Divn. "G"			
11	...	40th Divn. "Q"			

(6339) Wt. W160/M3016 1,500,000 10/17 McA & W Ltd (E 1898) Forms W3091.

Army Form W.3091.

WD 26

Cover for Documents.

Nature of Enclosures.

— War Diary —

Headquarters 120th Inf. Bde.

JULY. 1918.

VOLUME XXVI

Notes, or Letters written.

Instructions regarding War Diaries and Intelligence Summaries are contained in F. S. Regs., Part II. and the Staff Manual respectively. Title pages will be prepared in manuscript.

1.

WAR DIARY
or
~~INTELLIGENCE SUMMARY.~~
(Erase heading not required.)

JULY, 1918.
VOLUME XXVI.

Original

Army Form C. 2118.

Headquarters,
120th Infantry Brigade.

Place	JULY. 1918 Date	Hour	Summary of Events and Information	Remarks and references to Appendices
LA BELLE HOTESSE. C.21.d.0.3.	1st		Dispositions of Brigade :- 120th Infantry Brigade Headquarters ... 36A/C.21.d.0.3. 10th Battalion K.O.S.B. ... ... C.21.a.2.5. 15th Battalion K.O.Y.L.I. ... ... C.14.d.6.2. 11th Battalion Cameron Highrs ... ... C.14.c.7.7.	
			Instructions issued to Battalions that each in turn will occupy its own Sub-section of the WEST HAZEBROUCK LINE for a period of 4 days to be trained in all trench duties, sentry duties, reliefs etc. A number of Officers and N.C.Os. to be attached to Battalions to assist in the training of Trench Routine.	Appx.1.
	2nd	3-40 pm	120th Infantry Brigade was inspected by H.R.H. The Duke of CONNAUGHT, K.G.I., K.T. etc. at C.10.b.central (Sheet 36A)	Appx II
	3rd	8-15 pm	10th Battalion K.O.S.B. moved into its own Sub-section of the WEST HAZEBROUCK LINE for a period of 4 days in accordance with 120th Infantry Brigade No. 120/415 dated 1-7-18 (Appx.1)	
		5-15 pm	Lecture given by XV Corps Chemical Adviser to Commanding Officers and Company Commanders at Brigade Headquarters.	
	4th		Training generally carried out by Battalions; full use being made of Rifle and Lewis Gun ranges allotted.	
	5th		Football Field allotted to Battalions in turn for carrying out Inter-platoon and Inter-Company matches. Weekly Progress Report on Training forwarded to Divisional Headquarters.	Appx.111
	7th		11th Bn. Cameron Highlanders commenced its tour of 4 days in the WEST HAZEBROUCK LINE for training in trench routine.	
			2nd Lieut. H.E. TAYLOR, 15th Bn. K.O.Y.L.I. took over duties of Brigade Musketry Officer.	

D. D. & L., London, E.C.
(A8001) Wt. W1771/M2031 750,000 5/17 Sch. 52 Forms C2118/14

Instructions regarding War Diaries and Intelligence Summaries are contained in F. S. Regs., Part II. and the Staff Manual respectively. Title pages will be prepared in manuscript.

WAR DIARY
or
~~INTELLIGENCE SUMMARY.~~

(Erase heading not required.)

JULY, 1918.
VOLUME XXVI.

Army Form C. 2118.

Headquarters,
120th Infantry Brigade.

Place	JULY. 1918. Date	Hour	Summary of Events and Information	Remarks and references to Appendices
LA BELLE HOTESSE. C.21.d.0.3.	7th		40th Division Order No. 178 received, ordering a practice manning of the trenches in the Southern Section of the WEST HAZEBROUCK LINE by the 120th Infantry Brigade and affiliated Labour and R.E. Companies, on Wednesday 10th July, 1918.	
	8th	9 am	Divisional Commander (Major General Sir W.E.PEYTON, K.C.B., K.C.V.O., D.S.O.) inspected the 10th Bn. K.O.S.B.	
		8-30 pm	Revised Appendix 'A' to 120th Infantry Brigade Order No. 201 dated 25-6-18 issued.	Appx.IV.
		8-30 pm	120th Infantry Brigade Order No. 204 issued detailing a practice manning of the Southern Section of the WEST HAZEBROUCK LINE by Battalions of Brigade and affiliated Labour and R.E. Companies on Wednesday 10th inst.	Appx.V.
	9th	2 pm	15th Bn. K.O.Y.L.I. inspected by Divisional Commander.	
	10th		Practice manning of the Southern Section, WEST HAZEBROUCK LINE in accordance with 120th Infantry Brigade Order No. 204 dated 8th inst. carried out successfully.	
		8 pm	Amendments to 120th Inf. Bde. Order No. 201 and 202 issued.	Appx.VI.
	11th		15th Bn. K.O.Y.L.I. commenced its tour of 4 days in the WEST HAZEBROUCK LINE for training in trench duties.	
	12th		Weekly Progress report on Training forwarded to Divisional Headquarters.	Appx.VII.
	13th	9 am	11th Bn. Cameron Highlanders inspected while carrying out training by the Divisional Commander.	
	14th	11 am	Conference of Brigadiers at Divisional Headquarters.	
	15th	10 am	Conference of Battalion Commanders at Brigade Headquarters.	

D. D. & L., London, E.C.
(A8001) Wt. W1771/M2031 750,000 5/17 Sch. 52 Forms/C2118/14

Instructions regarding War Diaries and Intelligence Summaries are contained in F. S. Regs., Part II. and the Staff Manual respectively. Title pages will be prepared in manuscript.

WAR DIARY or ~~INTELLIGENCE SUMMARY~~.

(*Erase heading not required.*)

JULY, 1918.
VOLUME XXV1.

Army Form C. 2118.

Headquarters,
120th Infantry Brigade.

Place	Date	JULY Hour 1918	Summary of Events and Information	Remarks and references to Appendices
LA BELLE HOTESSE. C.21.d.0.3.	17th	10-45 pm	40th Division Order No. 182 received, cancelling 40th Division Order No. 175, Appendix 'A' and Amendments. In view of detachment of 119th Infantry Brigade to 1st Australian Division - setting forth distribution of troops of 40th Division with/attached Labour and R.E. Companies for the occupation of the WEST HAZEBROUCK LINE in the event of an attack on the Second Army front. Divisional Sector to be divided into two Brigade Sections; 120th Infantry Brigade to man the Southern Section.	
	18th		10th Bn. K.O.S.B. re urned to Camp from the WEST HAZEBROUCK LINE, the practice of occupying that line for instruction in trench duties being discontinued.	
		2-45 pm	120th Infantry Brigade Order No. 205 issued, cancelling 120th Infantry Brigade Order No. 201 dated 25-6-18 and revised Appendix 'A' issued 8-7-18. In the event of an attack on the Second Army front, the 40th Division (Less one Brigade) with attached troops will man the WEST HAZEBROUCK LINE, 120th Infantry Brigade with affiliated Labour and R.E. Companies shown in Appendix 'A' to man the Southern Section.	Appx.V111.
		2-45 pm	120th Infantry Brigade Order No. 206 issued detailing move of 120th Infantry Brigade Headquarters and 11th Bn. Cameron Highrs. on the 19th instant.	Appx.1X.
SERCUS. C.3.c.5.3.	19th	2 pm	Brigade Headquarters closed at LA BELLE HOTESSE, C.21.d.0.3., and re-opened at SERCUS, C.3.c.5.3. 11th Bn. Cameron Highrs. moved to Camp in C.3.a. in accordance with 120th Infantry Brigade Order No. 206 dated 18-7-18. Dispositions of Brigade :- Bde. Headquarters ... ... C.3.c.5.3. 10th Bn. K.O.S.B. ... ... C.21.a.2.5. 15th Bn. K.O.Y.L.I. ... ... C.14.d.6.2. 11th Bn. Cam. Highrs... ... C.3.a.9.3.	
			Weekly Progress Report rendered to Divisional Headquarters.	Appx. X.

D. D. & L., London, E.C.
(A8011) Wt. W1771/M2031 750,000 5/17 Sch. 52 Forms/C2118/14

Army Form C. 2118.

WAR DIARY
or
~~INTELLIGENCE SUMMARY.~~

(Erase heading not required.)

JULY, 1918.
VOLUME XXVI.

Headquarters,
120th Infantry Brigade.

Instructions regarding War Diaries and Intelligence Summaries are contained in F. S. Regs., Part II. and the Staff Manual respectively. Title pages will be prepared in manuscript.

Place	JULY Date 1918.	Hour	Summary of Events and Information	Remarks and references to Appendices
SERCUS. C.3.c.5.3.	20th		Brig. General C.J.HOBKIRK, C.M.G., D.S.O. having assumed temporary command of the 40th Division, Lieut.-Colonel, M. ARCHER-SHEE, D.S.O. assumes command of 120th Infantry Brigade.	
			Brigade Major (Captain H.G.EADY, M.C.) returned from leave.	
	21st		Divisional Church Parade service held in field at 36A/C.10.b.	
	22nd		A scheme to be adopted for a possible occupation of the EAST HAZEBROUCK LINE: reconnaissances carried out by Battalion Commanders.	
	23rd 24th 25th 26th 27th 28th 29th		Training generally carried out by Battalions in vicinity of Camp. Weekly Progress Report rendered to Divnl. H.Qrs (26th)	Appx XI
	30th		Divisional Commander (Major-General Sir W.E.PEYTON, K.C.B., K.C.V.O., D.S.O.) inspected Battalions of Brigade at training.	
			Staff Captain (Captain H.B.KERR, M.C.) proceeded to take up appointment with 80th American Division.	

M. Archer-Shee Lieut.-Colonel,
Commanding, 120th Infantry Brigade.

D. D. & L., London, E.C.
(A8001) Wt. W1771/M2031 750,000 5/17 Sch. 52 Forms/C2118/14

120th Inf. Bde. No. 120/415. S E C R E T.

Appx I

10th Garr. Bn. K.O.S.B.
15th Garr. Bn. K.O.Y.L.I.
11th Garr. Bn. Cam. Highrs.

H.Q. "G" 40th Division (for information).

1. Each Battalion in the Brigade will in turn occupy its own sub-section of the WEST HAZEBROUCK LINE for a period of 4 days, beginning as follows :-

10th Garr. Bn. K.O.S.B. ... July, 3rd.
15th Garr. Bn. K.O.Y.L.I. ... July, 7th.
11th Garr. Bn. Cam. Hrs. ... July, 11th.

2. Battalions will be disposed as if in the front system of defence and will be trained in all trench duties, sentry duties, reliefs etc.

3. In addition they will be employed on the construction of the EAST HAZEBROUCK LINE under the direction of C.E. XV Corps and orders of C.R.E., Corps Troops.
Units of this Brigade will be affiliated for purposes of work to 145 A.T. Coy. R.E.

4. A tracing is attached showing location of work to be done. Details will be forwarded later.

5. To assist Battalions in training their men in Trench Routine, a number of Officers and Warrant Officers or N.C.Os. will be attached by 31st Division to Battalions while in occupation of WEST HAZEBROUCK LINE.
Details will be forwarded later.

6. Transport Lines and Quartermasters stores will remain in present location.
Location of Battalion Headquarters chosen will be forwarded to Brigade Headquarters.

7. The above arrangements in no way alter instructions already issued that in case of necessity the 120th Infantry Brigade will man the WEST HAZEBROUCK LINE (vide 120th Infantry Brigade Order No. 201 dated 25-6-18).

8. ACKNOWLEDGE.

A B Kerr

Captain,
A/Brigade Major,
120th Infantry Brigade.

1-7-18.

Appx II

120th Infy. Bde. No. 120/474.

10th K.O.S.Bdrs
17th Worcestor
15th K.O.Y.L.I.
11th Cam. Highrs.

Inspection of 120th Infantry Brigade by H.R.H. The Duke of Connaught, K.G., K.T., etc. on 2nd July 1918.

1. The Brigade will be inspected at C.10.b. central (Sheet. 36.a) at 3.40 pm.

2. The 17th Garr. Battn. Worcester Regiment (Pioneers) will parade with 120th Infantry Brigade.

3. All battalions will parade as strong as possible and companies will be of equal strength and sized off before marching to the parade ground.

There is to be no selection of men, picked men are not to be placed in front ranks. The Duke of Connaught wishes to see the material of which Battalions are composed.

4. Dress - Fighting order, S.D. Caps to be worn. The Major-General desires Commanding Officers to ensure that all S.D. Caps are worn in the correct position.

6. On arrival at the centre of the front of the parade the Duke of Connaught will be received by a Rotal Saluto. Arms will then be sloped by order of the Brigadier.

Officers will come to the salute on the third motion of the 'Present Arms', and will remain at the salute until the second motion of the "Slope Arms".

Officers Commanding Battalions will arrange for this to be practised by all Officers before the parade.

7. The Adjutant of each Battalion and Right and Left markers for each Company will report to Staff Captain on the parade ground at 2.50 pm.

8. Battalions will march on to the markers at 3.15 pm.

9. The parade strength of each battalion will be wired to Brigade Headquarters at 10 am., 2nd July 1918.

10. The band of the 17th Garr. Bn. Worcester Regt (P) will play the Royal Salute and if the Duke of Connaught inspects the battalions they will play a slow march.

11. O.C., 10th K.O. Sco. Bordrs. will detail a bugler to report to the Staff Captain at 10 am., 2nd July.

12. A sketch map of the parade ground and positions of battalions is attached.

13. Acknowledge.

G W Archer

Lieut.,
A/Staff Captain,
120th Infantry Brigade.

1st July 1918.

BRIGADE ROUTINE ORDERS No. 131.

by

Brigadier General C. J. HOBKIRK, C.M.G., D.S.O.,

Commanding 120th Infantry Brigade.

2nd July 1918.

---

372. SPECIAL ORDER. 372.

On the conclusion of his inspection to-day H.R.H. The Duke of Connaught expressed great satisfaction at the appearance of the Brigade and wishes it to be known that it gave him great pleasure to meet so many old soldiers of regiments he has known so well and feels confident that they will sustain the high reputations of these Regiments.

T.W. Rucker, Lieut.,
A/Staff Captain,
120th Infantry Brigade..

----

appx III

120TH INFANTRY BRIGADE - TRAINING PROGRESS REPORT.

Musketry. 1. Training has been continued in the Care of Arms, judging distances and rapid loading. One tripod per battalion has been issued for aiming practices. Deliberate and rapid practices have been fired by all battalions on the range, chiefly at 100 yards. Battalions report that the standard of shooting is fair.

The Range at LA BELLE HOTESSE has been closed for two days for repairs.

Lewis Gun. 2. The average number of men in each battalion under training is 120. Instruction has been continued in mechanism, drill and stoppages. All teams have fired on the 20 yards range with fairly satisfactory results.

Drill. 3. Generally the men show greater steadiness on parade.

Improvement is also to be seen in the handling of arms and in turnout.

P. T. 4 The younger men have improved considerably with the daily training. A number of the men however are unlikely to reach the standard of agility required for Recreational Training.

Regimental Classes for training Instructors have been continued.

No Bayonet Fighting Course is available in this Area and the need for one will shortly be pressing.

Marching. 5. Short marches of from 4 - 5 miles have been carried out. There is still considerable room for improvement in march discipline.

Gas Drill 6. The standard of efficiency has improved. All Small Box Respirators have been tested in Lachrymatory Gas and very few defects discovered.

XV Corps Chemical Adviser lectured to Commanding Officers and Company Commanders on 3rd instant.

Bombing. 7. Classes in bombing have been started by one battalion this week.

S. O. S. 8. Regimental Classes have been held daily. Map reading has been studied and trenches located and marked on maps. Tests have also been fired on the Rifle Range.

Instruction of Officers 9. Lectures have been given to junior Officers on Map Reading, Platoon Organization and on simple Tactical Schemes.

The Brigade Signalling Class for beginners (consisting of 8 other ranks per battalion) has been running for a fortnight and satisfactory progress has been made in Visual Training(Flag) and in Buzzer Work.

Brig. General,
Comdg., 120th Infantry Brigade.

5-7-18

APPENDIX 'A' to 1 20th Infantry Brigade Order No. 201 dated 25-6-18 is cancelled, should be destroyed and the following substituted :-

Unit.	Location.	Approx. Strength		On Alarm to report	
		Rifles.	L.Gs.	To.	At.
Southern Sub-section				Officer&Guides 10th K.O.S.B.	Field at C.22.d.3.0. or field in prox. selected by O.C. 10th K.O.S.B.
10th K.O.S.B.		654	16		
258th T. Coy. R.E.	M.29.a.0.0.	171	1		
No.3 Labour Coy.	C.23.b.5.9.	250	1		
6 Labour Coy.	C.22.d.2.0.	356	1		
174 Labour Coy.	C.22.d.2.0.	244	1		
Centre Sub-section				Officer&Guides 15th K.O.Y.L.I	Field at C.16.d.2.9.
15th K.O.Y.L.I.		570	16		
No.92 Labour Coy.	T.11.d.6.8.	327	1		
31 Labour Coy.	T.18.c.2.7.	305	1		
110 Labour Coy. (all administrated by 26th Lab.Grp.)	N.27.c.6.6.	300	1		
35 Labour Coy.	C.8.b.central	351	1		
Northern Sub-section				Officer&Guides 11th Cam.Hrs.	Field at C.10.a.3.8.
11th Cam. Highrs.		637	16.		
No. 4 Labour Coy.	C.4.c.7.6.	229	1		
48 Labour Coy.	C.5.d.5.1.	290	1		
136 Labour Coy.	A.18.c.2.3.	260	1		
151 Labour Coy.	A.24.a.5.8.	250	1		

H. B. Kerr

Captain,
A/Brigade Major,
120th Infantry Brigade.

8-7-18.

Issued to all recipients of 120th Onf. Bde. Order No. 201.

appx V ~~E~~ 4

S E C R E T. ~~COPY NO~~

120TH INFANTRY BRIGADE ORDER No. 204.

****

Ref. Maps.
36.a. N.W.
36.a. N.E.
1/20,000.

8-7-18.

1. With reference to 120th Infantry Brigade Order No. 201 dated 25-6-18 and revised Appendix 'A' issued 8-7-18, a practice manning of the WEST HAZEBROUCK LINE will be carried out by 120th Infantry Brigade and affiliated Labour and R.E. Companies, on Wednesday 10th instant.

2. Battalions will be in position in the line by 10 a.m.

3. Affiliated Labour and R.E. Companies will rendezvous at the assembly places by 9-30 a.m., with the following exceptions. Nos. 3 and 48 Labour Companies will proceed direct to positions already allotted in Trench System.

4. Affiliated troops will not move from assembly positions into the Trench system until 10 a.m.

5. Owing to location of 258th Tunnelling Coy. R.E., Nos. 31, 92, 136 and 151 Labour Companies, only selected Officers and N.C.Os. from those Companies will carry out the practice scheme.

(a) Two busses will be at LE NIEPPE Cross Roads (T.11.a. 5.7.) at 8 a.m. to take to assembly position representatives from :-
258th Tunnelling Coy. R.E.
31st Labour Company.
92nd Labour Company.

(b) One buss will be at Cross Roads BELLE CROIX (B.13.a.) at 8 a.m. to take representatives of 136th and 151st Labour Companies to assembly position.

(c) 110 Labour Company need not be represented as it is shortly leaving the Area.

Group Commanders will detail the numbers from each Company who are to attend.

6. O.C., 64 Labour Group will detail 100 unarmed men for duty as stretcher bearers. They will report to O.C., 135th Field Ambulance at 36A/B.18.c.0.0. at 10 a.m.

7. Men of Labour Units will carry greatcoats and waterproof sheets but not blankets.

8. Arrangements will be made by battalions and Labour Coy. Commanders to give their men hot dinners in the trenches. If this is not practicable, haversack rations will be taken.

9. Details of 10th Garr. Bn. K.O.S.B. and 15th Garr. Bn. K.O.Y.L.I. will remain in Reserve in present camps. Names of Senior Officers left in charge will be submitted to Brigade Headquarters.

10/-

10. Reports on the practice will be submitted by Battalion, Labour Group and R.E. Company Commanders to Brigade Headquarters on Thursday, 11th instant.

11. ACKNOWLEDGE.

H.B. Kerr
Captain,
A/Brigade Major,
120th Infantry Brigade.

Issued through Signals
at 8.30 P/M

Issued to :-

Copy No.		
1.	...	G. O. C.
2.	...	Brigade Major,
3.	...	Staff Captain.
4.	...	War Diary.
5.	...	File.
6.	...	10th G.Bn. K.O.S.B.
7.	...	15th G.Bn. K.O.Y.L.I.
8.	...	11th G.Bn. Cam. Hrs.
9.	...	40th Division "G"
10.	...	40th Division "Q"
11.	...	135th Field Ambulance.
12. to 20		64th Labour Group.
21 to 24		26th Labour Group.
25	...	Labour Comdt. St. OMER.
26.	...	Lt.-Col. WHITE, ST MOMELIN
27.	...	XV Corps "G"
28.	...	Brigade Signals.
29.	...	258th T. Coy. R.E.

Appx VI

AMENDMENT TO
120TH INFANTRY BRIGADE ORDER NO.201
and
REVISED APPENDIX "A"
****

The following amendments will be made to 120th Infantry Brigade Order No. 201 dated 25-6-18 and Revised Appendix "A" issued 8-7-18.

Para 6 will be cancelled and the following substituted :-

"The following troops will be conveyed by bus from billets to their assembly positions, under arrangements which have been made by "Q" 40th Division.-

No. 31 Labour Company and No. 92 Labour Company will embus at LA NIEPPE: head of column facing South at T.11.a.5.7. and will proceed via RENESCURE, WARDRECQUES and BLARINGHEM, debussing at field C.16.d. 2.9.

No. 136 Labour Company and 151 Labour Company will embus at BELLE CROIX: head of column facing N.E. and immediately S. of Cross Roads at B.13.a.5.7. and will proceed via PONT ASQUIN and BLARINGHEM debussing at field C.10.a.8.8.

In the event of busses or lorries not being available, Units must be prepared to move by march route.

C.R.E. and Labour Group Commanders will be responsible for the embussing and debussing of troops under their command".

In REVISED APPENDIX "A"
under Southern Sub-section
Delete :- 258th Tunnelling Coy.R.E.,M.29.a.0.0. 171 1.

AMENDMENT TO
120TH INFANTRY BRIGADE ORDER NO.202
DATED - 26-6-18.
****

Para 2 will be cancelled and the following substituted :-
"Labour Companies which are not being embussed, will use most direct routes to Assembly Positions allotted in Revised Appendix "A" (issued 8-7-18) to 120th Infantry Brigade Order No. 201 dated 25-6-18".

ACKNOWLEDGE.

H.B. Kerr

Issued through Signals
at 8 p.m.
10th July, 1918.

Captain,
A/Brigade Major,
120th Infantry Brigade.

Issued to all recipients of 120th Infantry Brigade Orders No. 201 and 202.

****

Appx VII

120TH INFANTRY BRIGADE - TRAINING PROGRESS REPORT.

=*=

TRENCH DUTIES. 1.(a) Battalions have occupied the WEST HAZEBROUCK LINE for training in trench duties as follows :-

10th G. Bn. K.O.S.B. ... 3rd to 7th inst.
11th G. Bn. Cam. Hrs. ... 7th to 11th inst.

The 15th G. Bn. K.O.Y.L.I. are at present undergoing a period of 4 days in the above system.

(b) Valuable experience was gained during these tours of duty in a Trench System: but the standard of knowledge of actual trench routine as displayed by some companies was poor while there is also considerable room for improvement in trench discipline.

Assistance was given by experienced Officers and N. C. Os. from Units in the 31st Division.

MUSKETRY. 2. Training in rapid loading and aiming has continued. A Brigade Musketry Officer has been appointed to supervise all range routine discipline and better value has thus been obtained from the periods when the range is allotted to Units of this Brigade.

Standard of shooting by all battalions may be classes fair.

LEWIS GUN. 3. All Gun Teams have fired on the miniature range this week and have reached a fair state of efficiency.

DRILL. 4. The handling of arms is improving and the Classes for junior N.C.Os. under the R. S. Ms. are serving a useful purpose.

P. T. 5. Battalions are now erecting Assault Courses and training in Bayonet Fighting has commenced.

Inter-company competitions in all games under the heading of Recreational Training are being held.

MARCHING. 6. Marching in light order and for short distances has improved.

GAS DRILL. 7. The Standard Tests are carried out daily, with as a rule good results.

S. O. S. 8. Instruction is being continued regimentally for Scouts, Observers and Snipers. The tour of duty in the WEST HAZEBROUCK LINE afforded good training for these specialists.

INSTRUCTION OF OFFICERS. 9. Lectures have been held on Trench Routine and Pigeon Signal Service.

Brig. General,
Commanding, 120th Infantry Brigade.

12-7-18.

Appx VIII

S E C R E T.

COPY NO. 4

120TH INFANTRY BRIGADE ORDER NO. 205.

Ref. Maps.
36a N.W. 1/20,000
36a N.E. 1/20,000
EECKHOUT CASTEEL
Sheet 1/20,000

18-7-18.

1. 120th Infantry Brigade Order No. 201 dated 25-6-18 and revised Appendix 'A' dated 8-7-18 are cancelled and the following substituted.

2. In the event of an enemy attack on the Second Army front the 40th Division, less one Brigade, together with attached troops will man the WEST HAZEBROUCK LINE from D.25.c. in the South to V.6. central in the North. This Divisional Sector will now be divided into two Brigade Sections.

3. The 120th Infantry Brigade with attached troops shown in Appendix 'A' will man the Southern Section of this line.
Boundaries of Brigade Section are as follows :-

Southern Boundary.

A line drawn from D.25.c.5.8. to C.25.c.0.8.

Northern Boundary.

WALLON CAPPEL along the grid line to U.30.b.1.9. - U.30.b.8.6. - V.25.a.8.8.

4. For the purpose of defence the Brigade Section will be divided into three battalion sub-sections and will be held by units as follows :-

Southern Sub-section.

10th Bn. K.O.S.B. and attached troops.
Battn. H.Q. at C.23.d.8.9.

Centre Sub-section.

15th Bn. K.O.Y.L.I. and attached troops.
Battn. H.Q. at C.18.c.3.9.

Northern Sub-section.

11th Bn. Cam. Highrs. and attached troops.
Battn. H.Q. at U.30.c.0.6.

5. Boundaries of Sub-sections will be as follows ;-

Between 10th K.O.S.B. and 15th K.O.Y.L.I.

D.14.c.9.5. - D.14.c.1.4. - D.13.c.6.6. (Road inclusive to 10th K.O.S.B.) - C.18.c.8.2. - C.17.d.9.1. - C.16.c.5.8. (Road inclusive to 15th K.O.Y.L.I.)

Between 15th K.O.Y.L.I. and 11th Cam. Highrs.

D.7.b.9.4. - D.7.a.7.5. - C.12.a.9.4. - C.12.a.1.4. - C.11.b.7.1. - C.10.a.8.8. (Road inclusive to 15th K.O.Y.L.I.

6. In the event of an alarm being given -

(a) Battalions, less Details, will proceed to their positions in the line.

(b) Affiliated Labour and R.E. Companies, with certain exceptions to be notified later, will proceed by march route to Positions of Assembly as stated in Appendix 'A'

(c) The Senior Officer in charge of Details of each Battalion will report to Brigade Headquarters as soon as Details are ready to move to Assembly Positions in trenches in C.15.b. and C.10.c.

7. The defence of the line will be organised in depth, and in accordance with S.S. 210 - "The Division in Defence" - as far as troops are available but in any case troops will be disposed so as to hold both the Observation and the Main Line of Resistance. Where no Observation Line exists, already dug, battalions will push out Advance Posts in front of the existing Line of Resistance.

In making their dispositions, Commanding Officers must realize the comparative lack of mobility of the troops at their disposal, and the small number of Lewis Guns which can be manned. It must be impressed upon all ranks that they are to hold the line in which they are posted, whether it be the Observation or Main Line, to the last man. No withdrawal of troops will take place, even from the line of observation, unless orders to that effect are received from Brigade Headquarters.

8. Six guns of 120th Trench Mortar Battery will occupy positions allotted in WEST HAZEBROUCK LINE; the remaining two will remain in Reserve at Brigade Headquarters under O.C., 120th Trench Mortar Battery.

9. Rations for the day and one Iron Ration per man will be carried on the man.

10. Labour Group Commanders on the alarm will send to Brigade Headquarters a senior Officer for liaison duties.

11. O.C., 64th Labour Group will detail 100 unarmed men as stretcher bearers to report to 135th Field Ambulance at 36A/B.18.c.0.0.

12. Tracing is attached (forwarded to Battalions and 120th Trench Mortar Battery only) showing suggested dispositions. Battn. Comdrs. will forward schemes as approved by them to Bde.H.Q. as soon as possible.

13. Brigade Headquarters will be at C.3.c.5.3.

14. ACKNOWLEDGE.

H B Kerr
Captain,
A/Brigade Major,
120th Infantry Brigade.

Issued through Signals
at p.m.

APPENDIX 'A'
to
120TH INFANTRY BRIGADE ORDER NO.205 datod 18-7-18.

Unit.	Location	Approx. Strength Rifloc	L. Gs.	On Alarm to roport To.	At.
Southern Sub-section 10th Bn. K.O.S.B.				Officer & Guides 10th K.O.S.B.	Field at Approx. C.17.c.8.1.
No. 3 Labour Coy.	36A/C.23.b.5.9.	230	1.		
12 Labour Coy.	36A/C.5.d.9.5.	263	1		
164 Labour Coy.	36A/C.11.c.9.2.	416	1		
174 Labour Coy.	36A/C.22.d.2.0.	244	1		
(all administrated by 33rd Labour Group).					
Contro Sub-soction. 15th Bn.K.O.Y.L.I.				Officer& Guides 15th K.O.Y.L.I.	Field at C.18.d.2.9.
No. 4 Labour Coy.	36A/C.4.c.7.6.	229	1		
35 Labour Coy.	36A/C.8.b.cent.	351	1		
136 Labour Coy.	36A/A.18.c.2.3.	260	1		
151 Labour Coy.	36A/B.19.b.8.4.	250	1		
(all administrated by 64th Labour Group).					
Northern Sub-soction 11th Bn. Cam. Hrs.				Officer&Guides 11th Cam.Hrs.	Field in U.29.c.
No.31 Labour Coy.	27/T.18.c.2.7.	305	1		
92 Labour Coy.	27/T.11.d.6.8.	327	1		
138 Labour Coy.	27/N.35.b.2.5.	301	1		
(all administratod by 26th Labour Group).					
Brigado Roservo.					
173 Tunn. Coy.R.E.	27/I.2.b.8.6.	266	1	To occupy tronchos in C.4.b. & d. An Officer to roport to Bde. H.Q. when in position.	
Brigade Dotails Battn.	-	-	-	Seo para 6 (c)	

DISTRIBUTION.:-

Copy No. 1	...	G.O.C.
2	...	Brigade Major.
3.	...	Staff Captain.
4	...	War Diary.
5	...	File.
6	...	10th Bn. K.O.S.B.
7	...	15th Bn. K.O.Y.L.I.
8	...	11th Bn. Cam. Highrs.
9	...	120th T. M. Battery.
10	...	119th Infantry Brigade.
11	...	121st Infantry Brigade.
12	...	40th Division "G"
13	...	40th Division "Q"
14	...	40th Divnl. Train.
15	to 19	33rd Labour Group.
20	to 24	64th Labour Group.
25	to 28	26th Labour Group.
29	...	Lt.-Col. BUTLER, BLARINGHEM.
30	...	173rd Tunnelling Coy. R.E.
31	...	135th Field Ambulance.
32	...	Brigade Supply Officer.
33	...	O.C. Brigade Signals.
34	...	A.P.M., 40th Division.

AMENDMENT NO. 1
to
120TH INFANTRY BRIGADE ORDER NO. 205 dated 18-7-18.

==*=*=*=*=*=*=*=*=*=*=*=*=*=*=*=*

The following amendments will be made to 120th Infantry Brigade Order No. 205 dated 18-7-18 :-

1. <u>Para. 3.</u>

   <u>Northern Boundary</u> will be as follows :-

   WALLON CAPPEL along grid line to U.30.b.1.9. - U.30.b.8.6. - V.25.a.8.8. (road inclusive) - V.26.a.0.8. - V.26.central.

2. <u>APPENDIX 'A'</u>

   (a) Location of 33rd Labour Group is 36A/C.13.b.7.2.
   ,, ,, 64th ,, ,, ,, 36A/B.23.a.9.4.
   ,, ,, 26th ,, ,, ,, 27 /T.12.b.1.4.

   (b) Under Southern Sub-section insert :-

		Rifles	L.Gs.
63 Labour Coy.	36A/B.3.a.4.1.	290	1

   (c) Under Brigade Reserve

   Amend Location of 173rd Tunnelling Company R.E. to read 27/M.29.c.2.8.

3. ACKNOWLEDGE.

Captain,
A/Brigade Major,
120th Infantry Brigade.

<u>19-7-18.</u>

Issued to all recipients of 120th Inf. Bde. Order No.205.

====-====-ooOOOoo-=-=-=-=-=

ADMINISTRATIVE INSTRUCTIONS - OCCUPATION OF W. HAZEBROUCK LINE.

To accompany 120th Brigade Order No. 205.

Ref. Map:
1/40,000.
Sheets 27.
36a.

19th July 1918.

The Administrative Instructions issued with 120th Infantry Brigade Order No. 201 dated 25th June 1918 are hereby cancelled and should be destroyed.

1. Surplus kit.

(a) Units will arrange to form a dump in present quarters of all kit, blankets, stores, etc. not absolutely essential for fighting.

(b) Guard of 1 N.C.O., 3 O.R's. will be left with each Battalion Dump and will be provided with two days rations. Units will arrange for these men to be rationed.

(c) Dress will be fighting order with greatcoats.

2. Camps.

If the situation permits all tents and shelters will be struck and piled near a road ready for loading before the unit moves to the line.

3. Transport.

(a) Battalion Transport Lines and Quartermasters' Stores will be situated at approximately T.29.a. (Sheet 27) to which place transport will move under orders to be issued from these Headquarters.

(b) Captain L.J. TRITTON, 10th Battn. K.O. Sco. Bordrs. will be in charge of all transport on arrival at assembly position named.

(c) On the Alarm being given all available transport of attached Royal Engineer and Labour Companies will proceed to approximately T.29.a. and report to Officer i/c Brigade Transport.

(d) On arrival at new Transport Lines Captain TRITTON will detail one mounted orderly to report as soon as possible to Brigade Headquarters.

(e) Transport will not change its location from T.29.a. unless orders are received from either Brigade or Divisional Headquarters. If orders to this effect are received another mounted orderly who knows the new position will be sent to Brigade Headquarters.

(f) On the Alarm being given each battalion will detail one G.S. Limber wagon to report to O.C., 120th T. M. Battery for carrying Stokes Mortars and shells to the line. O.C., 120th T. M. Battery will be responsible for the drawing of required amount of T.M.C. from Brigade Dumps. The limbers will on completion of task return to their units.

5./. Rations.

5. Rations.

(a) Rations for the day and one iron ration per man will be carried forward, on the men.

(b) A supply of sandbags has already been issued to battalions. These are for carrying rations to the line after it has been manned. They should be used very sparingly as it may be impossible to get a further supply.

(c) The attention of Quartermasters is to be drawn to the comparative uselessness of sending forward fresh meat. The Brigade Supply Officer will arrange for preserved meat to be issued as far as possible but for the first two days a large percentage of fresh meat must be expected. Quartermasters will therefore cook as much of this meat as possible th the stores.

(d) Refilling point will be T.29.b.8.2 (Sheet 27).

6. Ammunition.

(a) 120 rounds S.A.A. per man and 2,000 rounds per Lewis gun will be taken forward by all units.

(b) Reserve S.A.A. dumps of 50 boxes S.A.A. are situate as follows :-

C.30.b.4.0. (Sheet 36a).
C.18.b.8.2. (-do-).
C.11.a.9.2. (-do-).
U.30.c.0.5. (Sheet 27).
U.28.b.8.0. (-do-).

(c) Officers Commanding Battalions will arrange for personnel to take charge of the dumps situate in their sectors. When it is necessary to draw on these dumps units will notify Brigade Headquarters.

(d) Brigade Reserve Ammunition Dumps are established as follows :-

No.1 ... C.21.a.6.5. ... Sheet 36a.
No.2 ... C.3 central. ... Sheet 36a.

(e) 10th K.O.Sco. Bordrs. will be responsible for No.1 Dump and 11th Cam. Highrs. for No.2 Dump. On receipt of these instructions one N.C.O. and one O.R. will be detailed to proceed to the Dumps and take charge and will relieve existing guards. These men will be rationed and relieved when necessary by their own units.

7. Medical Arrangements.

(a) 135th Field Ambulance will collect from the area within the following boundaries.

Southern Boundary. A line drawn from D.25.c.5.8 to C.28.c.0.8.

Northern Boundary. C.6.d.8.2 - C.6.c.0.5 - C.5.d.0. - C.4.d.5.2.

(b) 137th Field Ambulance will collect from the Northern Boundary of 135th Field Ambulance to left of Brigade Boundary.

(c) Advanced/

(c) Advanced Dressing Stations will be established as follows:-

By 135th Fd.Amb. at C.16.c.8.8. (Sheet 36a).
By 137th Fd.Amb. at U.20.b.9.1. (Sheet 27).

(d) Main Dressing Stations will be established at B.18.c.0.0 (Sheet 36.a) and T.18.c.8.7. (Sheet 27).

(e) The Corps Walking Wounded Collecting Station will be formed at T.22.a.3.4 (Sheet 27) for the Divisional Area.

(f) O.C., 64th Labour Group will detail 100 men from unarmed personnel for duty as stretcher bearers and they will report as early as possible to 135th Field Ambulance at B.18.c.0.0 (Sheet 36a). Care is to be taken that the men selected are of good physique and able to perform the duties which will be required of them.

8. Provost Arrangements.

(a) Straggler posts will be established as follows :-

1. Sheet 36a. C.13.c.7.3.
2. -do- . C.13.a.7.7.
3. -do- . C.1.b.3.2.
4. (-do-27). U.26.b.8.2.

(b) On the alarm being given each battalion will detail 2 N.C.Os. and 7 men to report to Brigade Headquarters for duty at these posts.

9. A copy of 40th Division Administrative Instructions for the occupation of W. HAZEBROUCK Line, dated 18.7.1918 is forwarded (to Battalions only) for information.

[signature]
Lieut.,
A/Staff Captain,
120th Infantry Brigade.

19.7.1918.

Amendment No.1 to Administrative Instructions issued with 120th Infantry Brigade Order No. 205.

Ref. Para.6. Cancel.

Reserve S.A.A. Dump situate at U.28.b.8.0.

Lieut.,
A/Staff Captain,
120th Infantry Brigade.

20.7.1918.

Amendment No.2 to Administrative Instructions - Occupation of W.HAZEBROUCK Line. To accompany 120th Brigade Order No.205.

Delete Paras. 1 and 2 and substitute following :-

1. Surplus kit, Tents, etc.

(a) Units will arrange to form a dump in present quarters, near a road, for all surplus kit, packs and stores not absolutely essential to fighting.

No lorries will be available for removing this kit, etc. and units will utilise 1st line transport to the best advantage to convoy this baggage to new transport lines. Returning ammunition and Ration limbers should also be utilised for this purpose.

(b) Blankets, Tents and Trench Shelters. Will be dumped on a lorry Route. So that, if lorries are available, these dumps may be cleared.

10th K.O.S.B.) In vicinity of camps on the
15th K.O.Y.L.I.) LA BELLE HOTESSE - LE CROQUET Road.
11th Camerons on road C.9.b.2.0. - C.10.a.8.8.

Units will wire exact location of these dumps.

If lorries are not available, units 1st line transport will be utilised if possible to clear - blankets being removed first.

(c) Guards will be left in charge of each battalion dump and will be rationed under battalion arrangements.

(d) Dress will be fighting order with greatcoats.

2. Ref. para. 5(d).

Amend refilling point to road T.19.b.8.2.

3. Reference para. 6(d).

Location of Brigade Reserve S.A.A. Dump No.1 to road C.21.a.9.1.

H.B. Kerr

Captain,
Staff Captain,
120th Infantry Brigade.

23.7.1918.

Appx IX

S E C R E T.

COPY NO. 4.

120TH INFANTRY BRIGADE ORDER NO.206.

Ref. Maps.
36a N.W. 1/20,000
36a N.E. 1/20,000
NECKHOUT CASTEEL
Sheet 1/20,000.

18-7-18.

1. The following moves will take place to-morrow, 19th instant.

120th Inf. Bde. Headquarters to Headquarters vacated by 121st Inf. Bde. at C.3.c.5.3.

11th Bn. Cam. Highrs. to Camp which is being vacated by 8th R. Irish Regt. at C.3.a. by 11 a.m.

2. Tents and Shelters at present occupied by 11th Cam. Highrs. will be moved by them under regimental arrangements. O.C., 11th Cam. Highrs. will also take over tents and shelters from 8th Irish Regt. at new Camp site. Numbers to be reported to this office.

3. Camp sites to be left thoroughly clean and certificates from Area Commandant or Billet Warden to be forwarded to Brigade Headquarters.

4. Brigade Headquarters will close at C.21.d.0.3. at 2 p.m. and will re-open at C.3.c.5.3. at the same hour.

5. ACKNOWLEDGE.

H B Kerr
Captain,
A/Brigade Major,
120th Infantry Brigade.

Issued through Signals at
2-45 p.m.

DISTRIBUTION:-

Copy No.		Copy No.	
1	G.O.C.	12	40th Division "G"
2	Brigade Major.	13	40th Division "Q"
3	Staff Captain.	14	40th Divnl. Train.
4	War Diary.	15	O.C. 26th Lab. Group.
5	File.	16	O.C., 33rd Lab. Group.
6	10th Bn. K.O.S.B.	17	O.C. 64th Lab. Group.
7	15th K.O.Y.L.I.	18	Lt-Col. BUTLER, BLARINGHEM
8	11th Bn. Cam.Hrs.	19	Bde. Supply Officer.
9	120th T. M. Bty.	20	Brigade Signals.
10	119th Inf. Bde.	21	A.P.M. 40th Division.
11	121st Inf. Bde.	22	Bde. Q. M. Sergt.
		23	135th Field Ambulance.

Appx X

120TH INFANTRY BRIGADE - TRAINING PROGRESS REPORT.

MUSKETRY. 1. A uniform course of six practices designed to suit the range at LA BELLE HOTESSE has been adopted. It is impossible to give any results as the range was only available on two days and on one of these shooting was interfered with by the rain.

Attention has been paid to rapid loading, to fire control and to the indication of targets.

LEWIS GUN. 2 Progress in training Lewis Gunners has been maintained although the specialist Instructors (Officers) lent by V111 Corps School have been withdrawn. The training of a second team per gun has been commenced by one Battalion.

DRILL 3. Close order drill and short ceremonial parades have been held daily. There is still considerable room for improvement one of the chief weaknesses being the lack of power of command on the part both of junior Officers and N.C.Os.

MARCHING. 4. Improving. The number of men falling out has been reduced partly owing to the worst cases having been evacuated to Base by A.D.M.S.

B.F.& P.T. 5. Instruction in Bayonet Fighting has been carried out daily. Recreational Training - Inter-company competitions are arousing keen interest.

GAS. 6. Satisfactory. Training in musketry etc. has been carried out while men are wearing masks. Gas drill has also been practised during the occupation of the WEST HAZEBROUCK LINE.

BOMBING. 7. Still in initial stages.

S.O.S. 8. Scouts are trained regimentally by Battalion Intelligence Officers. Progress satisfactory.

INSTRUCTION OF OFFICERS. 9. Special attention has been paid by means of lectures to impress upon all Platoon Commanders the importance of handling their own platoon and the need of cultivating the power of command.

Writing of messages has also been practised.

Lieut.-Colonel,
Comdg., 120th Infantry Brigade.

19th July, 1918.

Appx XI

120th INFANTRY BRIGADE - TRAINING PROGRESS REPORT.

MUSKETRY. 1. Considerable progress has been made by Battalions firing the special course, but musketry has been somewhat hampered by weather conditions and the state of the La BELLE HOTESSE Range.

LEWIS GUN. 2. Training shows good progress. The training of second teams per gun is proceeding, and instruction in A.A. work being given.

DRILL. 3. Company and Platoon ceremonial is being held daily, and Battalion ceremonial once a week.

Close order drill is improving, especially with regard to junior Officers and N.C.Os, who have received special attention.

Training in the preliminarystages of the platoon in the attack has begun.

MARCHING. 4. Route marches have been carried out, and the number of men falling out is becoming much reduced.

P.T.& B.F. 5. This is carried out daily. Great keenness is being shown inthis and in recreational training, which includes in one battalion, football between sides composed of whole platoons with three balls in play. this latter is producing a marked effect on the physical condiyion of the men.

GAS. 6. Gas drill is carried out daily, and other exercises are carried out while wearing masks.

BOMBING. 7. Elementary courses are in progress.

S. O. S. 8. SCouts are being trained regimentally by Battalion Intelligence Officers, especially with regard to night patrols. Progress is satisfactory.

INSTRUCTION OF OFFICERS. 9. Officers have been lectured on the platoon in the assault, and given special lectures on saluting and march dicipline. IN one Battalion a riding school has been formed.

Lieut.-Colonel,
Comdg., 120th Infantry Brigade.

26/7/1918

28031 W3125/M2250 1000m 6/17 M.R.Co.,Ltd. (1367) Forms W3091.

Army Form W. 3091.

WO 95/2607

Cover for Documents.

Nature of Enclosures.

~ War Diary ~

Headquarters 120th Infantry Brigade.

August 1918.

VOLUME XXVII

Notes, or Letters written.

Instructions regarding War Diaries and Intelligence Summaries are contained in F. S. Regs., Part II. and the Staff Manual respectively. Title pages will be prepared in manuscript.

Original ~~Duplicate~~

Page.1.

WAR DIARY
or
INTELLIGENCE SUMMARY.
(Erase heading not required.)

VOLUME XXVII.

AUGUST 1918.

Hd.Qrs. 120th Infantry Brigade.

Army Form C. 2118.

Place	Date	Hour	Summary of Events and Information	Remarks and references to Appendices
SERCUS.	1918. Aug. 1st.		Dispositions of Brigade :- Brigade Headquarters ... S.27/C.3.c.5.3. 10th K.O.S.B. ... ... C.21.a.2.5. 15th K.O.Y.L.I. ... ... C.14.d.6.2. 11th Cameron Hrs... ... C.3.a.9.3. 120th T.M.Battery ... LA BELLE HOTESSE.	
	2nd		15th K.O.Y.L.I. left for LUMBRES for 5 days intensive Battalion Musketry Course at Second Army School of Musketry. 17th Worcester Regt. (Pnrs.) moved to Camp vacated by 15th K.O.Y.L.I. (C.14.d.6.2) being at tactical disposal of G.O.C. 120th Infantry Bde. during absence of 15th K.O.Y.L.I. at LUMBRES on Battalion Musketry Course. Weekly Progress Report on Training forwarded to Divisional Headquarters.	Appx I
	3rd		2/Lieut. J.C.BARKER, 10th K.O.S.B., joined Bde. H.Q. as Bde. Intelligence Officer. Units engaged in training in vicinity of Camps.	
	4th	6 pm.	Captain T.KNOX-SHAW, M.C., Yorks & Lancs. Regt., assumed Staff Captaincy of 120th Infantry Brigade. Units engaged in training in vicinity of camps.	
	5th		Brigade Commander and Brigade Major attended Lecture and Demonstration on INFANTRY TRAINING, by Lieut.-General Sir IVOR MAXSE, K.C.B., C.V.O., D.S.O., Inspector-General of Training, at TERDEGHEM. Units in training.	
	6th		Units in training.	
	7th		10th K.O.S.B. replaced 15th K.O.Y.L.I. at Second Army Musketry Course, LUMBRES, the latter returning to Camp at C.14.d.6.2. 17th Worcester Regt. (Pnrs.) vacated Camp of 15th K.O.Y.L.I., returning to own camp, though still at tactical disposal of G.O.C. 120th Infantry Brigade. Units in training.	

D. D. & L., London, E.C. (A8001) Wt. W1771/M2031 750,000 5/17 Sch. 52 Forms/C2118/14

Instructions regarding War Diaries and Intelligence Summaries are contained in F. S. Regs., Part II. and the Staff Manual respectively. Title pages will be prepared in manuscript.

Army Form C. 2118.

WAR DIARY
or
INTELLIGENCE SUMMARY.
(Erase heading not required.)

VOLUME XXVII.

AUGUST 1918.

Hd.Qrs. 120th Infantry Brigade.

Place	Date	Hour	Summary of Events and Information	Remarks and references to Appendices
	1918 Aug.			
SERCUS.	8th	2 pm.	General Sir HERBERT.C.O.PLUMER, G.C.B., G.C.M.G., G.C.V.O., A.D.C., Commanding Second Army visited Brigade Headquarters. Units engaged in training in vicinity of camps.	
	9th.		Brigade Major reconnoitred line in LA MOTTE SECTOR (31st Divnl. Front) to be taken over by 120th Inf. Bde. from night 12/13th August. Units training in vicinity of camps.	
	10th	7.30 pm.	120th Inf. Bde. Order No. 207 issued. 120th Inf. Bde. will relieve the 121st Infantry Brigade in the Sector West of VIEUX BERQUIN on night 12/13th August 1918.	Appx II
		9 pm.	Brigadier-General C.J.HOBKIRK, C.M.G., D.S.O., resumed Command of 120th Inf.Bde. vice Lieut.-Colonel M. ARCHER-SHEE, D.S.O., 10th K.O.S.B. Units engaged in training in vicinity of camps.	
	11th		G.O.C. and Bde.Major reconnoitred line to be occupied by 120th Inf. Bde. from night 12/13th August 1918. Units training in vicinity of camps.	
	12th	9.45 p.m.	120th Inf. Bde. Order No. 208 issued, cancelling Order No. 207 dated 10:8:18. 120th Inf. Bde. will relieve part of the 92nd Inf. Bde. in the Right Brigade Sector of 31st Division Front (LA MOTTE Area) on the night 13/14th August. One Company of 92nd Inf. Bde. will be attached to 120th Bde., and the latter will be at the tactical disposal of 31st Divisional Commander.	Appx III.
	13th	6 pm.	Brigade Headquarters closed at SERCUS, S.27/C.3.c.5.3., and re-opened at same hour at FETTLE FARM, D.24.a.7.1.	
	Night 13/14th		120th Inf. Bde. and 1 Company of 11th E.Yorks Regt. (92nd Inf.Bde.) relieved 92nd Inf. Bde. in Right Brigade Sector of 31st Division front (LA MOTTE AREA) in accordance with 120th Inf. Bde. Order No. 208 dated 12:8:18.	
	14th	10 pm.	120th Inf. Bde. DEFENCE ORDERS issued for Right Sector of 31st Divn. front. For events, see Morning & Evening Wires and Daily Intelligence Summary. Casualties :- 1 O.R. Killed. 14 O.R. wounded.	Appx IV. Appx V. (a. & b.)

D. D. & L., London, E.C. (A8093) Wt. W1371/M2031 750,000 5/17 Sch. 52 Forms C2118/14

Instructions regarding War Diaries and Intelligence Summaries are contained in F. S. Regs., Part II. and the Staff Manual respectively. Title pages will be prepared in manuscript.

WAR DIARY
or
INTELLIGENCE SUMMARY.
(Erase heading not required.)

VOLUME XXVII.

AUGUST 1918.

Army Form C. 2118.

Page 3. Hd.Qrs. 120th Infantry Brigade.

Place	Date	Hour	Summary of Events and Information	Remarks and references to Appendices
	1918. Aug.			
FETTLE FARM. D.24.a. 7.1.	15th		Amendments to 120th Bde. Administrative Order of 10:8:18 issued. Amendments to 120th Bde. Defence Orders (App.II) of of 14:8:18 issued.	Appx VI Appx VII
		8 pm.	120th Inf. Bde. Order No. 209 issued. On night 17/18th August, the 10th K.O.S.B. will relieve 11th Cameron Hrs. in Support; the 11th Cameron Hrs. will relieve the 15th K.O.Y.L.I. in the line, and the 15th K.O.Y.L.I. will move back into Reserve. For events see Morning & Evening Wires and Daily Intelligence Summary. Casualties:- 4 O.R. Wounded.	Appx VIII Appx IX (a.&b.)
	16th		For events see Morning & Evening Wires and Daily Intelligence Summary. Casualties:- 2 O.R. Wounded.	Appx X (a.&b.)
	17th	2 am.	Inter-battalion relief carried out in accordance with 120th Inf. Bde. Order No. 209 dated 15:8:18. Dispositions :- Front Line ... ... 11th Cameron Hrs. Support " ... ... 10th K.O.S.B. Reserve " ... ... 10th K.O.Y.L.I. In the line ... ... 120th T. M. Bty. For events, see Morning and Evening Wires & Daily Intelligence Summary. Casualties :- 4 O.R. Killed. 4 O.R. Wounded.	Appx XI (a.&b.)
	18th		For events, see Morning and Evening Wires and Daily Intelligence Summary. Casualties :- 3 O.R. Killed. 3 O.R. Wounded.	Appx XII (a.&b.)
	19th		For events, see Morning and Evening Wires and Daily Intelligence Summary. Casualties :- 4 O.R. Killed. 1 O.R. Wounded.	Appx XIII (a.&b.)
	20th	3.30 p.m.	120th Inf.Bde. Order No. 210 issued. The 120th Inf. Bde. will take over the Right Battalion Sector of the 92nd Inf. Bde. on the left to-night. 10th K.O.S.B. will take over this new sector from the 10th E. Yorks Regt., 11th Cameron Hrs. will relieve the attached Coy. of 11th E. Yorks Rgt. on right to-night, the latter moving back to TIR ANGLAIS to the Support Area, moving one company to the "Z" line, one in area between "Z" and Reserve Line, keeping two in the Reserve Line.	Appx XIV

D. D. & L., London, E.C.
(A8001) Wt. W1771/M2031 730,000 5/17 Sch. 52 Forms/C2118/14

Instructions regarding War Diaries and Intelligence Summaries are contained in F. S. Regs., Part II. and the Staff Manual respectively. Title pages will be prepared in manuscript.

Army Form C. 2118.

WAR DIARY or INTELLIGENCE SUMMARY.

(Erase heading not required.)

VOLUME XXVII.

AUGUST 1918.

Page 4.

Hd.Qrs. 120th Infantry Brigade.

Place	Date	Hour	Summary of Events and Information	Remarks and references to Appendices
FETTLE FARM, D.24.a.7.1.	1918. Aug. 20th		For events, see Morning and Evening Wires and Daily Intelligence Summary. Casualties :- 3 OR wounded.	Appx XV & (a)
	21st		Reliefs carried out in accordance with 120th Inf. Bde. Order No. 210 dated 20:8:18.	
		12 noon.	120th Inf. Bde. Order No. 211 issued. An advance will be made to the line - Road from CUTLET CORNER to BECKET CORNER - F.26.c., thence back to PONT RONDIN, at an hour to be notified by Brigadier CENTRE Brigade (92nd). 10th K.O.S.B. and 11th Cameron Hrs. will conform to movements on their left, swinging forward ~~max~~ so as to reach the line PONT RONDIN - BECKET CORNER. 11th Camerons to keep in touch with left of 183rd Inf.Bde., and to try and swing forward their right to conform to the movement of that Bde., taking the line of the PONT RONDIN - NEUF BERQUIN Road as the limit of their advance at present.	Appx XVI
		3.45 p.m.	120th Inf. Bde. Order No. 212 issued. On night 21st/22nd August, the 10th K.O.S.B. will extend their left flank Northwards to F.19.d.2.6. taking over the line from 11th E.Yorks Regt. of 92nd Inf.Bde., and holding R.2. and R.3. subsectors with 3 companies in the line. On night 22/23rd, 119th Inf. Bde. will relieve the 10th K.O.S.B. in R.3 subsector, and the 15th K.O.Y.L.I. will relieve the 11th Camerons in R.1 subsector.	Appx XVII
	Night. 21/22nd.		The general line of 120th Bde. front was advanced by patrol action, the line of VIERHOUCK - PONT RONDIN - KEW CROSS - F.28.c.9.5. was reached in spite of a considerable amount of M.G. fire from K.6.d. 3 prisoners - stretcher bearers of 168 Regt. - were captured about K.6.b. as the result of this action. For other events, see Morning and Evening Wires and Daily Intelligence Summary. Casualties :- 3 OR wounded.	Appx XVIII (a-b)
	22nd	1.30 p.m.	120th Inf. Bde. Order No. 213 issued. At 5 p.m. 22nd August, G.O.C. 40th Division will assume Command of the front at present held by 31st Division from VIERHOUCK to F.14.c.3.5. On night 22/23rd, the following reliefs and readjustments of the line will take place on 120th Bde. front :- (a) The Royal Inniskillings, of the 119th Inf. Bde., will take over the R.3. Sector from 10th K.O.S.B. from F.25.a.7.0. northwards. (b) 10th K.O.S.B. will then extend their Southern Boundary to L.1.c.0.8., taking over from part of the 11th Cameron Hrs. (c) 15th K.O.Y.L.I. will relieve the 11th Cameron Hrs. in the R.1.subsector. Command of the present R.3. subsector to pass to G.O.C.119 Inf.Bde. at 7 a.m. 23:8:18.	Appx XIX

(A8031) Wt. W1771/M2031 750,000 5/17 Sch. 52 Forms/C2118/14

Instructions regarding War Diaries and Intelligence Summaries are contained in F. S. Regs., Part II. and the Staff Manual respectively. Title pages will be prepared in manuscript.

Army Form C. 2118.

WAR DIARY or INTELLIGENCE SUMMARY.

VOLUME XXVII.

AUGUST 1918.

(Erase heading not required.)

Headquarters, 120th Inf. Bde.

Place	Date 1918	Hour	Summary of Events and Information	Remarks and references to Appendices
FETTLE FARM - D.24.a. 7.1.	Aug. 5 pm.		40th Divisional Commander conferred with G.Os.C. 119th and 120th Infantry Bdes. at 120th Inf. Bde. Headquarters.	
	10.30 p.m.		120th Inf. Brigade Order No. 214 issued. At 4 p.m., 23rd inst., the 120th Inf. Brigade, in conjunction with 119th Infantry Bde. on left, and 183rd Inf. Bde. on right, will advance to the line - Cross Roads L.3.a.8.4. to BECKET CORNER. This line will be continued Southwards by 183rd Inf.Bde. 15th K.O.Y.L.I. will be on right and 10th K.O.S.B. on left. Fighting patrols to be pushed forward boldly, and artillery support given if desired.	Appx XX
	Night 22/23rd.		120th Inf. Bde. front was re-adjusted, in accordance with 120th Inf. Bde. Order No. 213 dated 22:8:18., the 119th Inf. Bde. taking over the front of the two left companies of the 10th K.O.S.B., the K.O.S.B. taking over the front of the left Company of the 11th Cameron Hrs., and the 15th K.O.Y.L.I. relieving the other two companies of the 11th Camerons. During the night the 119th Inf. Bde. made good the line ROOSTER FARM - BECKET CORNER - CUTLET CORNER.	
			For other events, see Morning and Evening Wires and Daily Intelligence Summary. Casualties. 6 O.R. Killed. 17 O.R. wounded.	Appx XXI (a. & b)
	23rd.	3.30 p.m.	120th Infantry Bde. Order No. 215 issued, ordering readjustments to be made in 120th Inf. Bde. front on completion of forward movement ordered for 23rd Aug., as per 120th Bde. Order No. 214 dated 22:8:18.	Appx XXII
		4.0 p.m.	Forward movement on 120th Bde. front commenced, as ordered in 120th Bde. Order No. 214 of 22:8:18. (For details see narrative attached - Appendix).	
			For other events, see Morning and Evening Wires and Daily Intelligence Summary. Casualties :- 1 Offr wounded. 24 O.R. wounded.	Appx XXIII (a)
	24th		For events, see Morning and Evening Wires and Daily Intelligence Summary. Casualties :- 2 Offrs wounded. 5 O.R. Killed. 19 O.R. wounded.	Appx XXIV
	25th	9.30 a.m.	Conference held at Brigade Headquarters between 40th Divisional Commander, G.Os.C. 119th and 120th Inf. Bdes. and Artillery Group Commanders.	
		3 pm.	120th Inf. Bde. Commander met Battalion Commanders in conference at H.Q. 15th K.O.Y.L.I.	
			For events, see Morning and Evening Wires and Daily Intelligence Summary. Casualties :- 1 O.R. Killed. 1 O.R. wounded. 2 O.R. missing.	Appx XXV (a)

Instructions regarding War Diaries and Intelligence Summaries are contained in F. S. Regs., Part II. and the Staff Manual respectively. Title pages will be prepared in manuscript.

Army Form C. 2118.

WAR DIARY
or
INTELLIGENCE SUMMARY.
(Erase heading not required.)

Page 6.

VOLUME XXVII.

AUGUST 1918.

Headquarters, 120th Infantry Brigade.

Place	Date	Hour	Summary of Events and Information	Remarks and references to Appendices
FETTLE FARM D.24.a.7.1.	1918 Aug. 26th	11.45 a.m.	120th Infantry Bde. Order No. 216 issued, ordering co-operation of 120th Inf. Bde. in attack to be carried out by 119th Inf. Bde. with the object of turning from the North the position at present held by the enemy, who holds the line of the LAU DICK from L.2.c.1.1. through BOWERY COTTAGES to RUE MARTIGNY.	Appx XXVI
		2.30 p.m.	Conference held at GRENADE FARM between 40th Divisional Commander and G.Os.C. 119th and 120th Inf. Bdes.	
			Capt. H.G.EADY, M.C.,R.E., Brigade Major, invested with Croix de Guerre at Investiture held at First Army Headquarters.	
		12	For events, see Morning and Evening Wires and Daily Intelligence Summary.	Appx XXVII (a)
			Casualties :- 2 O.R. wounded.	
	27th	12 a.m.	Order issued for attainment as early as possible of line indicated in 120th Bde. Order No. 216 dated 26:8:18. Heavy Artillery will assist by bombarding different points of enemy resistance at various intervals.	Appx XXVIII
			(For account of operations, see narrative attached - Appendix 'A').	Appx 'A'
			For other events, see Morning and Evening Wires and Daily Intelligence Summary.	Appx XXIX (a.+b)
			Casualties :- 1 O.R. Killed. 1 O.R. wounded.	
	28th	6 pm.	120th Inf. Bde. Order No. 217 issued. By dawn, 29th inst., all troops of 15th K.O.Y.L.I. in front line will be relieved by 11th Cameron Hrs., after attempt to gain new objective to-night. On completion of relief, O.C. 11th Camerons will assume command of the sub-sector.	Appx XXX
		6.45 p.m.	120th Inf. Bde. Order No. 218 issued. In the event of patrols being unable to seize RUE PROVOST and BOWERY COTTAGES to-night, the 120th Bde. will attack on 29th August, under a creeping barrage, to make good the line mentioned in 120th Inf. Bde. No. 120/426 dated 27:8:18.	Appx XXXI
			(For details of operations, see narrative attached - Appendix 'A').	Appx 'A'
			For other events, see Morning and Evening Wires and Daily Intelligence Summary.	Appx XXXII (a)
			Casualties :- 2 O.R. Killed 8 O.R. wounded.	
	29th.		Attack carried out in accordance with 120th Inf. Bde. Order No. 218 dated 28:8:18.	
			(For details, see narrative of operations attached - Appendix 'A').	Appx 'A'
			For other events, see Morning and Evening Wires and Daily Intelligence Summary.	Appx XXXIII
			Casualties 2 O.R. wounded. 1 O.R. missing.	

A6945 Wt. W14422/M1160 350,000 12/16 D. D. & L. Forms/C.2118/14.

Instructions regarding War Diaries and Intelligence Summaries are contained in F. S. Regs., Part II. and the Staff Manual respectively. Title pages will be prepared in manuscript.

WAR DIARY
or
INTELLIGENCE SUMMARY.

VOLUME XXVII.

AUGUST 1918.

(*Erase heading not required.*)

Army Form C. 2118.

Page 7.

~~Headquarters 120th Inf. Bde.~~

Place	Date	Hour	Summary of Events and Information	Remarks and references to Appendices
	1918. Aug.			
FETTLE FARM - D.24.a.7.1.	30th		120th Inf. Bde. Administrative Instructions issued for move of Brigade from line to WALLON CAPPEL.	Appx XXXIV
		3 pm.	Brigade Headquarters closed at FETTLE FARM, D.24.a.7.1. and re-opened at WALLON CAPPEL at same hour.	
WALLON CAPPEL.		7 p.m.	Move of 120th Inf. Bde. from line to WALLON CAPPEL area completed. Dispositions :-	
			Brigade Headquarters ... Schoolroom, WALLON CAPPEL.	
			10th K.O.S.B. ... 36/C.5.d.8.8.	
			15th K.O.Y.L.I. ... 27/U.24.c.2.4.	
			11th Cameron Hrs. ... 27/U.30.a.8.8.	
			120th T.M.Bty. ... WALLON CAPPEL.	
			For other events, see Morning ~~and~~ wire and Daily Intelligence Summary.	Appx XXXV (a, b)
			Casualties :- 12 O.R. wounded.	
	31st		Units engaged in cleaning up generally, etc.	

[signature]

Brigadier-General,
Commanding 120th Infantry Brigade.

A6945 Wt. W11422/M1160 350,000 12/16 D. D. & L. Forms/C./2118/14.

Bw Divn.

Appx I

120TH INFANTRY BRIGADE - TRAINING PROGRESS REPORT.

-

MUSKETRY. 1. Owing to lack of range facilities, little practical Musketry has been possible, but considerable progress has been made in rapid loading.

LEWIS GUN. 2. The second teams are now in training, and have fired a short course on the BELLE HOTESSE Lewis Gun Range.
Training in the tactical handling of the gun is proceeding, and shows satisfactory progress, though it is still rather in its elementary stage.

DRILL. 3. Close order and Ceremonial has been carried out daily, and there is considerable improvement in the steadiness of men on parade.
Platoons and Companies in Attack have also been practised daily, and sufficient progress has been made to enable these to be carried out as a scheme rather than as a drill.

P.T. & B.F. Improvement is satisfactory, and the general condition of men is steadily improving.

MARCHING. Route Marching is steadily improving, especially with regard to march discipline.

GAS. S.B.R. drill is carried out daily, and troops are exercised while wearing the respirator. Practise by night has also been started.

BOMBING. Elementary bombing classes are carried out daily, with a view to all men knowing how to throw a hand grenade, and as many as possible how to fire the rifle grenade.
Progress is satisfactory.

S.O.S. Practised daily under Battalion Scout Officers. Considerable progress in patrolling.

INSTRUCTION OF OFFICERS. Special lectures on all subjects have been given to officers, especially in Attack Formation.
Riding Schools have been formed.

Lieut.-Colonel,
Commanding 120th Infantry Bde.

2:8:18.

APPx II

COPY NO. 4

SECRET

120TH INFANTRY BRIGADE ORDER NO. 207.

10:8:18.

Ref.Map
attached
(only to Battns.)

1. The 120th Infantry Brigade will relieve the 121st Infantry Brigade in the Sector West of VIEUX BERQUIN on the night 12/13th instant.

2. All movement will be in accordance with attached March Table.
Battalion Transports will move to Transport Lines on the same day as the Battalions, in accordance with Administrative Instructions already issued.

3. Details of reliefs and advanced parties will be arranged by Battalions concerned, and Battalions of the 120th Infantry Brigade will assume similar dispositions to those adopted by the Battalions which they relieve.

4. All secret maps, aeroplane photographs, defence schemes, etc. will be taken over from units relieved, receipts given, and duplicates forwarded to this office by 6 p.m. 15th instant.

5. Completion of relief will be wired to both 120th and 121st Inf. Bde. Headquarters, using the following code words :-

15th K.O.Y.L.I.	...	SPRING
10th K.O.S.B.	...	SUMMER.
11th Cameron Hrs.	...	AUTUMN.
120th T.M.Bty.	...	WINTER.

6. Brigade Headquarters will close at its present location at 10 a.m., 13th inst., and re-open at the same hour at **D.17.a.7.3.** at which hour G.O.C. 120th Infantry Brigade will assume command of the sector.

7. ACKNOWLEDGE.

[signature]
Captain,
Brigade Major,
120th Infantry Brigade.

Issued through
Signals
at 7.30 p.m.

Distribution :-

Copy No.					
1	...	G.O.C.	12	...	119th Inf. Bde.
2	...	Bde.Major.	13	...	121st Inf. Bde.
3	...	Staff Captain.	14	...	31st Div. "G".
4	...	War Diary.	15	...	31st Div. "Q".
5	...	File.	16	...	135 Field Ambce.
6	...	10th K.O.S.B.	17	...	40th Div. Train.
7	...	15th K.O.Y.L.I.	18	...	Area Commandant, BLARINGHEM.
8	...	11th Camerons.			
9	...	120th T.M.Bty.	19	...	Bde.Supply Officer.
10	...	40th Div. "G".	20	...	Bde. Signals.
11	...	40th Div. "Q".	21	...	229 Field Coy.R.E.
11a	...	173 Tunng.Coy.	22 to.25		Labour Groups Nos. 26, 31, 33 & 64.

--*-*-*-*-*-*-*-*

MARCH TABLE TO ACCOMPANY 120TH INF. BRIGADE ORDER NO. 207.

Date	Unit.	From	To	Route	In relief of	Remarks
11th	15th K.O.Y.L.I.	MILL FONTAINE	Reserve Area about D.12.a. & c. and D.17.	March Route.	23rd Lancs. Fusiliers.	Hour of start & route to be notified later.
-Do-	120th T.M.Bty.	MILL FONTAINE	Reserve Area.	To march with 15th K.O.Y.L.I.		To be accommodated by 15th K.O.Y.L.I. Reconnaissance of T.M.positions occupied by 121 T.M.Bty. to be carried out night 11/12th and day of 12th.
-Do-	23rd Lancs.Fsrs.	Reserve Area.	SERCUS Area.			
12th	10th K.O.S.B.	LUMBRES.	Camp at LE NOIR TROU.	By bus.		To embuss at LUMBRES at 12 noon in busses bringing Battalion of 119th Bde. to LUMBRES.
-Do-	11th Camerons.	SERCUS Area.	Support Area.	By bus.	23rd Cheshire Regt.	To embuss at 10 a.m. at C.4.d.6.2. To debuss at D.3.central. Busses will return with 23rd Cheshire Regt.
-Do-	23rd Cheshire Rgt.	Support Area.	SERCUS Area.	-Do-		
Night 12/13	15th K.O.Y.L.I.	Reserve Area.	Line.		8th R.I.R.	
-Do-	120th T.M.Bty.	-Do-	-Do-		121 T.M.Bty.	
-Do-	8th R.I.R.	Line.	Reserve Area.			
-Do-	121 T.M.Bty.	Line.	Reserve Area.			
13th	10th K.O.S.B.	LE NOIR TROU	Reserve Area.	March Route.	8th R.I.R.	Hour of start 9 a.m.
-Do-	8th R.I.R.	Reserve Area.	SERCUS Area.			
-Do-	121 T.M.Bty.	-Do-	-Do-			

S E C R E T.

~~120th Infantry Brigade Administrative Order No. 2~~

120th Infantry Brigade Administrative Order No. 207.

Ref. Sheets :
27 & 36.a. (1/40,000).
36.a. N.E. (1/20,000).

10th August 1918.

1. Location of Units.

Brigade Headquarters	...	D.17.a.7.3.
Front Line Bn. H.Qrs.	...	E.14.d.5.3.
Support Bn. H.Qrs.	...	D.11.d.7.8.
Reserve Bn. H.Qrs.	...	D.12.a.3.2.
120th T. M. Battery.	...	D.18.c.8.4.
210 Fd. Coy., R.E.	...	D.5.c.9.1.

Transport Lines and Q.M. Stores.

Brigade Hd.Qrs and T.M. Battery.	...	D.8.d.3.0.
10th K.O.S.B. (from 8th R.Irish).	...	D.8.c.1.2.
15th K.O.Y.L.I. from 23rd Lancs Fus).	...	C.12.b.9.9.
11th Cam. Hrs. (from 23rd Cheshires).	...	C.12.b.9.9.
No.3 Coy. Train and Brigade Post Office.	...	C.14.c.2.8.
Refilling Point.	...	C.14.d.5.5.

2. Railhead.

(a) Railhead remains at EBBLINGHEM.
(b) All reinforcements arriving will be sent to Battalion Transport Lines.

3. Rations.

(a) Rations will be delivered to Transport Lines by No.3 Coy., Train.
(b) For the front line battalion rations are taken by limber to Battalion Headquarters and COBLEY HOUSE.
Rations for the two companies in the line to be taken to Company Headquarters by pack animals.
(c) For the battalions in Support and Reserve rations can be taken to all companies by limber, to Reserve by day, Support by night. (d) Limbers proceeding to the Company of the Support Battalion in "Z" Line via SANITAS CORNER must do so singly.
(e) Transport and pack animals are to be pushed as far forward as possible to save man-handling.
Carrying parties are not to be used for rations or water behind the Company Headquarters of the Companies in the line.
(f) Water. As the supply of petrol tins for water is very limited, steps must be taken to ensure that the same number of empty tins are returned each day as the numbers brought up full of water.
Unless this routine is rigidly enforced units in the line will not get sufficient water.
(g) Cookery. (1) For the front Line Battalion the bulk of the cooking should be done at the transport Lines.
(2) At present only 15 hot food Containers are available. Care must be taken to have these thoroughly scalded out each day, otherwise the food inside quickly gets tainted.

(3) For the /-

(3) For the Support and Reserve Battalions cooking can be done forward, provided every precaution to avoid smoke is taken.
(4) Cookers can in some cases be taken forward.

5. Ammunition.

(a) The Divisional Dump is situated in the S.A.A. Section 31st D.A.C. Lines - U.21.b.6.5.
(b) The Brigade Dump is established at - E.7.d.9.3. Units draw direct, notifying Brigade Headquarters of amounts drawn.
(c) Where not already in existence water proof recesses are to be constructed. Owing to the danger of ignition, sandbags are not to be employed, corrugated iron sheets being used instead.
(d) A careful check is to be kept of all S.A.A.. The promiscuous tearing open of the tin linings of S.A.A. Boxes is forbidden. Except in the cases of emergency, S.A.A. Boxes will be opened only on the order of an Officer.
The wooden lids must be worked frequently to prevent jamming.
Future ammunition returns and receipts will show separately the number of open and the number of unopened boxes.
(e) Loose bandoliers and clips of ammunition will not be left lying about the trenches but kept in the boxes.
(f) O.C., 120th T. M. Battery will arrange for the detonating of T.M.C. in the Brigade Dump as required.

6. R. E. DUMPS.

(a) The Main Divisional R.E. Dump is established at V.19.c.8.7 ... near CINQ RUES.
(b) A forward dump is located at BRICKSTACKS DUMP. E.20. b.7.0.
(c) All indents for R.E. Material should be submitted to this Headquarters.

7. Medical.

(a) The 31st Division evacuates all cases from the Brigade Sector.
(b) R.A.P. E.14.d.5.3.

Relay Posts. E.8.c.5.6.
E.19.b.8.3.

A.D.S. D.18.a.5.3. (Reserve A.D.S. D.9.d.1.8)

M. D. S. C.5.a.6.9.

Divisional Rest Station. ... T.18.a.9.9.

8. Cemeteries.

E.20.c.8.8.
GRAND HAZARD. D.8.c.9.6.
HAZEBROUCK. D.3.a.8.4.

Burials in other than authorised cemeteries are strictly forbidden.

9. Receipts.

At all inter-Unit reliefs, whenever trench stores, ammunition, rations, etc., are taken over or handed over, receipts must be exchanged and duplicate copies sent to Brigade Headquarters. It is pointed out that once a receipt has been given the recipient is responsible for the Stores, and any shortage subsequently discovered must be accounted for by him.

10. Trench Foot.

10. Trench Foot.

(a) In the event of continued wet weather, trench foot preventative measures will be carried out.

(b) Whale oil is available on application at Refilling Point.

(c) Clean socks can be obtained from 40th Divisional Clothing Store, RENESCURE.

11. Baths.

A Bath (capacity 100 men per hour) is being erected at FETTLE FARM D.24.c.7.6. for the use of Reserve Battalion.

Soyer stoves are available in billets of Reserve Battalion for heating water. Battalions can improvise baths by use Tarpaulin Sheets.

12. Clean Clothing Store.

Brigade Clean Clothing Store is located at Brigade Q.M. Stores, D.8.a.3.0.

(b) 31st Division Clean Clothing Store is at WALLON CAPPEL.

13. Gassed Clothing.

A stock of 500 S.D.Jackets and trousers together with underclothing is held as a Divisional Reserve for Gas Cases and is distributed between the Main Dressing Station and the 31st Divisional Clean Clothing Store, WALLON CAPPEL.

Such men as have been affected by Yellow Cross Gas will be sent to the main Dressing Station with a certificate signed by an Officer, stating that their clothing has been affected, when fresh clothing will be issued.

14. Salvage.

(a) The 31st Divisional Salvage Dump is located at WALLON CAPPEL.

(b) Salved stores of all sorts are to be conveyed there by returning ration limbers.

(c) It is to be impressed upon all men that itis their duty to collect and send back to the rear by ration parties etc., steel helmets, rifles, pieces of equipment, etc., however muddy or apparently useless..

(d) No man movin away from the line for any distance however short, on any duty whatsoever, should do so empty-handed.

(e) All empty Preserved Meat tins should be collected and sent to the 31st Divisional Solder kiln at WALLON CAPPEL.

15. Economy.

Waste paper, Jam cartons, dripping; tea, biscuit and other large tins, etc., will be returned to the Base through 40th Division.

16. Sanitation.

1. (a) Latrines of the bucket type only. Systematic burial of excreta is essential.

(b) On no account are food refuse and tins to be left lying about.

(c) Disciplinary action is to be taken against any man found throwing food refuse or tins over the parapet or parados.

2. (a) No.49 Sanitary Section located at B.22.d.6.5 administers the area.

(b) Indents /-

(b) Indents for requirements to be sent to this Office for transmission, through the Area Commandant, WALLON CAPPEL to 49 Sanitary Section.

(c) Approval of the indents will be notified to units by wire, when pioneers with tools must be sent to 49 Sanitary Section.

17. Ordnance.

The Brigade will continue to be administered by D.A.D.O.S 40th Division, located at T.18.c.2.8., EBBLINGHEM.

18. 18. Canteens.

WALLON CAPPEL U.23.c.20.25.
LE GRAND HAZARD. D.13.b.5.8.
There is a Y.M.C.A. at D.13.a.3.8.

19. Transport.

1. On the day of reliefs, Baggage wagons of the two units concerned may be retained after delivering supplies, in order to take up packs and blankets of the unit coming into reserve and remove those of the unit moving into the line.

2. Baggage wagons must be returned to No.3 Coy's Lines on completion.

20. Armourer Sergeant.

(a) The Armourer Staff Sergeant of 10th K.O.S.B. will report to the battalion in Reserve at 12 noon on the day following relief under arrangements to be made by O.C., 10th K.O.S.B. He will remain with the Reserve Battalion until all work required is completed.

(b) O.C., 120th T. M. Battery will apply to Brigade Headquarters if the services of Armourer Staff Sergeant are required.

21. Communication.

(a) A central telephone station will be established in the Transport Lines of 10th Bn. K.O.S.B.

The Battalion in Brigade Reserve will find the personnel (3 men) for the station, who will be attached to the 10th Bn. K.O.S.B. for rations and accommodation.

(b) The 15th Bn. K.O.Y.L.I. and 11th Bn. Cameron Highrs. will send a cyclist to be attached to the 10th Bn. K.O.S.B for rations and accommodation at the Transport Lines.

(c) A D.R.L.S. Service will be established as follows :-

LEAVE BDE. H.Qrs. D.17.a.7.3.	LEAVE 10th K.O.S.B. TRANSPORT LINES.
10 a.m.	10-45 a.m.
6 p.m.	5-45 p.m.

22. Baggage Wagons.

Baggage Wagons will be sent to Units on the night prior to the move.

After baggage has been cleared on the day of the move of units, all baggage wagons will be returned to No. 3 Coy. Train the same day as they will be required for supply services.

T Knox-Shaw

Captain,
Staff Captain,
120th Infantry Brigade.

APP^x III

COPY No.....

S E C R E T

120TH INFANTRY BRIG E ORDER NO. 208.

12:8:18.

1. 120th Infantry Brigade Order No. 207 is cancelled and the following substituted.

2. The 120th Infantry Brigade will relieve part of the 92nd Infantry Brigade on the night of the 13/14th in accordance with attached Relief Table.

3. The boundary between 120th Brigade and Brigade on the left will be :-
E.30.central - E.29 central - Valley Farm (inclusive to Brigade on left) SAWMILLS E.19.d.1.0 along track to D.24.a.8.0. - gird line through D.23. and D.21 central.

4. All arrangements for relief will be made by Commanders concerned, completion of reliefs being wired to 120th Brigade Headquarters by following code words :-

15th K.O.Y.L.I.	...	...	MORE
10th K.O.S.B.	...	...	HASTE
11th Cameron Hrs.	...	...	LESS
120th T.M.Battery	...	...	SPEED

5. One company of 11th E. Yorks will remain with the battalion of the 120th Brigade in the line, and will hold the extreme right of the line. This company will be under the tactical control of the Battalion Commander in the line, and will be relieved by other companies of the 92nd Brigade, under arrangements to be issued later.

6. All special maps, defence schemes, aeroplane photographs, etc. will be taken over from units relieved, receipts given, and duplicates of receipts forwarded to Brigade Headquarters by 6 p.m., 16th inst.

7. A map showing the position of platoons, and positions of posts on the flanks will be forwarded to Brigade H.Q. by noon 15th inst.

8. Brigade Headquarters will close at its present location at 6 p.m., at which hour it will re-open at FETTLE FARM, D.24.a.7.4., and G.O.C. 120th Brigade will assume command of the sector.

9. All transport lines will be taken over in accordance with Administrative Instructions already issued with 120th Inf. Brigade Order No. 207.

10. A C K N O W L E D G E.

[signature]
Captain,
Brigade Major,
120th Infantry Brigade.

Issued through Signals at 9.45 p.m.
To All Recipients of 120th Inf.Bde. Order No. 207 dated 10:8:18.

****

RELIEF TABLE TO ACCOMPANY 120TH INF. BDE. ORDER NO. 208.

Date	Unit	From	To	In relief of	Remarks.
13th	10th A.& S.H.	LE NOIR TROU	Reserve about D.17.b.	8th R.I.R.	Under arrangements between C.Os. concerned.
-Do-	11th Camerons	Support Centre Sector	Support Right Sector about E.25.b. & d. and E.27.d.	15th K.O.Y.L.I.	Relief to be complete by 9 p.m.
13/14th	15th K.O.Y.L.I.	Support	Line	1 Coy. 11th E. Yorks. 3 Coys 11th E.Lancs.	Under arrangements between C.Os.
-Do-	120th T.M.Bty.			121st T.M.Battery.	To be completed as early as possible.
-Do-	1 Coy. 11th E. Yorks.		Extreme right of line	1 Coy. 11th East Lancs.	Under arrangements between C.Os To come under tactical control of O.C., K.O.Y.L.I. on completion of relief.

Any routes in Divisional Area may be used.

The usual distances will be maintained on the line of march.

APPX IV

S E C R E T COPY NO.....

120TH INFANTRY BRIGADE.

DEFENCE ORDERS.

--*-*-*

14:8:18.

1. The 120th Brigade is holding the right sector of the 31st Division, with the 92nd Brigade of the 31st Division on the left, and the 183rd Brigade of the 61st Division on the right.

2. The boundaries of the area are as follows :-

NORTHERN BRIGADE BOUNDARY.

E.30 central - E.29 central - VALLEY FARM inclusive to Northern Brigade - SAWMILLS, E.19.d.1.0 - along track to D.24.a.8.0 - grid line through D.23 and D.21 central.

SOUTHERN BRIGADE BOUNDARY.

K.11.b.7.4. - K.4.a.6.0. - K.2.a.2.0. - along Canal through K.1.c. to D.30.c.7.3. - D.29.c.8.5. - D.29.a.8.2. - D.28.a.6.2. - D.28.c.6.5. - WEEVIL Crossing.

3. METHOD OF HOLDING THE SECTOR.

(a) The Sector will be held with one battalion in the Forward Zone and "Z" Line; one battalion in Support about the Reserve Line, and one battalion in Reserve about TIR ANGLAIS.

(b) The battalion in the Forward Zone will have two of its own companies and one company attached to it from the 92nd Brigade in the Forward Zone. The attached company will always be on the right. Its other two companies will garrison the "Z" Line. In addition, one company of the Support Battalion will garrison the Northern portion of the "Z" line, and will be under the tactical control of the C.O. of the Battalion holding the Forward Zone and "Z" Line.

(c) The Support Battalion will have one company in the Northern Sector of the "Z" Line, under the tactical control of the forward Battalion, as detailed in para. 3 (b), one company about E.27 central, and two companies in the Reserve Line.

(d) The Reserve Battalion is concentrated at LE TIR ANGLAIS.

4. LIAISON POSTS.

There are two liaison posts with the Brigade on the right :-

Front Line	...	120th Bde. post (attached Coy.)	...	K.11.b.7.6.
	...	183rd Bde. post	...	K.11.b.7.2.
"Z" Line.	...	120th Bde. Post	...	K.4.c.8.8.
	...	183rd Bde. Post	...	K.4.c.8.8.

5. The 120th Bde. front is covered by :-

(a) The 165th Bde. R.F.A., whose Headquarters are at SCALLOP FM. This comprises 3 - 18 pr.batteries, and 1 - 4.5 Howitzer battery.

(b) "A" Coy. 31st M.G. Battalion with Hd.Qrs. at E26a83

(c) Certain 6" Newton mortars, details of which will be issued later.

6. ACTION IN CASE OF ATTACK.

There are 3 kinds of warning signals :-
(i) S.O.S.
(ii) GAS.
(iii) "PERCY".

(i) S.O.S.

See Appendix I for general instructions.

The S.O.S. lines of the covering Artillery are as follows :-

"A" Battery (18-pdr.).

K.12.a.0.0. - K.12.a.60.55. - thence along line of the BECQUE - K.12.a.75.80.

"B" Battery. (18-pdr.)

K.12.a.75.80. - K.6.c.83.00. - K.6.c.98.83.

"D" Battery. (4.5" How.)

K.6.c.98.83. - K.6.b.0.0. - E.30.c.8.0.

"C" Battery. (18-pdr.)

E.30.c.8.0. - E.30. central.

(ii) GAS.

For general instructions as to giving alarm, etc., see Appendix 2.
Special precautions against gas shelling are to be taken in this sector, as it is particularly likely to occur in the BOIS D'AVAL area. Steps will be taken to thin out the troops in the gassed area as far as is possible, and to arrange for their periodical relief.
Our guns will not open fire if no hostile attack is suspected, except at the request of the infantry.

(iii) "PERCY".
If a hostile attack on our front seems to be impending, the code word "PERCY" will be sent.
The following action will then be taken at once :-
(a) Artillery will move into battle positions.
(b) No reinforcements will be sent, nor counter-attacks made in front of the "Z" line.
(c) The battalion in reserve will send two companies to reinforce the "Z" line. These companies will be under the tactical control of the C.O. of the battalion in the forward zone, who will be responsible for the

defence of the "Z" line, and may be stationed close behind the "Z" line instead of on it, if thought desirable.

(d) The 3 Companies of the Support Battalion not in the 'Z' line will remain as permanent garrisons of the works they are occupying.

(e) The two remaining companies of the Reserve Battalion will form a Brigade Reserve, for employment as the situation requires.

(f) That portion of the T.M.Battery not manning positions covering either the Forward Zone or "Z" line will remain in Brigade Reserve.

(g) The Details of the 3 Battalions of the Brigade will be formed into a composite company under the orders of the senior officer with them, and will occupy 3 posts in D.12 and D.18.a.

ACTION IN THE EVENT OF SURPRISE ATTACK BEFORE "PERCY" IS ISSUED.

In this case, the dispositions will follow as closely as is possible those made for "PERCY".

(a) Troops in the Forward Zone will hold out at all costs, but will not be reinforced.

The "Z" line will be reinforced as soon as possible as for "PERCY", but no counter-attack will be made in front of the "Z" line until the force of the enemy's attack has been broken.

7. WORKING PARTIES.

Working Parties will always move to their work fully equipped for fighting. In case of heavy bombardment or hostile action indicating an attack, working parties will at once man the nearest defences, reporting to the nearest unit (Battalion or Brigade Headquarters) that they have done so, and

If the situation does not require them to remain in these defences, instructions will be issued by the Brigade for them to rejoin their units.

8. RESPONSIBILITY FOR WORK.

The Battalion in the line is responsible for all work forward of the "Z" line. All battalions are responsible for the improvement and maintenance of all portions of that part of the line which they occupy. Responsibility for the work on the defences of the "Z" line rests with the Division.

9. ACKNOWLEDGE.

Captain,
Brigade Major,
120th Infantry Brigade.

Appendix I.

S. O. S. Signal.

1. USE.
The signal operates automatically as an order to the Artillery and Machine Guns to lay a barrage in front of our line, or on the enemy's lines, to assist the Infantry in breaking down an enemy attack.

2. WHEN USED.
The signal will only be used when the enemy actually attacks our lines in force, or is undoubtedly about to do so immediately.
The signal automatically causes a large expenditure of Artillery and Machine Gun ammunition; it should not, therefore, be used if there is time to obtain Artillery and Machine Gun support by ordinary means, or unless the officer ordering it is fully convinced that an attack in force, by the enemy, is being made or is immediately pending.
If the enemy are observed to be massing in rear of their lines, a demand for 'counter preparation' should be made in the usual way.

3. DEFINITION OF AREA.
For S.O.S. purposes, the Brigade occupies R.1. Section of the Divisional Front.
The Brigade on the left occupies R.2 and R.3 Sections.

4. BY WHOM MADE.
The S.O.S. call may be sent by any officer, infantry or artillery, who has assured himself that the condition mentioned in para. 2 exists. In very exceptional circumstances a senior N.C.O. may send an S.O.S. call, but he may not do so if an officer is present or within reasonable distance.

5. The S.O.S. signal can be made in 3 ways ,-

(a) By signal communications.
(b) By S.O.S. light signal.
(c) By a series of short blasts on the Strombus horn.

6. The normal procedure is as follows :-

(a) The officer who decides to send an S.O.S. signal will -
  (1) Order the firing of the S.O.S. light signal.
  (2) Instruct his signaller to send the S.O.S. message.
  (3) In appropriate cases (see para. (d) below) order the sounding of the S.O.S. Strombus horn.

(b) (1) The S.O.S. message consists of the letters "S.O.S. (followed by Battalion Sector) " only, e.g.- for this Brigade Front the message would read - "S.O.S. R.1".
It is repeated until answered.
No preliminary calling up of the distant office by its office call is to take place.

(2) For this purpose a prepared message form will be kept ready for signature in each Company and Battalion Signal Office.
This form will be signed by the Officer ordering the S.O.S. call to be sent, and completed by the signaller when it has actually been sent. The actual form will

subsequently be forwarded to Battalion and thence to Brigade Headquarters as soon as possible.

(3) The Battalion Signaller on receiving the message will automatically repeat it as follows in this order :-

To (i) The signal office of the covering artillery units.
(ii) Covering Machine Gun units.
(iii) Brigade Signal Office.
(iv) Companies other than the company which originated the call.
(v) Flank battalions.

(4) The Brigade Signal Office on receiving the message will automatically repeat in this order :-

To (i) The signal office of the covering Artillery Group.
(ii) The signal office of the covering Machine Gun Coy.
(iii) Divisional signal office.
(iv) Battalions other than the battalion which communicated the call.
(v) Flank Brigade Signal Offices (for information only).

(5) The order of precedence given in (3) and (4) above is so given as a guide only, but it should be understood that the S.O.S. call takes precedence of all other messages, and that all other traffic should be suspended for it. The S.O.S. call should, therefore, where circumstances permit, be sent simultaneously to all concerned.

(6) In the event of a breakdown of lines, any other suitable means of communication may be used.

(7) Every signal office will warn its own H.Q. of the S.O.S. message as instructed by those H.Q.

(c) (1) The S.O.S. Light Signal consists at present of a rifle grenade bursting into :-
RED over GREEN over YELLOW.

(2) Chains of repeating stations are established as follows :-

Sending Stn.	Repeating Station.
Any Coy. in R.1.	K.4.a.6.2. K.4.a.6.4. (Artillery).

(3) In order to confine the barrage to essential limits only, S.O.S. light signals will not be repeated by flank companies in the line or by repeating stations other than those in the xxxxxx chains given above.

(4) The signal will be repeated by the sending station until answered by artillery fire.

(d) (1) The strombos horn signal is a succession of short blasts lasting not more than 10 seconds each.

(2) The signal is taken up by all horns in the neighbourhood.

(3) It should therefore not be used when either of the other means is possible. It is intended only to cover the breakdown of signal communications combined with conditions which make it doubtful that the S.O.S. light signal will be seen.

(e) As soon as possible after sending the S.O.S., the officer who originated the call will inform his Battalion Commander of the situation.

7. REPEAT S.O.S. SIGNAL.

If any part of the front which is attacked is covered by a machine gun barrage, the S.O.S. signal should be repeated at 10 minutes interval if the continuation of the S.O.S. beyond that time is required. This should be done even if information has been passed to the Brigade that a prolongation of fire is desired, as it is difficult to pass this information on to individual machine guns.

8. TEST S.O.S. CALLS.

Frequent tests of the S.O.S. arrangements will be made. The procedure is exactly the same as for an actual S.O.S., except that the word "TEST" will be substituted for "S.O.S." in the message.

Artillery procedure is also the same, except that one round per Battery only will be fired.

Any Company Commander may make one "TEST" during his tour of duty in the line. He will note the following points and report them to his Battalion Commander by whom they will be transmitted through Infantry Brigade Hd.Qrs. to H.Q. Div. Artillery.

(a) Time of delivery of message to signaller.
(b) Time of transmission.
(c) Time of round fired by Battery.
(d) Result of fire.

The Battery should normally fire at once, as for an actual S.O.S., but is permitted to delay if another target is being engaged, or if hostile planes or balloons are observing. In the latter case, instead of firing one round the Battery will reply by a message " PLANE (followed by Section to which TEST referred)".

The Battalion Commander will enquire from the Battery Commander as to the cause of any delay or badly laid rounds.

No Tests will be made with light signals or Strombos horns.

9. Instructions as to sending S.O.S. and "TEST" calls will be hung in every Signal Office in the line.

10. CANCELLATION OF S.O.S.

When fire is no longer required, the message "CANCEL S.O.S." will be sent immediately. This message is distributed in the same way as the S.O.S. call.

--*-*-*-*-*-*-*-*-*-*-*-*

Appendix II.

ANTI - AIRCRAFT DEFENCE.

All Units are responsible for their own protection against attacks from the air, and should ensure that they are complete in A.A. small arms, sights and mountings, according to establishment.

The following are the chief considerations which will govern the defence of the area :-

(a) Fire will be opened on low-flying aeroplanes by rifles and Lewis guns, but in every case the sentry in front line posts will continue to watch the front.

(b) Lewis guns told off for anti-aircraft purposes in the line should not be placed at greater intervals than 500 yards. Positions may bechanged, but changes should be reported to Brigade Headquarters so that the anti-aircraft defence may be co-ordinated.

(c) Most implicit orders are necessary to ensure that no Lewis gun or rifle is to fire unless the "CROSS" on the hostile plane can be clearly seen with the naked eye. It is useless to fire at a range greater than 1,300 yards. This is to be made clear to every Lewis gunner, and steps will be taken to deal with those who fire wildly at aeroplanes obviously out of range.

(d) Anti-aircraft Lewis Guns will, as far as possible, be placed in groups of 4, or in pairs. If in groups of 4, they will be under an officer, or if in pairs under N.C.O's to be supervised by an officer.

Fire at night will not be opened unless :-

(i) The hostile aircraft can be seen against the sky.

(ii) The struts of the planes can be distinguished in the beams of the searchlight.

--*-*-*-*-*-*-*-*-*

Appendix III.

ANTI-GAS INSTRUCTIONS.

In the event of:-

A. **HEAVY GAS SHELLING OR GAS PROJECTOR SHOOTS.**

(1) Warning will be conveyed by :-

(a) Signal communications.
(b) sound signals - rattles
gongs
shouting ' Gas Shelling' after adjusting the Small Box Respirator,

BUT NOT STROMBOS HORNS.

(2) The telegram indicating heavy gas shelling or a projector shoot consists of the words "POISON HEAVY" (followed by the Battalion Sector or map square).

(3) The procedure for dealing with this message is the same as for the GAS message, except that it does not go higher than Divisional Headquarters and the D.G.O., unless the Gas Shelling is in a back area. In any case, the Divisional Signal Office will obtain the instructions of the General Staff before forwarding it higher, or to flank Divisions.

(4) The procedure for warning units occupying areas is also as above.

(5) The Signal on Rattles and Gongs will be taken up by similar instruments, but will NOT be taken up by Strombos Horns.

In the event of

B. **LIGHT GAS SHELLING.**

(1) Warning will be conveyed by :-
(a) signal communications.
(b) sound signals - rattles
gongs
shouting, as above,

BUT NOT STROMBOS HORNS.

(2) The telegram indicating Light Gas Shelling consists of the words "POISON LIGHT (followed by the Battalion Sector or map square)".

(3) The procedure for dealing with this message is the same as for the GAS message, except that it does not go higher than Infantry or Artillery Brigade Headquarters, unless the Gas Shelling is in rear of the line of Brigade Headquarters. In any case the Brigade Signal Office will obtain the instructions of the Brigade Staff before forwarding it higher.

(4) The procedure for warning units occupying areas is also as above.

(5) The Signal on Rattles and Gongs will be taken up by similar instruments, but NOT by Strombos Horns.

The expression "POISON" alone, or "POISON SHELL", is not to be used.

--*-*-*-*-*-* * -*-*-

120th Inf.Bde. No. 120/415.

SECRET

COPY NO......

120TH INFANTRY BRIGADE DEFENCE ORDERS

-

1. The following amendments are to be made to Appendix II "ANTI-AIRCRAFT DEFENCE".

   (a) After "or if in pairs" add "or single".

   (b) Add new para. as follows :-

   "An order board is to be provided at every post. Units will also arrange that the 'Letter and Colours of the Day' (particularly the latter) are communicated to each of their posts and understood by them.

   An additional reason for the restriction of A.A. Lewis Gun fire at night, particularly in back areas, is that the A.A. defences depend largely on listening for the location of hostile aeroplanes and that this is made more difficult if Lewis Guns fire unnecessarily."

2. With reference to (b) above, copies of a paper of orders for A.A.Lewis Gunners have been forwarded for distribution to each gun (vide 120th Inf. Bde. No. 120/401 dated 14:8:18 - to Battalions only). This paper should be pasted to a board of piece of tin and tied to the mounting or some part of the emplacement of the gun.

3. The Letters and Colours change daily at 12 noon and are to be communicated daily to A.A.Lewis Guns as if they were Passwords.

4. ACKNOWLEDGE (Units only).

A.O. Eade

Captain,
Brigade Major,
120th Infantry Brigade.

Issued to all recipients of 120th Inf. Bde. Defence Orders dated 13:8:18.

****

"A" Form.

Army Form C. 2121.
(In pads of 100.)

MESSAGES AND SIGNALS.

No. of Message ....

Prefix .... Code .... m. | Words. | Charge. | This message is on a/c of: | Recd. at ...... m.

Office of Origin and Service Instructions.

Priority

Sent At .... m. To .... By ....

Service.

App^x V

Date .... From .... By ....

(Signature of "Franking Officer.")

TO ~~[illegible]~~ JCA BUZO RUTU

Sender's Number.	Day of Month.	In reply to Number.	AAA
G 162	14		

Morning situation report AAA situation quiet AAA nothing to report AAA

Addsd ~~[illegible]~~ JCA repeated BUZO + RUTU

From RUQE

Place

Time 11.10 AM

The above may be forwarded as now corrected. (Z)

Censor. Signature of Addressor or person authorised to telegraph in his name.

* This line, except AAA, should be erased if not required.

Wt. W 3253/P511. 500,000 Pads. 1/18. B. & S. Ltd. (E2389.)

[illegible] Capt.

"A" Form.

MESSAGES AND SIGNALS.

Army Form C. 2121. (In pads of 100.)

No. of Message 60

Prefix SB Code DSp m. Words 18 Charge 1

Office of Origin and Service Instructions. 3 adds

Sent At 4.45 m. To YCA By

This message is on a/c of: 717 Service.

(Signature of "Franking Officer.")

Recd. at m. Date From By

Appx VI (a)

TO YCA BUZO RUTU

Sender's Number.	Day of Month.	In reply to Number.	AAA
* EW 14	14		

Evening Situation report AAA Situation unchanged aaa nothing to report.

Prisoner + material nil.

Added YCA repeated BUZO RUTU

From RUQE

Place

Time

The above may be forwarded as now corrected. (Z)

Censor. Signature of Addressor or person authorised to telegraph in his name.

Capt. Bothara

* This line, except AAA, should be erased if not required.

Wt. W 3253/P511. 500,000 Pads. 1/18. B. & S. Ltd. (E2389.)

Appx V (h)

CONFIDENTIAL.

120TH INFANTRY BRIGADE INTELLIGENCE SUMMARY.

RIGHT SECTOR

6 a.m. 13:8:18 to 6 a.m. 14:8:18.

A. OUR OPERATIONS.

(i) Infantry.

(ii) Patrols.

(iii) Artillery. Heavy Artillery fairly active, shelling back areas.

(iv) Machine Guns. Quiet.

(v) Trench Mortars. Quiet.

(vi) Aerial. One aeroplane crossed our line at E.30, and flew East, at 10 p.m.
Usual formations observed during the day.

B. ENEMY OPERATIONS.

(i) Infantry. Nil.

(ii) Artillery. 50 rounds were fired on our Front and Support Lines about 3.15 a.m.

(iii) Trench Mortars. Nil.

(iv) Machine Guns. Quiet.

(v) Aerial. One E.A. flew over our lines at 6.15 a.m. Height 2,000 feet.
10.20 p.m. One W.A. crossed our line at E.29, going N.W., and returned at 11.15 p.m.

C. VISIBILITY. Very misty from 3 a.m. to 6 a.m.

WG

J. C. Barker
2/Lieut.
Intelligence Officer,
120th Infantry Brigade.

14:8:18.

Army Form C. 2121.
(In pads of 100.)

Form.

MESSAGES AND SIGNALS.

No. of Message 10

Prefix Code m.	Words. 91	Charge.	This message is on a/c of:	Recd. at m.
Office of Origin and Service Instructions. Priority RUQE	Sent At 4.30 m. To YCA By Morse		ZL7 15 Service.	Date 0
			(Signature of "Franking Officer.")	From By

APPROVED

TO YCA BUZO RUFU

Sender's Number.	Day of Month.	In reply to Number.	
* MW 15	15		AAA

Morning situation report AAA
Posts in E 29d heavily
shelled AAA Also by
TM about E 30c 95.85 AAA
Weather fine wind slight

Addsd YCA repeated BUZO
RUFU

From RUQE
Place
Time 4.17 AM

The above may be forwarded as now corrected. (Z)

Censor. Signature of Addressor or person authorised to telegraph in his name.
[illegible] Capt
Bde. Major

* This line, except AAA, should be erased if not required.

Wt. W 3253/P511. 500,000 Pads. 1/18. B. & S. Ltd. (E2389.)

"A" Form
MESSAGES AND SIGNALS.

Army Form C. 2121
(In pads of 100.)

No. of Message 56

Prefix SB Code DD m.	Words	Charge.	This message is on a/c of:	Recd. at ......m.
Office of Origin and Service Instructions	12	1		
Priority / RUQE	Sent At 4 22 p m. To YCA By Mile		......Service. APP× VI (Signature of "Franking Officer")	Date 15 VIII From By

TO— YCA BUZO RUFU

Sender's Number.	Day of Month.	In reply to Number.	AAA
~~BM 2~~ EW15	15		

Situation quiet.

Added YCA repeated BUZO RUFU

From RUQE
Place
Time

The above may be forwarded as now corrected. (Z) T Frank Stawcliffe

Censor. Signature of Addressor or person authorised to telegraph in his name

* This line should be erased if not required.

Order No. 1625 Wt. W3253/ P 511 27/2 H. & K., Ltd. (E. 2634)

App^x VI(b)

CONFIDENTIAL.

120TH INFANTRY BRIGADE INTELLIGENCE SUMMARY.

RIGHT SECTOR.

6 a.m. 14:8:18 to 6 a.m. 15:8:18.

A. OUR OPERATIONS.

(i) Infantry. Our left company advanced their line slightly, which now runs E.30.a.2.4 - E.30.c.0.2.

(ii) Patrols.

(iii) Artillery. Very active firing on enemy trench system on the whole front all day. Harassing fire was increased after dark

(iv) Trench Mortars. Quiet.

(v) Machine Guns. Quiet.

(vi) Aerial. Usual formations were observed during the day.

B. ENEMY OPERATIONS.

(i) Infantry. Nil.

(ii) Artillery. Fairly quiet, became very active on our front line at E.29.d. at 9.30 p.m.

(iii) Trench Mortars. Quiet.

(iv) Machine Guns. Quiet during the day, but fairly active after dusk.

(v) Aerial. E.A. hovered over our line at 9 a.m., height 2,000 feet. E.A. flew over wood at E.28.c. at 3.40 p.m., but was driven off immediately by A.A. guns.

(vi) Visibility. Good during day. From 5 a.m. to 6 a.m. very poor.

T. Knox-Shaw

Captain,
for Intelligence Officer
120th Infantry Brigade.

15th Aug. 1918.

APPx VII

SECRET.

Administrative Instructions for LA MOTTE Area.

Ref. Sheets:
27.A., 36.A., (1/40,000). 15:8:1918.
36.A. N.E. (1,20,000).

120th Infantry Brigade Administrative Order No. 207 applies to the LA MOTTE Area with the following alterations.

(1) Delete para 1 and substitute :-
"Brigade Headquarters ... FETTLE FARM, D.24.a.8.1.
Front Line Battn.H.Qrs. .. E.26.d.9.8.
Support Battalion H.Qrs. . E.25.d.5.6.
Reserve Battn. H.Qrs. ... D.11d.7.8.
120th T. M. Battery. ... D.18.c.7.3.
211th Fd.Coy., R.E. ... D.5.c.9.1.

(2) Delete paras. 3(b), (c), (d) and substitute :-
(b) Rations can be delivered close to ~~the~~ all Company Headquarters by limber.
(c) Limbers passing the SAWMILLS,(E.19.d.1.2) by day must go singly at an interval of at least 100 yards.
(d) The main road passing the SAWMILLS is closed from 7.30 pm. to 9 pm., until further orders.

(3) Delete para. 5(b) and substitute :-
5(b) The Brigade dump is established at E.27.c.1.2.
Battalion dumps are located at E.28.a.3.2 and E.29.a.8.1.

(4) Add to para. 6(c) after "Headquarters" by 9 am.

(5) In.para.12, line 2 for D.8.a.3.0 read D.8.d.3.0.

(6) WATER.
(a) Water cart filling points exist at :-
GUNEWELE ... D.2.a.1.1.
WALLON CAPPEL U.28.b.5.7.
(b) Water points exist forward at :-
E.28.a.5.9.
E.19.b.9.7.

Captain,
Staff Captain,
120th Infantry Brigade.

15.8.1918.

War Diary APPx VIII

120th Inf.Bde. No. 120/415.

SECRET COPY NO. 5

120TH INFANTRY BRIGADE DEFENCE ORDERS

1. The following amendments are to be made to Appendix II "ANTI-AIRCRAFT DEFENCE".

   (a) After "or if in pairs" add "or single".

   (b) Add new para. as follows :-

   "An order board is to be provided at every post. Units will also arrange that the 'Letter and Colours of the Day' (particularly the latter) are communicated to each of their posts and understood by them.

   An additional reason for the restriction of A.A. Lewis Gun fire at night, particularly in back areas, is that the A.A. defences depend largely on listening for the location of hostile aeroplanes and that this is made more difficult if Lewis Guns fire unnecessarily."

2. With reference to (b) above, copies of a paper of orders for A.A.Lewis Gunners have been forwarded for distribution to each gun (vide 120th Inf. Bde. No. 120/401 dated 14:8:18 to Battalions only). This paper should be pasted to a board of piece of tin and tied to the mounting or some part of the emplacement of the gun.

3. The Letters and Colours change daily at 12 noon and are to be communicated daily to A.A.Lewis Guns as if they were Passwords.

4. ACKNOWLEDGE (Units only).

Captain,
Brigade Major,
120th Infantry Brigade.

Issued to Bns & Tmbty ~~all recipients~~ of 120th Inf. Bde. Defence Orders dated 13:8:18.

APPx 4 IX

SECRET COPY NO....

120TH INFANTRY BRIGADE ORDER NO. 209.

15:8:18.

1. On the night 17/18th August, the 10th K.O.S.B. will relieve the 11th Cameron Hrs. in Support: the 11th Cameron Hrs. will relieve the 15th K.O.Y.L.I. in the line, and the 15th K.O.Y.L.I. will move back into Reserve.

2. All arrangements for reliefs will be made between C.Os. concerned, but the relief of the 11th Cameron Hrs. by the K.O.S.B. will be complete by 9 p.m.

3. All special maps, etc. will be handed over to incoming battalions, and 11th Cameron Hrs. will take over all hot food containers and trench store petrol tins from battalion in line.

4. Battalions coming into their new positions will take over all working parties, in accordance with 120th Inf. Bde. No. 120/417 dated 14:8:18.
   All working parties for the night 17/18th, previously found by 11th Cameron Hrs., will be provided by the 10th K.O.S.B.

5. Completion of relief will be wired to Brigade H.Q. using following code words :-

   15th K.O.Y.L.I. ... ... DUCK.
   10th K.O.S.B. ... ... BOARD.
   11th Cameron Hrs. ... ... TRACK.

6. ACKNOWLEDGE.

[signature]

Captain,
Brigade Major,
120th Infantry Brigade.

Issued through
Signals
at 2 p.m.
*****

Distribution:-

Copy No. 1 ... G.O.C.
2 ... Bde.Major.
3 ... Staff Captain.
4 ... War Diary.
5 ... File.
6 ... 10th K.O.S.B.
7 ... 15th K.O.Y.L.I.
8 ... 11th Cameron Hrs.
9 ... 120th T.M.Bty.
10 ... 40th Divn. "G".
11 ... 31st Divn. "G".
12 ... 31st Divn. "Q".
13 ... 92nd Inf.Bde.
14 ... 183rd Inf.Bde.
15 ... "A" Coy. 31st M.G.Bn.
16 ... 165 Bde. R.F.A.
17 ... A.D.M.S., 31st Div.
18 ... C.R.E., 31st Div.
19 ... 40th Div. Train.
20 ... 119th Inf.Bde.
21 ... 121st Inf.Bde.
22 ... Bde.Supply Offr.
23 ... Bde.Signals.

A Form. Army Form C. 2121.
(In pads of 100.)

MESSAGES AND SIGNALS.

No. of Message 5

Prefix SB Code DAA m. | Words 30 | Charge.

Office of Origin and Service Instructions.

RUQE

Priority

Sent At 4.17 a m. To YCA By [illegible]

This message is on a/c of: Service.

APP

(Signature of "Franking Officer.")

Recd. at m. Date From By

TO YCA BUZO RUFU

Sender's Number.	Day of Month.	In reply to Number.	
* MW16	16		AAA

Morning situation report AAA situation on our front quiet aaa line advanced to E20a11 and E29d88 aaa E29d85 aaa

Addsd YCA repeated BUZO RUFU

Sent as E 30 A 11

From RUQE

Place

Time 4.5 a

The above may be forwarded as now corrected. (Z)

Censor. Signature of Addressor or person authorised to telegraph in his name.

[illegible] Brigade Major

* This line, except AAA, should be erased if not required.

Wt. W 3253/P511. 500,000 Pads. 1/18. B. & S. Ltd. (E2389.)

"A" Form.
MESSAGES AND SIGNALS.

Army Form C. 2121. (In pads of 100.)

No. of Message 47

Prefix SB Code m.	Words 31	Charge Text	This message is on a/c of:	Recd. at m.
Office of Origin and Service Instructions. Zadds. priority RUQE	Sent At 6.4 m. To ... By ...		APP Service. (Signature of "Franking Officer.")	Date From By

TO YCA BUZO ~~RUFU~~

Sender's Number.	Day of Month.	In reply to Number.	AAA
* G174	16		

Situation unchanged AAA Trench mortars have been active on 29.d.S.S. AAA Enemy aeroplane reported to be examining advanced posts on left flank.

Addsd YCA repeated BUZO RUFU

From RUQE
Place
Time

The above may be forwarded as now corrected. (Z)

T Vaughan Capt.

Censor. Signature of Addressor or person authorised to telegraph in his name.

* This line, except AAA, should be erased if not required.

Wt. W 3253/P511. 500,000 Pads. 1/18. B. & S. Ltd. (E2389.)

CONFIDENTIAL.

120TH INFANTRY BRIGADE INTELLIGENCE SUMMARY.

RIGHT SECTOR.

6 a.m. 15:8:18 to 6 a.m. 16:8:18.

A. OUR OPERATIONS.

(i)	Infantry.	Nil.
(ii)	Patrols.	See Patrol Report attached.
(iii)	Artillery.	Fairly active by day. Usual harassing fire by night.
(iv)	T.M's.	Quiet.
(v)	M.G's.	Quiet.
(vi)	Aerial.	Usual formations were observed.

B. ENEMY OPERATIONS.

(i)	Infantry.	Nil.
(ii)	Artillery.	Increased activity. Our Support Line at K.23.c. was heavily bombarded from 8.30 a.m. to 10.30 a.m. Bursts of about 20 - [illegible] mm. shells on GAUDESCURE ROAD at midnight, 12.45 a.m. and 1.55 a.m. Usual harassing fire during the night. (C.B.O. has been informed).
(iii)	M. G's.	Quieter than previous night.
(iv)	T.M's.	Nil.
(v)	Gas Shells	12.15 a.m. Gas Shelling of K.6.c. During the night, gas shells were mixed with H.E. along the Brigade Sector.
(vi)	Aerial.	E.A's. were observed to cross our lines as follows :- 1 at 8.50 a.m. 1 " 9.20 a.m. 5 " 12.10 p.m. 1 " 4.55 p.m. All were driven off by A.A. guns.

C. ENEMY INTELLIGENCE.

(i)	Movement.	Nil.
(ii)	Balloons.	Four balloons were observed up during day.

D. ENEMY DEFENCES. Listening post reports that enemy was at work on his wire opposite our line at K.6.a. and K.6.c. about 2 a.m. The wire here is an almost continuous belt of concertina.

E. MISCELLANEOUS. At 11.30 p.m. a Strombos Horn was sounded, apparently in NIEPPE FOREST or vicinity This was repeated on other horns. Respirators were worn until it was clear that no cloud gas was present.
The presence of gas was again detected about 4 a.m., though no shells were falling within 130 yds.

J. Parker 2/Lt
Intelligence Officer.
for G.O.C. 120th Infantry Brigade.

16:8:18.

P A T R O L   R E P O R T

RIGHT SECTOR

Unit.	Strength	Time of Leaving	Time of Returning	Route.	Object.	R e m a r k s.
15th K.O.Y.L.I.	1 Officer. 1 N.C.O. 5 O.Rs.	10.30 pm.	12.30 am.	K.6.c.6.4. to K.6.a.6.5.	Reconnoitre enemy wire and engage any hostile patrols.	Wire found to be an almost continuous belt of concertina. No hostile patrols were encountered.

J C Barker 2/Lt.
Intelligence Officer.
for G.O.C. 120th Inf Bde.

14/8/18.

SECRET

SHELLING REPORT

RIGHT SECTOR

6 a.m. 15:8:18 to 6 a.m. 16:8:18.

Time.	Area shelled	No. of rounds.	Calibre.	Remarks.
8.30 am. to 10.30 am.	Support Line at E.28.c.	Lively bombardment. Calibre mixed.		
2.15 pm.	K.4.a.	4	4.2	Direction of gun S.E.
M'night, 12.45 a.m and 1.15 a.m	CAUDESCURE ROAD.	Bursts of about 20 - 77 mm. shells.		
		GAS SHELLS.		
12.15 a.m.	K.6.a.	Gas Shelling. During the night gas shells were mixed with H.E. all over the Brigade front.		

J. C. Barker 2/Lt.
Intelligence Officer.
for G.O.C. 120th Infy Bde.

16/8/18.

"A" Form.
MESSAGES AND SIGNALS.

Army Form C. 2121
(In pads of 100)
No. of Message 87

Prefix SB Code BBA m. Words 14 Charge 9
Office of Origin and Service Instructions.
Priority.
3 adds RUQE

Sent At 4 14 m. To YCL By Maclean

This message is on a/c of: APP^x Service.
(Signature of "Franking Officer.")

Recd. at m. Date X1(a) From By

TO Y.C.A. RUFD. BUZO

Sender's Number.	Day of Month.	In reply to Number.	AAA
644	12		

Situation unchanged aaa Nothing to report aaa Added all Concerned.

From RUQE
Place
Time

The above may be forwarded as now corrected. (Z)
Censor. Signature of Addressor or person authorised to telegraph in his name.

*This line, except A A A, should be erased if not required.

Wt. W 3253/P511. 500,000 Pads 1/18. B. & S. Ltd. (E2389.)

"A" Form.
(In pads of 1...)

MESSAGES AND SIGNALS.

No. of Message 17

Prefix S.B. Code D.F.A. m. | Words 48 | Charge.

Office of Origin and Service Instructions.

RUQE

Priority

Sent At 4.36 a m. To YCA By Mole

This message is on a/c of: APPX XI Service.

(Signature of "Franking Officer.")

Recd. at ... m. Date ... From ... By ...

TO YCA BUZO RUFU

Sender's Number.	Day of Month.	In reply to Number.	AAA
* MW 17	17		

Morning situation report AAA

Left Coy heavily shelled about 11.45 pm and liaison post fr at E30 a 24 was driven out but believed now to have been re-established aaa SOS fired on this front from 11.50 pm to midnight aaa

Added YCA repeated BUZO RUFU

From RUQE
Place
Time 4.22 am

The above may be forwarded as now corrected. (Z)

Censor. Signature of Addressor or person authorised to telegraph in his name.

H.F.E. Capt. Bde Major

* This line, except AAA, should be erased if not required.

Wt. W 3253/P511. 500,000 Pads. 1/18. B. & S. Ltd. (E2389.)

CONFIDENTIAL.

Appx XI(a)

120TH INFANTRY BRIGADE INTELLIGENCE SUMMARY.

RIGHT SECTOR

6 a.m.16:8:18 to 6 a.m. 17:8:18.

A. OUR OPERATIONS.

(i) Infantry. The S.O.S. was received from the left Company at 11.40 p.m.
The left Liaison Post was forced to withdraw, but it is believed that same has now been re-established.
Full details are not yet to hand.

(ii) Patrols. Patrol Report attached.

(iii) Artillery. Fairly active.
A slow rate of fire was kept on the enemy trench system in front of our sector.

(iv) T.M's. 20 rounds were fired on hostile machine gun at E.30.d.0.6 at 4.25 a.m.
16 rounds were fired into enemy Strong Point at K.6.c.8.8.

(v) M.G's. During the day and night 6.000 rounds were fired on railways and tracks.
Low-flying E.A. was also driven off by L.G. fire at 1.5 p.m.

(vi) Aerial. Usual formations were observed over our line. One plane flew very low and fired on enemy trenches at 8.35 p.m.

B. ENEMY DEFENCES.

(i) Infantry. Fairly active.

(ii) Artillery. Increased activity.
Roads, tracks and trenches intermittently shelled by 7.7 cm. and 10.5 cm. guns.
The road at E.20.c.5.6. was shelled very heavily. Bursts of 7.7 cm. were fired on "Z" line at K.4.a.5.4. about m'night.
Road at K.5.d.central was heavily shelled at noon.
The area D.24.c. was shelled at 4.20 p.m. and 2 a.m.
20 shells - 10.5 cm. H.V. gun at 4.20 pm.
12 " - 10.5 cm. H.V. " at 2 a.m.
The gun was fired from OUTTERSTEENE ~~Sector~~ direction.
(C.B.O. has been informed).

(iii) M.G's. Quiet.

(iv) T.M's. Quiet.

(v) Gas Shells. Nil.

(vi) Aerial. E.A. flew over our new position but was driven off by L.G. fire at 1.5 p.m.
6 balloons were observed opposite our sector during the day.

(vii) Explosions. At 10 p.m. the shock of a heavy explosion was felt, but unaccompanied by any visible sign. No shelling was in progress at the time.

J. A. Barker 2/Lt.
Intelligence Officer,
for G.O.C. 120th Inf.Bde.

17:8:18.

PATROL REPORT

RIGHT SECTOR
6 a.m. 16:8:18 to 17:8:18 6 a.m.

Unit.	Strength.	Time.	Route.	Object.	Remarks.
15th K.O.Y.L.I.	1 Officer. 4 O.Rs	10 p.m. to 1.20 a.m.	K.6.a.6.0 to K.6.a.9.9. returned by same route.	To reconnoitre enemy posts.	No signs of enemy out in front. No enemy patrols seen.
11th E.Yorks R.	1 Officer. 3 O.Rs.	1 a.m. to 3.10 am.	K.6.c.5.4 to K.6.c.5.9.and returned by same route.	To reconnoitre enemy posts and obtain identifications if possible.	No enemy patrols were encountered, but voices were heard in a Northerly direction: noise ceased on investigation.
15th K.O.Y.L.I.	1 N.C.O. & 2 O.Rs. increased to 1 Offr. & 6 O.Rs.	9.30 a.m. to 11.45 a.m.	E.30.c.3.8 to E.30.c.4.0.	To examine ground in front of Coy. and locate enemy post.	Sound of a voice was heard in the direction of E.30.c.5.5. Patrol was strengthened to 1 Officer and 6 O.Rs. Investigations were made but no enemy could be found.

17/8/18.

J.L. Barker 2/Lt
Intelligence Officer.
for G.O.C. 120th Infy Bde

"A" Form.
MESSAGES AND SIGNALS.

Army Form C. 2121.
(In pads of 100.)

No. of Message.

Prefix SB Code DDP m. Words 17 Charge.

Office of Origin and Service Instructions.

Phng

RUGE

Sent
At m.
To
By

This message is on a/c of:

Service.

APPX XII (a)

(Signature of "Franking Officer.")

Recd. at m.
Date
From
By

TO YCA RUFU BUZO

Sender's Number.	Day of Month.	In reply to Number.	AAA
BM13	18		

Situation unchanged aaa Prisoners & material nil aaa added all concerned

From RUGE
Place
Time 4.15pm

The above may be forwarded as now corrected. (Z)

Censor. Signature of Addressor or person authorised to telegraph in his name.

* This line, except AAA, should be erased if not required.

Wt. W 3253/P511. 500,000 Pads 1/18. B. & S. Ltd. (E2380.)

"A" Form.
MESSAGES AND SIGNALS.

No. of Message ....

Prefix 2 KM Code DR m.	Words. 22	Charge. text	This message is on a/c of:	Recd. at 13 m.
Office of Origin and Service Instructions. RUQE	Sent At 4.8 am To YCA By Shew		.... Service. APP × XII	Date .... From .... By ....
Pri. M. 3 adds			(Signature of "Franking Officer.")	

TO	YCA	BUZO	RUFU	

Sender's Number.	Day of Month.	In reply to Number.	AAA
* MW 18	18		

Morning situation report AAA

Situation quiet and nothing to report aaa

Added YCA repeated BUZO RUFU

From RUQE
Place
Time 4 am

The above may be forwarded as now corrected. (Z)

Censor. Signature of Addressor or person authorised to telegraph in his name

* This line, except AAA, should be erased if not required.

Wt. W 2252/P511. 500,000 Pads. 1/18. B. & S. Ltd. (E2388)

APPX XII (b)
War Diary

CONFIDENTIAL.

120TH INFANTRY BRIGADE INTELLIGENCE SUMMARY.

R I G H T   S E C T O R

6 a.m. 17:8:18 to 6 a.m. 18:8:18.

A. OUR OPERATIONS.

(i) Infantry. Nil.
(ii) Patrols. See report attached.
(iii) Artillery. Slow rate of fire maintained throughout period.
(iv) M.G's. 2000 rounds were fired on tracks and trenches on a line G.24.d.2.1. - G.24.d.8.8.
(v) T.M's. Quiet.
(vi) Aerial. The usual formations were observed over the enemy's lines. In every case they were engaged by A.A. guns, but no combats were seen.

B. ENEMY OPERATIONS.

(i) Infantry. Inactive.
(ii) Artillery. Active.
Area K.5.a.8.8. was shelled with 7.7 cm. during afternoon.
Left Company received considerable attention, and frequent bursts throughout the period.
Centre Company was shelled with 4.2 cm. and 5.9 cm., mixed with gas shells, which fell mostly between the front and "Z" line.
The Right Company, "Z" line, was heavily shelled by 5.9 cm. about 3 p.m., also from 2.15 a.m. to 3.15 a.m.

(iii) M.G's. Fairly quiet.
Left Coy. report gun to be firing on No. 2 Mule Track from North.
(iv) T.M's. Quiet.
E.M. fired with accuracy on Left Coy. at 11.45 p.m. True bearing on flash was 106° from E.29.d.6.7.
(v) Gas Shells. One shell on Left Coy. at 3 a.m.
Gas shells were fired on Right Coy. about midnight.
(vi) Aerial. E.A's crossed the line at - 8.40 a.m. and 9 a.m. These were immediately driven off by A.A. fire. Height 3,000 feet.
(vii) Balloons. Balloons were seen up at the following times :-
1 up from 5 a.m. to 6.30 a.m.
2 " " 7.30 am. to 8.5 a.m.
3 " " 12 noon to 12.15 a.m.

C. ENEMY INTELLIGENCE.

(i) Lights. Enemy put up a quantity of double red lights along the front at 8.30 p.m. and 5 a.m., with the result that his artillery opened on a line from K.5.b.9.8. to K.5.d.3.4.
During his artillery action, he sent up white lights which burst into stars.

D. **ENEMY DEFENCES.**

(i) New Work.

A trench has been dug approximately 60 yds. in length from F.25.c.8.5., and running north.

E. **MISCELLANEOUS.**

(i) Identifications. Left Brigade report " Shoulder strap and identicy disc from German killed gives identification 7th Company 2nd Battn. 111th I.R. ", which was obtained at E.24.c.20.08.

(ii) Visibility.
Poor. Ground mist.

[signature]

Intelligence Officer,
for G.O.C. 1[illegible]th Inf.Bde.

18:3:18.

"A" Form.
Army Form C. 2121.
(In pads of 100.)

MESSAGES AND SIGNALS.

No. of Message 16

Prefix 1 MB.	Code DX	m.	Words. 19	Charge.	This message is on a/c of:	Recd. at 2.12 m.
Office of Origin and Service Instructions.			Sent		Service.	Date
2 XB			At 4.7 p.m.			From
3 adds			To YCa			By
PRIORITY			By [illegible]		Signature of "Franking Officer."	
RVQE						

APPX [illegible]

TO YCA. RUEV. BUZO

Sender's Number.	Day of Month.	In reply to Number.	AAA
* Bu 2[illegible]	[illegible]		

Situation unchanged aaa
Prisoners captured nil
aaa [illegible]

From	RVQE
Place	
Time	4.3 p

The above may be forwarded as now corrected. (Z) [illegible]

Censor. Signature of Addressor or person authorised to telegraph in his name.

*This line, except **A A A**, should be erased if not required.

Wt. W 3253/P511. 500,000 Pads 1/18. B. & S. Ltd. (E2389.)

S E C R E T

P A T R O L   R E P O R T

RIGHT SECTOR.

6 a.m. 17:8:18 to 6 a.m. 18:8:18.

Unit.	Strength.	Time.	Route.	Object.	R e m a r k s.
15th K.O.Y.L.I.	1 Officer. 14 O.Rs.	10 p.m. to 11.15 p.m.	E. 30.a.3.4 to E.30.c.4.2.	To cover relief.	No enemy seen. Relief was carried out uninterrupted.

18/8/18.

J. A. Barker 2/Lt.
Intelligence Officer
for G.O.C. 120th Infy Bde

HOSTILE SHELLING REPORT.

6 a.m. 17:8:18 to 6 a.m. 18:8:18.

RIGHT SECTOR

Enemy artillery very active.

Area K.5.a.8.8. was shelled with 7.7 cm. during afternoon.

Left Company received considerable attention and frequent bursts throughout the period.

Centre Coy. was shelled with 4.2 cm. and 5.9 cm., mixed with gas shells., which fell mostly between the front and "Z" lines.

The Right Company was heavily shelled by 5.9 cm. about 3 p.m., also from 2.15 a.m. to 3.15 a.m.

Intelligence Officer,
for G.O.C., 120th Infantry Bde.

18:8:18.

"A" Form.
MESSAGES AND SIGNALS.

Army Form C. 2121 (In pads of 100)

No. of Message

Prefix SB Code DBA m. Words 21 Charge 1

Office of Origin and Service Instructions. RUQE

Priority 3 adds

Sent At 4.16a m. To YCA By MOC

This message is on a/c of: Service.

APPx

(Signature of "Franking Officer.")

Recd. at m.

Date

From XIII

By

TO YCA BUZO RUFU

Sender's Number.	Day of Month.	In reply to Number.	AAA
G2	19		

Morning situation AAA
situation unchanged aaa 4th Army report aaa ~~[illegible]~~ all
~~[illegible]~~

Addsd YCA repeated BUZO RUFU

From RUQE
Place
Time 4.15a

The above may be forwarded as now corrected. (Z)

Censor. Signature of Addressor or person authorised to telegraph in his name.

*This line, except AAA, should be erased if not required.

Wt. W 3253/P511. 500,000 Pads. 1/18. B. & S. Ltd. (E2389.)

for GOC 15th Bde.

APP^x XIII (b)

CONFIDENTIAL.

120TH INFANTRY BRIGADE INTELLIGENCE SUMMARY.

RIGHT SECTOR.

6 a.m. 18:8:18 to 6 a.m. 19:8:18.

A. OUR OPERATIONS.

(i) Infantry Nil.
(ii) Patrols. Reports attached.
(iii) Artillery. Active.
The enemy' trenches and rear works were consistently shelled during the period.
Centre Company. Enemy's front shelled from 10 a.m. to 10.30 a.m. and from 3.20 p.m. to 3.45 p.m.
Right Company. Normal.
Left Company. Heavy shelling from 8.15 p.m. to 10.30 p.m.
(iv) T.M's. Quiet.
(v) M.G's. 3.500 rounds were fired on tracks and trenches during the period.
(vi) Aerial. Usual formations observed.
9 planes crossed enemy lines very low at 11 a.m.

B. ENEMY OPERATIONS.
(i) Infantry. Nil.
(ii) Artillery. Normal *K4a*
Area K.4.a. was shelled at 12.45 p.m., 20 rds. 5.9 Cm.
Heavy barrage was put down round our front and support lines at 1.45 p.m.
Left Coy. Heavy shelling from 8.30 p.m. to 9 p.m., otherwise quiet.
Centre Coy. Shelled by 77 mm. at 2.15 p.m., and 4.2 also from 5 p.m. to 6 p.m.
Usual bursts during period.
Right Coy. Roads in K.5.c. and d. were shelled consistently. The Coy. front was shelled by 5.9 from 11 p.m. to 3 a.m.
BEAULIEU FARM was shelled intermittenly from 6 p.m. to 8 p.m. The guns that shelled the front line are firing from S.E. direction. (C.B.O. has been informed).
(iii) M.G's. Quiet during day.
One gun active at 11 a.m., which was firing from PONT RONDIN.
No. 1 Mule Track and right "Z" line were swept about 9 p.m.
Gun was being fired from *K12a*
(iv) T.M's. Quiet.
(v) Gas Shells. 3 fell immediately behind advanced posts of Left Coy. at 2 p.m.
(vi) Aerial. Only one plane crossed our lines during the day - at 6 p.m. but was not seen to return.

C. ENEMY INTELLIGENCE.
(i) Movement. Nil.
(ii) Explosions. An explosion was felt and fire observed due East *of E29d E.1.*
A slight explosion was observed E.S.E. at 2.15 p.m.
(iii) Balloons. 3 balloons ascended when our barrage commenced at 11 a.m. 5 were observed up at 1.30 p.m.
(iv) Lights. Green and red lights were fired along our front at 2 p.m. and 8 p.m.
D. ENEMY DEFENCES. Nil.
Visibility. Low until 10 a.m. when sun came out and ground mist cleared. Low visibility at 7.30 p.m.

19/8/18

Intelligence Officer
for G.O.C. 120th Infy Bde

PATROL REPORTS
RIGHT SECTOR.
From 6 a.m. 18:8:18 to 6 a.m. 19.:8:18.

Unit	Strength	Time	Route.	Object.	Remarks.
11th Cameron Hrs.	1 N.C.O. 3 Men.	9.30 p.m. to 12 m'nt.	E.29.b.8.6. E.30.a.1.6. E.30.3.5. E.30.a.3.3. turned north re-entering line at E.29.b.8.0.	To get in touch with enemy.	No signs of enemy. When patrol was at E.30.a.1.6. they were fired on by sniper, approx. E.30.a.4.0. Search was made but sniper's post could not be located.
10th E.Yorks R.	1 Officer. 2 Men.	11.15 p.m. to 12.55 a.m.	K.6.c.4.6. K.11.b.7.9.	To ascertain whether or no there are any enemy posts this side of the BECQUE.	Having gone forward from K.6.c.4.6. we set out in a direction E. crossing a ditch 20 yds. N.E. of a small bush, we there found a tape which we followed for some distance, we then saw the BECQUE on our right, and so proceeded to follow it, after having walked between 250 to 300 yds. we moved to our right, and there discovered a German post unoccupied, but containing a supply of German stick bombs. Continuing to the right, we discovered two enemy dug-outs, both of which had appearence of having been used lately, but were then empty. Here the BECQUE broadened and from there to the road there was apparently no bridge. We then returned to our line.
11th Cameron Hrs.	1 Officer. 3 Men.	2 a.m. to 3.15 a.m.	E.29.b.8.0. E.30.a.1.0.	To locate sniper that fired on No. 1 Patrol.	The sniper fired, but he could not be located, owing to the thigh-high thistles & corn round about that post.

19/8/18.

[signature] Intelligence Officer
for G.O.C. 120th Inf Bde

"A" Form.

S B MESSAGES AND SIGNALS.

Army Form C. 2121.
(In pads of 100.)

No. of Message 10

Prefix Code DA m.	Words 14	Charge.	This message is on a/c of:	Recd. at m.
Office of Origin and Service Instructions. 3 adds Priority RUQE	Sent At m. To By		APPX Service. (Signature of "Franking Officer.")	Date From By

TO	YCA	BUZO	RUFU

Sender's Number.	Day of Month.	In reply to Number.	AAA
MW 20	20		

Morning situation AAA
Situation normal

Addsd YCA repeated BUZO RUFU

From RUQE
Place
Time

The above may be forwarded as now corrected. (Z)

Censor. Signature of Addressor or person authorised to telegraph in his name.

* This line, except AAA, should be erased if not required.

Wt. W 3253/P511. 500,000 Pads. 1/18. B. & S. Ltd. (E2389.)

"A" Form.
MESSAGES AND SIGNALS.

Army Form C. 2121.
(In pads of 100)

No. of Message 117

Prefix SB Code 87 m. Words 96 Charge 1

Office of Origin and Service Instructions.
RVQE
PLY
2 adds ...

Sent
At 4.39 m.
To YCA
By ...

This message is on a/c of: .... Service.

(Signature of "Franking Officer.")

Recd. at ... m.
Date 20 VIII 18
From
By

App^x^ XIV (a)

TO YCA ...

Sender's Number.	Day of Month.	In reply to Number.	AAA
*B442	20		

Situation apparently unchanged aaa Patrols moving towards KEW CROSS but no report yet received aaa addsd YCA Rptd all concerned

From
Place RVQE
Time 4.25 pm

The above may be forwarded as now corrected. (Z)

Censor. Signature of Addressor or person authorised to telegraph in his name.

* This line, except AAA, should be erased if not required.

Wt. W 3253/P511. 500,000 Pads. 1/18. B. & S. Ltd. (E2389.)

CONFIDENTIAL.

120TH INFANTRY BRIGADE INTELLIGENCE SUMMARY.

RIGHT SECTOR.

6 a.m. 19:8:18 to 6 a.m. 20:8:18.

A. OUR OPERATIONS.

(i) Infantry. No change on Brigade front.
Progress was made by troops on right at 10 a.m., and later at 5 p.m.
Right Coy. of Left Battalion have now advanced their right flank along approximate line _ E.30.a.07.30 _ E.29.b.05.90.
A liaison post consisting of 4 men from our left Coy., and 1 N.C.O and 5 men from Left Bn. has been formed.

(ii) Patrols. Our patrols are periodically moving over front day and night with a view of obtaining information and knowledge of enemy's intentions
A patrol went out at 10 a.m. to reconnoitre positions N.W. of the BECQUE. Two hostile M.G's fired on patrol from S.E. side of BECQUE. No casualties were suffered. Strength of patrol 1 Officer, 1 N.C.O. & 1 man.
Later, at 10 p.m. another patrol was arranged to take out a Lewis gun. It went forward to K.11.b8.7.where they fired on a troublesome gun, and effectively silenced same. On its return, this patrol stated they had observed another gun in a barn at K.11.b.9.4. 8 rifle grenades and 1 L.G.magazine were sufficient for this gun; the patrol then pushed forward to ascertain, if possible, the damage. The barn was in silence.
Whilst on the bank of the BECQUE this patrol was enfiladed by a M.G. fired from approx. K.12.a.78.90.
The Centre Coy. patrol of 2 officers at ~~xx~~2.15 p.m. reported they had shot a Boche. It appears that he, on being asked to surrender commenced shouting, and got his rifle, evidently with the intention of firing. As he had comrades apparently at hand, there was no alternative but to shoot him and retire. Circumstances prevented an immediate search.
There appear~~s~~ to be no posts W. of BECQUE.
For further patrols, see attached report.

(iii) Artillery. Our artillery was active during period.
Areas in rear of line were systematically harassed.
A barrage opened at 5 p.m. from approx. K.12.a. to K.17.a.

(iv) T.M's. Quiet.

(v) M.G's. Quiet during day. Occasional bursts of fire during night.

(vi) Aerial. Active throughout period. Strong formations flew over enemy lines at 6.30 a.m. One of our 'planes brought down an enemy balloon in flames at 1.45 p.m. Three machines flew very low, firing into enemy's lines at 5.30 p.m.

B. ENEMY OPERATIONS.

(i) Infantry. Nil.

(ii) Artillery. Normal.

Front shelled at intervals. Whizzbangs were very troublesome on left Coy. front, especially from 1.20 a.m. to 2.5 a.m.

Gas shells/ were occasionally mixed with H.E. over our front.

Area K.11.b.7.9. shelled from 10 a.m. to 4 p.m. with 5.9 and 4.2.

Right Support Coy. shelled at 11.30 a.m. and intermittently during day. A slow rate of fire by 4.2s. was kept up all day on GAUDESCURE/ area and K.5.b. CAUDESCURE area again shelled from 1 a.m. to 3.30 a.m. No. 1 Mule Track, GOMBERT FM. and BEAULIEU FM. shelled during the afternoon.

(iii) M.G's. Quiet during day, but active at night.

M.G. suspected in farm at K.11.b.9.4. was silenced by 6 rifle grenades and 1 magazine.

M.G. fire from K.12.a.10.75 very active.

(iv) T.M's. Quiet.

(v) Aerial. Below normal.

One E.A. shot down in enemy's lines at 10 am.

C. ENEMY INTELLIGENCE.

Movement. Individual movement observed during the morning.

D. MISCELLANEOUS

(i) The Right Coy. of Battalion on left have advanced their right flank along approx. line E.30.a.07.80 - E.29.b.95.50. A liaison post has been formed.

(ii) A fire on extreme right of front was started by our shelling, and burned from 5.45 a.m. to 6.30 a.m.

(iii) Two enemy O.B's. were brought down in flames by our planes about 11.30 a.m. Two other balloons seen to fire on the right about midday; cause not known.

[signature]
Intelligence Officer,
for G.O.C. 120th Inf.Bde.

20:8:18

SECRET

COPY NO. 4

120TH INFANTRY BRIGADE ORDER NO. 210.

20:8:18.

1. The 120th Infantry Brigade will take over the Right Battalion Sector of the 92nd Infantry Brigade on the left to-night.

2. The new Northern Brigade Boundary of the Brigade will run as follows :-

   E.22.central - Road Junction E.30.b.0.7. - F.26.c.0.0. - L.3.a.0.0. - L.5.d.0.5.

3. The 10th K.O.S.B. will take over this new sector from the 10th East Yorks Regt., and will carry on the latter's Patrol Scheme.
   All arrangements will be made between C.Os. concerned. Special maps, etc. will be taken over as usual.

4. The 11th Cameron Hrs. will relieve the attached Company of the 10th East Yorks Regt. on the right to-night. On relief this attached Company will move back to TIR ANGLAIS.
   The most careful arrangements must be made to ensure that the strictest liaison is maintained with the unit on the right.

5. The 15th K.O.Y.L.I. will move from TIR ANGLAIS to the Support Area, moving one Company to the "Z" Line, one in the area between "Z" and Reserve Line, keeping two in the Reserve Line.
   The camp at TIR ANGLAIS will be left standing, and will be handed over to the 10th East Yorks Regt.

6. Completion of relief will be wired as under :-

10th K.O.S.B.	...	STICK.
15th K.O.Y.L.I.	...	NO.
11th Cameron Hrs.	...	BILLS.

7. ACKNOWLEDGE.

Issued through
Signals
at 8.30 p.m.

Captain,
Brigade Major,
120th Infantry Brigade.

Distribution :-

Copy No.					
1	...	G.O.C.	12.	...	40th Div. "G".
2	...	Bde. Major.	13	...	92nd Inf.Bde.
3	...	Staff Captain.	14	...	183rd Inf.Bde.
4	...	War Diary.	15	...	223rd Fd.Coy.R.E.
5	...	File.	16	...	C.R.E., 31st Divn.
6	...	10th K.O.S.B.	17	...	A.D.M.S. 31st Divn.
7	...	15th K.O.Y.L.I.	18	...	165 Bde.R.F.A.
8	...	11th Cameron Hrs.	19	...	"D" Coy. 31st M.G.Bn
9	...	120th T.M.Bty.	20	...	Bde. Signals.
10	...	31st Divn. "G".	21	...	Bde.Supply Officer.
11	...	31st Divn. "Q".	22	...	"X" 31st M.T.M.Bty.

1/2B
2XB

"A" Form.

Army Form C. 2121.
(In pads of 100.)

MESSAGES AND SIGNALS.

No. of Message 10

Prefix .... Code DBK m. | Words 36 | Charge. each

Office of Origin and Service Instructions. 3 adds

RUQE

Sent At 4 17 a m. To YCA By Morley

This message is on a/c of: 7 1 7 Service.

(Signature of "Franking Officer.")

Recd. at ...... m. Date ...... From ...... By ......

TO YCA

APPx XVI

Sender's Number.	Day of Month.	In reply to Number.	AAA
* BM 13	2		

no change in situation of right Bde general situation aaa Heavy hostile shelling about K5b K6a aaa 3 prisoners 188 Regt captured about K6b (already reported) aaa

Addsd YCA rptd RUFU and BUZO

From RUQE
Place
Time 4.10 am.

The above may be forwarded as now corrected. (Z)

Censor. Signature of Addressor or person authorised to telegraph in his name.

* This line, except AAA, should be erased if not required.

Wt. W 3253/P511. 500,000 Pads. 1/18. B. & S. Ltd. (E2389.)

Appx XV(a)

CONFIDENTIAL.

[illegible] INFANTRY BRIGADE INTELLIGENCE SUMMARY

RIGHT SECTOR.

8 a.m. 20:9:18 to 8 a.m. 21:9:18.

A. OUR OPERATIONS.

(i) Infantry.

The general line was advanced by patrol action and by 7.15 p.m. the line of [illegible] - [illegible] CROSS - F.25.c.9.5 was reached. Considerable amount of M.G. fire was met with from K.8.d.

3 prisoners - stretcher bearers of 188 Regt. - were captured about K.8.b.

(ii) Artillery.

Harassing fire was kept up on L.2.a., F.25.c. & d. and [illegible], during the afternoon.

Night firing was carried out from 8.00 p.m. to 4.30 a.m. on roads and tracks.

(iii) T.M's. Nil.

(iv) M.G's. Little activity.

(v) Aerial. Usual formations seen.

B. ENEMY OPERATIONS.

(i) Infantry. Only slight opposition met with during the day.

(ii) Artillery. Considerable shelling of forward areas, especially in K.13.d. and K.8.b., and on the "Z" line.

(iii) T.M's. Quiet.

(iv) M.G's. Considerable activity from K.8.d.

(v) Aerial. 8.35 p.m. one enemy aeroplane over K.2[illegible], driven off by A.A. fire.

(vi) Movement. None observed.

(vii) Snipers. Only slight activity, chiefly from K.8.d.

(viii) General. Enemy was continually sending up green and red lights.

Explosion observed in F.19.d.4.3.

(B.) [illegible]

21:9:18.

For Intelligence Officer
[illegible] Infantry Bde

App x XVII

S E C R E T.

COPY NO. 4.

120TH INFANTRY BRIGADE ORDER NO. 221.

31-8-18.

1. The 31st Division has reached the line F.14.c.3.8. along the Road through BLEU and BRACKEN FARM and the track to F.23.c.9.5. - NEW CROSS - PONT RONDIN - VIERHOUCK.
The 92nd Infantry Brigade report little opposition on their front. The 94th Infantry Brigade report some opposition from their left.
The 29th Division line runs North from HULLEBERT FARM.
The 61st Division left is at GHENT HOUSE in E.12.d., and they are moving forward.

2. The next bound will be the line Road from CUTLET CORNER to SECRET CORNER - F.26.c. thence back to PONT RONDIN.
The advance to this line will be made at an hour to be selected by Brigadier CENTRE Brigade and notified later.
Touch must be maintained between left of 120th Infantry Brigade and right of 92nd Infantry Brigade, and 10th K.O.S.B. and 11th Cameron Hrs. will conform to movement on their left, swinging forward so as to reach the line PONT RONDIN - SECRET CORNER.
The 11th Cameron Hrs., as already ordered, will keep in touch with the left of the 183rd Infantry Brigade which is at present at GHENT HOUSE in E.12.d. and is advancing, and will try and swing forward their right to conform to the movement of the 183rd Infantry Brigade, taking the line of the PONT RONDIN - NEUF BERQUIN Road as the limit of their advance at present.

3. The strictest liaison must be kept with flanking Units and reports sent in as frequently as possible.

4. ACKNOWLEDGE.

Issued through
Signals
at 12 noon.

Captain,
Brigade Major,
120th Infantry Brigade.

DISTRIBUTION:-

Copy No 1 ... G.O.C.
2 ... Brigade Major.
3 ... Staff Captain.
4 ... War Diary.
5 ... File.
6 ... 10th K.O.S.B.
7 ... 15th K.O.Y.L.I.
8 ... 11th Cam. Hrs.
9 ... 120th T. M. Battery.
10 ... 92nd Inf. Bde.
11 ... 183rd Inf. Bde.
12 ... 168th Bde. R.F.A.

APPX XVIII

SECRET

COPY NO. 4

120TH INFANTRY BRIGADE ORDER NO. 212.

21:8:18.

1. On night 21st/22nd, the 10th K.O.S.B. will extend their left flank northwards to F.19.d.2.6., taking over the line from the 11th E. Yorks Regt., of the 92nd Inf. Brigade, and holding R.2. and R.3. subsectors with 3 companies in the line.

2. After completion of relief, the northern boundary of the Brigade will run as follows :-

E.16.central - Road Junction E.18.c.1.2. - F.27.central.

3. All arrangements for relief will be arranged direct between C.Os. concerned.

4. All maps, aeroplane photos, dumps, etc. will be taken over, receipts given, and duplicates forwarded to this office.

5. 10th K.O.S.B. will submit disposition sketch within 24 hours of relief.

6. Completion of relief will be wired by code word :-

GILDY.

7. 15th K.O.Y.L.I. will be prepared to furnish carrying parties for the two battalions in the line to-night. All arrangements will be made direct.

8. On night 22nd/23rd, 119th Infantry Brigade will relieve the 10th K.O.S.B. in R.3. subsector, and the 15th K.O.Y.L.I. will relieve the 11th Camerons in R.1. subsector. The inter-battalion boundary between 10th K.O.S.B. and 15th K.O.Y.L.I. will then be brought further South.

9. ACKNOWLEDGE.

Captain,
Brigade Major,
120th Infantry Brigade.

21:8:18.

Issued through
Signals
at 3.45 p.m.
****

DISTRIBUTION:-

Copy. No.		Copy. No.	
1	G.O.C.	12	31st Div. "Q".
2	Bde. Major	13	92nd Inf.Bde.
3	Staff Capt.	14	183rd Inf.Bde.
4	War Diary.	15	"D" Coy. 31 M.G.Bn.
5	File.	16	165 Bde.R.F.A.
6	10th K.O.S.B.	17	A.D.M.S. 31st Div.
7	15th K.O.Y.L.I.	18	C.R.E.
8	11th Camerons.	19	223 Field Coy.R.E.
9	120th T.M.Bty.	20	Bde. Supply Officer.
10	40th Div. "G".	21	"X" 31 T.M.Bty.
11	31st Div. "G".	22	Bde. Signals.

"A" Form.
C. 2121.
(In pads of 100.)

MESSAGES AND SIGNALS.

No. of Message 22

Prefix SB Code DDa m.	Words 20	Charge 1	This message is on a/c of:	Recd. at m.
Office of Origin and Service Instructions. Priority gadd RUQE	Sent At 4.36a m. To JCH By		Service (Signature of "Franking Officer.")	Date From By

TO YCA BUZO AAAX

Sender's Number.	Day of Month.	In reply to Number.	
* G 11	22		AAA

Morning situation AAA Situation normal aaa Considerable gas shelling forward area.

Addsd YCA repeated BUZO RUFU

From RUQE
Place
Time

The above may be forwarded as now corrected. (Z)

Censor. Signature of Addressor or person authorised to telegraph in his name.

*This line, except **A A A**, should be erased if not required.

Wt. W 3253/P511. 500,000 Pads. 1/18. B. & S. Ltd. (E2389.)

GOC Bde.

"A" Form.

Army Form C. 2121.
(In pads of 100.)

MESSAGES AND SIGNALS.

No. of Message 119

Prefix ...... Code ...... m. | Words 37 | Charge.

Office of Origin and Service Instructions.

RUQE

3 adds

Sent At 4.30 m. To ...... By ......

This message is on a/c of: ...... Service. (Signature of "Franking Officer.")

Recd. at ...... m. Date 22. VIII. 18 From ...... By ......

SIGNALS

TO

APPx XVIII (a) XIX (a)

Sender's Number. BM45 | Day of Month. 22 | In reply to Number. | AAA

From

Place

Time

The above may be forwarded as now corrected. (Z)

Censor. Signature of Addressor or person authorised to telegraph in his name.

* This line, except **AAA**, should be erased if not required.

Wt. W 3253/P511. 500,000 Pads. 1/18. B. & S. Ltd. **(E2389.)**

APPx ~~XXXXXXX~~ XIX (b)

CONFIDENTIAL.

120TH INFANTRY BRIGADE INTELLIGENCE SUMMARY.
RIGHT SECTOR.
6 a.m. 21:8:18 to 6 a.m. 22:8:18.

A. OUR OPERATIONS.

(i) Infantry. Very active/ Patrol action.
One prisoner was taken by our left Battn. of the 188 Regt.

(ii) Patrols. Front constantly patrolled to keep in touch with the enemy.
~~(For further patrols see attached report)~~.

(iii) Artillery. Fairly active. Harassing fire was maintained during period on enemy's rear areas.

(iv) T.M's. Quiet.

(v) M.G's. Fairly quiet.

(vi) Aerial. Usual formations observed during the period.
At 7 p.m. strong formations patrolled the enemy lines.

B. ENEMY OPERATIONS.

(i) Infantry. Nil. Scouts very active.

(ii) Snipers. Snipers active, especially on left Battn.front.

(iii) Artillery. Very active on front line. Heavy barrage put down on forward companies of left Battalion at 6 p.m. "Z" line and tracks leading from "Z" line to front line were harassed during the night, especially in the neighbourhood of KEW CROSS. Area E.30.a. was heavily bombarded from 1.45 p.m. to 2.15 p.m. by 5.9s.

(iv) M.G's. Quiet during the day. Active during night sweeping roads and tracks. M.G. nest approx. F.25.d.4.0.

(v) T.M's. Quiet.

(vi) Gas Shells. On whole of Right Battalion front, gas shells were often mixed with H.E. At 2 p.m. about 10 gas shells fell between the BROQUE and COURONNE - PONT RONDIN road. At 11 p.m. KEW CROSS neighbourhood was very heavily shelled with gas, which slowly drifted across our front, and respirators had to be worn at intervals until 5 a.m. The gas could easily be detected, as it caused violent sneezing.

(vii) Aerial. Normal. Two 'planes patrolled our front from noon to 2 p.m. making repeated attempts to cross our lines, but were driven off each time by A.A. fire.

(viii) Balloons. 11 a.m. One balloon was seen up at a bearing of 88°. 1.30 p.m. to 4 p.m. 5 enemy balloons were seen up at bearings of 77°, 88°, 94°, 100° and 107°.
The above bearings were taken from E.28.a.4.5.

C. ENEMY INTELLIGENCE.

(i) Lights. Red, green and white lights were fired along the Brigade front. The white lights ascended to a great height and were very bright.
From 11.30 p.m. onwards "flaming onions" went up at intervals from the direction of "RUE PROVOST".

(ii) Movement. Individual movement observed all along our line.

J. W. Barker

for Brigadier-General, S/Keiw

22:8:18. Commanding 120th Infantry Brigade.

APPx ~~XXXXIII~~ XX

S E C R E T COPY NO. 4

120TH INFANTRY BRIGADE ORDER NO. 213.

22:8:18.

1. At 8 p.m. 22nd August, G.O.C. 40th Division will assume Command of the front at present held by 31st Division from VIERHOUCK to F.14.c.3.6.

2. On night 22nd/23rd the following reliefs and readjustments of the line will take place on the 120th Infantry Brigade front :-
   (a) The Royal Inniskillings, of the 119th Inf.Bde., will take over the R.3. Sector from the 10th K.O.S.B., from F.25.a.7.0. northwards.
   (b) The 10th K.O.S.B. will then extend their Southern boundary to L.1.c.0.8., taking over from part of the 11th Cameron Hrs.
   (c) The 15th K.O.Y.L.I. will relieve the 11th Cameron Hrs in the R.1. Subsector.

3. After completions of reliefs, the Brigade boundaries will be as follows :-
   (a) <u>Northern Boundary</u> :-
   F.25.c.7.0. - Road Junction E.30.b.0.5. - E.22 central - E.22.a.3.5. - along LA MOTTE road to E.20.b.7.0. - E.13.c.5.5. - E.17.a.0.0.
   (b) <u>Southern Boundary</u> :-
   L.7.c.9.0. - Road Junction K.11.b.9.1. - K.11.b.3.4. - K.4.a.8.0. - K.2.a.3.0. - K.1.c.5.2. - along track to CHATEAU in D.30.c.
   (c) <u>Inter-battalion Boundary</u> :-
   L.2.c.2.1. - Road Junction L.1.c.0.8. - GARE BAUDGHE (inclusive to Southern Battalion) to East end of Light Railway in F.25.a.

4. The newly-adjusted fronts will be held by each battalion with two companies in the forward area, and two companies in support, in or about the "Z" line.
   The 11th Cameron Hrs. will keep one company in the "Z" Line astride the inter-battalion boundary, one company about E.27, and two companies in the Reserve Line.
   Battalion Headquarters of battalions in the line and reserve will remain as they are at present.

5. All details of reliefs will be arranged direct between C.Os. concerned.

6. All special maps of the front, aeroplane photos, defence schemes, details of dumps, etc. will be handed over on relief.

7. Particular care will be given to maintenance of liaison posts on flanks, especially on the right of the Brigade with the 183rd Infantry Bde.

8. Battalions will forward sketches of their dispositions to these Headquarters within 24 hours of completion of reliefs.

9. Completion of relief will be notified to these Headquarters by the following code words :-

   15th K.O.Y.L.I. ... ... ROACH.
   10th K.O.S.B. ... ... PERCH.
   11th Cameron Hrs. ... ... BREAM.

10. Command of the present R.3. subsector will pass to 119th Inf. Bde. at 7 a.m. on 23rd August, up to which hour all

relieving /

troops in the present 120th Inf. Bde. forward area will be under the orders of G.O.C. 120th Infantry Bde.

11. Full details as to tactical and administrative policies to be adopted on the front will be issued later.

12. ACKNOWLEDGE.

Issued through
Signals
at 1.30 p.m.
=========

Captain,
Brigade Major,
120th Infantry Brigade.

<u>DISTRIBUTION</u> :-

Copy No.		
1	...	G.O.C.
2	...	Brigade Major.
3	...	Staff Captain.
4	...	War Diary.
5	...	File.
6	...	10th K.O.S.B.
7	...	15th K.O.Y.L.I.
8	...	11th Cameron Hrs.
9	...	120th T.M.Bty.
10	...	40th Divn. "G".
11	...	40th Divn. "Q".
12	...	119th Inf. Bde.
13	...	121st Inf. Bde.
14	...	183rd Inf. Bde.
15	...	223rd Field Coy. R.E.
16	...	229th Field Coy. R.E.
17	...	C.R.E., 40th Division.
18	...	A.D.M.S. 40th Division.
19	...	-Ditto-
20	...	40th Divnl. Train.
21	...	Bde. Supply Officer.
22	...	Bde. Signals

=========================

ADMINISTRATIVE INSTRUCTIONS No. 213.

RIGHT BRIGADE.

Ref. Sheets 27 and 36a.

1. Transport Lines of battalions are xxxxxxxxxx located at PAPOTE - D.16.d.1.2.
Brigade Headquarters Transport Lines are at present at D.8.d.3.1 but will move shortly to D.16.d.1.2.

2. Water. Is obtained from following water cart refilling points :-
(1) CUNEWELE.
(2) HAZEBROUCK.

3. Ammunition. (a) The Divisional Dump is situated in the lines of the S.A.A. Section, 40th D.A.C., at U.21.b.6.5.
(b) Brigade dumps are established at :-
Brigade Hd.Qrs ... D.24.a.8.1.
"B" Ride ... E.27.c.2.3.
(c) Demands for ammunition will be submitted to reach Brigade Headquarters by 8 am. daily.

4. (a) R.E.Dumps.
Divisional Dump ... V.19.c.8.7.
Brickstacks Dump ... E.20.b.7.0.
Forestry Dump ... E.28.c.2.3.
Operation Dump ... E.27.d.9.9.
(end of No.2 Mule track).
(b) All indents for material will be forwarded to reach Brigade Headquarters by 9 am. daily. Brigade Headquarters will submit requirements to affiliated R.E. Company.

5. Railhead.
E B B L I N G H E M.

6. Refilling Point.
Location of re-filling point and No.3 Coy., A.S.C. Train will be notified later.

7. Reserve rations and water.
Rations are dumped for the LA MOTTE Defences at -
D.30.d.2.6.
E.20 central.

8. Tramway System.
Runs from E.20.b.7.0 to K.3.a.3.8 with branches running East as under :-
(1) E.27.a.0.4 to E.27.b.1.8.
(2) E.27.c.2.3 forking at E.27.c.7.3 to E.27.d.9.9 and K.3.b.9.8.
Push trucks are kept under a guard at E.20.b.7.0 and receipts must be given for all trucks issued.

9. Baths. A bath is being erected near FETILE FARM, D.24.a.7.6., for the use of the Reserve Battalions in the line. It will have capacity for 100 men per hour.

10. Clean Clothing Store. Divisional Clean Clothing Store will be established at WALLON CAPPEL.
Units indent direct on the Divisional Baths Officer and draw from Divisional Stores with 1st line transport

11. Gassed Clothing. Such men as have been affected with Yellow

Cross/

Cross Gas will be sent to the Divisional Main Dressing Station with a certificate signed by an officer stating that their clothing has been affected, when fresh clothing will be issued.

12. Salvage. All salvage collected will be sent by units direct to Divisional Salvage dump at WALLON CAPPEL. A solder kiln for the recovery of solder is situated at Divisional Salvage Dump.

13. Ordnance. D.A.D.O.S. opens at WALLON CAPPEL at 12 noon, 24th August.

14. Medical Arrangements.

(a) 135th Fd. Ambce. will be responsible for the evacuation from forward area.

(b) Relay Posts - E.19.b.8.3.
K.3.a.3.7.
K.4.a.5.4.
A. D. S. - D.18.a.5.3.
Reserve A.D.S. - D.9.d.1.8.
M. D. S. - C.5.a.6.9.

15. Provost Arrangements.

Locations of Battle stops, P. of W. cages and Stragglers Posts :-

First Position - Battle Stops.

D.20.d.0.3 - D.20.b.9.4 - D.16.b.4.1 - D.10.b.6.7 - D.11.b.3.7.

Stragglers Collecting Station and Advanced P. of W. Cage :-

D.9.b.4.2.

16. Divisional Canteens.

Wallon CAPPEL	.....	U.23.c.20.35.
LE GRAND HAZARD	.....	D.13.b.3.9.

17. Cemeteries.

No burials will take place except in the cemeteries authorised in Corps and Divisional Routine Orders.

18. Divisional Reception Camp.

Remains in present location.

T. Knox-Shaw

Captain,
Staff Captain,
120th Infantry Brigade.

23.8.1918.

DISTRIBUTION:-

Copy No. 1	...	G.O.C.
2	...	Brigade Major.
3	...	Staff Captain.
4	...	War Diary.
5	...	File.
6	...	10th K.O.S.B.
7	...	15th K.O.Y.L.I.
8	...	11th Cameron Hrs.
9	...	120th T. M. Bty.
10	...	40th Division "G".
11	...	119th Inf. Bde.
12	...	[illegible]rd Inf. Bde.
13	...	[illegible]rd Field Coy. R.E.
14	...	1[illegible] Bde. R.F.A.
15	...	Bde. Signals.
16	...	"D" Coy.31st M.G.Bn.

War Diary

APPX XXI

SECRET

COPY NO. 4

120TH INFANTRY BRIGADE ORDER NO. 214.

22:8:18.

1. On completion of relief to-night, the 120th Infantry Bde. line will run from COCHIN CORNER along the road PONT RONDIN - KEW CROSS - thence to F.28.c.7.4.

2. 119th Inf. Bde. are trying to-night to get on to the general line ROOSTER FARM - BECKET CORNER - CUTLET CORNER.
   183rd Inf. Bde. on our right are on the line CHAPELLE DUVELLE - RUE MONTIGNY, and from there have a defensive flank to COCHIN CORNER.

3. At 4 p.m., 23rd inst., the 120th Inf. Bde., in conjunction with 119th Inf. Bde. on the left, and 183rd Inf. Bde. on the right, will advance to the line Cross Roads L.3.c.8.4. to BECKET CORNER. This line will be continued Southwards by 183rd Bde. 15th K.O.Y.L.I. will be on the right, and 10th K.O.S.B. on the left.

4. The Right Boundary of the advance will be the line of the road from L.13.b.2.7. to Cross Roads L.3.c.8.4., on which line touch will be continuously maintained with 183rd Bde. on the right.
   The Left Boundary of the advance will be the line of the road from KEW CROSS to BECKET CORNER, on which line touch will be continuously maintained with 119th Infantry Bde.
   Inter-battalion boundary will be the line of the stream from PONT RONDIN to its junction with the LAUDICK in L.1.b.7.3., thence along the ditch from L.1.b.8.1. to L.~~1~~2.b.7.8.

5. The advance will be made with fighting patrols, supported by platoons, and will be made in two main bounds - one, to the line of the LAUDICK, and the second to the final objective.

6. Fighting patrols must push forward boldly, and must endeavour to work round any local point which is holding up the advance. To assist in this, two Stokes Mortars with teams will be allotted to each battalion. All arrangements for parties for the necessary carrying of ammunition, etc. will be made direct between O.C., 120th T.M.Battery and Battalion Commanders concerned.

7. In the event of the general advance being held up by machine gun fire from enclosures along the line of BISHOP'S CORNER - BECKET CORNER, arrangements have been made for artillery to fire a 10-minutes burst on this line of enclosures from BISHOP'S CORNER to F.28.d.7.4. when called for by Company Commanders.
   The signal for this artillery support to be put down will be the firing of 3 Very Lights in succession, fired from Company Headquarters.

8. Joint Battalion Headquarters will be formed by 15th K.O.Y.L.I. and 10th K.O.S.B. at present 15th K.O.Y.L.I. Headquarters - K.6.a.8.7.

9. The ~~xxxxxx~~ greatest attention must be paid to the forwarding of frequent reports, and to keeping the closest touch with units on flank.

10. ACKNOWLEDGE.

Issued through
Signals
at 10.30 p.m.

Captain,
Brigade Major,
120th Infantry Brigade.

"A" Form
Army Form C. 2121
(In pads of 100.)

MESSAGES AND SIGNALS.

No. of Message............

Prefix...........Code...........m. Words Charge.
Office of Origin and Service Instructions.
This message is on a/c of: ....Service.
Sent At ....m. To By
(Signature of "Franking Officer.")
Recd. at......m. Date.......... From By

APPx XXII(a)

TO: MEVI RUPE RUFU ART GROUP

Sender's Number.	Day of Month.	In reply to Number.	AAA
Bn 45	23		

Line of posts reported established as follows aaa ROOSTER FARM to L1.b73 L1d70 L7b63 aaa Touch is maintained throughout the line and with unit on right flank at COCHIN CORNER aaa Right Coy reports a line of [illegible] west of LAUDICK from BOWERY COTTAGES to L2c11 and enemy posts east of this aaa Enemy [illegible] active on this flank of the front aaa (Btn on right believed back

From
Place
Time

The above may be forwarded as now corrected. (Z)
Censor. Signature of Addressor or person authorised to telegraph in his name
* This line should be erased if not required.

Order No. 1625. Wt. W3253/ P 511. 27/2. H. & K., Ltd. (E. 2634).

Army Form C. 2121.
(In pads of 100.)

MESSAGES AND SIGNALS.

No. of Message...........

Prefix......... Code .... m. | Words. | Charge.

Office of Origin and Service Instructions.

Priority

Sent
At........... m.
To...........
By...........

This message is on a/c of:
.... *Service.*
Signature of "Franking Officer."

Recd. at...... m.
Date..........
From..........
By..........

Appx XXII

TO	MEVI	RUFU	BUZO	RURE

Sender's Number.	Day of Month.	In reply to Number.	AAA
* MW 23	23		

Situation report AAA [illegible]

Addsd MEVI repeated RUFU BUZO RURE

From RURE
Place
Time

The above may be forwarded as now corrected. (Z)
Censor. Signature of Addressor or person authorised to telegraph in his name.
[illegible] for G.O.C. Bde

*This line, except **A A A**, should be erased if not required.
Wt. W 3253/P511. 500,000 Pads. 1/18. B. & S. Ltd. **(E2389.)**

"A" Form
Army Form C. 2121
(In pads of 100.)

MESSAGES AND SIGNALS.

No. of Message...........

Prefix..........Code..........m.	Words	Charge.	This message is on a/c of:	Recd. at......m.
Office of Origin and Service Instructions	Sent		.............Service.	Date...........
Sheet 2	At ....m.			From ....
	To			
	By		(Signature of "Franking Officer.")	By..........

TO

Sender's Number.	Day of Month.	In reply to Number.	AAA

on original line) aaa
Intense MG fire met
with from BOWERY
COTTAGES aaa

From KUGE
Place
Time

The above may be forwarded as now corrected. (Z)

Censor. Signature of Addressor or person authorised to telegraph in his name

* This line should be erased if not required.

Order No. 1625. Wt. W3253/ P 511. 27/2 H. & K., Ltd. (E. 2634).

Army Form C. 2121
(In pads of 100.)

...Form

MESSAGES AND SIGNALS.

No. of Message............

Prefix..............Code..............m. | Words | Charge.

Office of Origin and Service Instructions

Copy

Sent

At ....m.

To ....

By ....

This message is on a/c of:

..............Service.

(Signature of "Franking Officer")

Recd. at......m.

Date..............

From ....

By..............

TO Btns and TMB

Sender's Number.	Day of Month.	In reply to Number.	AAA
	23		

The Divl Cmdr wishes all troops of this Bde who have been engaged to be told how much he appreciates their good work in this days fighting and the Brigdr wishes to thank CO's officers and men for their highly successful advance under difficult conditions

From

Place

Time

The above may be forwarded as now corrected. (Z)

Censor. Signature of Addressor or person authorised to telegraph in his name

* This line should be erased if not required.

Order No. 1625. Wt. W3253/ P 511. 27/2 H. & K., Ltd. (E. 2634).

War Diary

A PPx XXII (b)

CONFIDENTIAL.

120TH INFANTRY BRIGADE INTELLIGENCE SUMMARY.
RIGHT SECTOR
6 a.m. 22:8:18 to 6 a.m. 23:8:18.

A. OUR OPERATIONS.

(i) Infantry. Nil.

(ii) Patrols. Constant patrols went out to a depth of 300 to 500 yards.
The Line on the right was advanced to the line of the PONT RONDIN - COCHIN CORNER road.
Situation quiet.

(iii) Artillery. Quiet during day. Usual harassing fire at night.

(iv) T.M's. Nil.

(v) M.G's. Nil.

(vi) Aerial. Usual formations observed.

B. ENEMY OPERATIONS.

(i) Infantry. Nil.

(ii) Artillery. Active.
Continuous shelling of sector with H.E. mixed with gas shells ("Mustard").
100 rounds 10.5 cm. fell on Eastern edge of AVAL WOOD.
K.24. and K.8. received 300 rounds 10.5 cm.
Severe shelling of all forward areas during the night.

(iii) M.G's. Quiet.

(iv) T.M's. Quiet.

(v) Aerial. Normal.
One E.A. over CAUDESCURE, driven off by A.A.fire.
One E.A. crossed our lines at E.30 about 9 a.m. Seen to circle round HAZEBROUCK, re-crossing the line at E.24 about 9.30 a.m.

C. MISCELLANEOUS.

Two enemy O.B's. brought down in flames by one of our 'planes about 6 a.m.
Two O.B's. up during morning on true bearing 93° and 85° from E.29.c.50.00.
Observation indifferent.

(Sd) R.C. Barker.

for Brigadier-General,
Commanding 120th Infantry Bde.

23:8:18.

War Diary

APPx XXIII

SECRET. COPY NO. 4....

120TH INFANTRY BRIGADE ORDER No.215.

23-8-18.

1. On completion of the forward movement to-night, the 120th Infantry Brigade front will be readjusted as follows :-

(a) The Southern boundary will be altered to the grid line from K.4.central to L.5.central at 11.30 p.m., 23rd August, by which hour all troops of 120th Infantry Brigade will be clear of the area South of that line. This area will then be taken over by 183rd Infantry Brigade.

(b) The 11th Cameron Hrs. will withdraw their companies from the "Z" line and the E.27.area, and will dispose all 4 companies in the Reserve Line and the LA MOTTE SWITCH. Any accommodation that can be found in or West of the Reserve Line within the Brigade Area may be utilised by this Battalion.

The 10th K.O.S.B. will relieve all troops of 15th K.O.Y.L.I. in the final line reached, and will hold the outpost line with two companies, keeping two companies in Support about E.30. and K.6.a. and b.

The 15th K.O.Y.L.I. on relief will place three companies in the "Z" line, keeping as few troops as possible in the CAUDESCURE portion of this line, and one company in the area about E.27.

(c) Any M.Gs. or T.Ms. in the area to be vacated will be withdrawn by 11-30 p.m.

2. On completion of this adjustment, Battalion Headquarters will be as follows :-

15th K.O.Y.L.I.	...	GRENADE FARM E.20.b.7.0.
10th K.O.S.B.	...	Advanced Headquarters - by GARS BRUGGHE. Rear Headquarters - E.26.d.

3. All reliefs will be arranged direct between C.Os. concerned.

4. Completion of reliefs and moves will be wired as follows :-

10th K.O.S.B.	(Completion of relief)	...	SUN
15th K.O.Y.L.I.	(" " move)	...	MOON.
11th Cameron Hrs	(" " ")	...	STAR

5. ACKNOWLEDGE.

Issued through Signals at 3-30 p.m.

Captain,
Brigade Major,
120th Infantry Brigade.

APPx "A"

23rd August.

On the night 22/23rd, the 120th Infantry Brigade front was re-adjusted, the 119th Inf. Bde. taking over the front of the two left companies of the 10th K.O.S.B., the K.O.S.B. taking over the front of the left company of the 11th Camerons, and the 15th K.O.Y.L.I. relieving the other two companies of the 11th Camerons.

During the night the 119th Inf. Bde. made good the line ROOSTER FARM - BECKET CORNER - CUTLET CORNER.

At 10.30 p.m. 22nd, orders were issued to the 10th K.O.S.B. and 15th K.O.Y.L.I. to advance their line by means of strong fighting patrols, in co-operation with Bdes. on the flanks, to the line Cross Roads L.3.c.8.4. to BECKET CORNER, the advance to begin at 4 p.m. In the event of the advance being generally held up by hostile M.G. fire, artillery co-operation had been arranged. As soon as the advance began at 4 p.m., the enemy put a heavy artillery barrage down, but it was chiefly along the VIEUX BERQUIN - COCHIN CORNER Road. Very heavy machine gun fire from the direction of BOWERY COTTAGES, and a strong belt of undamaged wire along the West side of the LAUDICK held up the attack of the right Coy. of the 15th K.O.Y.L.I., who could not get beyond the LAUDICK, while the battalion on their right could not get forward of their original line at COCHIN CORNER.

The left company of the K.O.Y.L.I. also met with strong M.G. resistance, but advanced some 700 yds. as far as the LAUDICK, capturing some prisoners and 1 machine gun, the whole crew of which was either killed or captured.

The Company of the K.O.S.B. were held up early in the attack by strong M.G. fire from their immediate front, and the 119th Inf. Bde. were asked to demonstrate against these M.Gs. in the hope of forcing their withdrawal by threatening their rear, but owing to difficulties in communication this information could not be got through to the 119th Bde. in time. Later in the day, the K.O.S.B. succeeded in forcing their way across the LAUDICK and eventually joined up with the 119th Bde. at ROOSTER FARM, taking a few prisoners and driving off with Lewis gun and rifle fire enemy patrols which endeavoured to drive them from the newly-gained line.

At the end of the operation the line ran from ROOSTER FARM to East of DENVER, thence to COCHIN CORNER, where they were in touch with the 183rd Infantry Brigade.

Casualties were :-

	Officers.	O.R.
10th K.O.S.B. ...	2	21
15th K.O.Y.L.I. ...	-	6.

27th August.

On the 27th inst., orders were issued for the 119th Inf. Bde. to attack across the front of the 120th Inf. Bde., making good the line from BECKET CORNER to BISHOPS CORNER, capturing RUE PROVOST and BOWERY COTTAGES from the North, and mopping up the ground between the BECKET CORNER - BISHOPS CORNER Road and the LAUDICK. The 15th K.O.Y.L.I. were to co-operate advancing at Zero plus 90 to make good the line from BISHOPS CORNER southwards to join up with the 183rd Inf. Bde.

At/

At 10 a.m., the attack of the 119th Inf. Bde. opened, and BISHOPS CORNER was soon taken.

At 11.30 a.m., the 15th K.O.Y.L.I. started to advance, and at once met with intense M.G. fire from BOWERY COTTAGES, RUE PROVOST and RUE MONTIGNY. The Battalion on their right were unable to move from COCHIN CORNER. The right company of the 15th K.O.Y.L.I. again got to the West edge of the LAUDICK, where they encountered the wire in front of BOWERY COTTAGES, and as the 119th Bde. attack on the latter strong point did not materialise, they were unable to advance, and eventually swung back their right to join up with the 183rd Bde. who were still at COCHIN CORNER.

The left Company of the 15th K.O.Y.L.I. met with heavy M.G. fire from houses on the DENVER - BISHOPS CORNER Road, and from RUE PROVOST, but succeeded eventually in turning the M.G. that was giving the chief trouble on the DENVER Road, capturing the gun, and killing most of the crew. This was not completed till late in the afternoon. No touch had been gained with the 119th Inf. Bde., but towards 7 p.m. a platoon was pushed down the DENVER - BISHOPS CORNER Road, and touch was gained with the 119th Bde. at L.2.d.9.9., and a final line was formed from COCHIN CORNER - L.1.d.85.10., and thence along the road to L.2.d.9.9.

28th & 29th August.

During the day of the 28th, BOWERY COTTAGES, RUE PROVOST and all the points of enemy resistance were engaged at different times by all calibres of artillery, and at 7 p.m., patrols from the two forward companies of the 11th Cameron Hrs. were ordered to try and gain the points BOWERY COTTAGES and RUE PROVOST. If they were successful, the two companies were to move forward and make good the line from BISHOPS CORNER to RUE PROVOST - thence through BOWERY COTTAGES to COCHIN CORNER.

Immediately the patrols moved out, the enemy put down a heavy artillery barrage mixed with gas, forcing the troops to put on respirators, and effectually stopping the advance. Later in the evening, patrols succeeded in getting in to BOWERY COTTAGES, but found the plantation alongside still strongly held with M.Gs.

In the event of this patrol action being unsuccessful, orders had been issued for a set attack to be made on 29/8/18 from the line DENVER - BISHOPS CORNER, under a creeping barrage. Accordingly at 1.30 p.m. on 29th one company advanced under a creeping barrage on RUE PROVOST, which was soon reported captured. A second company then advanced through RUE PROVOST, turned South, and captured BOWERY COTTAGES, all objectives being gained by 2.45 p.m. Except for some artillery fire, hostile fire was slight, but considerable trouble was caused after the objectives had been taken by enfilade M.G.fire from the direction of ACTON CROSS.

Casualties of 11th Cameron Hrs. - 29 O.R.

****

Army Form C. 2121.
(In pads of 100.)

MESSAGES AND SIGNALS.

No. of Message..........

Prefix......... Code.......... m. | Words. | Charge.

Office of Origin and Service Instructions.

Priority

Sent
At............ m.
To............
By............

This message is on a/c of:
.... Service.
(Signature of "Franking Officer.")

APP x XXIV

Recd. at...... m.
Date..........
From..........
By..........

TO MEVI RUFU RUPE

Sender's Number.	Day of Month.	In reply to Number.	AAA
G 32	24		

Morning situation AAA Unchanged quiet night AAA Weather fine slight mist

Addsd MEVE repeated RUFU RUPE

From RUQE
Place
Time 4.22 AM

The above may be forwarded as now corrected. (Z)

Censor. Signature of Addressor or person authorised to telegraph in his name.

[illegible]
for [illegible] Bde.

*This line, except AAA, should be erased if not required.

Wt. W 3253/P511. 500,000 Pads. 1/18. B. & S. Ltd. (E2389.)

War Diary

CONFIDENTIAL.

APPx XXIV(a)

120TH INFANTRY BRIGADE INTELLIGENCE SUMMARY.
RIGHT SECTOR
6 a.m. 23:8:18 to 6 a.m. 24:8:18.

A. OUR OPERATIONS.

(i) Infantry. At 4 p.m., in conjunction with operations on our flanks, we advanced our line on the Brigade front. Heavy machine-gun and artillery fire was met with from about 4.10 p.m. onwards, especially from L.1.b., houses in L.2.b. and d., and BOWERY COTTAGES. The houses in L.2. b. and d. were taken on with Stokes mortars and artillery, and by about 7 p.m. one platoon was reported almost on the line of the LAUDICK - L.1.b. 7.3 - L.1.d.7.0. The right company of the right battalion managed to work forward to the line of the LAUDICK, but was out of touch with the troops on the right. They found the West bank of the LAUDICK fairly strongly wired, with strong enemy M.G. posts on the Eastern side, and they were eventually forced to swing back their right again to COCHIN CORNER, where the left of the battalion on the right was found to be resting.

The left battalion was strongly opposed at first, but eventually pushed forward across the LAUDICK to the line ROOSTER FARM - L.1.b.7.3. The enemy launched a counter-attack on this line, but it was driven off by our rifle and Lewis gun fire.

By 11 p.m. troops were reported in touch all along the line, and with units on both flanks, with posts being consolidated along this line - ROOSTER FARM - L.1.b.7.3. - L.1.d.7.0. - COCHIN CORNER.

(ii) Patrols. Constant patrolling to keep in touch with enemy.

(iii) Artillery. Co-operation between infantry and artillery was most effective. In response to signal from our infantry, the artillery put down 10 minutes intense fire on the M.G's from BISHOP'S CORNER to F.28.d.6.4. Further support was given at the request of the infantry.

(iv) M.G's. Nil.

(v) T.M's. Co-operated with infantry operations.

(vi) Aerial. Strong formations were observed over enemy lines during the period.

B. ENEMY OPERATIONS.

(i) Infantry. A counter-attack was directed against our left battalion, which was beaten off by our fire.

(ii) M.G's. Very active whilst our troops were advancing.

M.G's located at L.2.d.5.4., these continued firing throughout the night.

(iii) Artillery. Very active.

At 3.30 p.m. 20 rds. 18-pdr. shrapnel were fired over E.29 central.

From 3.40 p.m. to 3.50 p.m. about 100 rds. of 10.5 cm. and 7.7 mm. were fired between KEW CROSS and LA COURONNE.

At 4.10 p.m. the enemy put down a barrage of 15 cm., 10.5 cm. and 7.7 mm. on the KEW CROSS - COCHIN CORNER road, lasting till 5 p.m.

E.23.c. and E.22.c. also received much attention during the afternoon.

Active harassing fire during the night. Some heavy calibre gas shells fell near VERT RUE.

(iv) T.M's. Quiet.

(v) Gas Shells. Some heavy-calibre gas shells fell near VERT RUE, also 6 or 8 fell about K.4.b.

(vi) Aerial. Inactive.

C. MISCELLANEOUS.

Visibility. Daybreak to 9 a.m. very misty, dull and poor throughout period.

(Sgd) J.C. Barker

2/Lieut.,
for Brigadier-General,
Commanding 120th Infantry Brigade.

24:8:18.

Wardiary

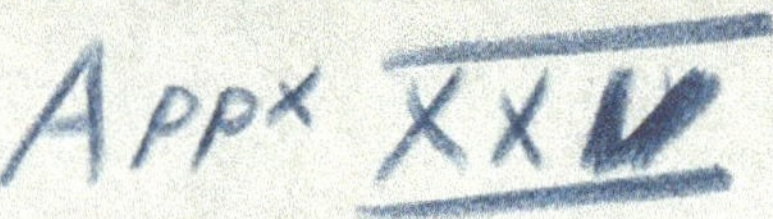

CONFIDENTIAL.

120TH INFANTRY BRIGADE INTELLIGENCE SUMMARY
RIGHT SECTOR

6 a.m. 24:8:18 to 6 a.m. 25:8:18.

A. OUR OPERATIONS.

(i) Infantry. Posts established yesterday were further consolidated.

(ii) Patrols. (a) 2/Lieut. J. Parker (15th K.O.Y.L.I) and 6 men proceeded from our posts at L.1.b.8.4. and L.1.b. 7.2. at 8 p.m. to reconnoitre the LAUDICK from L.1.b.7.4. to L.1.d.95.20. The patrol left the above-mentioned posts, proceeded to the LAUDICK at L.1.b.7.4., along the bed of the stream (which is practically dry) to L.1.d.9.6. The patrol observed single shots fired from approx. L.1.b.9.3., apparently a sniper. Enemy M.G. fired at intermediate intervals from approx. L.2.c.5.5. (judging by report). It is presumed that the sniper comes up at dusk, as there was no sniping during the day, 2/Lieut. J. Parker having investigated that portion of the LAUDICK between 4.30 p.m. and 6 p.m. the same day. The patrol returned at 9.30 p.m. by the same route.

(b) Another patrol consisting of 2/Lieut. S. Scarr (15th K.O.Y.L.I.) and 2 men left their post at L.1.d.6.1. at 8 p.m. to reconnoitre ground up to the LAUDICK. The patrol proceeded 50 yds. N. of road running from [illegible] CORNER to BISHOP'S CORNER and parallel with same until they reached point L.1.d.9.2. They found the enemy holds a post at L.2.c.2.1. where the LAUDICK crosses the road. Post was located by hearing the occupants talking. M.G. postwas located about L.2.c.4.6. by sound and direction of fire.
M.G. post was also located by sound and direction of fire at L.8.a.2.6., position was later confirmed by observing 5 enemy stood upright on the top of the post - 3 of these men were shot by patrol, enemy stretcher bearers were afterwards seen (through field glasses) carrying the bodies away. This post is still active. Patrol returned to our lines at 9.15 p.m.

(c) One Sergt. and 3 men (10th K.O.S.B.) left the post at F.26.d.7.6. at 11 p.m. to get in touch with enemy. They proceeded to F.26.c.8.5. when fired on by M.G. from F.26.d.4.6. M.G. & snipers were also located ~~ak~~ in line of trees running from L.2.b.0.4. to L.2.b.1.8. Otherwise no sign of enemy between [illegible] CORNER and L.1.b.9.9.

(d) One Officer and 5 O.R. (10th K.O.S.B.) left their post at L.1.b.6.8. to get in touch with enemy and locate M.G. positions. The patrol went forward to a depth of 300 yds., and heard enemy speaking, just at that moment a M.G. opened fire from approx. L.2.c.6.8. (judging by report and direction of fire). Patrol returned at 1 a.m.

(e) One Officer and 5 O.R. (10th K.O.S.B.) left our position at L.1.d.2.5. to get in touch with enemy and locate M.G. positions, at 1.30 a.m. The patrol proceeded from L.1.d.2.5. to L.1.b.4.5., L.1.b.9.8., L.1.b.9.3. and L.1.b.3.9. and returned to post at 2.30 a.m. No enemy patrols or signs of enemy seen. There is a line of trip wire about 50 yds. in front of our post.

(iii) Artillery. Usual harassing fire.

(iv) T.M's. Nil.
(v) M.G's. Normal.
(vi) Aerial. At 3.30 p.m. one of our 'planes shot down an enemy balloon which fell in flames, a second balloon was brought down at 5 p.m.

Usual formations were observed during the period.

B. ENEMY OPERATIONS.

(i) Infantry. Nil.

(ii) Artillery./ Considerable shelling round COBLEY COTTAGE between 5 and 6 p.m., also at 4 a.m.

/ Active

A barrage was put down on E.30.a. and c. from 12 noon to 12.30 p.m.

At about 11.15 p.m., in response to Red Signals fired from point opposite our left company, right battalion, a heavy barrage was put down on the road from KEW CROSS to GENET ~~XXXX~~ CORNER and L.1.a. and b., about half an hour later this ceased on Green Signals being fired. E.29.a. received about 25 rounds 77 mm. between 8 p.m. and 8.40 p.m.

E.28.b. and K.5. received much attention.

(iii) M.G's. Fairly active. (See Patrols).
(iv) Snipers. Active at night.
(v) T.M's. Nil.
(vi) Gas Shells. At 8.15 p.m. a few gas shells were fired into back areas.
(vii) Aerial. E.A. observed flying westwards at 8 p.m., which was engaged by A.A. fire.

Brigadier-General,
Commanding 120th Infantry Brigade.

25:8:18.

"A" Form.
MESSAGES AND SIGNALS.

Army Form C. 2121.
(In pads of 100.)
No. of Message

Prefix S.B. Code m. | Words. | Charge.
Office of Origin and Service Instructions.
Priority
RUGE

Sent At m. To By

This message is on a/c of: Service
(Signature of "Franking Officer.")

Recd. at m.
Date
From
By

APPX XXVI

TO MEVI RUPE RUTU

Sender's Number.	Day of Month.	In reply to Number.	AAA
G41	26		

Situation report AAA

~~Situation unchanged.~~

Addsd MEVI repeated RUPE RUTU

From RUQE
Place
Time

The above may be forwarded as now corrected. (Z)
Censor. Signature of Addressor or person authorised to telegraph in his name
F. Kemm Maj
Cdr Bde

* This line, except AAA, should be erased if not required.
Wt. W 3253/P511. 500,000 Pads. 1/18. B. & S. Ltd. (E2388.)

K.4.a., K.5. & E.29.b. also received a few rounds of gas.

(VI) Aerial. 1 E.A. flew over CORNET PERDU about 8.15 a.m., driven off by A.A. fire.

(VII) Balloons. Two balloons were [illegible] opposite [illegible] front

26/8/18

[illegible] Barker
Capt. [illegible]
for Brig. General,
Commanding [illegible] Bde.

APP× XXVII

SECRET. COPY NO....

120TH INFANTRY BRIGADE ORDER NO. 216.

26:8:18.

1. The enemy is holding the line of the LAUDICK from L.2.c.1.1. through BOWERY COTTAGES to RUE MARTIGNY.
   It is proposed to turn this position from the North.

2. On a date and at an hour to be notified later, the 119th Infantry Brigade will attack from BECKET CORNER on both sides of the BLEU - BISHOP'S CORNER Road.

3. Objective and boundaries are shown on attached map.
   The 61st Division will extend the objective from RUE PROVOST through L.14.b.7.7. to L.14.d.8.2.

4. The attack will be carried out by two companies which will make good the line of the road as far South as BISHOP'S CORNER inclusive. They will be followed by two companies for mopping up. These Companies will turn Westwards as soon as the line of the road is established and mop up the area between the road and the LAUDICK, including the BISHOP'S CORNER - DENVER Road.
   In addition a special party will be told off to capture BOWERY COTTAGES from the North.

5. The attack will be carried out under a creeping barrage of fifty four 18-pdrs. which will extend from about GILLIE FARM to the LAUDICK. The barrage will be thickest on the left.

   (a) The creeping barrage will come down on a line 300 yds. in advance of the ROOSTER FARM - BECKET CORNER Road, and will move forward at the approximate rate of 100 yds. in 3 minutes to the line BOWERY COTTAGES - RUE PROVOST - PRINCE FARM, where it will remain as a protective barrage till zero plus 75 when it creeps forward again to a line about 300 yards South of the above road, to allow the moppers-up to enter BOWERY COTTAGES.
   At Zero plus 90 this protective barrage will begin to roll up from West to East. As the guns lift off they will switch on to the line PRINCE FARM - REGAL FARM.

   (b) In addition to the creeping barrage there will be a standing barrage mixed with smoke on the LAUDICK from L.1.b.65.25. to L.14.b.7.7. The barrage will remain on this line until Zero plus 72, when it will stop.

   (c) The Heavy Artillery will put down a standing barrage mixed with smoke on the line GILLIE FARM - PRINCE FARM, searching 400 yards Eastwards, to protect the left flank of the attack. This barrage will cease at Zero plus 110.

   (d) A Heavy Artillery standing barrage will be put down on the line of the road BISHOP'S CORNER to L.2.c.15.15.
   At Zero plus 21 lifts on to line BOWERY COTTAGES - RUE PROVOST - L.9.a.8.8. - ACTON CROSS. This barrage will roll off at following times :-

Zero plus 65	off	BOWERY COTTAGES.
Zero plus 90	off	RUE PROVOST.
Zero plus 100	off	L.9.a.8.8.
Zero plus 106	off	REGAL LODGE.
Zero plus 130	off	YATTON FARM and ACTON CROSS.

6/.

6. Details of Machine Gun co-operation will be issued later, but O.C., 15th K.O.Y.L.I. will get into immediate touch with O.C. M.G. Company covering 120th Inf.Bde., to arrange the support for co-operation of mobile guns.

7. The action of 120th Infantry Brigade will be to move forward on completion of the operation of the 119th Infantry Brigade, and take over the Southern portion of the objective, from BOWERY COTTAGES to BISHOP'S CORNER.

8. Prior to Zero hour, all troops holding the line from ROOSTER FARM to DENVER will be withdrawn to a line shown roughly as a red dotted line on the attached map, in order to avoid our own barrage.
During the time that the two companies of the 119th Infantry Brigade are mopping up the area between the objective and the LAUDICK, troops on the front of the 120th Inf. Bde. must withhold fire. In the event of any of the enemy being driven on to our lines, they must be made prisoner without endangering mopping-up parties who are behind them.

9. At Zero plus 90, 15th K.O.Y.L.I. will advance from the direction of DENVER with their left flank on the DENVER - BISHOP'S CORNER Road and their right flank in touch with the 61st Division on the Southern boundary, and will take over the line BOWERY COTTAGES - RUE PROVOST - BISHOP'S CORNER, making good any portion of this line the moppers-up have been unable to seize.
A special party should be detailed to deal with isolated enemy posts in the ruined houses along the DENVER - BISHOP'S CORNER Road. To assist in dealing with any enemy posts O.C. 120th T. M. Battery will place two mortars and teams at the disposal of O.C., 15th K.O.Y.L.I., all arrangements being made direct between Os.C. concerned.

10. The 184th Infantry Brigade, of 61st Division, on our right will be moving forward in co-operation with 15th K.O.Y.L.I. with their left flank moving along the Southern boundary with a view to gaining the objective shown on the attached map.
The strictest touch must be kept between 15th K.O.Y.L.I. and the troops on their right during the advance.

11. O.C., 10th K.O.S.B. will hold a force in readiness to form a defensive flank facing S.E. in the event of the whole of the objective not being obtained, and must be prepared at a moment's notice to re-occupy all the ground vacated by the troops prior to Zero.

12. The signal that the various objectives gave been reached will be three WHITE VERY LIGHTS fired in quick succession.

13. After Zero plus 130 the S.O.S. line for the artillery will be about 200 yards in advance of the objective shown on the map.

14. Watches will be synchronized on Y day as follows :-

A Staff Officer from 120th Brigade Headquarters will be at Joint Battalion Headquarters at 7.30 p.m. on Y day.

15. If the objective is reached and the situation permits, the area South of the line K.4. central - L.3. central will be handed over tp 61st Division on Z/Z plus 1 night, under arrangements which will be notified later, and 120th Inf.Bde. will be pulled altogether out of the line.

16. ACKNOWLEDGE.

Captain,
Brigade Major,
120th Infantry Brigade.

Issued thro'
Signals
at 11.45 a.m.
****

DISTRIBUTION :-

Copy No. 1	...	G.O.C.
2	...	Brigade Major.
3	...	Staff Captain.
4	...	War Diary.
5	...	File.
6	...	10th K.O.S.B.
7	...	15th K.O.Y.L.I.
8	...	11th Cameron Hrs.
9	...	120th T. M. Battery.
10	...	184th Inf. Bde.
11	...	119th Inf. Bde.
12	...	121st Inf. Bde.
13	...	40th Divn. "G".
14	...	165 Bde. R.F.A.
15	...	229th Fd. Coy. R.E.
16	...	M. G. Coy.
17	...	104th Bn. M.G.Corps.
18	...	1st Heavy Bde. R.G.A.
19	...	Liaison Officer.
20	...	A.D.M.S.
21	...	135th Field Ambce.
22	...	17th Worcester Rgt. (Pnrs.)
23	...	Bde. Signals.

****

EDITION 7.
SHEET 36A N.E.
SECRET
Merris
Outtersteene
Vieux Berquin
Bleu
la Couronne
Doulieu
Pont Rondin
Rue Provost
Rue Montigny
Neuf Berquin
Vierhouck
FRONT LINE
Old Boundary
Southern Div
Old Boundary
Garbedoen Farm
Terrapin House
Auk House
Verity Crossing
Slogan Farm
Kismet House
Drone House
Alert Crossing
Scandal Crossing
Celery Copse
President Cross
Trois Tilleuls
Noote Boom
Lynde Farm
Lesage Farm
The 3 Farms
Despot Farm
Frisco Farm
Torn Farm
Labis Farm
Haute Maison
Dromena
Corin
Gaul Farm
Orb House
Hullebert Farm
Cutlet Corner
Benefit Row
Pent House
la Becque
Tiger Farm
le Verrier
Bracken Farm
Pont Wemeau
Cute Farm
Gillie Farm
Pola Mill
Becket Corner
Rooster Farm
Kew Cross
Gombert Farm
Gars Brugghe
Bishops Corner
Acton Cross
Aileron Farm
la Brielle Farm
Prince Farm
Shue Farm
le Cornet Perdu
Denver
Yatton Farm
Puxton Cross
Genet Corner
Regal Lodge
Dank Cottage
Welyn Farm
Bowery Cottages
Cent House
Gochin Corner
Salsey Farm
Kennet Cross
Fal Farm
Sinbad Farm
Hutton Mill
Turtle Farm
Bronco Farm
Dirk Cottages
Cobalt Cottages
Petit Bois Bridge
Atom Farm
Pullet Farm
Hemeria Chapel
Yam Farm
Leam Farm
Coney Cottage
Trompe Bridge
Worle Farm
Robermetz
Obos Cottage
Wandle Farm
Faggot Farm
College

"A" Form.

Army Form C. 2121.
(In pads of 100.)

MESSAGES AND SIGNALS.

No. of Message........

Prefix 2 X B. Code ... m. Office of Origin and Service Instructions. RUQE Priority 3 adds	Words. 27	Charge. Text	This message is on a/c of: .... Service. APPX (Signature of "Franking Officer.")	Recd. at ...... m. Date ...... From ...... By XXVIII
	Sent At 4 20a m. To YPZ By [illegible]			

TO MEVI RUPE RUTU

Sender's Number.	Day of Month.	In reply to Number.	AAA
G 49	27		

Morning Situation AAA Situation unchanged AAA BAWEY [illegible] reported to be [illegible] [illegible] [illegible] MEVI [illegible] RUPE RUTU

~~Added MEVI~~ Repeated RUPE RUTU

From RUQE
Place
Time

The above may be forwarded as now corrected.
(Z) [signature] for [illegible]

Censor. Signature of Addressor or person authorised to telegraph in his name

* This line, except AAA, should be erased if not required.

Wt. W 3253/P511. 500,000 Pads. 1/18. B. & S. Ltd. (E2359.)

War Diary

CONFIDENTIAL.

APPx XXVIII (a)

120TH INFANTRY BRIGADE INTELLIGENCE SUMMARY.
RIGHT SECTOR
6 a.m. 26:8:18 to 6 a.m. 27:8:18.

A. OUR OPERATIONS.

(i) Infantry. Nil.

(ii) Patrols. Active patrolling was carried out by our front line battalions during the night, but nothing of interest to report.

(iii) Artillery. Normal.
Usual harassing fire during the night.

(iv) T.M's. Nil.

(v) M.G's 2,500 rounds were fired on tracks and light railways during the period.

(vi) Aerial. Usual formations were observed flying over the lines, but no combats seen.

B. ENEMY OPERATIONS.

(i) Infantry. Nil.

(ii) Artillery. Fairly quiet throughout the period.
K.4.a., K.5.a. and b., and K.12.a. and b. received much attention during the day.
East edge of AVAL WOOD received several bursts during the day, mostly 77 mm. and 10.5 cm.

(iii) M.G's. Tracks and rear communications were swept at intervals during the night.

(iv) T.M's. Nil.

(v) Gas Shells. During the night a few gas shells were mixed with H.E. round CAUDESCURE.

(vi) Aerial. Inactive.

C. ENEMY INTELLIGENCE.

(i) Movement. Nil.

(ii) Defences. Nil.

(ii) Explosions. Nil. BOWERY COTTAGES were seen to be on fire during the evening, and were still burning at the time of writing this report.

J. C. Banks Capt.
for Brigadier-General,
Commanding 120th Infantry Bde.

27:8:18.

APP^x ~~XXXXX~~ XXIX

120th Infantry Brigade No. 120/428. SECRET

15th K.O.Y.L.I.
11th Cameron Hrs.
119th Inf. Bde.)
184th Inf. Bde.) For information.
40th Division "G".)

1. The objective line given in 120th Infantry Brigade Operation Order No. 216 is to be attained as early as possible.

2. With this end in view, the Heavy Artillery, during the 28th instant, will bombard at different times BOWERY COTTAGES, RUE PROVOST and other points of enemy resistance.

3. At 7 p.m., 28th instant, strong active patrols will be pushed out from both Companies of the 11th Cameron Hrs. to try and seize these points, the Northern Company patrols moving on RUE PROVOST, and the Southern on BOWERY COTTAGES.

4. In the event of these points being seized, the two Companies of 11th Camerons will at once move forward to take up the line from BISHOP'S CORNER along the objective line to L.9.a.2.8.- thence to line of RUE PROVOST - COCHIN CORNER Road, including BOWERY COTTAGES. The dividing point between Companies on this line will be L.8.b.5.5.

The forward movement will be carried out directly under the orders of the Company Commanders, who must ensure that the patrols mentioned in para. 3 send reliable reports to Company Headquarters.

5. In the event of patrols being unable to seize these points, they will report accordingly to the Company Commanders, and a regular attack under a creeping barrage from the line of the DENVER - BISHOP'S CORNER Road will be made Southwards by the Camerons on the 29th instant. Full details will be issued later.

Captain,
Brigade Major,
120th Infantry Brigade.

27:8:18.
12 p.m.

"A" Form.
MESSAGES AND SIGNALS.

Army Form C. 2121.
(In pads of 100.)
No. of Message

Prefix ... Code ... m. | Words. | Charge.
Office of Origin and Service Instructions.
Priority

Sent
At ... m.
To
By

This message is on a/c of: ... Service.
(Signature of "Franking Officer.")

APP XXXX

Recd. at ... m.
Date
From
By

TO MEVI RUPE RUTU

Sender's Number.	Day of Month.	In reply to Number.	AAA
G 55	28		

Morning situation AAA Situation unchanged AAA Enemy artillery fairly active AAA

Added MEVI repeated RUPE RUTU

From RUQE
Place
Time

The above may be forwarded as now corrected. (Z)
Censor. Signature of Addressor or person authorised to telegraph in his name.

* This line, except AAA, should be erased if not required.

Wt. W 3253/P511. 500,000 Pads. 1/18. B. & S. Ltd. (E2385.)

"A" Form

MESSAGES AND SIGNALS.

Army Form C. 2121
(In pads of 100.)

No. of Message.........

Prefix.........Code.........m.	Words	Charge.	This message is on a/c of:	Recd. at......m.
Office of Origin and Service Instructions	35		..........Service.	Date..........
	Sent			From..........
	At..........m.			
	To..........			
	By..........		(Signature of "Franking Officer.")	By..........

TO

Sender's Number.	Day of Month.	In reply to Number.	AAA
BM77	28		

From

Place

Time

The above may be forwarded as now corrected. (Z)

Censor. Signature of Addressor or person authorised to telegraph in his name

* This line should be erased if not required.

Order No. 1625 Wt. W3253/ P 511 27/2 H. & K., Ltd. (E. 2634).

K.	W	M.
1 O.R.	3 O.R.	1 O.R.
	9 O.R.	
	1 Off.	

SECRET

120TH INFANTRY BRIGADE INTELLIGENCE SUMMARY.
RIGHT SECTOR.
6 a.m. 27:8:18 to 6 a.m. 28/8/18.

A. OUR OPERATIONS.

(i) Infantry. We advanced our line to the line of the BISHOP'S CORNER - DENVER Road, and towards BOWERY COTTAGES. Intense hostile M.G. fire was met from BOWERY COTTAGES, in front of which a strong line of wire runs, from RUE PROVOST and from a house on the BISHOP'S CORNER - DENVER Road. This last gun was eventually enveloped and captured.

12 prisoners and 1 M.G. were reported during operations.

(ii) Artillery. Active during operations. Usual harassing fire at night.

(iii) M.G's. Active during operations.

(iv) T.M's. 4 T.M's were brought into action, two along the DENVER - BISHOP'S CORNER Road to assist in the capture of the M.G. located there, and two by BOWERY COTTAGES, into which 50 rounds were fired before the mortars were damaged by hostile fire.

(v) Aerial. Contact patrols carried out from 12 noon until about 2 p.m. Aeroplanes flying low over lines.

B. ENEMY OPERATIONS.

(i) Infantry. Nil.

(ii) Artillery. At 11 a.m. enemy laid down a barrage from BRACKEN FARM,-F.19.c.,-ROOSTER FARM - F.25.d. to L.2.b. Bombardment ceased at 1 p.m.

Area around VERTE RUE and GOMBERT FARM was shelled intermittently throughout the day with 5.9 cm., 4.2 cm., and 77 mm.

LA COURONNE and KEW CROSS also received great attention, the shelling becoming intense from 6.45 p.m. to 7 p.m.

(iii) M.G's. Very active.

(iv) T.M's. Quiet.

(v) Aerial. Strong formations active between 10 a.m. and 11 a.m. At 12.45 p.m. - 1.30 p.m. two E.A. patrolled our line, one of them dropping four white lights over KEW CROSS.

(vi) O.B's. One enemy O.B. seen opposite our front during the operations. Others were observed on grid bearings 79°, 82° and 108°. from K.F.a.5.5.

An enemy O.B. was destroyed by one of our 'planes.

G. [illegible]

Fires were observed during the morning behind enemy's lines.

[signature] Lieut
for Brig.-General,
Commanding 120th Infantry Bde.

[illegible]

App× XXXI

SECRET COPY NO. 15

120TH INFANTRY BRIGADE ORDER NO. 217.

28:8:18.

1. By dawn 29th instant, all troops of the 15th K.O.Y.L.I. in the front line will be relieved by the 11th Cameron Hrs.
   Relief of the forward Company of the 15th K.O.Y.L.I. will not begin until after the attempt to gain the new objective to-night.

2. On completion of relief, O.C. 11th Cameron Hrs. will assume Command of the Sector, and will hold the line with one Company from BISHOP'S CORNER to L.2.c.8.6., - one Company just North of that line, - one Company from the present junction with 184th Infantry Brigade to L.2.c.8.6., and one Company in Support about K.12.b. and d.

3. All arrangements will be made direct between C.Os. concerned.

4. Completion of relief will be wired to Brigade H.Qrs. by word :-

   SNOOKER.

5. In the event of the action to-night being successful, O.C., 11th Cameron Hrs. will take over the newly gained line and modify his dispositions accordingly.

6. ACKNOWLEDGE.

[signature]
Captain,
Brigade Major,
120th Infantry Brigade.

Issued thro'
Signals
at 6 p.m.

DISTRIBUTION :-

Copy No.		
1	...	G.O.C.
2	...	Brigade Major.
3	...	Staff Captain.
4	...	War Diary.
5	...	File.
6	...	10th K.O.S.B.
7	...	15th K.O.Y.L.I.
8	...	11th Cameron Hrs.
9	...	120th T.M.Bty.
10	...	119th Inf. Bde.
11	...	184th Inf. Bde.
12	...	40th Division "G".
13	...	185 Bde. R.F.A.
14	...	Bde. Supply Officer.
15	...	Bde. Signals.
16	...	121st Inf. Bde.

S E C R E T COPY NO. . .

120TH INFANTRY BRIGADE ORDER NO. 218.

28:8:18.

1. In the event of patrols being unable to seize RUE PROVOST and BOWERY COTTAGES to-night, the 120th Infantry Brigade will attack to-morrow, 29th inst., to make good the line mentioned in 120th Inf. Bde. No. 120/426 dated 27:8:18.

2. The attack will be carried out from the line from BISHOP'S CORNER to L.2.c.8.6. under a creeping barrage, by one Company of the 11th Cameron Hrs., who will make good the line of the road from L.9.a.4.9. to L.8.b.3.5. One platoon will also be detailed from this Company to form a line of posts facing East, to connect BISHOP'S CORNER with the left of this objective.

This Company will be closely followed by a second Company of the 11th Cameron Hrs., who will pass through the first objective and move S.W. to capture BOWERY COTTAGES, eventually making good the line from L.8.b.3.5. to BOWERY COTTAGES inclusive.

Arrangements must be made for this second Company of Camerons to be in position North of the BISHOP'S CORNER - DENVER Road between BISHOP'S CORNER and L.2.a.7.0. by dawn 29th instant.

Objectives are shown on attached map.

3. The signal that RUE PROVOST has been captured will be the firing of two VERY LIGHTS; and that BOWERY COTTAGES have been captured, the firing of three VERY LIGHTS.

4. The Company of the Camerons on the line due South from DENVER will be withdrawn West of the line of the Light Railway by dawn 29th instant. They must be prepared to swing round immediately BOWERY COTTAGES have been captured to make good a line from BOWERY COTTAGES to the present junction with the 184th Infantry Brigade.

5. Full details of artillery barrages will be issued later.

6. ZERO hour will be 1·30 p.m. 29th inst.
Watches will be synchronised from Bde Hqrs [illegible] to be notified later

7. A contact 'plane will fly over the area at 4 p.m. and will call for flares by either sounding a Klaxon horn or firing a light. Troops must be instructed to light these flares on this signal, ~~XXXXXXXXXXXXXXXXXXXXXXXXXXXXXXXXXXXXXX~~.

8. All prisoners will be sent back to Battalion Hd.Qrs. at E.26d.d.9.5., where they will be handed over to an officer to be detailed by 10th K.O.S.B. K.O.S.B. will also provide 1 N.C.O. and 6 men to report at Headquarters mentioned above at 2 p.m. 29th inst., to act as escorts for these prisoners, who will be sent back to Bde.Hd.Qrs. All papers on any officer prisoners are to be taken from them and sent down with them. Papers on O.R. prisoners will not be touched.

9. On night 29/30th on completion of this operation, the front held by 120th Infantry Brigade will probably be taken over by the 61st Division, under arrangements which will be issued later.

10. ACKNOWLEDGE.

Captain,
Brigade Major,
120th Infantry Brigade.

Issued thro'
Signals
at 6.45 p.m.
****

<u>DISTRIBUTION</u> :-

Copy No.		
1	...	G.O.C.
2	...	Bde.Major.
3	...	Staff Captain.
4	...	War Diary.
5	...	File.
6	...	10th K.O.S.B.
7	...	15th K.O.Y.L.I.
8	...	11th Cameron Hrs.
9	...	120th T. M. Bty.
10	...	119th Inf. Bde.
11	...	184th Inf. Bde.
12	...	165 Bde. R.F.A.
13	...	1st Heavy Bde. R.G.A.
14	...	40th Division "G".
15	...	"D" Coy. 104th M.G.Bn.
16	...	135 Field Ambulance.

****

"A" Form.

MESSAGES AND SIGNALS.

Army Form C. 2121.
(In pads of 100.)

No. of Message ....

Prefix .... Code .... m. | Words. | Charge.

Office of Origin and Service Instructions.

Priority

Sent

At .... m.

To

By

This message is on a/c of:

Service.

(Signature of "Franking Officer.")

Recd. at .... m.

Date ....

From

By ....

APPx XXXIII

TO MEVI RUPE RUTU

Sender's Number.	Day of Month.	In reply to Number.	AAA
	29		

Morning situation AAA

[illegible]

Added MEVI Repeated RUPE RUTU

From RUPE

Place

Time

The above may be forwarded as now corrected. (Z)

Censor. Signature of Addressor or person authorised to telegraph in his name

[illegible signature]

* This line, except AAA, should be erased if not required.

Wt. W 3253/P511. 600,000 Pads. 1/18. B. & S. Ltd. (E2389.)

CONFIDENTIAL.

APP^x XXXII (a)

120TH INFANTRY BRIGADE INTELLIGENCE SUMMARY.
RIGHT SECTOR.
6 a.m. 28:8:18 to 6 a.m. 29:8:18.

A. OUR OPERATIONS.

(i) Infantry. At dusk an attempt was made to advance our line on a front from just West of BISHOP'S CORNER along the road to DENVER, and from thence to COCHIN CORNER, under cover of fighting patrols. Our patrols of the Right Company were successful in gaining an entrance into BOWERY COTTAGES (see Patrols), but owing to a heavy enemy barrage [the adjacent plantation was found to be strongly held with M.G.s.] mixed with gas, which was put down on our left Company, they were unable to advance. The patrols of the Right Company were then withdrawn, and the whole consolidated in their previous positions.

(ii) Patrols. At 7 p.m., the 15th K.O.Y.L.I. sent out 3 fighting patrols, each consisting of 1 Sergt. and 9 men, under 2/Lt. J.C.WATERTON, to move forward covering the advance of the main party. No. 1 Patrol reports :-

"At 7 p.m. we moved forward from L.7.b.6.6. to L.8.a.9.2 No enemy were encountered and BOWERY COTTAGES were unoccupied. Enemy machine gun posts and sniper were located in the adjacent plantation. We returned by same route."

No.2 Patrol reports :-

"We moved forward at 7 p.m. from L.7.b.5.3. to L.8.c.4.9. We entered several unoccupied dugouts along the road, also located enemy M.G. in plantation, from which Very Lights were fired. We returned by same route. "

No. 3 Patrol reports :-

"At 7 p.m. the patrol moved forward from L.7.d.0.4. to L.7.d.9.3. and on to L.8.c.0.4., entering several recently-occupied shelters which contained German ammunition. No enemy encountered. We returned by same route".

All patrols encountered slight wire entanglement which presented no serious obstacle.

(iii) Artillery. Our heavy artillery bombarded enemy positions in L.8.a. and b. at intervals during the day.

Usual harssing fire during the night.

(iv) T.M's. Quiet.

(v) M.G's. Over 3,000 rds. were fired on tracks and enemy positions during the period.

(vi) Aerial. Usual formations seen.

B. ENEMY OPERATIONS.

(i) Infantry. Nil.

(ii) Artillery. Quiet until 7 p.m. when a heavy barrage mixed with gas was put down on our advanced positions, particularly on road from BISHOP'S CORNER to DENVER.

Fairly active throughout the night and early this morning. Area E.22.a. and c. received much attention during the day.

(iii) Snipers. Sniper was located in plantation in L.8.a.

(iv) T.M's. T.M's fired from the direction of BOWERY COTTAGES into L.2.c.

(v) Gas Shells. Gas Shells were mixed with H.E. and a barrage put down at 7 p.m.

(vi) Aerial. Active at daybreak.

J.A. Barker 2/Lieut.
for Brig.-General,
Comdg.120th Infantry Bde.

29:8:18.

CONFIDENTIAL.

Grc

APPx XXIV

120TH INFANTRY BRIGADE INTELLIGENCE SUMMARY
RIGHT SECTOR.
6 a.m. 29th Augt. to 6 a.m. 30th Aug.

A. OUR OPERATIONS.

(i) Infantry. At 1.30 p.m. we advanced our line on the Brigade front. At 2.53 p.m. the first objective (RUE PROVOST) was reported as having been taken, and our second objective (BOWERY COTTAGES) was reported complete by 3.30 p.m. Our line then ran BISHOP'S CORNER - L.3.c.7.5. - RUE PROVOST - BOWERY COTTAGES - COCHIN CORNER.

Later in the day the Brigade on our right advanced their line to RUE MONTIGNY, and joined up with our line at RUE PROVOST.

(ii) Artillery. Our artillery gave our infantry much support. The co-operation between the infantry and artillery was most effective.

(iii) M.G's. M.G's. co-operated with infantry operations. 2000 rounds were also fired on tracks and enemy positions during the period.

(iv) T.M's. Quiet.

(v) Aerial. Very active. Contact patrols were carried out during operations.

About 7 p.m. very strong formations were observed flying East.

B. ENEMY OPERATIONS.

(i) Infantry. Nil.

(ii) Artillery. Fairly active on forward positions throughout the period.

From 5 p.m. to midnight, VIEUX BERQUIN, COCHIN CORNER and RUE PROVOST were heavily shelled with 77 mm. and 5.9s.

About 6.45 p.m. GARS BRUGGHE area received much shrapnel.

(iii) M.G's. Quiet. One gun fired from ACTON CROSS during operations.

(iv) T.M's. Nil.

(v) Gas Shells. One gas shell fell near VERTE RUE at 6.30 p.m. During the operations some gas shells were mixed with the enemy's barrage.

(vi) Aerial. Only one E.A. crossed our line, which was immediately driven off by A.A. fire.

C. ENEMY INTELLIGENCE.

(i) Movement. Nil.

(ii) Explosions. Frequent explosions noticed behind enemy lines during the night.

Several fires were observed, especially in the direction of ESTAIRES.

J. Barker Maj
for Brigadier-General,
Commanding 120th Infantry Bde.

30:8:18.

S E C R E T.   120th Inf. Bde. No. 120/474.

APPX XXXV

120TH INFANTRYB BRIGADE ADMINISTRATIVE INSTRUCTIONS.

1. Battalions will move to-morrow to Camps located as under :-

(a) 120th Inf. Bde. H.Qrs. ... WALLON CAPPEL.
(b) 10th Bn. K.O.S.B. ... 36A/C.5.d.8.8.
(c) 15th Bn. K.O.Y.L.I. ... 27 /U.24.c.2.4.
(d) 11th Bn. Cam. Hrs. ... 27 /U.30.a.8.8.
(e) 120th T. M. Bty. ... School at WALLON CAPPEL.

2. (i) For Camp (b) 200 shelters will be delivered at 1 p.m. O.C., 10th K.O.S.B. will arrange for a party to be there to take them over at that hour.

(ii) In Camp (c) there are about 70 tents. 20 of these tents must be handed over to the 10th K.O.S.B. in exchange for 50 trench shelters. Details of exchange to be arranged between Commanding Officers concerned.

(iii) For Camp (d) D.A.D.O.S. will deliver 20 tents and 140 shelters at 1 p.m. O.C., 11th Cam. Highrs. will arrange for a party to be there to take over and erect.

3. Transport Lines will move to-morrow as under :-

120th Infantry Brigade to WALLON CAPPEL.
10th K.O.S.B. will take over from 23dr Lancs.Frs.C.5.c.8.8.
15th K.O.Y.L.I. " " " " 8th R. Irish R.C.5.d.5.5.
(these lines may not be vacated until 31st instant in which case, temporary lines for the night must be found in the same field).
11th Cam. Hrs. will take over from 23rd Cheshires R. C.6.b.2.4.

4. Baggage Wagons will report to Units Transport Lines at 9 a.m. on 30th instant.

5. Two Motor lorries will report for each Battalion at LA PAPOTE at 9 a.m. on 30th instant. These lorries are to do two journeys.

6. The Transport Lines at LA PAPOTE will be handed over to the 119th Infantry Brigade and a duplicate of the receipts for stores and camp equipment handed over will be forwarded to this office.

7. The 119th Infantry Brigade will send representatives to take over trench stores by 12 noon 30th instant. Duplicates of receipts to be forwarded to this office.

8. Horse Ambulances will report as under :-

One for 10th K.O.S.B. at TIR ANGLAIS at 1 p.m.
One for 15th K.O.Y.L.I. at LA MOTTE at 1-30 p.m.
One for 11th Cam. Hrs. at BRICKSTACKS(E.20.b.6.0.) at 1 p.m.

Battalions must arrange to send representatives to act as guides.

29-8-18.

Captain,
Staff Captain,
120th Infantry Brigade.

35807. W16879/M1879 500,000 3/17 R.T. (1074) Forms/W3091/3

Army Form W.3091.

WO 28

Cover for Documents.

Nature of Enclosures.

War Diary.

Headquarters 120th Infantry Brigade.

September 1918.

VOLUME XXVIII

Notes, or Letters written.

ORIGINAL

Instructions regarding War Diaries and Intelligence Summaries are contained in F. S. Regs., Part II, and the Staff Manual respectively. Title pages will be prepared in manuscript.

Page 1.

WAR DIARY
or
INTELLIGENCE SUMMARY.
(Erase heading not required.)

VOLUME XXVIII.

SEPTEMBER 1918.

H.Q. 120th Infantry Brigade.

Army Form C. 2118.

Place	Date 1918.	Hour	Summary of Events and Information	Remarks and references to Appendices
WALLON CAPPEL.	Sep. 1st		Brigade in Divisional Reserve. Dispositions :- Brigade Headquarters ... Schoolroom, WALLON CAPPEL. 10th K.O.S.B. ... S.36/C.5.d.8.8. 15th K.O.Y.L.I. ... S.27/U.24.c.2.4. 11th Cameron Hrs. ... S.27/U.30.a.8.8. 120th T. M. Bty. ... WALLON CAPPEL. ~~Casualties:- 2 OR Killed 11 OR wounded.~~ Units engaged in cleaning up generally.	
	2nd		Units training in vicinity of camps, in accordance with Training Programme 120/428 dated 2:9:18. ~~Casualties:- 2 OR Killed.~~	~~Appx. I~~
	3rd		Rehearsal of Brigade Ceremonial at Parade Ground U.18.a. and c. ~~Casualties:- 4 OR wounded.~~	
	4th		At a Ceremonial Parade held at U.18.a. and c., in which all units of 120th Inf. Bde. participated, Major-General Sir W.E.PEYTON, K.C.B., K.C.V.O., D.S.O., Commanding 40th Division, presented Military Medal ribbands in connection with operations 14/15th August 1918. Recipients of ribbands were :- No. 238072 Pte. H. W. CARTER ... 15th K.O.Y.L.I. No. 64391 Pte. A. G. WARD ... -Do-	
	5th		Battalions practicing Outpost and Advanced Guard Schemes in vicinity of camps.	
	6th		Outpost and Advanced Guard Scheme carried out by Brigade.	~~Appx. II~~
	7th		120th Brigade Sports held.	Appx.III
	8th		Units engaged in training in vicinity of camps.	
	9th	11.45 a.m.	Brigade Commander met Os.C. Battns. and Quartermasters in conference at Brigade Headquarters.	

A6945 Wt. W11422/M1160 350,000 12/16 D. D. & L. Forms/C./2118/14.

Instructions regarding War Diaries and Intelligence Summaries are contained in F. S. Regs., Part II. and the Staff Manual respectively. Title pages will be prepared in manuscript.

Page 2.

WAR DIARY or INTELLIGENCE SUMMARY. H.Q. 120th Infantry Brigade.

VOLUME XXVIII.
SEPTEMBER 1918.

Army Form C. 2118.

(Erase heading not required.)

Place	Date	Hour	Summary of Events and Information	Remarks and references to Appendices
	1918.			
WALLON CAPPEL.	10th	6 pm.	120th Inf. Bde. Order No. 219 issued, ordering move of Brigade to Support Line (STEENWERCK Sector) in relief of 121st Inf. Bde. on 11th and 12th September, 1918.	Appx.IV
	11th	8.15 p.m.	120th Inf.Bde. Order No. 220 issued. 120th Bde. will relieve 119th Bde. in the Advanced Guard positions of 40th Divisional front on night 13/14th Septr., in accordance with Relief Table issued.	Appx.V
WINK COTTAGE, A.20.b.3.3.	12th	1 p.m.	Brigade Headquarters closed at WALLON CAPPEL, and re-opened at WINK COTTAGE, A.20.b.3.3. (West of STEENWERCK) at same hour.	
		5 p.m.	Move of 120th Inf.Bde. to Support Line, in relief of 121st Inf.Bde., completed in accordance with 120th Bde. Order No. 219 dated 10:9:18. Dispositions :- Brigade Headquarters ... ... WINK COTTAGE, A.20.b.3.3. 10th K.O.S.B. ... ... LE GRAND BEAUMART. 15th K.O.Y.L.I. ... ... A.21.d.4.3. 11th Cameron Hrs... ... ... PONT WEMEAU. 120th T. M. Bty. ... ... A.20.b.5.6.	
	Night 13/14th		120th Inf.Bde. relieved 119th Inf.Bde. in Advanced Guard positions in Right (STEENWERCK) Sector of 40th Div. front, in accordance with 120th Inf.Bde. Order No. 220 dated 11:9:18. Dispositions :- 10th K.O.S. B. in LINE ... H.Q. B.20.b.4.1. 15th K.O.Y.L.I. " SUPPORT... H.Q. B.19.b.3.5. 11th Camerons " RESERVE... H.Q. B.25.a.3.5. 120th T.M.Bty. " LINE ... H.Q. A.30.b.3.9.	
	14th	10 a.m.	Brigade Headquarters closed at WINK COTTAGE, A.20.b.3.3. and re-opened at LOWER FARM, A.24.c.6.8. at same hour. G.O.C. 120th Inf. Bde. assumed Command of Right (STEENWERCK) Sector of 40th Divisional front.	

A6945 Wt. W11422/M1160 350,000 12/16 D. D. & L. Forms/C./2118/14.

Instructions regarding War Diaries and Intelligence Summaries are contained in F. S. Regs., Part II, and the Staff Manual respectively. Title pages will be prepared in manuscript.

Page 3.

WAR DIARY
or
INTELLIGENCE SUMMARY.
(*Erase heading not required.*)

VOLUME XXVIII.
SEPTEMBER 1918.
H.Q. 120th Infantry Bde.

Army Form C. 2118.

Place	Date	Hour	Summary of Events and Information	Remarks and references to Appendices
LOWER FM. A.24.c.6.8.	1918. 14th		For events, see Evening Wire and Daily Intelligence Summary. Casualties :- NIL.	Appx V above
	15th	8 pm.	120th Inf. Bde. Order No. 221 issued, ordering inter-battalion reliefs for night 16/17th September 1918, as follows :- 11th Cameron Hrs. to relieve 15th K.O.Y.L.I. in Support Area. 15th K.O.Y.L.I. " " 10th K.O.S.B. in Line. 10th K.O.S.B. to move to Reserve Area.	Appx.VI
			For events, see Morning and Evening Wires and Daily Intelligence Summary. Casualties :- 1 Officer wounded. 2 OR. wounded.	Appx VII (a. & b.)
	Night 16/17th		Inter-battalion reliefs completed in accordance with 120th Inf. Bde. Order No. 221 dated 15:9:18. Dispositions :- 15th K.O.Y.L.I. ... ... FRONT LINE. 11th Cameron Hrs. ... ... SUPPORT. 10th K.O.S.B. ... ... RESERVE. 120th T. M. Bty. ... ... LINE.	
			For events, see Morning and Evening Wires and Daily Intelligence Summary. Casualties :- 1 OR. Killed 6 OR. wounded.	Appx VIII (a. & b.)
	17th		120th Inf. Bde. INSTRUCTIONS No. 1 issued, laying down Defensive Policy for Brigade front - Right (STEENWERCK) Sector.	Appx IX
			For events, see Morning and Evening Wires and Daily Intelligence Summary. Casualties :- 1 OR Killed. 4 OR. wounded.	Appx X (a. & b.)
	18th	2 pm.	120th Inf. Bde. Order No. 222 issued, ordering inter-battalion reliefs on night 19/20th Septr. as follows :- 10th K.O.S.B. to relieve 11th Cameron Hrs. in SUPPORT Area. 11th Cameron Hrs " " 15th K.O.Y.L.I. in LINE. 15th K.O.Y.L.I. to move back into RESERVE.	Appx XI

A6945 Wt. W11422/M1160 350,000 12/16 D. D. & L. Forms/C./2118/14.

Instructions regarding War Diaries and Intelligence Summaries are contained in F. S. Regs., Part II. and the Staff Manual respectively. Title pages will be prepared in manuscript.

Page 4.

WAR DIARY
or
INTELLIGENCE SUMMARY.
(Erase heading not required.)

VOLUME XXVIII.

SEPTEMBER 1918.

H.Q. 120th Infantry Bde.

Army Form C. 2118.

Place	Date	Hour	Summary of Events and Information	Remarks and references to Appendices
LOWER FM. A.24.c.6.8.	1918. Septr.			
	18th		For events, see Morning and Evening Wires and Daily Intelligence Summary. Casualties :- 1 Officer & 1 OR missing. 3 OR wounded.	Appx XII (a. & b.)
	Night 19/20th		Inter-battalion reliefs carried out, in accordance with 120th Infantry Brigade Order No. 222 dated 18:9:18. Dispositions :- 11th Cameron Hrs. ... ... FRONT LINE. 10th K.O.S.B. ... ... SUPPORT. 15th K.O.Y.L.I. ... ... RESERVE. 120th T. M. Bty. ... ... LINE.	
			For events, see Morning and Evening Wires and Daily Intelligence Summary. Casualties :- 2 OR killed. 2 OR wounded.	Appx XIII (a. & b.)
	20th		For events, see Morning and Evening Wires and Daily Intelligence Summary. Casualties :- 1 Officer wounded. 1 OR killed. 1 OR wounded.	Appx XIV (a. & b.)
	21st		120th Inf. Bde. Order No. 223 issued. On night 22/23rd Septr. the 120th Inf. Bde. will be relieved in the line by 121st Inf. Bde.	Appx XV
			For events, see Morning and Evening Wires and Daily Intelligence Summary. Casualties :- 1 Officer & 5 OR wounded.	Appx XVI (a. & b.)
	22nd		For events, see Morning and Evening Wires and Daily Intelligence Summary. Casualties :- 3 OR wounded.	Appx XVII (a. & b.)
	23rd	12.50 a.m.	Relief of 120th Inf. Bde. in line by 121st Inf. Bde. completed, in accordance with 120th Infantry Brigade Order No. 223 dated 21:9:18.	
		10 am.	Brigade Headquarters closed at LOWER FARM, A.24.c.6.8, and re-opened at WINK COTTAGE, A.20.b.3.3. at same hour. Dispositions of Brigade :- Bde. H.Q. ... ... WINK COTTAGE, A.20.b.3.3. 10th K.O.S.B... ... GRAND BEAUMART. 15th K.O.Y.L.I. ... PONT WEMEAU.	

A6945 Wt. W11422/M1160 350,000 12/16 D. D. & L. Forms/C./2118/14.

Army Form C. 2118.

Instructions regarding War Diaries and Intelligence Summaries are contained in F. S. Regs., Part II, and the Staff Manual respectively. Title pages will be prepared in manuscript.

WAR DIARY
or
INTELLIGENCE SUMMARY.
(Erase heading not required.)

Page 5.

VOLUME XXVIII.
SEPTEMBER 1918
H.Q. 120th Inf. Bde.

Place	Date	Hour	Summary of Events and Information	Remarks and references to Appendices
WINK COTTAGE A.20.b.3.3.	1918. Sepr. 23rd.		Dispositions of Brigade (Contd) :- 11th Cameron Hrs. ... ... A.21.d. 120th T. M. Bty. ... ... A.20.b.5.6. For other events, see Morning ~~and Evening~~ Wires ~~and Daily Intelligence Summary~~. Casualties :- 1 O.R. wounded.	~~Appx XVII (not)~~ Appx XVIII
	24th		Brigade in Divisional Reserve. Units engaged in cleaning up generally. Casualties :- 1 O.R. wounded.	
	25th		Conference between Divisional Commander, Brigade Commander and Brigade Major at H.Q. 120th Inf. Brigade. Units training in vicinity of camps. Casualties :- 1 O.R. wounded.	
	26th		-Do- -Do- -Do-	
	27th		-Do- -Do- -Do- Conference between Divisional Commander and G.Os.C. 120th and 121st Inf. Bdes. at Headquarters 121st Inf.Bde., LOWER FARM, A.24.c.6.8.	
	28th		Units training in vicinity of camps.	
	29th	~~xxpm~~	-Do- -Do- -Do-	
	30th	7 pm.	120th Infantry Bde. Order No. 224 issued, ordering relief by 120th Inf. Bde. of 121st Inf. Bde. on the Right Brigade Front, STEENWERCK Sector, on the night 1st/2nd Octr.1918. in accordance with relief table issued.	Appx XIX

C.J. Hobkirk [signature]
Brigadier-General,
Commanding 120th Infantry Brigade.

A6945 Wt. W11422/M1160 350,000 12/16 D. D. & L. Forms/C./2118/14.

Appx III
120th
Sept 7th
1918.
Brigade
Sports
A.M.D.

1. 100 yds. ... ... 2 Heats ... ... 10.30 a.m.
Entries limited to 3 per Bn., and 3 per Bde.H.Qrs. and T.M.Bty.

2. Bicycle Tortoise Race - Heats ... ... 10.45 a.m.
Open to Runners only. 50 yds. between strings. Last man in wins. Touching ground disqualifies.

3. Tug-of-War ... 2 Heats ... ... 11.0 a.m.
1 team of 10 men per Bn., and 1 per Bde.H.Qrs. and T.M.Bty.
Best of 3 pulls. 9 ft.pull.

4. 440 yds. (1st and 2nd) ... ... 11.30 a.m.
2 entries per Bn., & 1 per Bde. H.Q. and T.M.Bty.

5. Relay Sack Race (Prizes to men of winning team) 11.45 a.m.
1 team per Bn., and 1 per Bde.H.Q. and T.M.Bty. combined. Team to be 4 men from one Coy. Each man to go 25 yards.

6. Veterans Race - 100 yds. (1st - 2nd - 3rd) ... 12 noon.
Men of 45 and over. 1 yard start for every year over 45.

7. Company Team 2 - 220 yds. (Prizes to men of
Relay Race. 2 - 440 yds. winning team) 12.15 p.m.

1 Team per Bn., and 1 per T.M.Bty. & Bde. H.Q. combined. Team to be 4 men from one Company.

--------- I N T E R V A L -------- 12.30 p.m. - 1.30 p.m

8. Final Tug-of-War (Prizes to men of winning team) ... 1.30 p.m.
Best of 3 pulls.

9. Final Bicycle Race (1st - 2nd) ... 1.45 p.m.
(As for No.2).

10. 2½ miles Cross-country 10 prizes ... 2.0 p.m.
Team of 10 men per Bn., and 10 per Bde. & T.M.B.combined.
8 first home to count.
1st home 8 pts., 2nd 7 pts.,etc.

11. 440 yds. Open to all comers 1st - 2nd ... 2.0 p.m.

12. 100 yds. Officers 120th Bde. (Sweepstake) 2.30 p.m.

12a. 100 yds OR FINAL (1st & 2nd) 2.40 P.M.

13. Officers Jumping on Horseback. (Sweepstake) 2.45 p.m.
(Open to Regtl.Officers only, excluding C.Os. and 2nds.-in-Command).

14. Officers Horses Jumping. Cup Presentation ... 3.15 p.m.
(Open to 120th Brigade)
Cup - Presented by Brigade Major.

15. Officers Horses Jumping. (Cup Presentation) 3.45 p.m
(Open to all comers)
Cup - Presented by G.O.C.

16. N.C.Os. and O.R. Jumping. (1st - 2nd - 3rd) 4.15 p.m
Transports of 120th Brigade.

17. Transport N.C.Os. & O.R. Mule Race (1st 2nd 3rd) ... 4.45 p.m
120th Bde. only. - No saddlery, spurs or stick.

17a.

18. Band Race ... 1st - 2nd ... 5.0 p.m.

==*=*=*=*=*=*=*=*=*=*=*=*=*=*=*=*

EVENTS NOS. 14 & 15.- Entrance fee 10 francs to go to General Fund.

* * * *

APPX IV

S E C R E T. COPY NO. 3.

120TH INFANTRY BRIGADE ORDER No.319.

Ref. Map. Parts of 27 S.E., 28 S.W.
36a N.E. 36 N.W.
1/20,000.

10-9-18.

1. The 120th Infantry Brigade will relieve the 121st Infantry Bde. in Brigade Support on the 11th and 12th September, 1918.

2. (a) The Units of 120th Infantry Brigade, less transport, will move by Bus in accordance with the attached Embussing Table - Appendix 'A'.

(b) The Transport of Units will move by road in accordance with attached March Table - Appendix 'B'

3. (a) Units must be ready to embuss 15 minutes before the hour at which the convoy is timed to start.

(b) Parties of 25 O.R. under an Officer or N.C.O. must be detailed beforehand for each bus.

(c) Each man will take his pack and blanket in the lorry with him except the 11th Bn. Cameron Highrs.

(d) 11th Bn. Cameron Highrs. will carry all packs and blankets in three motor lorries which will proceed to PONT WEMEAU.

4. (a) Units moving in the morning must debuss speedily to allow the lorries to return for the second journey.

(b) No lorries in the morning will be allowed to take stores to Transport Lines.

5. (a) Baggage wagons will report to Units on the evening prior to their move.

(b) Two lorries in the afternoon will be available for each battalion to move surplus stores and rear party. These lorries will move with convoy to debussing point.

6. (a) Rations will be delivered to Units transport lines in the new area on the day Units move forward.

(b) Units on the day of their move will arrange that guides that know the way to their new transport lines meet the supply wagons at OUTLET CORNER at 12 noon.

7. (a) All tents, shelters and Camp equipment in the Camps now occupied will be left standing.

(b) All Camps must be left clean and tidy. Units leaving early must leave behind parties to clean up.

8. The 10th K.O.S.B. and 15th K.O.Y.L.I. on arrival in the new Area come under the Command of G.O.C. 121st Infantry Brigade for tactical purposes.

9. Units will report by wire to Headquarters of 120th Inf. Bde. their arrival in their new Camps.

10. Brigade Headquarters will close at WALLON CAPPEL and open at WINK COTTAGE at 1 p.m. 12th inst. at which hour the G.O.C. 120th Inf. Bde. will assume Command of the Brigade in Support.

11. ACKNOWLEDGE.

Captain,
Brigade Major,
120th Infantry Brigade.

Issued at 6 p.m.

DISTRIBUTION :-

Copy No 1 ... G.O.C.
2 ... Brigade Major.
3 ... Staff Captain.
4 ... War Diary
5 ... File.
6 ... 10th Bn. K.O.S.B.
7 ... 18th Bn. K.O.Y.L.I.
8 ... 11th Bn. Cam. Highrs.
9 ... 120th T. M. Battery.
10 ... 121st Inf. Bde.
11 ... 40th Division.
12 ... No. 3 Coy. Divnl. Train.
13 ... Officer i/c M. T. Convoy.
14 ... Brigade Signals.

=-=-=-=-=-=-=-=-=-=-=-=-=

S E C R E T.

APPENDIX 'A'

MOVE OF 120TH INFANTRY BRIGADE - EMBUSSING TABLE

Issued with 120th Infantry Brigade Order No. 219.

Serial No.	UNIT	DATE.	No. of BUSSES	TIME	EMBUSSING POINT.	R O U T E.	DEBUSSING POINT.	DESTINATION.	TAKING OVER CAMP FROM	REMARKS
1.	10th K.O.S.B.	11th	20	8 a.m.	G.5.b.9.3.	HAZEBROUCK-LABREARDE - CAESTRE - METEREN - BAILLEUL - BAILLEUL STATION - S 21.d.8.3 - S 27 a.9.1. - S 27.d.9.0. - A.4.a. and c.	A.16.c.3.0	GRAND BEAUMONT.	8th Bn. R. Irish Rgt.	
2.	15th K.O.Y.L.I	11th	3	8 a.m.	G 5.b.9.3.		- do - = do -	A.21.d.4 3.	23rd Cheshires.	
3.	15th K.O.Y.L.I.	11th	21	2 p.m.	U.24.c.2.7.		- do - - do -	A.21.d.4.3.	23rd Cheshires.	
4.	10th K.O.S.B. Rear Party.	11th	2	2 p.m.	U.24.c.2.7.		- do -	F.23.d.2.1	if roads permit.	
5.	Hd.Qrs. 120th Infantry Bde.	12th	1	8 a.m.	WALLON CAPPEL		- do -	A.20.b.3.3.	Hd. Qrs. 121 st Inf. Bde.	
6.	11th Cam. Hrs.	12th	21	8 a.m.	U.24.c.2.7.		- do -	PONT WEMEAU	23rd Lancs. Fusrs.	
7.	Hd.Qrs.120th Infantry Bde.	12th	6	2 p.m.	WALLON CAPPEL		- do -	A.20.b.3.3.		
8.	120th T.M.Bty.	12th	4	2 p.m.	WALLON CAPPEL		- do -	A.20.b.5.6	121st T.M.B.	
9.	11th Cam. Hrs.	12th	8	2 p.m.	U.24.c.2.7.		- do -	PONT WEMEAU		

(a) After the convoy leaves METEREN an interval of 200 yards will be maintained between every 6 lorries.
(b) Lorries return by the same route except through BAILLEUL where lorries will keep to lorry circuit.
(c) In the morning ALL lorries will return as soon as units have debussed
(d) In the afternoon two lorries per unit may proceed with stores to transport lines - if roads permit.

---------ooo0Oooo---------

S E C R E T.

APPENDIX 'B'

MARCH TABLE FOR TRANSPORT OF 120TH INFANTRY BRIGADE.

Map refce. Sheet 36A N.E. 1/20,000   Issued with 120th Infantry Brigade Order No. 219.

Serial No.	UNIT.	DATE	TIME	STARTING POINT.	R O U T E.	DESTINATION	TAKING OVER LINES OF	REMARKS.
1.	10th K.O.S.B.	11th	7 a.m.	G.5.b.5.0.	LA MOTTE - VIEUX BERQUIN - F.13.a.3.2. - OUTLET CORNER - PONT WEMEAU	F.23.d.2.1.	8th R. Irish R.	
2.	15th K.O.Y.L.I.	11th	1 p.m.	U.24.c.2.7.		F.30.c.1.2.	23rd Cheshires.	
3.	11th Cam. Hrs.	12th	7 a.m.	U.30.b.3.5.		PONT WEMEAU	23rd Lanc. Frs.	
5.	Headquarters 120th Inf. Bde.	12th	10 a.m.	WALLON CAPPEL		A.20.b.4.7.	Headquarters 121st Inf. Bde.	

25 yards distance will be maintained between every 6 Vehicles.

===========ooo000ooo===========

SECRET

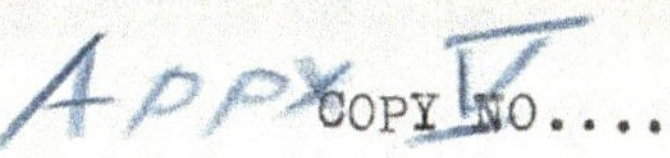

COPY NO....

120TH INFANTRY BRIGADE ORDER NO. 220.

11:9:18.

1. The 120th Infantry Brigade will relieve the 119th Infantry Brigade in the advanced guard positions on the night 13/14th September, in accordance with attached Relief Table.

2. All reliefs will be arranged direct between C.Os. concerned, but routes to be taken by units moving forward will conform to the instructions issued by 119th Infantry Brigade to their units being relieved.

3. All special maps, aeroplane photographs, etc. will be taken over on relief.

4. The Brigade boundaries on completion of relief will be as follows :-

   Northern:- Grid line through B.13.central and B.18.central.

   Southern:- Grid line through H.7.central and H.10.central.

5. The 31st Division will be on the North of the Brigade, and the 61st Division on the South.

6. Completion of relief will be wired to Brigade Headquarters, using following code words :-

10th K.O.S.B.	... ...	SILK.
15th K.O.Y.L.I.	... ...	SATIN.
11th Cameron Hrs	... ...	COTTON.
120th T. M. Bty	... ...	RAGS.

7. 120th Infantry Brigade Headquarters will close at WINK COTTAGE and re-open at LOWER FARM, A.24.c.6.8. at 10 a.m. on 14th instant, at which hour G.O.C. 120th Infantry Brigade will assume command of the Sector.

8. Up to 10 a.m. 14th inst., all troops in the forward area will be under the tactical control of G.O.C. 119th Infantry Brigade.

9. ACKNOWLEDGE.

Captain,
Brigade Major,
120th Infantry Brigade.

Issued at
8.15 p.m.
****

DISTRIBUTION :-

Copy No. 1	... G.O.C.	9.	... 120th T.M.Battery.
2	... Bde.Major.	10	... 40th Division "G".
3	... Staff Capt.	11	... 119th Inf. Bde.
4	... War Diary.	12	... 121st Inf. Bde.
5	... File.	13	... No. 3 Coy. Div. Train.
6	... 10th K.O.S.B.	14	... A.D.M.S. 40th Divn.
7	... 15th K.O.Y.L.I.	15	... C.R.E. 40th Divn.
8	... 11th Cameron Hrs.	16	... Brigade Signals.

==*=*=*=*=*=*=*

RELIEF TABLE TO ACCOMPANY 120TH INFANTRY BRIGADE ORDER NO. 220.

NIGHT 13/14th Septr. 1918.

Unit.	From	To	In relief of	Hd.Qrs.	Remarks.
10th K.O.S.B.	LE GRAND BEAUMONT.	LINE.	12th N. Staffs. Regt.	B.20.b.4.1.	
15th K.O.Y.L.I.	A.21.d.4.3.	SUPPORT.	13th R.Inniskilling Fsrs.	B.19.b.3.5.	(1 Coy. TANDY FARM. (1 Coy. PUNGENT FARM. (1 Coy. TIG FARMS. (1 Coy. WATERLANDS.
11th Camerons.	PONT WEMEAU.	RESERVE.	13th E. Lancs. Regt.	B.25.a.3.5.	All 4 Coys. along the line through B.19.c. & B.25.a.
120th T.M.Bty.	A.20.b.5.6.	LINE.	119th T. M. Bty.	A.30.b.3.9.	

"A" Form.

Army Form C. 2121.
(In pads of 100.)

MESSAGES AND SIGNALS.

No. of Message

Prefix Code m.	Words. 14	Charge	This message is on a/c of:	Recd. at m.
Office of Origin and Service Instructions. Priority three addrs JUVO	Sent At m. To By		APPx V (6) Service. (Signature of "Franking Officer.")	Date From By

TO DAFA MAKU JUME

Sender's Number.	Day of Month.	In reply to Number.	
* G/12	15		AAA

Morning situation AAA

Situation quiet

Addsd DAFA repeats MAKU JUME

From JUVO
Place
Time

The above may be forwarded as now corrected. (Z) [illegible] Capt.

Censor. Signature of Addressor or person authorised to telegraph in his name.

* This line, except AAA, should be erased if not required.

Wt. W 3253/P511. 500,000 Pads. 1/18. B. & S. Ltd. (E2389.)

"A" Form.
(In pads of ...)

MESSAGES AND SIGNALS.

No. of Message

Prefix ... Code ... m.	Words.	Charge.	This message is on a c of:	Recd. at ... m.
Office of Origin and Service Instructions.	Sent		Appx ... Service.	Date 5 (c)
Priority WR	At ... m.			From
	To			
	By		(Signature of "Franking Officer.")	By

TO DAFA MAKU JUME

Sender's Number.	Day of Month.	In reply to Number.	AAA
G 17	15		

Evening situation aaa
situation unchanged aaa
nothing to report aaa

Addsd DAFA repeated MAKU JUME

From JUVO
Place
Time 4.8 P.m.

The above may be forwarded as now corrected. (Z) WE
Censor. Signature of Addressor or person authorised to telegraph in his name.

* This line, except AAA, should be erased if not required.

Wt. W 3253/P511. 500,000 Pads. 1/18. B. & S. Ltd. (E2389.)

CONFIDENTIAL.

War Diary APP V

120TH INFANTRY BRIGADE INTELLIGENCE SUMMARY.

RIGHT SECTOR.

From 6 a.m. 14:9:18 to 6 a.m.15:9:18.

A. OUR OPERATIONS.

(i) Infantry. An observation post was established at the LAUNDRY B.29.c.5.9., from where excellent observation of both banks of the LYS can be obtained. Patrols reconnoitred the bridge at B.29.c.7.7., which was found demolished, and the river found still in flood. Another patrol located an enemy M.G. post, which is only manned at night, among the debris on East side of river LYS at point B.29.c.8.6. The post is apparently vacated by day, and steps are being taken to deal with the post by night with Stokes mortars.
A third patrol reconnoitred the bridge at H.4.c.1.5. The approaches and first 20 yds. were found in a good condition, but further reconnaissance was stopped by heavy hostile M.G. fire across the bridge. The patrol waited for 1¾ hrs. close to the bridge in the hopes of any of the enemy coming across, but no hostile movement took place.

(ii) Artillery. Usual harassing fire, especially heavy on area B.18.a. and c. by night.

(iii) Aircraft. At 1 p.m. one of our planes shot down an enemy O.B. over ARMENTIERES.
A contact plane called for flares at 6.30 a.m. and again at 6.45 p.m.

(iv) M.G. and T.M. 20 rds. T.M. fired at enemy movement round suspected M.G. emplacement at B.23.b.95.55.

B. ENEMY OPERATIONS.

(i) Infantry. Nil.

(ii) Artillery. Chiefly counter-battery work. 50 rds. 77 mm. fired on NIEPPE SWITCH about B.22.d.5.9.

(iii) Gas Shelling. About 300 gas shells fired into area about B.19.

(iv) M.G. & T.M. Enemy M.G's active during night from B.29.c.8.6. and from vicinity of LAUNDRIES in H.5.a.
A few rounds from a light Minnenwerfer fell about LA HAYE FARM.

(v) Aircraft. Some activity between 7 a.m. and 11 a.m., one plane making several efforts to cross our lines. A.A. fire drove it off each time.
At 7 a.m. enemy plane dropped flares just West of our line in B.23.b.

(vi) Balloons. Enemy balloon, bearing 58° from LA HAYE FARM brought down. Two more enemy balloons rose at 9.20 a.m. on bearings 91° and 166° from LA HAYE FARM

C. (i) MOVEMENT. No movement observed except about suspected M.G. position in A.23.b.95.55.

(ii) Nil.

(iii) Nil.

(iv) Nil.

(v) Pigeons seen to be released from tree at B.29.c.90.25.

(vi) Copy of Order of 12th Inf. Division dated 22:8:18 picked up in PONT DE NIEPPE (attached).

Brigadier-General,
Commanding 120th Infantry Brigade.

15:9:18.

APP^x VI

SECRET COPY NO. ..

120TH INFANTRY BRIGADE ORDER NO. 221.

15:9:18.

1. On the night 16/17th September, the following reliefs will take place :-

   (a) The 11th Bn. Cameron Hrs. will relieve the 15th Bn. K.O.Y.L.I. in the Support Area.

   (b) The 15th K.O.Y.L.I. will relieve the 10th Bn. K.O.S.B. in the line.

   The 10th K.O.S.B. on relief will move back into the Reserve Area, taking over the accommodation vacated by the 11th Cameron Hrs.

2. All arrangements will be made direct between C.Os. concerned.

3. No movement of troops will take place before 7.30 p.m., and all movements will be in small parties.

4. All special maps, aeroplane photographs, etc., hot food containers and petrol tins will be handed over by Battalions to relieving Battalions.

5. Completion of relief will be wired to Brigade Headquarters, using following code word :-

   M E T Z.

6. Disposition maps, showing dispositions down to platoons, will be forwarded by 15th K.O.Y.L.I. and 11th Cameron Hrs. to Brigade Headquarters by 6 p.m. 17th instant.

7. 15th K.O.Y.L.I. will ensure that details for patrols keeping communication with Brigade on right are handed over to 11th Cameron Hrs.

8. A C K N O W L E D G E.

Issued through Signals at 8 p.m.

[signature]

Captain,
Brigade Major,
120th Infantry Brigade.

DISTRIBUTION :-

Copy No.		Copy No.	
1 ...	G.O.C.	10 ...	40th Division "G".
2 ...	Bde. Major.	11 ...	182nd Inf. Bde.
3 ...	War Diary.	12 ...	93rd Inf. Bde.
4 ...	Staff Captain.	13 ...	331st Bde. R.F.A.
5 ...	File.	14 ...	64th H.A. Group.
6 ...	10th K.O.S.B.	15 ...	Bde. Supply Officer
7 ...	15th K.O.Y.L.I.	16 ...	39th Bn. M.G.C.
8 ...	11th Cameron Hrs.	17 ...	Bde. Signals.
9 ...	120th T. M. Bty.	18 ...	137th Field Ambulance.

****

"A" Form.

Army Form C. 2121.
(In pads of 100.)

MESSAGES AND SIGNALS.

No. of Message

Prefix ... Code ... m.	Words.	Charge.	This message is on a/c of:	Recd. at ... m.
Office of Origin and Service Instructions.	Sent		Service.	Date
	At ... m.		APP VII	From
	To			
	By		(Signature of "Franking Officer.")	By

TO DAFA MAKU JUME

Sender's Number.	Day of Month.	In reply to Number.	AAA
* G 10	14		

Evening Situation AAA Normal AAA Hostile Sniping activity very great AAA Enemy artillery active on back areas during early morning and HIEPPE SWITCH line shelled with 77 mm from about 12 noon to 12.45 pm.

Added DAFA repeated MAKU JUME

From JUVO

Place

Time

The above may be forwarded as now corrected. (Z)

Censor. Signature of Addressor or person authorised to telegraph in his name.

Capt.
Bde Major.

* This line, except AAA, should be erased if not required.

Wt. W 3253/P511. 500,000 Pads. 1/18. B. & S. Ltd. (E2389.)

War Diary APPx VII

CONFIDENTIAL

120th INFANTRY BRIGADE INTELLIGENCE SUMMARY.

RIGHT SECTOR.

From 6 a.m. 13:9:18 to 6 a.m. 14:9:18.

OUR OPERATIONS. A.

(1) Infantry. During the night 13/14th Septr. the 120th Brigade relieved the 119th Brigade in the Divisional Advanced Guard . Our forces are disposed thus :- The left flank is held by the 10th K.O.S.B. as far as B.28.b.central. The right flank as far as JESUS FARM by the 15th K.O.Y.L.I., with two companies in Support along the NIEPPE System - B.22.d. & b. - B.16.b &d. one company in TAFFY FARM Area. The 11th Camerons in Brigade Reserve lie on the line LOWLAND FARM - ORPHANS REST.

Our line runs :-

JESUS FARM (B.26.d.40.10) - H.3.a.central - H.3.b.7.5. - B.28.d.30.35 - B.28.b.3.4. - MANCHESTER KEEP - B.23.d.84.70 - B.23.b.80.62 - B.17 d.40.33 - B.17 a.54.10 - posts at B.17.d. 10.87 - H.3.c.68.95.

(2) Artillery. Our gnus continually harassed the enemy.

(3) Aircraft. There has been considerable aerial activity which increased towards evening.

(4) T.M's. Our T.M. Battery having established itself in PONT DE NIEPPE fired 64 rounds on buildings known to be held by the enemy. Many direct hits were obtained.

B.

ENEMY OPERATIONS.

(1) Infantry The day passed quietly.

(2) Artillery. The enemy guns were unusually quiet until 5.30 p.m. At that hour the area about B.20.c.2.8. was shelled with 77 mm. and gas shells. (There had been troop movements just previously).
At 7.30 p.m. a concentration of 5.9s. was put down about B.19.c.7.7.
During the night and early morning, the area in A.24.d. and the vicinity of LOWER FARM, A.24.c.7.8. received attention with 5.9s.

(3) M.G's. Enemy M.G's fired throughout the day on our posts in the forefield. Snipers were active, firing from buildings on outskirts of PONT DE NIEPPE, B.24.a.20.15. Our L.Gs. maintained a vigorous retaliation.

C.

Intelligence. General. Small enemy groups still cling tenaciously to the outskirts of PONT DE NIEPPE.

[signature] for Brig.-General,
Commanding 120th Infantry Bde.

"A" Form.
Army [illegible]
(In pads of [illegible])

MESSAGES AND SIGNALS.

No. of Message

Prefix .... Code .... m.

Words. 21 Charge. 1

Office of Origin and Service Instructions:

JKMO

Priority

3 adds

Sent

At .... m.

To

By

This message is on a/c of:

..... Service.

(Signature of "Franking Officer.")

Recd. at .... m.

Date

From

By

App^x VIII (a)

TO DAFA MAKU JUBE

Sender's Number.	Day of Month.	In reply to Number.	AAA
* G 17	16		

Morning Situation AAA [illegible] unchanged ordinary harassing fire AAA Neighbourhood Pistol farm B20 b4 0 heavily shelled between 4 and 6.30 pm

Added DAFA repeated MAKU JUBE

From JUVO

Place

Time

The above may be forwarded as now corrected. (Z)

Censor.

Signature of Addressor or person authorised to telegraph in his name.

[illegible signature]

* This line, except **AAA**, should be erased if not required.

Wt. W 3253/P511. 500,000 Pads. 1/18. B. & S. Ltd. **(E2389.)**

MESSAGES AND SIGNALS. No. of Message

Prefix ... Code ... m.	Words.	Charge.	This message is on a c of:	Recd. at ... m.
Office of Origin and Service Instructions.	Sent		Service.	Date
Priority HQr	At ... m.		App* VIII (6)	From
	To			
	By		(Signature of "Franking Officer.")	By

TO	DAFA	MAKU	JUBE

Sender's Number.	Day of Month.	In reply to Number.	AAA
* G 21	16		

Evening situation AAA

Situation unchanged aaa 77 MGs active about B 27 c & d aaa slight shelling from right 7 H about B 23 d 55 aaa considerable enemy aerial activity during morning

Addsd DAFA repld MAKU JUBE

From	JUVO
Place	
Time	4 pm

The above may be forwarded as now corrected. (Z)

Censor. Signature of Addressor or person authorised to telegraph in his name.

* This line, except AAA, should be erased if not required.

Wt. W 3253/P511. 500,000 Pads. 1/18. B. & S. Ltd. (E2389.)

Lar APP x VIII

CONFIDENTIAL

120TH INFANTRY BRIGADE INTELLIGENCE SUMMARY.
RIGHT SECTOR.
From 6 a.m. 15:9:18 to 6 a.m.16:9:18.

(a) OUR OPERATIONS.

(i) INFANTRY. A liaison post has been established at Bridge H.3.c.3.7. and we are now in constant touch with Battalion on our right.

(ii) ARTILLERY. Usual harassing fire, more active by night.
Approximately 20 rounds were fired on O.P. NOTRE DAME CHURCH, B.30.d.

(iii) AIRCRAFT. About 5.30 p.m., our aeroplanes shot down E.A. in direction of Jute Factory B.29.b.
Enemy balloon shot down S.E. of ERQUINGHAM, evening 15th inst.

(iv) M.G's, T.M's, etc. 10.50 a.m. 15th, 2 rds. T.M. fired at enemy observer about B.18.c.2.4. O.K. reported.
4 a.m. 16th, 21 rds. fired on targets B.24.c.1.8., B.24.c.2.7., B.24.c.3.6.
5 a.m. 2 rds. on suspected M.G. emplacement at B.18.c.2.4.

(b) ENEMY OPERATIONS.

(i) INFANTRY. Nil.

(ii) ARTILLERY. Counter-battery work throughout the day.
About 6 rds. 77 mm. fired in direction of TAFFY FARM B.22.c.35.95., and few rds. in NIEPPE SWITCH B.22.d.5.9.
70-100 rds. 5.9 fired on POSTON FARM B.20.b.3.0. between 2 p.m. and 7.30 p.m. Objective apparently battery behind the hedge.
Heavy shelling throughout night on battery positions and roads.
Posts intermittently shelled during the night with 77 mm.

(iii) GAS SHELLING. About 8.30 p.m. 20 gas shells fell in B.19.b. and d.

(iv) M.G's, T.M's, etc. 20 rds. T.M. fired into PONT DE NIEPPE about 11 a.m. from direction B.24.c.2.2.
At 1.30 p.m. 3 T.M's fell about B.23.b.1.5 from B.24.a.3.1. M.G's active by night - Posts located at house B.24.c.1.8. and B.24.c.3.5.

(v) AIRCRAFT E.A. crossed our lines in B.23 at 2 p.m., but driven off by A.A. fire. Returned at 2.30 p.m. re-crossing line in B.29. At 6.30 p.m., E.A., red fusilage, white tail and green planes, flew low over our lines - driven off by A.A. and M.G. fire. At 10.30 p.m. E.A. flew over PONT DE NIEPPE, but later driven off by A.A. fire. E.As. active over our back area throughout day. Bomb dropped near LOWER FARM B.25.c.2.6. at 6.45 p.m.

(vi) BALLOONS. O.B. observed at grid bearing of 81° from B.22.a.4.0.

(c) INTELLIGENCE.

(i) MOVEMENT. Transport was heard during the night from our post in GOSPEL VILLA.

(ii) ENEMY DEFENCES. Camouflage erected at B.18.c.2.4., but observation from B.23.b.4.3. still effective.

(iii), (iv), (v), and (vi) Nil.

W. Archer for Lieut

Brigadier-General,
Commanding 120th Infantry Brigade.

16:9:18.

Form. (In pads of 100.)

MESSAGES AND SIGNALS.

No. of Message

Prefix ... Code ... m.	Words.	Charge.	This message is on a/c of:	Recd. at ... m.
Office of Origin and Service Instructions.	Sent		Service.	Date
Priority	At ... m.			From
	To			
	By		(Signature of "Franking Officer.")	By

Appx II (a)

TO DAFA MAKU JUBE

Sender's Number.	Day of Month.	In reply to Number.	AAA
* G 25	17		

Morning Situation AAA

Situation unchanged [illegible]

relief of SUVO by [illegible]

completed [illegible]

Addsd DAFA rptd MAKU JUBE

From SUVO

Place

Time

The above may be forwarded as now corrected. (Z)

Censor. Signature of Addressor or person authorised to telegraph in his name.

[illegible] Bde

* This line, except AAA, should be erased if not required.

Wt. W 3253/P511. 500,000 Pads. 1/18. B. & S. Ltd. (E2389.)

"A" Form. Army Form C. 2121.
(In pads of 100.)

MESSAGES AND SIGNALS.

No. of Message

Prefix ...... Code ...... m. | Words. | Charge.

Office of Origin and Service Instructions.

Priority

Sent
At ...... m.
To
By

This message is on a c of:
Service.
APP X (a)
(Signature of "Franking Officer.")

Recd. at ...... m.
Date
From
By

TO DAFA MAKU JUBE

Sender's Number.	Day of Month.	In reply to Number.	AAA
G 31	17		

Evening Situation AAA
Situation quiet aaa
Nothing report

Addsd DAFA rptd MAKU JUBE

From JOVO
Place
Time 4 12 pm

The above may be forwarded as now corrected. (Z)

Censor. Signature of Addressor or person authorised to telegraph in his name.

* This line, except AAA, should be erased if not required.

Wt. W 3253/P511. 500,000 Pads. 1/18. B. & S. Ltd. (E2389.)

War Diary App^x X

CONFIDENTIAL.

180TH INFANTRY BRIGADE INTELLIGENCE SUMMARY
RIGHT SECTOR.
6 a.m. 16:9:18 to 6 a.m. 17:9:18.

(a) OUR OPERATIONS.

(i) INFANTRY. Our patrols were active during the night.
A machine gun post was located in house at S.18.c.1.9. This post was occupied by about 40 of the enemy. 3 machine guns were located in house in S.17.d.8.4. These M.G's cross fired with another at S.24.a.1.1.
Snipers fired on patrols from S.23.b.9.7.
(ii) ARTILLERY. Harassing fire was maintained throughout the period. Enemy back areas were heavily shelled from 10 p.m. to midnight.
(iii) AIRCRAFT. Strong formations were observed during the day.
About 8.15 a.m. three of our machines coming from the direction of ARMENTIERES were attacked by 8 E.As. (2 of which were triplanes) over S.20. One single-seater E.A. was shot down, and crashed in S.20.central. The pilot was dead.
(iv) M.G's & T.M's. Cross roads and suspected enemy posts were engaged by our M.G's during the period.
Trench mortars were quiet.

(b) ENEMY OPERATIONS.

(i) INFANTRY. Nil.
(ii) ARTILLERY. Fairly active.
PONT DE NIEPPE was fired on by light field guns and a few heavies at dawn.
Much counter-battery work was carried out during the night. Considerable attention was paid to areas S.16 and S.21.
(iii) GAS SHELLS KELLOW CROSSING received a few gas shells at 10 p.m.
About midnight, a few gas shells fell in area of battalion on our right, and the gas slowly drifted over into our area.
(iv) M.G's & T.M's. Active. (See our Infantry).
PONT DE NIEPPE was swept at intervals by M.G's during the night. Trench Mortars were active at intervals Light T.M's were fired from S.18.c. and S.18.d.5.0. Heavy T.M's were fired from S.24.c.
(v) AIRCRAFT. More active than usual, many attempts being made to cross our lines, but driven off by our fighting patrols.
One E.A. brought down (See our Aircraft).
(vi) BALLOONS. Nil.

(c) INTELLIGENCE.

(i) MOVEMENT. Nil.
(ii) GENERAL. Nil.

J. Barker
Capt
for Brigadier-General
Commanding 180th Infantry Brigade.

17:9:18.

HOSTILE SHELLING REPORT

From 6 a.m. 16:9:18 to 6 a.m. 17:9:18.

Time.	Area Shelled.	Calibre.	No. rds.	Direction or bearing.	Remarks.
8.50 p.m.	B.26.a.5.3.	4.2	3	South.	
11.30 p.m.	B.26.b.8.8.	77 mm.	10	South-East.	
1.25 a.m.	B.26.b.8.8.	77 mm.	10	-Do-	
5.15 a.m.	B.26.a.5.2.	77 mm.	20	-Do-	
5.50 a.m.	B.25.b.	4.2	14	ARMENTIERES.	

17:9:18.

CBarker 2/Lt
for Brigadier-General,
Commanding 120th Infantry Brigade.

S E C R E T

APPx 4 XI

COPY NO.....

120TH INFANTRY BRIGADE ORDER NO. 222.

18:9:18.

1. On the night 19/20th September, the following reliefs will take place :-

(a) The 10th K.O.S.B. will relieve the 11th Cameron Hrs. in the Support Area.

(b) The 11th Cameron Hrs. will relieve the 15th K.O.Y.L.I. in the line.

The 15th K.O.Y.L.I. on relief will move back into the Reserve Area, taking over the accommodation vacated by 10th K.O.S.B.

Dispositions of Battalions will be in accordance with 120th Inf. Bde. Instructions No. 1 dated =17:9:18.

2. All arrangements will be made direct between C.Os. concerned.

3. No movement of troops will take place before 7.30 p.m., and all movements will be in small parties.

4. All special maps, aeroplane photographs, etc., hot food containers and petrol tins will be handed over by Battalions to relieving Battalions.

5. Completion of relief will be wired to Brigade Headquarters, using following code word :-

D U D

6. Disposition maps, showing dispositions down to Platoons, will be forwarded by 11th Cameron Hrs. and 10th K.O.S.B. to Brigade Headquarters by 6 p.m. 20th inst.

7. 11th Cameron Hrs. will ensure that details for patrols keeping communication with Brigade on right are handed over to 10th K.O.S.B.

8. Special attention is called to 120th Inf. Bde. No. 120/426 dated 18:9:18 regarding wiring of forward posts.

9. ACKNOWLEDGE.

Issued thro'
Signals
at 2 p.m.

Captain,
Brigade Major,
120th Infantry Brigade.

DISTRIBUTION:-

Copy No.1	G.O.C.	10	40th Divn. "G".
2	Bde.Major.	11	182nd Inf.Bde.
3	War Diary.	12	94th Inf.Bde.
4	Staff Capt.	13	331st Bde.R.F.A.
5	File.	14	64th H.A. Group.
6	10th K.O.S.B.	15	Bde. Supply Officer.
7	15th K.O.Y.L.I.	16	"C" Coy.39th M.G.Bn.
8	11th Camerons.	17	137th Field Ambulance.
9	120th T.M.Bty.	18	224th Field Coy. R.E.
		19	Bde. Signals.

****

MESSAGES AND SIGNALS.

No. of Message

Prefix SB Code m.	Words. 16	Charge.	This message is on a/c of:	Recd. at m.
Office of Origin and Service Instructions.	Sent		Service.	Date
	At m.		App^x XII (a)	From
	To			
	By		(Signature of "Franking Officer.")	By

TO DAFA MAKU JUBE

Sender's Number.	Day of Month.	In reply to Number.	AAA
* G 34	18		

Morning situation AAA

Situation quiet and heavy artillery action about [illegible] passed all night AAA

Addsd DAFA rptd MAKU JUBE

From JUVO

Place

Time 4 3 am

The above may be forwarded as now corrected. (Z)

Censor.

Signature of Addressor or person authorised to telegraph in his name.

* This line, except **AAA**, should be erased if not required.

Wt. W 3253/P511. 500,000 Pads. 1/18. B. & S. Ltd. **(E2389.)**

MESSAGES AND SIGNALS

Prefix ...... Code ...... m.	Words. Charge.	This message is on a/c of:	Recd. at ...... m.
Office of Origin and Service Instructions.	Sent	Service	Date
Priority / HQ	At ...... m.	Appx XII (6)	From
	To		
	By	Signature of "Franking Officer."	By

TO DAFA MAKU JUBE

Sender's Number.	Day of Month.	In reply to Number.	AAA
* G41	18		

Evening Situation AAA [illegible]

[illegible]

[illegible]

Added DAFA reptd MAKU JUBE

From JUVO

Place

Time

The above may be forwarded as now corrected. (Z)

Censor. Signature of Addressor or person authorised to telegraph in his name

* This line, except AAA, should be erased if not required.

Wt. W 3253/P511. 500,000 Pads. 1/18. B. & S. Ltd. (E2389.)

App^x XII

CONFIDENTIAL.

120TH INFANTRY BRIGADE INTELLIGENCE SUMMARY.

RIGHT SECTOR.

6 a.m. 17:9:18 to 6 a.m. 18:8:18.

(a) OUR OPERATIONS.

(i) INFANTRY. Nil.
(ii) ARTILLERY. Normal. At 5.30 a.m. heavy barrage was put down on our left.
(iii) AIRCRAFT. Very active. Strong formations were observed flying over our lines, which frequently crossed the enemy lines, meeting with heavy A.A. fire.
(iv) M.G's & T.M's. M.G's fired on enemy positions, roads and light railways during the period. T.M's were fairly active.
At 10.20 a.m. we fired 12 rounds on enemy T.M. position at B.24.c.2.2., and at 4.30 p.m. 12 rounds on M.G. position at B.18.c.2.4. where enemy movement had been seen during the day. At 2 a.m. 10 rds. were fired on targets B.29.b.9.9. and B.24.c.1.8. - suspected T.M. positions.

(b) ENEMY OPERATIONS.

(i) INFANTRY. At 4.30 p.m. one of the enemy was seen moving at B.18.c.2.4. Brushwood and timber at this point would seem to indicate an enemy post. At 7.50 p.m. a German was seen to look over the top of ruined house on North side of road at B.24.c.1.8.
(ii) ARTILLERY. Normal in forward areas; very active in back areas, chiefly firing on roads and batteries.
The support lines of right Coy. were shelled intermittently during the day.
Area B.16. a. and b., B.19.a. and B.21.b. and d. received much attention during the day.
Area 24.a. and c. received over 250 rounds between 8 p.m. and 4 a.m.
At 5.30 a.m. enemy artillery replied vigorously on usual targets.
(iii) GAS SHELLING. B.19.b.central received 3 rds. of gas at 10.25 am. Between midnight and 2 a.m. gas was mixed with H.E. in B.27.
(iv) M.G's & T.M's. M.G's active, especially on right Coy. front. M.G. fired from B.24.c.1.8. M.G. was active in H.3.c. or d.
T.M's. From 10.30 a.m. to 11 a.m. and from 8 p.m. to 9 p.m. area B.29.b. was bombarded by heavy Minnenwerfers which fired from approximately B.18.d.1.8.
Light Minnenwerfers fired on post at B.23.b.8.1. from B.24.c.2.2.
Two light Minnenwerfers fired from right of PONT DE NIEPPE into village.
(v) AIRCRAFT. E.A. repeatedly tried to cross our lines during the day, but were driven off each time by A.A. fire.
(vi) BALLOONS. One balloon was seen up on our front from 3 p.m. to 41 4.15 p.m. at a true bearing of 90° from B.28.b.49.58.

(c) ENEMY INTELLIGENCE.

(i) LIGHTS. Red lights were fired along Brigade front at intervals during our barrage at 5.30 a.m. No action observed.

[signature] Barker
for Brigadier-General,
Commanding 120th Infantry Brigade.

18:9:18.

"A" Form.

Army Form C. 2121. (In pads of 100.)

MESSAGES AND SIGNALS.

No. of Message..........

Prefix ..... Code ..... m.	Words 35	Charge	This message is on a/c of:	Recd. at ..... m.
Office of Origin and Service Instructions.	Sent		App^x XIII (a) Service.	Date
	At..... m.			From
	To			
	By		(Signature of "Franking Officer.")	By

TO DAFA PANI JUBE

Sender's Number.	Day of Month.	In reply to Number.	AAA
G4	19		

Morning situation AAA Quiet ... very ... fire ... gas ... Sells in P20C for 2 hours from 1 AM

Addsd DAFA Repd PANI JUBE

From TUVO

Place

Time 4.10 AM

The above may be forwarded as now corrected. (Z)

Censor. Signature of Addressor or person authorised to telegraph in his name

*This line, except AAA, should be erased if not required.

Wt. W 3253/P511. 500,000 Pads. 1/18. B. & S. Ltd. (E2389.)

"A" Form.
MESSAGES AND SIGNALS.

Army Form C. 2121.
(In pads of 100.)
No. of Message............

Prefix......... Code.......... m. | Words. | Charge. | This message is on a/c of: | Recd. at...... m.

Office of Origin and Service Instructions.

Priority

Sent
At........... m.
To...........
By...........

Service.

(Signature of "Franking Officer.")

Date.........
From
By

Appx XIII (a)

TO DAFA PANI JUBE

Sender's Number.	Day of Month.	In reply to Number.	AAA
* G11	19		

Evening situation AAA Situation normal aaa artillery quiet

Addsd DAFA rptd PANI JUBE

From JOVO
Place
Time

The above may be forwarded as now corrected.

Censor.

(Z) TNS Capt

Signature of Addressor or person authorised to telegraph in his name.

*This line, except A A A, should be erased if not required.

Wt. W 3253/P511. 500,000 Pads. 1/18. B. & S. Ltd. (E2389.)

J Cpe
Bothmafer

Appx XIII

CONFIDENTIAL.

120TH INFANTRY BRIGADE INTELLIGENCE SUMMARY.
RIGHT SECTOR.
6 a.m. 18:9:18 to 6 a.m. 19:8:18

(a) OUR OPERATIONS .

(i) INFANTRY. Nil.
(ii) ARTILLERY. Normal during the day; very active from 10 p.m. to 2 a.m. Usual harassing fire on enemy positions and back areas was maintained throughout the period.
(iii) AIRCRAFT. Aerial activity normal.
(iv) M.G's. Harassing fire was carried out at intervals. Many targets were engaged by our fire.
(v) T.M's. 12 noon - fired 6 rounds on B.18.c.1.3 and B.17.d.7.5. Enemy sent up one white Very light.
3.15 p.m. - fired 6 rds. on the above targets.
5.30 p.m. - 5 more rds. were fired on these targets.

(b) ENEMY OPERATIONS.

(i) INFANTRY. Nil.
(ii) ARTILLERY. Normal during the day, but very active after dusk, firing on cross roads and battery positions.
Areas B.19.c., B.20.a. and c. and B.25.a. received much attention, especially during the night. Area B.30.a. was shelled intermittently throughout the period.
(iii) GAS SHELLS. Gas was often mixed with H.E. during the period. Area B.20.a. and c. was heavily shelled with 'sneezing' gas and "Yellow Cross" shells from 1.15 a.m. to 2.30 a.m. 300 rds. were received in this area, but the gas was carried away by the S.W. wind.
(iv) M.G's. Usual searching fire along railway and roads in B.22.a. M.G. position located at B.29.c.80.62. M.G. very active at B.28.b.3.8.
(v) T.M's. Activity below normal. A few rds. were fired on post at B.28.b.9.5. just after flares had been lit in answer to call from contact planes at 6.35 a.m. Suspected Battery at B.30.d.60.20. Two T.M's fired on bearing of 144° and 139° from B.22.b.60.90.
(vi) AIRCRAFT. Normal. 4 E.As. flew over NIEPPE at a height of 6,000 ft. at 6.25 p.m. 1 E.A. flew over NIEPPE at 2,000 ft. at 6.30 p.m., driven off immediately by A.A.fire.
(vii) BALLOONS. One up from 3 p.m. to 5.30 p.m. on true bearing of 92 degrees from B.28.b.49.58. One up 12.30 p.m. to 3 p.m. 49½ degrees from B.27.b.70.10. One up 1.30 p.m. to 3 p.m. 90 degrees from B.27.b.70.10.

(c) INTELLIGENCE.

(i) MOVEMENT. Enemy O.P. suspected in tree across river at B.29.c.90.65.
(ii) FIRES. Fire observed on bearing of 37° from B.27.b.70.10. from 4.15 p.m. to 5.5 p.m.
(iii) EXPLOSION. Slight explosion at 11.30 a.m. followed by clouds of grey smoke at bearing of 25° from B.27.b.70.10.

[signature]
Brigadier-General,
Commanding 120th Infantry Brigade.

19:9:18.

"... Form.
MESSAGES AND SIGNALS.

Army Form C. 2121.
(In pads of 100.)

No. of Message ....

Prefix .... Code .... m.	Words.	Charge.	This message is on a/c of:	Recd. at .... m.
Office of Origin and Service Instructions.	Sent		.... Service.	Date
Private	At .... m.		APPX XIV(a)	From
	To			
	By		(Signature of "Franking Officer.")	By

TO DAFA PANI JUBE

Sender's Number.	Day of Month.	In reply to Number.	AAA
G12	20		

Morning situation AAA Situation unchanged AAA Usual counter battery firing on both sides AAA

Ref Order 222 DUD

Addsd DAFA rptd PANI JUBE

From JUVO

Place

Time

The above may be forwarded as now corrected.	(Z)
Censor.	Signature of Addressor or person authorised to telegraph in his name.

*This line, except AAA, should be erased if not required.

Wt. W 3253/P511. 500,000 Pads. 1/18. B. & S. Ltd. (E2389.)

"A" Form.
MESSAGES AND SIGNALS.

Army Form C. 2121.
(In pads of 100.)
No. of Message..........

Prefix.......... Code.......... m. | Words. | Charge.
Office of Origin and Service Instructions.

This message is on a/c of:

Service.

(Signature of "Franking Officer.")

Sent
At.......... m.
To..........
By..........

Recd. at .... m.
Date
From
By

APP X XIII (6)

TO DAFA PANI JUBE

Sender's Number.	Day of Month.	In reply to Number.	AAA
G 17	20		

Evening Situation AAA

Situation unchanged aaa

[illegible] generally very quiet aaa [illegible] [illegible] [illegible] aaa HQ POC evacuated strong shelling.

Addsd DAFA Rptd PANI JUBE

From JUVO
Place
Time

The above may be forwarded as now corrected. (Z)

Censor. Signature of Addressor or person authorised to telegraph in his name.

Capt.

*This line, except AAA, should be erased if not required.

Wt. W 3253/P511. 500,000 Pads. 1/18. B. & S. Ltd. (E2389.)

Appx XIV

CONFIDENTIAL.

120TH INFANTRY BRIGADE INTELLIGENCE SUMMARY.
RIGHT SECTOR.
6 a.m. 19:9:18 to 6 a.m. 20:9:18.

(a) OUR OPERATIONS.

(i) INFANTRY. Our patrols were active during the night. Lieut. ALLISON and 2 O.R. left our lines at H.3.a.5.1. at midnight to reconnoitre the bank of the LYS 400 yds. to right and left of H.3.c.5.7. No enemy were encountered, neither was the patrol fired on.

(ii) ARTILLERY. Normal during the day, more active after dusk. Harassing fire was maintained on enemy forward areas and roads during the period.

(iii) AIRCRAFT. Normal during morning, more active in the afternoon, being engaged with much A.A. fire.

(iv) M.G's. Normal. Harassing fire was carried out and many targets engaged.

(v) T.M's. Fairly quiet.
21 rounds were fired on enemy M.G.position in vicinity of B.17.d.7.4. at 5 a.m.

(b) ENEMY OPERATIONS.

(i) INFANTRY. Nil.

(ii) ARTILLERY. Fairly quiet during the day, very active after dusk. Areas B.15.b. and d., B.16.a. and c., B.21.d., and B.27.b. received much attention throughout the period. About 7.30 p.m. area A.30.c. received 45 shells - 5.9 & 77 mm. Back areas were shelled with heavy calibre during the night.

(iii) GAS SHELLS. About 200 rounds of "Yellow Cross" fell in the vicinity of HOLLEBECQUE FARM between midnight and 4 a.m.

(iv) M.G's. Below normal.

(v) T.M's. Fairly quiet. A few rounds fell in the vicinity of PONT DE NIEPPE during the night.

(vi) AIRCRAFT. Normal.
One E.A. flew over our lines at 8.55 a.m. and was immediately driven off by A.A. fire.
E.As. flew over our lines at 4.25 p.m., 5 p.m. and 5.25 p.m. All were engaged by A.A. fire.

(c) ENEMY INTELLIGENCE.

(i) MOVEMENT. Nil.

[signature]
for Brigadier-General,
Commanding 120th Infantry Bde.

20:9:18

Appx XV

SECRET.

COPY NO. 4

120TH INFANTRY BRIGADE ORDER NO. 223.

21-9-18.

1. On the night 22nd/23rd September, the 120th Infantry Brigade will be relieved in the line by the 121st Infantry Brigade in accordance with attached relief table.

2. All arrangements for relief will be made by C.O's. concerned.

3. No movement will be made by relieving battalions East of STEENWERCK before 7 p.m., and all movement will be made in small parties.

4. Priority of movement will be given to incoming Units.

5. All defence instructions, Special maps, Aeroplane photographs, and all trench stores will be handed over to incoming Units and receipts obtained. These receipts will be forwarded to Brigade Headquarters by 6 p.m. 24th instant.

6. Completion of relief will be wired by code word :-

U N I T Y.

and completion of moves of 120th Infantry Brigade Units to new Areas will be wired to Brigade Headquarters.

7. 120th Infantry Brigade Headquarters will close at present location and reopen at WINK COTTAGE, A.20.b.3.3. at 10 a.m. 23rd inst., at which hour G.O.C. 121st Infantry Brigade will assume Command of the Sector.

8. All administrative details of relief will be issued by Staff Captain.

9. ACKNOWLEDGE.

Issued through Signals at 8 p.m.

Captain,
Brigade Major,
120th Infantry Brigade.

DISTRIBUTION:-

Copy No. 1 ... G.O.C.
2 ... Bde. Major.
3 ... Staff Captn.
4 ... War Diary.
5 ... File.
6 ... 10th K.O.S.B.
7 ... 15th K.O.Y.L.I.
8 ... 11th Cam. Hrs.
9 ... 120th T.M.Bty.
10 ... 40th Divn. "G"
11 ... 40th Divn. "Q"
12 ... 119th Inf. Bde.
13 ... 121st Inf. Bde.
14 ... 183rd Inf. Bde.
15 ... 94th Inf. Bde.
16 ... 331st Bde. R.F.A.
17 ... 64th H. A. Group.
18 ... "C" Coy. 39th M.G.Bn.
19 ... 137th Field Ambce.
20 ... 224th Field Coy. R.E.
21 ... "L" Special Coy. R.E.
22 ... Bde. Supply Officer.
23 ... Bde. Signals.

RELIEF TABLE TO ACCOMPANY 120TH INFANTRY BRIGADE ORDER NO. 223.

Serial No.	Unit.	From	To	In relief of	Remarks.
1.	23rd Cheshires	A.21.d.	Line.	11th Cameron Hrs.	To move before 8th R.I. Regt.
2.	11th Cameron Hrs.	Line.	A.21.d.		To give way to any incoming troops.
3.	8th Rl.Irish Regt.	A.16.c.	Support.	10th K.O.S.B.	
4.	10th K.O.S.B.	Support.	GRAND BEAUMART		- Do- -do- -do-
5.	23rd Lancs.Fusrs.	PONT WEMEAU.	Reserve	15th K.O.Y.L.I.	
6.	15th K.O.Y.L.I.	Reserve.	PONT WEMEAU.		-Do- -do- -do-
7.	121st T.M.Bty.	A.20.b.5.6.	Line.	120th T.M.Bty.	
8.	120th T.M.Bty.	Line.	A.20.b.5.6.		-Do- -do- -do-

"A" Form.

Army Form C. 2121.
(In pads of 100.)

MESSAGES AND SIGNALS.

No. of Message..........

Prefix........ Code........ m. | Words. | Charge

Office of Origin and Service Instructions.

Priority

Sent
At........ m.
To
By

This message is on a/c of:
.... Service.
(Signature of "Franking Officer.")

Recd. at ...... m.
Date
From
By

App XVI (c)

TO DAFA PANL JUPI

Sender's Number.	Day of Month.	In reply to Number.	AAA
G 26	21		

Enemy Situation AAA Situation

quiet and nothing to

report

Added DAFA Repd PANL JUPI

From JUVO
Place
Time

The above may be forwarded as now corrected. (Z)

Censor. Signature of Addressor or person authorised to telegraph in his name

*This line, except **AAA**, should be erased if not required.

Wt. W 3253/P511. 500,000 Pads. 1/18. B. & S. Ltd. (E2389.)

"A" Form
MESSAGES AND SIGNALS.

Army Form C. [illegible]
(In pads of 100.)

No. of Message ....

Prefix...... Code ....m	Words	Charge	This message is on a/c of:	Recd. at........m.
Office of Origin and Service Instructions	Sent		..........Service.	Date..........
	At..........m.			From..........
	To..........			
	By..........		(Signature of "Franking Officer.")	By..........

Appx XVI (a)

TO DAFA PANE JUBE

Sender's Number.	Day of Month.	In reply to Number.	AAA
BM 271	21		

Situation report aaa Situation normal aaa Enemy machine guns active throughout night but artillery quiet aaa

addsd DAFA rptd PANE and JUBE

From JAVD
Place
Time

The above may be forwarded as now corrected. (Z)

Censor. .... T.B. Khan? Capt
[illegible] of Addressor or person authorised to telegraph in [illegible] name

* This line should be erased if not required.

(18.65.) Wt. W12952/M1204. 187,500 Pads. 1/17 H.P.[illegible] (E. 812).

App^x XVI

CONFIDENTIAL.

120TH INFANTRY BRIGADE INTELLIGENCE SUMMARY.

RIGHT SECTOR

6 a.m. 20:9:18 to 6 a.m. 21:9:18.

(a) OUR OPERATIONS.

(i) INFANTRY. A patrol of 1 N.C.O. and 3 men left our post at B.17.d.3.0. to reconnoitre along trench to road at B.23.b.8.6. Patrol reports trench clear of enemy. No enemy fire from N.E. side of trench. M.G. opened fire from approx. B.23.b.9.5. Patrol returned at 10.45 p.m.

A second patrol was sent out to inspect our wire. Route taken from B.23.d.7.7. to B.29.a.05.75. Patrol report a good belt of wire with gaps in places.

(ii) ARTILLERY. Slight activity during the day, increasing towards dusk. Enemy back areas were subjected to usual harassing fire.

(iii) M.G's. Quiet during the day.
Enemy cross roads and tracks were harassed after dusk, and enemy M.G. positions were fired on during the night.

(iv) T.M's. During the night 30 rds. were fired on M.G. positions in the vicinity of B.29.b.9.8.

(v) AIRCRAFT. Usual formations were observed over our lines during the day with increased activity about 5 p.m. About 11.30 a.m. one of our planes dropped 3 bombs in the direction of ARMENTIERES.

(b) ENEMY OPERATIONS.

(i) INFANTRY. Nil.

(ii) ARTILLERY. Slight activity during the day, increasing about 4.30 p.m. TAFFY FARM was harassed by whizz-bangs throughout the period. About 5 p.m. this Farm was heavily bombarded by whizz-bangs for 45 minutes. There was light scattered shelling of forward areas and harassing fire on cross roads and battery positions in back areas during the night. Areas B.15.b., B.16.a., B.17.b., and B.22. received much attention during the period.

(iii) GAS SHELLING. "Sneezing" gas was reported in B.22. and B.27.c. about 3.20 a.m.

(iv) M.G's. M.G's were seen to fire from house at H.3.d.75.45. and about H.4.b.65.65.

(v) T.M's. Quiet.

(vi) AIRCRAFT. Below normal. At 6.45 p.m. 7 E.A. flying along our front from S. to N. were driven off by A.A. fire.

(vii) BALLOONS. Hostile balloons were observed as follows:-
9.30 a.m. to 11.40 a.m. T.B. $93\frac{1}{2}^{\circ}$ from B.22.a.4.0.
5.30 p.m. to 6.55 p.m. T.B. 168° from B.22.a.4.0

(c) INTELLIGENCE.

(i) MOVEMENT. Movement was seen in factory chimney in B.29.b.65.50.

(ii) FIRES. Fires were observed at T.B. 133° from B.16.d.8.1. At 8.30 p.m. a fire in ARMENTIERES, which burned throughout the night.

(iii) <u>GENERAL</u>. M.G. fires down NIEPPE Road from approx. B.24.c.05.75. M.G. is suspected in Factory chimney at B.29.b.65.50.

At 9.30 p.m. noises were heard coming from direction of H.4.c.5.5. It appears as though enemy are dismantling light railway. Noise of transport was heard about 10.30 p.m. at H.4.c.3.1.

[signature] for Brigadier-General,
Commanding 120th Infantry Bde.

21:9:18.

Army Form C. 2121.
(In pads of 100.)

MESSAGES AND SIGNALS.

No. of Message...........

Prefix ... Code ... m.	Words. 2	Charge 4	This message is on a/c of:	Recd. at ...... m.
Office of Origin and Service Instructions. JUHA Priority	Sent At ... m. To ... By ...		... Service. (Signature of "Franking Officer.")	Date ... From ... By ...

APPx XVII (a)

TO DAFA PANI JUPI

Sender's Number.	Day of Month.	In reply to Number.	AAA
G 30	22		

Morning situation [illegible]

Addsd DAFA rptd PANI JUPI

From JUVO
Place
Time

The above may be forwarded as now corrected. (Z)

Censor. Signature of Addressor or person authorised to telegraph in his name.

*This line, except AAA, should be erased if not required.

Wt. W 3253/P511. 500,0 c Pads 1/18. B. & S. Ltd. (E2089.)

"A" Form.
Army Form C. 2121.
(In pads of 100.)

MESSAGES AND SIGNALS.

No. of Message ....

Prefix ...... Code ...... m.	Words.	Charge		Recd. at ...... m.
Office of Origin and Service Instructions.	Sent		This message is on a/c of:	Date ......
	At ...... m.		...... Service.	From
	To			
	By		(Signature of "Franking Officer.")	By ......

AAA I/III (?)

TO DAFA PANI JUPI

Sender's Number.	Day of Month.	In reply to Number.	AAA
* G36	22		

Evening Situation AAA Situation quiet aaa a few 77s fired a [illegible] B28 F38 aaa nothing else [illegible]

Addsd DAFA 1 pdr PANI JUPI

From JUVO

Place

Time 3 5(?)

Priority

The above may be forwarded as now corrected.

(Z)

Censor.

Signature of Addressor or person authorised to telegraph in his name.

[illegible] Capt

* This line, except AAA, should be erased if not required.

Wt. W 3253/P511. 500,000 Pads. 1/18. B. & S. Ltd. (E2389.)

War Diary APP^x XVII

CONFIDENTIAL.

120TH INFANTRY BRIGADE INTELLIGENCE SUMMARY.
RIGHT SECTOR.
6 a.m. 21:9:18 to 6 a.m. 22:9:18.

(a) OUR OPERATIONS.

(i) INFANTRY. Nil.
(ii) ARTILLERY. Our ~~shelling~~ artillery maintained harassing fire in enemy's forward areas and roads. At night our harassing fire increased, especially on roads.
(iii) AIRCRAFT. Great activity all day. Strong formations were seen to cross the enemy's lines on many occasions.
(iv) M.G's 500 rds. were fired into houses in H.3.d.5.3. - H.3.d.6.4. - H.3.d.7.4., which are enemy M.G. posts. Cross Roads, tracks and light railways were harassed during the night and many targets were engaged by our fire.
(v) T.M's. During the night many rds. were fired on suspected M.G. and T.M. positions.

(b) ENEMY OPERATIONS.

(i) INFANTRY. Nil.
(ii) ARTILLERY. Quiet during the day. Between 3.15 p.m. and 4.45 p.m. 100 rds. (5.9s) fell in the vicinity of HOLLEBEQUE FARM, later, between 7.15 p.m. and 7.45 p.m. 60 rds. 5.9s. fell in the same area. The enemy bombarded our Support Lines with H.E. mixed with gas from 8 p.m. to 8.15 p.m. Area B.24.c. was shelled intermittently throughout the night. Back areas were subjected to harassing fire throughout the night.
(iii) GAS SHELLING. 6 gas shells fell near Railway Crossing in B.21.a.
(iv) M.G's. Active. Areas B.16.b. and d., and B.22.a. and c. were swept by M.Gs. during the night. Roads in B.29.a. were also harassed by M.G. fire
(v) T.M's. 15 rds. fell in PONT DE NIEPPE at 6.30 p. .
35 rds. of searching fire were fired into B.28.b.1.8 about midnight.
(vi) AIRCRAFT. Quieter than usual. Two E.A. tried to cross our lines at 11.30 a.m., but were driven off by A.A. fire.
(vii) BALLOONS. Nil.

(c) ENEMY INTELLIGENCE.

(i) GENERAL. An escaped Portuguese prisoner was found in our lines about 10.30 a.m.
3 small bombs were dropped on NIEPPE at 10.22 pm.
A whizz-bang battery, used for sniping, appears to have 2 guns approx. H.6.b., these guns are very active in the vicinity of TAFFY FARM.

[signature]
for Brigadier-General,
Commanding 120th Infantry Bde.

22:ix:18.

"A" Form.
MESSAGES AND SIGNALS.

Army Form C. 2121.
(In pads of 100.)
No. of Message..........

Prefix........ Code.......... m. | Words. | Charge.
Office of Origin and Service Instructions.

Sent
At.......... m.
To..........
By..........

This message is on a/c of:
.... Service.
(Signature of "Franking Officer.")

APP^x XVIII

Recd. at...... m.
Date..........
From..........
By..........

TO DAFA PANI JUPI

Sender's Number.	Day of Month.	In reply to Number.	AAA
G 40	23		

Morning Situation AAA

Ref JUVO Order 223 UNITY

Added DAFA rptd PANI JUPI

From JUVO
Place
Time

Priority

The above may be forwarded as now corrected. (Z)

Censor. Signature of Addressor or person authorised to telegraph in his name.

for ? Bde

*This line, except AAA, should be erased if not required.

Wt. W 3253/P511. 500,0.0 Pads. 1/18. B. & S. Ltd. (E2389.)

Appx XIV

SECRET COPY NO. 2

120TH INFANTRY BRIGADE ORDER NO. 224.

30:9:18.

1. The 120th Infantry Brigade will relieve the 121st Infantry on the Right Brigade Front on the night 1st/2nd October, in accordance with attached relief table.

2. All arrangements for relief will be made direct between C.Os. concerned.

3. (a) All special maps, aeroplane photographs, defence instructions, and trench and area stores, including hot food containers, will be taken over and receipts given.

   (b) Instructions as to Defence of STEENWERCK Line will be handed over to Battalions relieved.

   (c) Special care will be taken to ensure that all details of work on defensive systems are taken over.

4. Sketches showing dispositions down to platoons will be submitted to Brigade Headquarters by 12.00, 3rd prox.

5. No movement will be made East of STEENWERCK before ~~xxxxxx~~ 19.00.

6. Completion of reliefs will be wired by following code word :-

N A P C O.

7. Brigade Headquarters will close at WINK COTTAGE and re-open at TOUQUET PARMENTIER, B.21.a.9.5. at 10.00 on 2nd Octr., at which hour G.O.C. 120th Infantry Bde. will assume command of the sector.

8. A C K N O W L E D G E.

Issued through Signals at 7 p.m.

H. L. Eady
Captain,
Brigade Major,
120th Infantry Brigade.

DISTRIBUTION:-

Copy No.				
1	G.O.C.		13	121st Inf. Bde.
2	Bde. Major.		14	182nd Inf. Bde.
3	Staff Capt.		15	331st Bde. R.F.A.
4	War Diary.		16	64th H.A.G.
5	File.		17	"B" Coy. 39th M.G.Bn.
6	10th K.O.S.B.		18	137th Fd.Ambce.
7	15th K.O.Y.L.I.		19	-Do- Adv.Dg.Stn.
8	11th Camerons.		20	224 Field Coy.R.E.
9	120th T.M.Bty.		21	"L" Special Coy.R.E.
10	40th Divn. "G".		22	Bde. Supply Officer.
11	40th Divn. "Q".		23	Bde. Signals.
12	119th Inf. Bde.		24	40th Div. Train.

#=#=#=#=#=#=#=#=#

RELIEF TABLE TO ACCOMPANY 120TH INFANTRY BRIGADE ORDER NO. 224.

Serial No.	Unit.	From	To	In Relief of	Headquarters.	Remarks.
1.	15th K.O.Y.L.I.	PADDY FARM, A.11.c.2.8.	LINE Left.	23rd Cheshires.	B.22.b.3.6.	23rd Cheshire H.Q. at present at TOUQUET PARMENTIER. 15th K.O.Y.L.I. will go into new H.Q. at B.22.a.3.6. a.3.6
2.	10th K.O.S.B.	GRAND BEAUMART.	LINE, Right.	8th Royal Irish Regt.	PUNGENT FARM, B.26.a.2.6.	To arrange march with 15th K.O.Y.L.I. so that K.O.Y.L.I. have priority of movement.
3.	11th Camerons.	TRIMBLE FARM.	RESERVE.	23rd Lancs. Fusiliers.	LETT FARM, B.25.c.3.6.	Not to move off till 10th K.O.S.B. are clear.
4.	120th T.M.Bty.	A.21.a.4.6.	LINE	121st T.M.Bty.	A.24.a.6.4.	

Vol 29

(6392) Wt. W6192/P875 1,500,000 4/18 McA & W Ltd (E 2815) Forms W3091/4. Army Form W.3091.

Cover for Documents.

Nature of Enclosures.

War Diary
Headquarters 120th Inf. Bde.
October 1918.

VOLUME XXIX

Notes, or Letters written.

ORIGINAL

SECRET

Army Form C. 2118.

Instructions regarding War Diaries and Intelligence Summaries are contained in F. S. Regs., Part II. and the Staff Manual respectively. Title pages will be prepared in manuscript.

Page 1.

WAR DIARY

or

~~INTELLIGENCE SUMMARY.~~

(Erase heading not required.)

VOLUME XXIX.

OCTOBER, 1918.

Headquarters, 120th Infantry Brigade.

Place	Date OCTOBER 1918	Hour	Summary of Events and Information	Remarks and references to Appendices
WINK COTTAGE A.20.b.3.3.	Night 1/2nd		120th Infantry Brigade relieved the 121st Infantry Brigade in the Right Brigade front in accordance with 120th Infantry Brigade Order No. 224 dated 30-9-18.	
			Dispositions of Headquarters :-	
			10th Bn. K. O. S. B. ... ... Sheet 36/B.26.a.2.8. 15th Bn. K.O.Y.L.I. ... ... B.22.a.3.6. 11th Bn. Cameron Hrs. ... ... B.25.c.3.6. 120th T. M. Battery ... ... A.24.a.6.4.	TKS
TOUQUET PERMENTIER B.21.a.9.5.	2nd	1000	120th Infantry Brigade Headquarters closed at WINK COTTAGE, 36/A.20.b.3.3., and re-opened at TOUQUET PARMENTIER 36/B.21.a.9.5.	
		1800	Headquarters and reserve personnel of 120th Trench Mortar Battery moved from A.24.a.6.4. to TOUQUET PARMENTIER, A.21.b.9.5.	TKS
			For events see Evening wire and Daily Intelligence Summary.	Appendix I (a & b)
			Casualties :- NIL	
	~~3rd.~~		During the day we took over the line as far South as the Corps Boundary. We advanced our Right flank to road running South from 36/H.6.d.8.2. to Corps Boundary - Grid line 36/H.11., I.11., J.11.	TKS
			For events see morning and evening wires and Daily Intelligence Summary.	Appendix II (a & b)
			Casualties :- NIL.	
	4th		During the day we advanced our line in conjunction with troops on the right to a line about 36/I.9.b.0.2. to I.9.b.3.7.	TKS
			For events see morning and evening wires and Daily Intelligence Summary. CASUALTIES :- NIL	Appendix III (a & b)

A6945 Wt. W11422/M1160 350,000 12/16 D. D. & L. Forms/C./2118/14.

Army Form C. 2118.

Instructions regarding War Diaries and Intelligence Summaries are contained in F. S. Regs., Par. II. and the Staff Manual respectively. Title pages will be prepared in manuscript.

Page 2.

WAR DIARY

or

~~INTELLIGENCE~~ SUMMARY.

(*Erase heading not required.*)

VOLUME XXIX.
OCTOBER, 1918.

Headquarters,
120th Infantry Brigade.

Place	Date OCTOBER 1918	Hour	Summary of Events and Information	Remarks and references to Appendices
TOUQUET PARMENTIER B.21.a.9.5.	5th		During the night 4/5th we altered the line on our right flank to conform with the Company on our right.	TRS
			Line now runs :- 36/I.9.b.30.70 - I.8.b.60.45. - I.9.b.55.20. - I.9.c.9.8. where we are in touch with troops on our right.	
		1650	120th Infantry Brigade Order No. 225 issued. 120th Infantry Brigade will relieve the 119th Infantry Brigade in the Outpost Positions on night 5/6th and 6/7th October. On completion of relief 120th Infantry Brigade will operate as Advanced Guard to the 40th Division.	Appendix IV
		1650	120th Infantry Brigade Instructions No. 1 issued stating composition of Advanced Guard. Advanced Guard Brigade will be responsible for the defence of the NIEPPE System in addition to the Outpost Line.	Appendix V
	night 5/6th		11th Bn. Cameron Highrs. relieved the 10th Bn. K.O.S.B. in Outpost Position of 120th Infantry Brigade front.	TRS
			15th Bn. K.O.Y.L.I. moved from NIEPPE to Support Area ~~xxxxxxxx~~ about HOUPLINES, relieving the 13th E. Lancs. Regt. (119th Infantry Brigade).	
			For further events see morning and evening wires and Daily Intalligence Summary.	Appendix VI (a & b)
			Casualties :- 2 O.R. Killed.	
	Night 6/7th		15th Bn. K.O.Y.L.I. moved from Support Area about HOUPLINES and relieved the 12th N. Staffs Regt. (119th Infantry Brigade) in the line in accordance with 120th Infantry Brigade Order No. 225 dated 5th.	TRS
			For events see morning and evening wires and Daily Intelligence Summary.	Appendix VII (a & b)
			Casualties :- 1 O.R. Killed 5 O.R. wounded.	
	7th	1000	120th Infantry Brigade Headquarters closed at TOUQUET PARMENTIER, B.21.a.9.5. and re-opened at 36/H.11.b.4.6.	TRS

Instructions regarding War Diaries and Intelligence Summaries are contained in F. S. Regs., Par. II. and the Staff Manual respectively. Title pages will be prepared in manuscript.

WAR DIARY

or

~~INTELLIGENCE SUMMARY~~. Headquarters, 120th Infantry Brigade.

(Erase heading not required.)

VOLUME XXIX.
OCTOBER, 1918.

Army Form C. 2118.

Page 3.

Place	Date OCTOBER 1918.	Hour	Summary of Events and Information	Remarks and references to Appendices
H.11.b.4.6.	7th		Dispositions of Brigade :-	
			Brigade Headquarters ... ... 36/H.11.b.4.6. 10th Battn. K.O.S.B. ... ... In Reserve in ERQUINGHEM and H.5.d. 15th Battn. K.O.Y.L I. ... ... In Outpost Line. 11th Battn. Cam. Highrs .. .. In Support about HOUPLINES.	THS
			For events see morning and evening wires ~~and Daily Intelligence Summary~~.	Appendix VIII (a + b).
			Casualties :- 1 OR Killed 5 OR wounded	
	8th	2000	120th Infantry Brigade Order No. 226 issued ordering Inter-battalion reliefs on night 9/10th October.- 10th Bn. K.O.S.B. to relieve 11th Cam. Highrs in Support. 11th Bn. Cam. Hrs. to relieve 15th K.O.Y.L.I. in Outpost Line. 15th K.O.Y.L.I. to move back into the ERQUINGHEM AREA.	Appendix IX THS.
			For events see morning and evening wires and Daily Intelligence Summary.	Appendix X (a + b)
			Casualties :- 1 Offr & 1 OR. Missing 1 OR. wounded.	
	night 9/10th		Inter-battalion reliefs completed in accordance with 120th Infantry Brigade Order No. 226 dated 8-10-18. Dispositions :- 10th Bn. K.O.S.B. ... ... In Support. 15th Bn. K.O.Y.L.I. ... ... In ERQUINGHEM AREA. 11th Bn. Cam. Hrs. ... ... In Outpost Line.	THS
			For events see morning and evening wires and Daily Intelligence Summary.	Appendix XI (a + b)
			Casualties :- 1 OR Killed 1 OR wounded 22 OR. Gassed	
	10th		For events see morning and evening wires and Daily Intelligence Summary. CASUALTIES :- 2 Offrs + 1 OR. wounded 1 Offr + 37 OR. Gassed.	THS Appendix XII (a + b)

Instructions regarding War Diaries and Intelligence Summaries are contained in F. S. Regs., Par. II, and the Staff Manual respectively. Title pages will be prepared in manuscript.

Page 4.

WAR DIARY

or

~~INTELLIGENCE SUMMARY~~.

(*Erase heading not required.*)

VOLUME XXIX.
OCTOBER, 1918.

Headquarters,
120th Infantry Brigade.

Army Form C. 2118.

Place	OCTOBER Date 1918.	Hour	Summary of Events and Information	Remarks and references to Appendices
H.11.b.4.6.	11th	1820	Orders issued for one Company of 10th Bn. K.O.S.B. to carry out a Minor Operation on 12th instant to gain an identification and make good the line of INCANDESCENT SUPPORT as far North as the Road 36I.5.d.5.5. and will also send a party to mop up INCANDESCENT Front Line as far North as the road.	Appendix XIII TLS
			For events see morning and evening wires and Daily Intelligence Summary.	Appendix XIV (a & b)
			Casualties :- 1 OR. wounded.	
	12th	05[illegible]5	A Minor Operation was carried out by "A" Company, 10th Bn. K.O.S.B. Line now runs as follows :- North of Railway from I.11.a.6.3. - along INCANDESCENT TRENCH - to road at I.5.d.3.6. Posts pushed out in direction of L'EPINETTE to join 11th Cam. Highrs. and are being pushed into INCANDESCENT SUPPORT. No identifications were obtained as the enemy withdrew directly our advance was perceived.	TLS
		1150	120th Infantry Brigade Order No. 228 issued. 120th Infantry Brigade will be relieved in the Advanced Guard Position by the 121st Infantry Brigade on the night 13/14th October.	Appendix XV
			For events see morning and evening wires and Daily Intelligence Summary.	Appendix XVI (a & b)
			Casualties :- 2 OR. Killed 7 OR. Gassed	
	13th		The line gained yesterday was consolidated and posts established to connect up with the main line on the left. The general line now runs as follows :- 36/C.28.a.2.2. - I.5.a.5.7. I.5.c.0.8. - I.5.c.4.3. - I.5.c.9.3. - along INCANDESCENT TRENCH to railway at I.11.a.6.3. where we are in close liaison with the troops on our right.	TLS
	night 13/14		Relief carried out in accordance with 120th Infantry Brigade Order No. 228 dated 12-10-18.	
			For events see morning and evening wires and Daily Intelligence Summary.	Appendix XVII (a & b)
			Casualties :- NIL	

A6945 Wt. W11422/M1160 350,000 12/16 D. D. & L. Forms/C./2118/14.

Instructions regarding War Diaries and Intelligence Summaries are contained in F. S. Regs., Part II. and the Staff Manual respectively. Title pages will be prepared in manuscript.

Army Form C. 2118.

WAR DIARY or INTELLIGENCE SUMMARY.

(Erase heading not required.)

VOLUME XXIX.
OCTOBER, 1918.

Page 5.

Headquarters, 120th Infantry Brigade.

Place	Date	Hour	Summary of Events and Information	Remarks and references to Appendices
TOUQUET PARMENTIER B.21.a.9.5.	14th	10.00	120th Infantry Brigade Headquarters closed at H.11.b.4.6. and re-opened at TOUQUET PARMENTIER, B.21.a.9.5.	
			Dispositions :- Brigade Headquarters ... TOUQUET PARMENTIER. 10th Bn. K.O.S.B. ... 36/B.9.d.7.6. 15th Bn. K.O.Y.L.I. ... B.29.a.2.3. 11th Bn. Cam. Hrs. ... H.3.a.6.2. 120th T. M. Battery ... B.9.c.2.6.	TWB
			Defence Instructions for NIEPPE System issued to Units.	Appendix XVIII
	16th	07.00	120th Infantry Brigade Order No. 229 issued. 40th Division will be ready to advance in an Easterly direction in conjunction with the 59th and 31st Division. In the event of Advanced Guard moving forward, the 120th Infantry Brigade will be prepared to Support the 121st Infantry Brigade or move through the 121st Infantry Brigade if the situation admits and requires it.	Appendix XIX TWB
		14.00	120th Infantry Brigade Headquarters closed at TOUQUET PARMENTIER and re-opened at H.11.b.4.6. Units ordered by wire to move and occupy positions detailed in para 5 of 120th Infantry Brigade Order No. 229.	
			Dispositions taken up as follows :- Brigade Headquarters ... H.11.b.4.6. 10th Bn. K.O S.B. ... C.26.b.8.0. 15th Bn. K.O Y.L.I. ... H.12.b.3.7. 11th Bn. Cam. Hrs. ... H.4.d.5.7. 120th T. M. Bty. ... H.12.c.6.7.	TWB
			120th Infantry Brigade Instructions No. 3 issued.	Appendix XX
		23.20	Wire (BM 4) sent to all Units ordering Brigade to be clear of present positions by	

A6945 Wt. W11422/M1160 350,000 12/16 D. D. & L. Forms/C./2118/14.

Instructions regarding War Diaries and Intelligence Summaries are contained in F. S. Regs., Par. II. and the Staff Manual respectively. Title pages will be prepared in manuscript.

Army Form C. 2118.

WAR DIARY
or
INTELLIGENCE SUMMARY.
(*Erase heading not required.*)

VOLUME XXIX.
OCTOBER, 1918.

Page 6.

Headquarters,
120th Infantry Brigade.

Place	Date	Hour	Summary of Events and Information	Remarks and references to Appendices
H.11.b.4.6.	16th	23.20	(Cont). 10.00 hours 17th and concentrate as follows :- Brigade Headquarters ... about C.28.b. 10th Bn. K.O.S.B. ... at C.18.d. 15th Bn. K.O.Y.L.I. ... at C.30.central 11th Bn. Cam. Hrs. ... at I.6.a. 120th T. M. Bty. ... about C.22.b. & d.	TUS
	17th		Move carried out in accordance with wire B.M. 4 of 16th. Dispositions:- Brigade Headquarters ... J.1.central. 10th Bn. K.O.S.B. ... LA CROIX AU BOIS. 15th Bn. K.O.Y.L.I. ... CHAMPREUILLE (C.26.d.) 11th Bn. Cam. Highrs. ... LA PREVOTE (J.1.d.). 120th T. M. Battery. ... J.1.d.	TUS
	18th	01.30	120th Infantry Brigade Order No. 230 issued. Enemy withdrawing Eastwards through ROUBAIX and TOURCOING. 40th Division is to continue to advance. 120th Infantry Brigade will be about WAMBRECHIES by 12.00 hours 18th inst.	Appendix XXI.
		09.30	Brigade Headquarters closed at J.1.central and re-opened at WAMBRECHIES (E.26.c.7.0.) 10th Bn. K.O.S.B. ... WAMBRECHIES E.26.d.3.2. 15th Bn. K.O.Y.L.I. ... - do - E.26.d.0.5. 11th Bn. Cam. Highrs. ... - do - K.2.a.5.9. 120th T. M. Battery ... - do - K.1.b.9.4.	TUS
			Brigadier General C.J.HOBKIRK, C.M.G., D.S.O. proceeded to ENGLAND for six months tour of duty. Brigadier General The Hon. W.P.HORE-RUTHVEN, C.M.G., D.S.O. assumed Command of the Brigade vice Brigadier General HOBKIRK.	

A6945 Wt. W11422/M1160 35,6000 12/16 D. D. & L. Forms/C./2118/14.

Instructions regarding War Diaries and Intelligence Summaries are contained in F. S. Regs., Part II, and the Staff Manual respectively. Title pages will be prepared in manuscript.

Army Form C. 2118.

WAR DIARY *or* INTELLIGENCE SUMMARY.

(Erase heading not required.)

VOLUME XXIX.
OCTOBER, 1918.

Page 7.

Headquarters,
120th Infantry Brigade.

Place	Date	Hour	Summary of Events and Information	Remarks and references to Appendices
WAMBRECHIES.	18th	22.08	Units notified by wire (BM24) that Brigade will move to ST ANDRE on 19th instant.	
ST ANDRE.	19th		Move carried out in accordance with wire BM 21 of 18th instant.	JMS
			Dispositions :-	
			Brigade Headquarters ... ST ANDRE (36/K.14.a.7.0.)	
			10th Bn. K.O.S.B. ...)	
			15th Bn. K.O.Y.L.I. ...) Billetted in MONASTRY	
			11th Bn. Cam. Hrs. ...) in	
			120th T. M. Bty. ...) 36/ K.14.a.	
	20th		Working parties found by the Brigade to work under the supervision of the 109th Railway Company at K.21.a.2.9. (One Battalion & two Companies from 09.00 to 13.00 and one Battalion and two Companies from 13.00 to 17.00). One hour devoted to drill and training of specialists by all Companies.	JMS
	21st		In addition to one hour devoted daily to drill and the training of specialists by all Companies - Battalion Commanders to arrange that all Companies which are not working on the railway in the morning, to spend one hour on Musketry.	
		15.00	Conference held at Brigade Headquarters. The Major General Commanding the 40th Division addressed Battalion Commanders, Seconds-in-Command, Company Commanders and O.C., 120th T. M. Battery laying stress on the lessons learnt during the last three months. (i) Need for training Officers and N.C.Os. in leadership and initiative. (ii) Necessity for more definite instructions to subordinate commanders. (iii) Rôle of an Advanced Guard and necessity for better communications. (iv) Billeting organisation	JMS
	22nd		Class of Instruction for Signallers commenced at Brigade Headquarters under the Brigade Signalling Officer, 10 other ranks per Battalion attending.	JMS

A6945 Wt. W11422/M1160 350,000 12/16 D. D. & L. Forms/C./2118/14.

Instructions regarding War Diaries and Intelligence Summaries are contained in F. S. Regs., Par. II, and the Staff Manual respectively. Title pages will be prepared in manuscript.

Page 8.

WAR DIARY or INTELLIGENCE SUMMARY.

(Erase heading not required.)

VOLUME XXIX.
OCTOBER, 1918.

Army Form C. 2118.

Headquarters,
120th Infantry Brigade.

Place	Date	Hour	Summary of Events and Information	Remarks and references to Appendices
ST ANDRE.	23rd		Working parties found by the Brigade for work on the Railway at K.21.a.2.9. (One Battalion & 2 Companies from 09.00 to 13.00 and 1½ Battns. from 13.00 to 17.00)	TRS
			One hour devoted to Musketry by all Companies.	
	24th) 25th)		--- ditto ---	
	26th		1½ Battalions employed on Railway at ST ANDRE. 1½ Battalions ,, ,, ,, at LA MADELEINE.	TRS
			No training carried out.	
	27th		--- ditto ---	
		10.00	120th Infantry Brigade Order No. 231 issued, detailing move of Brigade to vicinity of LANNOY, on 28th October, 1918.	Appendix XXII
		14.15	Conference held at Brigade Headquarters, at which were present - G.O.C., Brigade Major, Commanding Officers and Adjutants. (1) Owing to the under strength of Battalions it was decided to organise Companies on three platoon basis and, if necessary, subdivide platoons into three sections - 2 rifle and 1 Lewis Gun Section. (2) Necessity for Officers to be sent to conduct personnel from Reception Camp to Units to prevent straggling emphasised. (3) C.Os. complained of the shortage of supplies for Divisional Canteen.	TRS
	28th		The Brigade left ST ANDRE at 08.30 and arrived at LANNOY at 12.30. Battalions marching well on the whole and considering the distance (about 10 miles) the number of men who fell out (about 69) was not excessive, as it was the first occasion on which the Brigade had marched in close formation. The whole Brigade was comfortably billeted in LANNOY.	TRS

A6945 Wt. W11422/M1160 35,000 12/16 D. D. & L. Forms/C./2118/14.

VOLUME XXIX.
OCTOBER, 1918.

Army Form C. 2118.

WAR DIARY
or
INTELLIGENCE SUMMARY.
(*Erase heading not required.*)

Instructions regarding War Diaries and Intelligence Summaries are contained in F. S. Regs., Par. II. and the Staff Manual respectively. Title pages will be prepared in manuscript.

Page 9.

Headquarters,
120th Infantry Brigade.

Place	Date	Hour	Summary of Events and Information	Remarks and references to Appendices
LANNOY.	28th	(Cont).	Conference attended by C.Os., Adjutants and Staff was held at Brigade Headquarters at 17.30 hours at which the G.O.C. raised points noticed during the march of the Brigade. (2) Arranged bounds of billeting area. (3) Decided on four hours training daily.	TAS
	29th	05.00	G.O.C. left Headquarters with G.S.O. 3 to visit the line. At dawn enemy heavily shelled the area. The G.O.C. was slightly wounded in the back. Battalions training - musketry on range. Riding School for Officers.	TAS
	30th) 31st)		Battalions training.	TAS

W. Ruthven Brigadier General,
Commanding, 120th Infantry Brigade.

A6945 Wt. W11422/M1160 350,000 12/16 D. D. & L. Forms/C./2118/14.

DUPLICATE

SECRET

Army Form C. 2118.

Instructions regarding War Diaries and Intelligence Summaries are contained in F. S. Regs., Part II. and the Staff Manual respectively. Title pages will be prepared in manuscript.

Page 1.

WAR DIARY
or
~~INTELLIGENCE SUMMARY.~~
(Erase heading not required.)

VOLUME XXIX.

OCTOBER, 1918.

Headquarters, 120th Infantry Brigade.

Place	OCTOBER 1918	Hour	Summary of Events and Information	Remarks and references to Appendices
WINK COTTAGE A.20.b.3.3.	Night 1/2nd		120th Infantry Brigade relieved the 121st Infantry Brigade in the Right Brigade front in accordance with 120th Infantry Brigade Order No. 224 dated 30-9-18.	TUS
			Dispositions of Headquarters :-	
			10th Bn. K. O. S. B. ... ... Sheet 36/B.26.a.2.6. 15th Bn. K.O.Y.L.I. ... ... B.22.a.3.6. 11th Bn. Cameron Hrs. ... ... B.25.c.3.6. 120th T. M. Battery ... ... A.24.a.6.4.	
TOUQUET PARMENTIER B.21.a.9.5.	2nd	1000	120th Infantry Brigade Headquarters closed at WINK COTTAGE, 36/A.20.b.3.3., and re-opened at TOUQUET PARMENTIER 36/B.21.a.9.5.	TUS
		1800	Headquarters and reserve personnel of 120th Trench Mortar Battery moved from A.24.a.6.4. to TOUQUET PARMENTIER, A.21.b.9.5.	
			For events see Evening wire and Daily Intelligence Summary.	Appendix I (a).
			Casualties :- NIL.	
	3rd.		During the day we took over the line as far South as the Corps Boundary. We advanced our Right flank to road running South from 36/H.6.d.8.2. to Corps Boundary - Grid line 36/H.11., I.11., J.11.	TUS
			For events see morning and evening wires and Daily Intelligence Summary.	Appendix II (a & b)
			Casualties :- NIL.	
	4th		During the day we advanced our line in conjunction with troops on the right to a line about 36/I.9.b.0.2. to I.9.b.3.7.	TUS
			For events see morning and evening wires and Daily Intelligence Summary.	Appendix III (a & b)
			CASUALTIES :- NIL	

A6945 Wt. W11422/M1160 35,000 12/16 D. D. & L. Forms/C./2118/14.

Instructions regarding War Diaries and Intelligence Summaries are contained in F. S. Regs., Par. II. and the Staff Manual respectively. Title pages will be prepared in manuscript.

Page 2

Army Form C. 2118.

WAR DIARY
or
INTELLIGENCE SUMMARY.
(Erase heading not required.)

VOLUME XXIX.
OCTOBER, 1918.

Headquarters,
120th Infantry Brigade.

Place	OCTOBER 1918	Hour	Summary of Events and Information	Remarks and references to Appendices
TOUQUET PARMENTIER B.21.a.9.5.	5th		During the night 4/5th we altered the line on our right flank to conform with the Company on our right. Line now runs :- 36/I.9.b.30.70 - I.8.b.60.45. - I.9.b.55.20. - I.9.c.9.8. where we are in touch with troops on our right.	TRS
		1650	120th Infantry Brigade Order No. 225 issued. 120th Infantry Brigade will relieve the 119th Infantry Brigade in the Outpost Positions on night 5/6th and 6/7th October. On completion of relief 120th Infantry Brigade will operate as Advanced Guard to the 40th Division.	appendix IV
		1650	120th Infantry Brigade Instructions No. 1 issued stating composition of Advanced Guard. Advanced Guard Brigade will be responsible for the defence of the NIEPPE System in addition to the Outpost Line.	appendix V TRS
	night 5/6th		11th Bn. Cameron Highrs. relieved the 10th Bn. K.O.S.B. in Outpost Position of 120th Infantry Brigade front. 15th Bn. K.O.Y.L.I. moved from NIEPPE to Support Area ~~relieving~~ about HOUPLINES, relieving the 13th E. Lancs. Regt. (119th Infantry Brigade).	
			For further events see morning and evening wires and Daily Intalligence Summary.	appendix VI (a & b)
			Casualties :- 2 O.R. Killed.	
	Night 6/7th		15th Bn. K.O.Y.L.I. moved from Support Area about HOUPLINES and relieved the 12th N. Staffs Regt.(119th Infantry Brigade) in the line in accordance with 120th Infantry Brigade Order No. 225 dated 5th.	TRS
			For events see morning and evening wires and Daily Intelligence Summary.	appendix VII (a & b).
			Casualties :- 1 O.R. Killed 5 O.R. wounded	
	7th	1000	120th Infantry Brigade Headquarters closed at TOUQUET PARMENTIER, B.21.a.9.5. and re-opened at 36/H.11.b.4.6.	TRS

A6945 Wt. W11422/M1160 350,000 12/16 D. D. & L. Forms/C./2118/14.

Instructions regarding War Diaries and Intelligence Summaries are contained in F. S. Regs., Par. II. and the Staff Manual respectively. Title pages will be prepared in manuscript.

Army Form C. 2118.

WAR DIARY
or
~~INTELLIGENCE SUMMARY~~.
(Erase heading not required.)

Page 3.

VOLUME XXIX.
OCTOBER, 1918.

Headquarters,
120th Infantry Brigade.

Place	Date OCTOBER 1918.	Hour	Summary of Events and Information	Remarks and references to Appendices
H.11.b.4.6.	7th		Dispositions of Brigade :-	TBS
			Brigade Headquarters ... ... 36/H.11.b.4.6.	
			10th Battn. K.O.S.B. ... ... In Reserve in ERQUINGHEM and H.5.d.	
			15th Battn. K.O.Y.L I. ... ... In Outpost Line.	
			11th Battn. Cam. Highrs .. .. In Support about HOUPLINES.	
			For events see morning and evening wires ~~and Daily Intelligence Summary~~.	Appendix VIII (a & b)
			Casualties :- 1 OR killed 5 OR wounded	
	8th	2000	120th Infantry Brigade Order No. 226 issued ordering Inter-battalion reliefs on night 9/10th October.-	Appendix IX
			10th Bn. K.O.S.B. to relieve 11th Cam. Highrs in Support.	TBS
			11th Bn. Cam. Hrs. to relieve 15th K.O.Y.L.I. in Outpost Line.	
			15th K.O.Y.L.I. to move back into the ERQUINGHEM AREA.	
			For events see morning and evening wires and Daily Intelligence Summary.	Appendix X (a & b)
			Casualties :-	
	night 9/10th		Inter-battalion reliefs completed in accordance with 120th Infantry Brigade Order No. 226 dated 8-10-18.	TBS
			Dispositions :-	
			10th Bn. K.O.S.B. ... ... In Support.	
			15th Bn. K.O.Y.L.I. ... ... In ERQUINGHEM AREA.	
			11th Bn. Cam. Hrs. ... ... In Outpost Line.	
			For events see morning and evening wires and Daily Intelligence Summary.	Appendix XI (a & b)
			Casualties :-	
	10th		For events see morning and evening wires and Daily Intelligence Summary.	TBS Appendix XII (a & b)

A6945 Wt. W11422/M1160 350,000 12/16 D. D. & L. Forms/C.2118/14.

Instructions regarding War Diaries and Intelligence Summaries are contained in F. S. Regs., Par. II. and the Staff Manual respectively. Title pages will be prepared in manuscript.

WAR DIARY
or
INTELLIGENCE SUMMARY.
(Erase heading not required.)

VOLUME XXIX.
OCTOBER, 1918.

Army Form C. 2118.

Page 4.

Headquarters,
120th Infantry Brigade.

Place	Date OCTOBER 1918.	Hour	Summary of Events and Information	Remarks and references to Appendices
H.11.b.4.6.	11th	1820	Orders issued for one Company of 10th Bn. K.O.S.B. to carry out a Minor Operation on 12th instant to gain an identification and make good the line of INCANDESCENT SUPPORT as far North as the Road 36I.5.d.5.5. and will also send a party to mop up INCANDESCENT Front Line as far North as the road.	Appendix XIII TRS
			For events see morning and evening wires and Daily Intelligence Summary.	Appendix XIV (a & b)
			Casualties :- 1 OR wounded	
	12th	0525	A Minor Operation was carried out by "A" Company, 10th Bn. K.O.S.B. Line now runs as follows :- North of Railway from I.11.a.6.3. - along INCANDESCENT TRENCH - to road at I.5.d.3.6. Posts pushed out in direction of L'EPINETTE to join 11th Cam. Highrs. and are being pushed into INCANDESCENT SUPPORT. No identifications were obtained as the enemy withdrew directly our advance was perceived.	TRS
		1150	120th Infantry Brigade Order No. 228 issued. 120th Infantry Brigade will be relieved in the Advanced Guard Position by the 121st Infantry Brigade on the night 13/14th October.	Appendix XV
			For evenys see morning and evening wires and Daily Intelligence Summary.	Appendix XVI (a & b)
			Casualties :- 2 OR Killed. 7 OR Gassed.	
	13th		The line gained yesterday was consolidated and posts established to connect up with the main line on the left. The general line now runs as follows :- 36/C.28.a.2.2. - I.5.a.3.7. I.5.c.0.8. - I.5.c.4.3. - I.5.c.9.3. - along INCANDESCENT TRENCH to railway at I.11.a.6.3. where we are in close liaison with the troops on our right.	TRS
	night 13/14		Relief carried out in accordance with 120th Infantry Brigade Order No. 228 dated 12-10-18.	TRS
			For events see morning and evening wires and Daily Intelligence Summary.	Appendix XVII (a & b)
			Casualties ;- Nil	

A6945 Wt. W11422/M1160 350,000 12/16 D. D. & L. Forms/C./2118/14.

Army Form C. 2118.

VOLUME XXIX.
OCTOBER, 1918.

Instructions regarding War Diaries and Intelligence Summaries are contained in F. S. Regs., Part II. and the Staff Manual respectively. Title pages will be prepared in manuscript.

WAR DIARY
or
INTELLIGENCE SUMMARY.
(*Erase heading not required.*)

Page 5.

Headquarters,
120th Infantry Brigade.

Place	Date	Hour	Summary of Events and Information	Remarks and references to Appendices
TOUQUET PARMENTIER B.21.a.9.5.	14th	10.00	120th Infantry Brigade Headquarters closed at H.11.b.4.6. and re-opened at TOUQUET PARMENTIER, B.21.a.9.5.	TMJ
			Dispositions :- Brigade Headquarters ... TOUQUET PARMENTIER. 10th Bn. K.O.S.B. ... 36/B.9.d.7.6. 15th Bn. K.O.Y.L.I. ... B.29.a.2.3. 11th Bn. Cam. Hrs. ... B.3.a.6.2. 120th T. M. Battery ... B.9.c.2.6.	
			Defence Instructions for [illegible] System issued to Units.	Appendix XVIII
	16th	07.00	120th Infantry Brigade Order No. 229 issued. 40th Division will be ready to advance in an Easterly direction in conjunction with the 59th and 31st Division. In the event of Advanced Guard moving forward, the 120th Infantry Brigade will be prepared to support the 121st Infantry Brigade or move through the 121st Infantry Brigade if the situation admits and requires it.	Appendix XIX
		14.00	120th Infantry Brigade Headquarters closed at TOUQUET PARMENTIER and re-opened at H.11.b.4.6. Units ordered by wire to move and occupy positions detailed in para 5 of 120th Infantry Brigade Order No. 229.	TMJ
			Dispositions taken up as follows :- Brigade Headquarters ... H.11.b.4.6. 10th Bn. K.O.S.B. ... C.26.b.3.0. 15th Bn. K.O.Y.L.I. ... H.12.b.3.7. 11th Bn. Cam. Hrs. ... H.4.1.b.7. 120th T. M. Bty. ... H.12.c.6.7.	
			120th Infantry Brigade Instructions No. 3 issued.	Appendix XX
		23.20	Wire (BM 4) sent to all Units ordering Brigade to be clear of present positions by	

A6945 Wt. W11422/M1160 350,000 12/16 D. D. & L. Forms/C./2118/14.

Instructions regarding War Diaries and Intelligence Summaries are contained in F. S. Regs., Par. II, and the Staff Manual respectively. Title pages will be prepared in manuscript.

Army Form C. 2118.

WAR DIARY
or
INTELLIGENCE SUMMARY.
(Erase heading not required.)

VOLUME XXIX.
OCTOBER, 1918.

Page 6.

Headquarters,
120th Infantry Brigade.

Place	Date	Hour	Summary of Events and Information	Remarks and references to Appendices
H.11.b.4.6.	16th	23.20	(Cont). 10.00 hours 17th and concentrate as follows :- Brigade Headquarters ... about C.28.b. 10th Bn. K.O.S.B. ... at C.18.d. 15th Bn. K.O.Y.L.I. ... at C.3 .central 11th Bn. Cam. Hrs. ... at I.6.a. 120th T. M. Bty. ... about C.22.b. & d.	
	17th		Move carried out in/accordance with wire B.M. 4 of 16th.	TMS
			Dispositions:- Brigade Headquarters ... J.1.central. 10th Bn. K.O.S.B. ... LA CROIX AU BOIS. 15th Bn. K.O.Y.L.I. ... CHAMPREUILLE (C.26.d.) 11th Bn. Cam. Highrs. ... LA PREVOTE (J.1.d.). 120th T. M. Battery. ... J.1.d.	
	18th	01.30	120th Infantry Brigade Order No. 230 issued. Enemy withdrawing Eastwards through ROUBAIX and TOURCOING. 40th Division is to continue to advance. 120th Infantry Brigade will be about WAMBRECHIES by 12.00 hours 18th inst.	Appendix XXI
		09.30	Brigade Headquarters closed at J.1.central and re-opened at WAMBRECHIES (E.26.c.7.0.) 10th Bn. K.O.S.B. ... WAMBRECHIES E.26.d.3.2. 15th Bn. K.O.Y.L.I. ... - do - E.26.d.0.5. 11th Bn. Cam. Highrs. ... - do - K.2.a.5.9. 120th T. M. Battery ... - do - K.1.b.9.4.	TMS
			Brigadier General C.J.HOBKIRK, C.M.G., D.S.O. proceeded to ENGLAND for six months tour of duty. Brigadier General The Hon. W.P.HORE-RUTHVEN, C.M.G., D.S.O. assumed Command of the Brigade vice Brigadier General HOBKIRK.	

A6945 Wt. W11422/M1160 350,000 12/16 D. D. & L. Forms/C./2118/14.

Instructions regarding War Diaries and Intelligence Summaries are contained in F. S. Regs., Par. II, and the Staff Manual respectively. Title pages will be prepared in manuscript.

Page 7.

WAR DIARY
or
INTELLIGENCE SUMMARY.
(Erase heading not required.)

VOLUME XXIX.
OCTOBER, 1918.

Army Form C. 2118.

Headquarters,
120th Infantry Brigade.

Place	Date	Hour	Summary of Events and Information	Remarks and references to Appendices
WAMBRECHIES.	18th	22.08	Units notified by wire (BM24) that Brigade will move to ST ANDRE on 19th instant.	
ST ANDRE.	19th		Move carried out in accordance with wire BM 21 of 18th instant.	
			Dispositions :-	
			Brigade Headquarters ... STANDRE (36/K.14.a.7.0.)	
			10th Bn. K.O.S.B. ...)	
			15th Bn. K.O.Y.L.I. ...) Billetted in MONASTRY	
			11th Bn. Cam. Hrs. ...) in	
			120th T. M. Bty. ...) 36/ K.14.a.	
	20th		Working parties found by the Brigade to work under the supervision of the 109th Railway Company at K.21.a.2.9. (One Battalion & two Companies from 09.00 to 13.00 and one Battalion and two Companies from 13.00 to 17.00). One hour devoted to drill and training of specialists by all Companies.	
	21st		In addition to one hour devoted daily to drill and the training of specialists by all Companies - Battalion Commanders to arrange that all Companies which are not working on the railway in the morning, to spend one hour on Musketry.	
		15.00	Conference held at Brigade Headquarters. The Major General Commanding the 40th Division addressed Battalion Commanders, Seconds-in-Command, Company Commanders and O.C., 120th T. M. Battery laying stress on the lessons learnt during the last three months.	
			(i) Need for training Officers and N.C.Os. in leadership and initiative.	
			(ii) Necessity for more definite instructions to subordinate commanders.	
			(iii) Role of an Advanced Guard and necessity for better communications.	
			(iv) Billeting organisation	
	22nd		Class of Instruction for Signallers commenced at Brigade Headquarters under the Brigade Signalling Officer, 10 other ranks per Battalion attending.	

A6945 Wt. W11422/M1160 35,000 12/16 D. D. & L. Forms/C./2118/14.

Instructions regarding War Diaries and Intelligence Summaries are contained in F. S. Regs., Par. II, and the Staff Manual respectively. Title pages will be prepared in manuscript.

Page 8.

WAR DIARY
or
INTELLIGENCE SUMMARY.
(Erase heading not required.)

VOLUME XXIX.
OCTOBER, 1918.

Army Form C. 2118.

Headquarters,
120th Infantry Brigade.

Place	Date	Hour	Summary of Events and Information	Remarks and references to Appendices
ST ANDRE.	23rd		Working parties found by the Brigade for work on the Railway at K.21.a.2.9. (One Battalion & 2 Companies from 09.00 to 13.00 and 1½ Battns. from 13.00 to 17.00)	TKS
			One hour devoted to Musketry by all Companies.	
	24th) 25th)		--- ditto ---	TKS
	26th		1½ Battalions employed on Railway at ST ANDRE. 1½ Battalions ,, ,, ,, at LA MADELEINE.	TKS
			No training carried out.	
	27th		--- ditto ---	
		10.00	120th Infantry Brigade Order No. 231 issued, detailing move of Brigade to vicinity of LANNOY, on 28th October, 1918.	Appendix XXII
		14.15	Conference held at Brigade Headquarters, at which were present - G.O.C., Brigade Major, Commanding Officers and Adjutants.	TKS
			(1) Owing to the under strength of Battalions it was decided to organise Companies on three platoon basis and, if necessary, subdivide platoons into three sections - 2 rifle and 1 Lewis Gun Section.	
			(2) Necessity for Officers to be sent to conduct personnel from Reception Camp to Units to prevent straggling emphasised.	
			(3) C.Os. complained of the shortage of supplies for Divisional Canteen.	
	28th		The Brigade left ST ANDRE at 08.30 and arrived at LANNOY at 12.30. Battalions marching well on the whole and considering the distance (about 10 miles) the number of men who fell out (about 69) was not excessive, as it was the first occasion on which the Brigade had marched in close formation. The whole Brigade was comfortably billeted in LANNOY.	TKS

A6945 Wt. W11422/M1160 350,000 12/16 D. D. & L. Forms/C./2118/14.

Army Form C. 2118.

Instructions regarding War Diaries and Intelligence Summaries are contained in F. S. Regs., Part II, and the Staff Manual respectively. Title pages will be prepared in manuscript.

VOLUME XXIX.
OCTOBER, 1918.

WAR DIARY
or
INTELLIGENCE SUMMARY.
(Erase heading not required.)

Page 9.

Headquarters,
120th Infantry Brigade.

Place	Date	Hour	Summary of Events and Information	Remarks and references to Appendices
LANNOY.	28th	(Cont).	Conference attended by C.Os., Adjutants and Staff was held at Brigade Headquarters at 17.30 hours at which the G.O.C. raised points noticed during the march of the Brigade. (2) Arranged bounds of billeting area. (3) Decided on four hours training daily.	TWS
	29th	05.00	G.O.C. left Headquarters with G.S.O. 3 to visit the line. At dawn enemy heavily shelled the area. The G.O.C. was slightly wounded in the back. Battalions training - musketry on range. Riding School for Officers.	TWS
	30th) 31st)		Battalions training.	TWS

W. Ruthven Brigadier General,
Commanding, 120th Infantry Brigade.

A6945 Wt. W11422/M1160 350,000 12/16 D. D. & L. Forms/C./2118/14.

"A" Form
MESSAGES AND SIGNALS.

Army Form C. 2121
(In pads of 100.)

No. of Message..........

Prefix.......Code.......m.	Words	Charge.	This message is on a/c of:	Recd. at......m.
Office of Origin and Service Instructions	Sent		App I (a)	Date..........
	At ....m.		..........Service.	From ....
	To			
	By		(Signature of "Franking Officer")	By..........

TO DAFA
JUZA
JURE

Sender's Number.	Day of Month.	In reply to Number.	AAA
G 31	2		

Evening Situation AAA
Situation quiet AAA
nothing to report.

Addsd DAFA repeated
JUZA and JURE

From JUV ①
Place
Time

The above may be forwarded as now corrected (Z) Priority

Censor. Signature of Addressor or person authorised to telegraph in his name
Capt.

* This line should be erased if not required.

Order No. 1625. Wt. W3253/ P 511. 27/2 H. & K., Ltd. (E. 2634)

Appendix I

S E C R E T.

INTELLIGENCE REPORT - 180TH INFANTRY BRIGADE.
R I G H T   S E C T O R.

6 a.m. 1-10-18 to 6 a.m. 2-10-18.

"A" OUR OPERATIONS.

1. INFANTRY. Nil.

2. ARTILLERY. Counter Battery work was carried out throughout the period.
Enemy positions and back areas were harassed during the night.

3. AERIAL. Single machines were observed during the morning, increased activity later.

4. M. Gs. Enemy positions and tracks were harassed by M.G. fire.

5. T. M. Quiet.

"B" ENEMY OPERATIONS.

1. INFANTRY. Nil.

2. ARTILLERY. Below normal.
Area B.18.c. was lightly shelled at 20.30

3. M. Gs. Normal.
M.G.position located at B.29.c.8.9.

4. T.Ms. Nil.

5. AERIAL. Below normal.

"C" ENEMY INTELLIGENCE.

EXPLOSIONS. Four explosions were heard from the direction of ARMENTIERES between 04.30 to 06.30. There was no shelling at the time.

Brigadier General,
Commanding, 180th Infantry Brigade.

==========================

SHELLING REPORT.

Right Sector.

Period-06.00, 1/10/18 to 06.00, 2/10/18.

Time.	Area Shelled.	No. Rds.	Calibre.	Directn.	Remarks.
20.30.	B.16.c.	12.	5.9.	S.E.	*

* Enemy Artillery quiet throughout the period.

H. Barker Capt.
for. Brigadier General,
Commanding 120th Infantry Brigade.

2/10/18.

"A" Form

Army Form C. 2121
(In pads of 100.)

MESSAGES AND SIGNALS.

No. of Message...........

Prefix........Code........m.	Words	Charge.	This message is on a/c of:	Recd. at......m.
Office of Origin and Service Instructions	Sent		..........Service.	Date..........
	At........m.			From ....
	To			
	By		(Signature of "Franking Officer")	By..........

TO — JUZA 178th Inf Bde

Sender's Number.	Day of Month.	In reply to Number.	AAA
	3		

Cancelled DAFA repeated JUZA and 178 Inf Bde

From JUVO
Place
Time

The above may be forwarded as now corrected. (Z)

Priority

Censor. Signature of Addressor or person authorised to telegraph in his name

* This line should be erased if not required.

Order No. 1625 Wt. W3253/ P 511 27/2 H. & K., Ltd. (E. 2634)

"A" Form

Army Form C. 2121
(In pads of 100.)

MESSAGES AND SIGNALS.

No. of Message............

Prefix..............Code..............m. | Words | Charge.

Office of Origin and Service Instructions

Sent
At ....m.
To ....
By ....

This message is on a/c of:
..........................Service.
(Signature of "Franking Officer")

Recd. at......m.
Date..............
From ....
By..............

Appx II (6)

TO DAFA
JUZA
JUGU

Sender's Number.	Day of Month.	In reply to Number.	AAA
939	3rd		

Evening quiet AAA forward companies believed working forward to obtain touch with JUZA

AAA
Prisoners since morning of 1st NIL AAA during last six hours NIL Wounded DAFA reports JUZA and JUGU

From TUVO
Place
Time

The above may be forwarded as now corrected. (Z)

.... Censor.

Signature of Addressor or person authorised to telegraph in his name
[signature] Capt.

* This line should be erased if not required.

Order No. 1625. Wt. W3353/ P 511. 27/2 H. & K., Ltd. (E. 2634).

Appendix II

CONFIDENTIAL.

INTELLIGENCE REPORT - 120TH INFANTRY BRIGADE.
RIGHT SECTOR.
06.00 2-10-18 to 06.00 3-10-18

"A" OUR OPERATIONS.

1. INFANTRY. During the day we took over the line as far South as the Corps Boundary. We then advanced our right flank to the road running South from H.6.b.8.2. to Corps Boundary, where we are in touch with the Division on our Right. Posts were established along the railway from B.29.d. to H.6.b.8.2.
Patrols are pushing forward to obtain touch with 119th Infantry Brigade.

2. ARTILLERY. Quiet during the day. Slight activity during the night.

3. AERIAL. Usual formations were observed: flying very low over the enemy's lines.

"B" ENEMY OPERATIONS.

1. INFANTRY. Nil.

2. ARTILLERY. Occasional rounds fell in PONT de NIEPPE, which were fired at a longer range than usual. Area H.5.d/1.1. received a few shells.

3. M. Gs. Nil.

4. T. Ms. Nil.

5. GAS SHELLS. Occasional Gas Shells fell in B.28.a.

6. AERIAL. Signle E.As. attempted to cross our lines during the day but were driven off by A.A. fire.

"C" ENEMY INTELLIGENCE.

1. FIRES. Several fires and explosions were observed in rear of enemy lines during the period

2. MOVEMENT. Movement was observed at B.30.b.6.9. and C.19.c. 26.72. during the morning.

3-10-18.

Brigadier General,
Commanding 120th Infantry Brigade.

HOSTILE SHELLING REPORT.
****

Right Sector.

Period - 06.00. 2/10/18. to 06.00. 3/10/18.

Enemy artillery very quiet.

Occasional shells fell in PONT DE NIEPPE,

and H.5.d.

J. C. Barker Capt.
for Brigadier General,
Commanding 120th Infantry Brigade.

3/10/18.

"A" Form
MESSAGES AND SIGNALS.

Army Form C. 2121
(In pads of 100.)

No. of Message............

Prefix..............Code..............m.	Words	Charge.	This message is on a/c of:	Recd. at........m.
Office of Origin and Service Instructions	Sent		........................Service.	Date............
	At..........m.			From ....
	To..............			
	By		(Signature of "Franking Officer")	By..............

TO { [illegible] [illegible] [illegible]

Sender's Number.	Day of Month.	In reply to Number.	AAA
G60.	4		

Morning	quiet	AAA	Line
held	as	reported	last
night	AAA	One	Coy
moving	against	[illegible]	[illegible]
position	[illegible]	[illegible]	[illegible]
[illegible]	AAA	night	quiet.

From [illegible]
Place
Time

The above may be forwarded as now corrected (Z)

....
Censor. Signature of Addressor or person authorised to telegraph in his name

* This line should be erased if not required.

Order No. 1625. Wt. W3253/ P 511. 27/2 H. & K., Ltd. (E. 2634)

Army Form C. 2121 (In pads of 100.)

"A" Form

MESSAGES AND SIGNALS.

No. of Message............

Prefix..............Code..............m.	Words	Charge.	This message is on a/c of:	Recd. at......m.
Office of Origin and Service Instructions	Sent		............................Service.	Date............
	At ....m.			From ....
	To			
	By		(Signature of "Franking Officer")	By............

TO DAFA / JUBA / JUGU

Sender's Number.	Day of Month.	In reply to Number.	AAA
346	6		

... AAA

Situation unchanged ...

Prisoners Nil

... DAFA, JUBA and JUGU

From	JUGU
Place	
Time	

The above may be forwarded as now corrected (Z)

.... Censor.

Signature of Addressor or person authorised to telegraph in his name

* This line should be erased if not required.

Order No. 1625. Wt. W3253/ P 511. 27/2 H. & K., Ltd. (E. 2634)

CONFIDENTIAL.

Appendix III

INTELLIGENCE REPORT - 120TH INFANTRY BRIGADE.
RIGHT - SECTOR.
08.00 3-10-18 to 08.00 4-10-18.

"A" OUR OPERATIONS.

1. INFANTRY. During the day we advanced our line in conjunction with troops on the right, to a line about I.9.b.0.2 to I.9.b.5.7. A strong party of the enemy with M.Gs. were met in the trenches about I.3.d. and b., and another hostile M.G. was in action in I.2.d. The left company was held up N.E. of CHAPELLE D'ARMENTIERES by more M.Gs., and troops on the right were also held up. CHAPELLE D'ARMENTIERES was heavily shelled all the afternoon and as the company in I.9.b. was being enfiladed from I.3.d. and was not in touch on the right it was decided to withdraw the company to a line just E. of CHAPELLE D'ARMENTIERES. Patrols were pushed out N.E. during the day as far as C.27.d., but no touch was gained with 119th Infantry Brigade. By dawn to-day the line in I.9.b. was re-established and patrols were pushed out towards I.11.a. to try and gain touch with 119th Infantry Brigade. Enemy M.Gs. and a light T.M. were in action about I.10.b. and the forward advance was held up. Steps are being taken to deal with/hostile /these nests with T. Ms.

2. ARTILLERY. Very active.

3. AERIAL. Very active. Strong formations were observed to cross the enemy lines meeting with heavy A.A. fire. No. combats seen.

4. M.Gs. Quiet.

5. T.Ms. Quiet.

"B" ENEMY OPERATIONS.

1. INFANTRY. (see our operations).
2. ARTILLERY. Very active throughout the period. East side of ARMENTIERES. was heavily shelled by H.V. guns from 16.00 to 18.00. Areas I.1.d., I.2.c., I.7.b. and I.8.a. were heavily shelled by 5.9s. and 4.2s. during the afternoon. Scattered shelling of forward areas was reported throughout the night.
3. AERIAL. Very active. Repeated attempts were made to cross our lines during the period. At 14.00 four E.As. crossed our lines bringing down one of our O.Bs. in flames.
4. M.G. During the afternoon and evening enemy M.Gs. fired from level crossing at I.3.d.30.00., during the night this M.G. retired to a position approx. I.10.b.7.5.
5. T.Ms. T.Ms. are reported to be firing from I.10.b.7.5.
6. GAS SHELLS. Nil.

"C" ENEMY INTELLIGENCE.

1. GENERAL. Many fires and dense clouds of smoke were observed opposite our front. A large fire burned all night on a true bearing of 152° from B.17.d.58.20. During the morning an officer and one other rank encountered a strong working party dismantling railway in I.9. and 10. Three of the enemy were shot. The Officer and one O.R. withdrew being outnumbered. The working party dispersed.

[signature]

for Brigadier General,
Commanding, 120th Infantry Brigade.

HOSTILE SHELLING REPORT.

Right Sector.

Period-06.00 3/10/18. to 06.00 4/10/18.

ENEMY ARTILLERY.

Very active throughout the period.

East side of ARMENTIERES was heavily shelled by H.V. guns from 16.00 to 18.00.

Areas I.1.d., I.2.c.,I.7.b. and I.8.a. were heavily shelled by 5.9s and 4.2s during the afternoon.

Scattered shelling of forward areas was reported throughout the night.

Brigadier General,
4/10/18. Commanding 120th Infantry Brigade.

Appendix IV

S E C R E T. COPY NO. 4

120TH INFANTRY BRIGADE ORDER NO. 225.

5-10-18.

1. The 120th Infantry Brigade will relieve the 119th Infantry Brigade in the outpost positions on the night 5/6th and 6/7th October in accordance with attached table of reliefs.

2. All arrangements for relief will be made direct between C.Os. concerned.

3. Boundries on completion of relief will be as follows :-

Northern. Grid line through C.16.central and C.17.central.
Southern. I.10.central I.11.central.

4. The 11th Bn. Cameron Highrs., are relieving the 1?th Bn. K.O.S.B. in the outpost position of the 1?th Infantry Brigade front on the night 5/6th October. If the 11th Bn. Cameron Highrs. are not squeezed out of the line by the 119th Infantry Brigade extending as far south as [illegible] Southern Boundary, the 15th Bn. K.O.Y.L.I. will take over on the night 6/7th the portion of the outpost line still occupied by the 11th Bn. Cameron Highrs.

5. All special maps, aeroplane photographs, etc. and all trench stores will be taken over from Units being relieved.

6. Dispositions of battalion in the line, giving locations of all posts, will be sent to Brigade Headquarters by [illegible] 7th inst.

7. Completion of relief will be wired by the following code word :-

"BUCKSHEE"

8. Brigade Headquarters will close at [illegible] and re-open at a site to be notified later at 1000 7th inst. at which hour G.O.C. 120th Infantry Brigade will assume Command of the sector.
Up to 1000 7th inst., all troops in the outpost area will be under the tactical control of G.O.C., 119th Infantry Brigade.

9. On completion of relief dispositions of 120th Infantry Brigade will be as follows :-

Brigade Headquarters	...	To be notified later.
15th Bn. K.O.Y.L.I.	...	In outpost line.
11th Bn. Cam. Highrs.	...	In [illegible]
10th Bn. K.O.S.B.	...	In [illegible] and [illegible]

10. ACKNOWLEDGE.

Issued through Signals
at 16 15

Captain,
Brigade Major,
120th Infantry Brigade.

<u>DISTRIBUTION</u>.:-

Copy No. 1 ... G.O.C.
2 ... Brigade Major.
3 ... Staff Captain,
4 ... War Diary.
5 ... File.
6 ... 10th K.O.S.B.
7 ... 15th K.O.Y.L.I.
8 ... 11th Bn. Cam. Hrs.
9 ... 120th T. M. Battery.
10 ... 40th Division "G"
11 ... 40th Division "Q"
12 ... 119th Inf. Bde.
13 ... 121st Inf. Bde.
14 ... 176th Inf. Bde.
15 ... 330th Bde. R.F.A.
16 ... 331st Bde. R F.A.
17 ... 39th Bn. M.G.C.
18 ... "A" Coy. 39th Bn. M.G.C.
19 ... "C" Coy. - do -
20 ... 64th H. A. Group.
21 ... 137th Field Ambce.
22 ... A.D.S. 137th Fd. Ambce.
23 ... 224th Field Coy. R.E.
24 ... Bde. Supply Officer.
25 ... Brigade Signals.
26 ... 40th Div. Train.

[illegible] INFANTRY BRIGADE ORDER NO. [illegible] dated 5-10-1[illegible].

Serial No.	Date	UNIT.	FROM	TO	IN RELIEF OF	H. Qrs.	REMARKS.
1	October 7/8th	[illegible]	[illegible]	Support Area about HOUPLINES.	11th [illegible] Lancs. [illegible]	[illegible]	
[illegible]	7/8th	11th Cam. Hrs.	[illegible] Area	Line - 1?0th Inf. Bde. Front.	1?th [illegible]	[illegible].7.	
[illegible]	7/8th	1?th [illegible]	Line - 1?0th Bde. Front.	[illegible] Area		[illegible]	
[illegible]	?/7th	1?th [illegible]	Support Area about HOUPLINES.	LINE.	1?th N.Staffs.R.	C.??.c.7.?.	
5.	?/7th	1?th N.Staffs.	LINE	Support Area about HOUPLINES.		C.??.c.?.5.	
6.	7/8th	11th Cam. Hrs.	CHAPELLE D' ARMENTIERES Area.	Support Area about HOUPLINES.	13th N.Staffs.R.	C.?.c.?.5.	

Appendix V

SECRET.

COPY NO. 1

120TH INFANTRY BRIGADE INSTRUCTIONS NO. 1.

5-10-18.

1. On completion of relief of the 119th Infantry Brigade the 120th Infantry Brigade, with attached troops, will operate as the Advanced Guard to the Division.

2. The Advanced Guard will be composed as follows :-

Adv. Guard Commander ... G.O.C. 120th Inf. Bde.

120th Infantry Brigade.
331st Bde. R.F.A.
"A" Coy. 39th Bn. M.G.C.
½ Coy. XV Corps Cyclist.

3. The Advanced Guard Brigade will be responsible for the defence of the NIEPPE System South of the LYS in addition to the Outpost Line.

For this purpose the Reserve Battalion will keep a nucleus garrison of 1 Company in the NIEPPE System from the LYS to the Division Southern boundary.

Machine Gun positions for the defence of this portion of the LYS line are being reconnoitred and will be notified later.

The responsibility for the defence of the rest of the NIEPPE system will be with the 119th Infantry Brigade, who are being withdrawn into that neighbourhood.

4. The following communications are being opened up and maintained under the direction of the C.R.E. :-

(a) A main route running forward through ORVILLE JUNCTION - ERQUINGHEM - Southern edge of ARMENTIERES - CHAPELLE D'ARMENTIERES.

(b) Supplementary route through LE BIZET - C.14.a., c and d, to C.20.b. and d to bridge at C.20.d.9.0. A connection with the main route will be made East of the LYS as soon as possible.

(c) Pontoon bridges exist :-

H.2.c.1.9.
H.3.c.4.7.
H.4.c.1.4.
C.20.d.9.0.

(d) Foot bridges exist at :-

H.3.d.5.5.
C.15.d.6.8.
another is under construction at
C.21.d.3.5.

5. In two or three days time R.E. assistance will be available for the improvement of forward and second line defences.

H. Earle

Captain,
Brigade Major,
120th Infantry Brigade.

To all recipients
of 120th Inf.Bde.
Order 225 dated
5-10-18.

"A" Form

Army Form C. 2121
(In pads of 100.)

MESSAGES AND SIGNALS.

No. of Message..........

Prefix..............Code..............m. | Words | Charge.
Office of Origin and Service Instructions

Sent
At ....m.
To
By

This message is on a/c of:
..........................Service.
VI
(Signature of "Franking Officer")

Recd. at......m.
Date..............
From ....
By..............

TO JV21

Sender's Number. ·950· | Day of Month. | In reply to Number. | AAA

Situation no change AAA enemy artillery active in and about ARMENTIERES especially near Railway Station.

JV21.

From
Place
Time

The above may be forwarded as now corrected (Z)

Censor. Signature of Addressor or person authorised to telegraph in his name

* This line should be erased if not required.

Order No. 1625. Wt. W3253/ P 511. 27/2 H. & K., Ltd. (E. 2634)

MESSAGES AND SIGNALS. No. of Message..........

Prefix..........Code..........m. Office of Origin and Service Instructions	Words	Charge.	This message is on a/c of: ....Service. (Signature of "Franking Officer")	Recd. at......m. Date.......... From.......... By..........
	Sent At ....m. To .... By			

TO DAFA JUZA JUZI

Sender's Number.	Day of Month.	In reply to Number.	AAA
Bm. 49	5th		

evening situation AAA Exact position of line not clear Shut Btn. on right report they are now across our front with their left resting on the railway AAA Quiet day on front AAA Shrapnel & Gas barrage put down in 1.10 C at about 15.40. AAA Prisoners NIL.

From JUVO
Place
Time

The above may be forwarded as now corrected (Z)

Censor. Signature of Addressor or person authorised to telegraph in his name

Captain

* This line should be erased if not required.

Order No. 1625. Wt. W3253/ P 511. 27/2 H. & K., Ltd. (E. 2634).

Appendix VI

CONFIDENTIAL.

INTELLIGENCE REPORT - 180TH INFANTRY BRIGADE.
RIGHT - SECTOR.
0600 4-10-18 to 0600 5-10-18.
****

"A" OUR OPERATIONS.

1. INFANTRY During the period we altered the line of our right flank to conform with the Company on our right. The line now runs I.9.b.30.70. - I.9.b.[illegible] - I.9.b.55.20. - I.9.c.9.8. where we are in touch with the troops on our right.

   At 1600 patrols gained touch with 119th Inf. Brigade at H.3.d.3.6.

2. ARTILLERY. Normal. Enemy areas were harassed throughout the period.

3. AIRCRAFT. Active. Strong formations were seen crossing the enemy's lines meeting with heavy A.A. fire.

4. M. Gs. Quiet.

5. T. Ms. Nil.

"B" ENEMY OPERATIONS.

1. INFANTRY. Nil.

2. ARTILLERY. Active. The following areas suffered spasmodic shelling by 5.9s. throughout the period. CHAPELLE D' ARMENTIERES, the railway in I.1. and HOUPLINES SWITCH. Our front was subjected to scattered shelling by 4.2s and 7.7 mm throughout the period. Between 1930 and 2015 20 shells, heavy calibre, fell in H.22.central. At 2300, 12 rounds fell into NIEPPE village.
3. AERIAL. Normal. Attempts to cross our lines were made by single E.As. all of which were driven off by our A.A. fire
4. M.Gs. and T.Ms. Fairly active throughout the period. Most of M.Gs. and T.Ms. in I.10.b. was dealt with by our Artillery.
5. GAS SHELLS. B.16.d. was shelled with gas and H.E. mixed at 2300.
6. BALLOONS. Three balloons were seen up opposite our front at 0700 and four at 1015.

"C" ENEMY INTELLIGENCE.

Fires Several fires were observed opposite our front during the period. A large fire was observed on a grid bearing of 177° from H.12.b.5.7.

[signature] Barker
Capt.
for Brigadier General,
Commanding, 1[illegible]0th Infantry Brigade.

HOSTILE SHELLING REPORT.

Right Sector.
Period-06.00 4/10/18. to 06.00 5/10/18.

Time.	Area Shelled.	Rds.	Calibre.	Direction.	Remarks.
19.30. to 10.15.	B.23.cenl.	20.	Heavy.	E.S.E.	--
23.00	NIEPPE.	12.	,,	E.S.E.	--
	CHAPELLE D'ARMENTIERES, ARMENTIERES STN. HOUPLINES STN*		5.9.	115° Grid H.12.b.5.7.	Spasmodic shelling throughout the period.

* Our Front was subjected to scattered shelling by 4.2s & 77mm. Throughout the period.

5/10/18.

Brigadier General,
Commanding 120th Infantry Brigade.

"A" Form

Army Form C. 2121
(In pads of 100.)

MESSAGES AND SIGNALS.

No. of Message..........

Prefix..........Code..........m.	Words	Charge.	This message is on a/c of:	Recd. at......m.
Office of Origin and Service Instructions	Sent		....................Service.	Date..........
	At ....m.			From ....
	To			
	By		(Signature of "Franking Officer")	By..........

TO

Sender's Number.	Day of Month.	In reply to Number.	AAA

From

Place

Time

The above may be forwarded as now corrected. (Z)

Censor. Signature of Addressor or person authorised to telegraph in his name

* This line should be erased if not required.

Order No. 1625. Wt. W3353/ P 511. 27/2 H. & K., Ltd. (E. 2634)

MESSAGES AND SIGNALS. No. of Message..........

Prefix........Code........m.	Words	Charge.	This message is on a/c of:	Recd. at......m.
Office of Origin and Service Instructions	Sent		.................Service.	Date........
	At ....m.			From ....
	To		....	
	By		(Signature of "Franking Officer")	By..........

TO DAFA JUZA JUZ1

Sender's Number.	Day of Month.	In reply to Number.	AAA
G161.	6		

Evening Situation AAA. [illegible]

Addsd DAFA repeated JUZA and JUZ1

From JUVU
Place
Time

The above may be forwarded as now corrected (Z)
Censor. Signature of Addressor or person authorised to telegraph in his name

* This line should be erased if not required.

Order No. 1625. Wt. W3253/ P 511. 27/2 H. & K., Ltd. (E. 2634).

CONFIDENTIAL.

Appendix VIII

INTELLIGENCE REPORT - 120TH INFANTRY BRIGADE.
RIGHT - SECTOR.
06.00 5-10-18 to 0600 6-10-18.
==*=*=*=*=*=*=*=*=*=*=*=*=*

"A" OUR OPERATIONS.

1. INFANTRY. At 18.00 our forward company advanced along CENTRAL AVENUE and occupied HEADQUARTERS WALK from I.10.b. 3.5. to I.10.a.9.0. where touch was gained with the troops on our right. Further advance was rendered impossible owing to heavy M.G. fire from approx. I.4.d.95.40.
We are not in touch with 119th Infantry Brigade on our left. Our patrols met a partol of 1 Officer and 8 O.Rs. from the Division on our right at GRAND PORTE EGAL FARM, but no signs of 119th Infantry Brigade could be found there.
During the night patrols were pushed forward to reconnoitre, they report that INCARNATE TRENCH is strongly held by the enemy.
2. ARTILLERY. Harrasing fire on enemy positions and back areas was continuous.
3. AERIAL. Normal. Usual formations were seen flying low over enemy lines.
4. M.Gs. and T.Ms. Quiet.

"B" ENEMY OPERATIONS.

1. INFANTRY. About 10.00 M.G. and sniper were very active from approx. I.10.a. 7.7. but they withdrew shortly afterwards.
2. ARTILLERY. ARMENTIERES Station was again heavily shelled throughout the period.
Our front was subjected to spasmodic bursts during the day.
During the night heavy searching fire was directed against areas I.1., I.2., I.7., and I.8. probably our advanced gun positions.
Between 23.05. and 23.45 counter battery work was carried out by 4.2s in area I.8.a. about 40 rounds being fired. Guns fired from S.E.
3. AERIAL. Low flying single E.As. crossed our lines at 0900, 13.00, and 18.00
4. GAS SHELLS Occasional Gas shells were mixed with H.E. At 04.45 a heavy barrage of mustard gas mixed with 4.2. and 5.9 was put down on our Support Lines in areas C.21.d. and C.22.c. The barrage decreased about 05.45 and ceased at 06.00 No apparent enemy infantry action followed.
5. M.Gs. Noemal. (see infantry)
6. T.Ms. Nil.

"C" ENEMY INTELLIGENCE.

1. FIRES. Two fires were seen S.E. of our front.

[signature]

for Brigadier General,
Commanding, 120th Infantry Brigade.

6-10-18.

HOSTILE SHELLING REPORT.

RIGHT SECTOR.

ARMENTIERES STN. was again heavily shelled throughout the period. Our front was subjected to spasmodic bursts during the day. During the night heavy searching fire was directed against areas I.1.,I.2.,I.7.,and I.8., probably our advanced gun positions.

Between 22:05. and 24.45. counter battery work was carried out by 4.2s in area I.8.a.,about 40 rounds were fired. Gun fired from S.E.

At 04.45 a heavy barrage of mustard gas mixed with H.E. was put down on our support lines in areas C.21.d. and C.22.c. The barrage decreased about 05.45 and ceased at 06.00. No apparent enemy infantry action followed.

J C Barker ? ??

for. Brigadier General.

6-10-18. Commanding, 120th Infantry Brigade.

Prefix..............Code..............m.	Words	Charge.	This message is on a/c of:	Recd. at......m.
Office of Origin and Service Instructions	Sent		........................Service.	Date..........
	At ....m.			From..........
	To			
	By		(Signature of "Franking Officer.")	By..........

TO DAFA PAN[illegible]

Sender's Number.	Day of Month.	In reply to Number.	AAA
Km 61	7		

Situation unchanged AAA In touch with 7/21 on right AAA Patrols report no enemy encountered within 400 yards of line AAA Enemy artillery quiet AAA [illegible] DAFA lighted flares

From DWD
Place
Time 5.50

The above may be forwarded as now corrected. (Z)

Censor. Signature of Addressor or person authorised to telegraph in his name

* This line should be erased if not required.

Order No. 1625. Wt. W3253/ P 511. 27/2 H. & K., Ltd. (E. 2634)

Prefix..............Code...............m. | Words | Charge.

Office of Origin and Service Instructions

Sent

At ....m.

To ....

By ....

This message is on a/c of :

..........................Service.

....

(Signature of "Franking Officer.")

Recd. at......m.

Date..............

From ....

By..................

TO DAFA
JUZA
JUZI

Sender's Number.	Day of Month.	In reply to Number.	AAA
563	7th		

Morning situation AAA

[illegible]

Addsd DAFA repeated JUZA and JUZI

From JUVO

Place

Time

The above may be forwarded as now corrected (Z)

.... Censor.

Signature of Addressor or person authorised to telegraph in his name

Capt

* This line should be erased if not required.

Order No. 1625. Wt. W3253/ P 511. 27/2 H. & K., Ltd. (E. 2634).

Appendix IX

S E C R E T. COPY NO. 4

120TH INFANTRY BRIGADE ORDER NO. 226.

8-10-18.

1. On the night 9/10th October, the following reliefs will take place :-

(a) The 10th Bn. K.O.S.B. will relieve the 11th Bn. Cameron Highrs. in Support.

(b) The 11th Bn. Cameron Highrs. will relieve the 15th Bn. K.O.Y.L.I. in the Outpost Line.

(c) The 15th Bn. K.O.Y.L.I., on relief, will move back into the ERQUINGHEM Area.

2. All details of relief will be arranged direct between C.Os. concerned.

3. Special attention will be paid by O.C., 11th Bn. Cameron Highrs. to taking over liaison posts with troops on the flanks.

4. All special maps, aeroplane photographs and trench stores will be taken over by relieving Units.

5. On completion of relief the two Companies of the 10th Bn. K.O.S.B. North of ARMENTIERES will be under the tactical control of O.C. 11th Bn. Cameron Highrs. as laid down in Instructions No. 2 dated 7-10-18.

6. Completion of reliefs will be wired to Brigade Headquarters using following code word :-

"RABBITS"

7. Detailed dispositions will be forwarded by O.C. 11th Bn. Cameron Highrs. by last D.R. 10th instant.

8. The policy of work will be continued as ordered in Instructions No. 2.

9. ACKNOWLEDGE.

Issued through Signals
at 20.00

H. [signature]
Captain,
Brigade Major,
120th Infantry Brigade.

Copy No. 1 G.O.C.
2 Bde. Major.
3. Staff Captn.
4. War Diary.
5. File.
6. 10th K.O.S.B.
7. 15th K.O.Y.L.I.
8. 11th Cam. Hrs.
9. 120th T.M.Bty.
10. 40th Div. "G"
11. 40th Div. "Q"
12. 119th Inf. Bde.
13. 121st Inf. Bde.
14. 176th Inf. Bde.
15. 94th Inf. Bde.
16. 330th Bde. R.F.A.
17. 331st Bde. R.F.A.
18. "A" Coy. 39th Bn. M.G.C.
19. 137th Fd. Ambce.
20. A.D.S. - do -
21 ... 224th Field Coy. R.E.
22 ... Bde. Supply Officer.
23 ... Bde. Signals.
24 ... 40th Divnl. Train.

MESSAGES AND SIGNALS. No. of Message...........

Prefix............Code 0355 m. | Words | Charge.

Office of Origin and Service Instructions

JUVO

Sent At 358 m. To 1022 By

This message is on a/c of: ....Service.

(Signature of "Franking Officer")

Recd. at......m. Date........... From .... By...........

TO DAFA JUZI PANI

Sender's Number. 964 | Day of Month. 8th | In reply to Number. | AAA

Morning situation AAA

Added DAFA repeated JUZI and PANI

From JUVO

Place

Time

The above may be forwarded as now corrected (Z)

Censor. Signature of Addressor or person authorised to telegraph in his name

Capt

* This line should be erased if not required.

Order No. 1625. Wt. W3253/ P 511. 27/2 H. & K., Ltd. (E. 2634).

Prefix..............Code..............m. | Words | Charge.

Office of Origin and Service Instructions

Sent

At ....m.

To ....

By ....

This message is on a/c of :

..............................*Service.*

(Signature of "Franking Officer")

Date..............

From ....

By..........

TO

Sender's Number. | Day of Month | In reply to Number. | AAA

From

Place

Time

The above may be forwarded as now corrected (Z)

Censor. Signature of Addressor or person authorised to telegraph in his name

* This line should be erased if not required.

Order No. 1625. Wt. W3253/ P 511. 27/2 H. & K., Ltd. (E. 2634)

CONFIDENTIAL.

Appendix X

INTELLIGENCE REPORT , 120TH INFANTRY BRIGADE.
RIGHT SECTOR.
06.00 7-10-18 to 06.00 8-10-18.

"A" OUR OPERATIONS.

1. INFANTRY. During the period posts were established by the left and centre front line companies as follows :-
Lewis Gun Post :- C.16.c.~~xxxxx~~ 75.05., C.22.c.95.80., C.28.a.95.95., C.28.c.90.90.
Infantry Posts :- C.22.b.10.45., C.28.b.10.55.
Right Coy established posts at I11 a 06 & I5 c 22
At 12.00 a patrol consisting of one Officer and 3 O.Rs. proceeded along SPAIN AVENUE, and NEWBURN to reconnoitre road at C.28.b.70.45.
The patrol proceeded as far as C.28.b.24.35. and report two Germans seen North of road at approx. C.28.b.central.

2. ARTILLERY. Normal. Usual harassing fire was carried out, which increased towards dusk.

3. AERIAL. Usual artillery observers crossed our lines during the day but no strong formations were seen.

4. M. Gs. Normal.

5. T. Ms. Nil.

"B" ENEMY OPERATIONS.

1. Infantry. Nil.

2. ARTILLERY. Below normal. Our forward areas were subjected to light scattered shelling throughout the period.
Our back areas were harassed during the night.

3. AERIAL. One E.A. flew over CHAPELLE D'ARMENTIERES at 06.40
Two E.As. crossed our lines at 09.10 and returned at 09.35.
Single E.As. flew over our lines at 14.10 - 15.06 - 16.49.
All the above were drived off by A.A. fire.

4. M. Gs. Normal.

5. T. Ms. Nil.

"C" ENEMY INTELLIGENCE.

1. MOVEMENT. (see Infantry).

2. GENERAL. Visibility very low. Very little E.A.A. fire during the day, the A.A. guns which fired seemed to be well in rear of enemy's lines, and the shells were bursting very low and forward of our Support Lines.

J. Barker Y/H.
for Brigadier General,
Commanding, 120th Infantry Btigade.

8-10-18.

HOSTILE SHELLING REPORT.

Right Sector.

Period-06.00 7/10/18. to 06.00 8/10/18.

Time	Area shelled.	Calibre.	No. Rounds.	Direction.	Remarks.
06.18 to 06.50.	I 3.d.80.30. I 4.a.25.40. I 3.a.50.15.	4.2.	12.	E.S.E.	Salvoes of three.
10.20.to 11.05.	I 9.b.centl.	5.9.	11.	S.E.	Shrapnel.
13.10 to 14.05.	I.1 a. & c.	5.9.	8.	S.E.	do.
15.15.to 16.05.	I 7.a.& c.	4.2.	14.	E.S.E.	do.
17.00 to 17.15.	I 8.b.	5.9.	14.	E.S.E.	do.
21.45.to 22.00.	I 8.c.	4.2.	14.	E.S.E.	H.E,

J.C. Barker Capt.

for Brigadier General,

Commanding 120th Infantry Brigade.

8/10/18.

MESSAGES ...

Prefix..............Code..............m. | Words | Charge.

Office of Origin and Service Instructions

Sent. At ....m. To .... By ....

This message is on a/c of: .... Service. XI

(Signature of "Franking Officer")

Date........ From .... By........

TO DAFA PANI JUZ (a)

Sender's Number.	Day of Month.	In reply to Number.	AAA
G 70	9		

Morning wire AAA

[illegible]

From JUVO

Place

Time

The above may be forwarded as now corrected (Z)

Censor. Signature of Addressor or person authorised to telegraph in his name

Priority

* This line should be erased if not required.

Order No. 1625. Wt. W3253/ P 511. 27/2 H. & K., Ltd. (E. 2634).

"A" Form.

Army Form C.[illegible]
(In pads of 100.)

[ME]SSAGES AND SIGNALS.

No. of Message ....

[illegible] .... Code .... m.	Words	Charge	This message is on a/c of:	Recd. at .... m.
Office of Origin and Service Instructions.	Sent		.... Service.	Date ....
	At .... m.			From ....
	To			
	By		(Signature of "Franking Officer.")	By ....

TO DHQ3 PAN[illegible]

Sender's Number.	Day of Month.	In reply to Number.	AAA
[illegible]576	9		

Evening situation [illegible]

[illegible]

Addsd DAFA [illegible] PAVI and JUZI

From	JUVO
Place	
Time	

The above may be forwarded as now corrected. (Z)

.... Censor. .... Signature of Addressor or person authorised to telegraph in his name

[illegible signature]

* This line, except AAA, should be erased if not required.

Wt. W 3253/P511. 500,000 Pads. 1/18. B. & S. Ltd. (E2389.)

Appendix XI

CONFIDENTIAL.

INTELLIGENCE REPORT - 120TH INFANTRY BRIGADE.
RIGHT SECTOR
06.00 8-10-18 to 06.00 9-10-18.

"A" OUR OPERATIONS.

1. INFANTRY. A Lewis Gun post has been established at C.22.b.40.45. also an Infantry Post at C.22.a.95.80.
A patrol of one Officer and 3 O.Rs. penetrated along EDMEADE AVENUE as far as C.22.b.85.45. without opposition.

2. ARTILLERY. Active by day, increased activity after dusk. 18 pdrs fired salvoes at intervals from 21.00 to 03.00. Heavies were very active throughout the night.

3. AERIAL. Active. Strong formations were observed flying low over enemy's lines. Increased enemy A.A. fire especially in forward Areas.

4. M. Gs. M.G. positions have been established as follows :-

C.28.a.15.20.	I.4.d.2.1.
C.22.c.30.40.	I.4.d.3.1.
C.22.c.32.45.	I.4.a.4.4.
C.22 a.80.45.	I.3.d.7.6.

Suspected enemy positions, tracks and light railways were swept during the night.

5. T. Ms. Quiet.

"B" ENEMY OPERATIONS

1. INFANTRY. Nil.
2. ARTILLERY. Increased activity. Two guns firing from a grid bearing of 108° from I.8.a.0.2. were very active throughout the day, fire being directed from O.Bs. at grid bearings of 139° and 124° from I.8.a.0.2., the following targets being engaged I.2.a., I.12.d. and I.1.a. and b.
ARMENTIERES was shelled intermittently. Heavy duds are reported to have fallen in areas H.12.d. and H.18.b.
Our forward areas were subjected to light scattered shelling throughout the period. The following areas received much attention C.21.b. and d. I.3.d. and I.4.b.
3. AERIAL. Two E.As. flew over CHAPELLE D'ARMENTIERES at 09.20, height 3.000 feet. Two E.As. flew over areas C.20., C.21, C.26. and C.27.at a height of 3.000 feet from 14.35 to 14.55
Heavy A.A. fire was directed at all the above.
4. M. Gs. Very active throughout the night. Suspected M.G. position at I.11.a.8.6.
5. T. Ms. Nil.
6. GAS SHELLS. A barrage of gas and H.E. mixed was laid down on road running through C.27.a. and C.27.d. from 01.65 to 02.45
7. BALLOONS. Three balloons were up throughout the day at the following T. Bs, from I.2.a.10.48, 60°, 89° and 130°

[signature] for
Brigadier General,
Commanding, 120th Infantry Brigade.

9-10-18.

HOSTILE SHELLING REPORT.

Right Sector.

Period-06.00 8/10/18 to 06.00 9/10/18.

ENEMY ARTILLERY.

Increased activity.

2 guns firing from a grid bearing of 108° from I 8.a.0.2 were very active throughout the day, fire being directed from O.Bs at grid bearings of 139° and 124° from I 8.a0.2., the following targets being engaged:- I.2.a., I.12.d.and 1.a. and b.

ARMENTIERES was shelled intermittently.

Heavy "duds" are reported to have fallen in areas H.12.d. and H.18.b.

Our forward areas were subjected to light scattered shelling throughout the period.

The following areas received much attention:- C.21.b.and d.,I.3.d. and I.4.b.

[signature]

Brigadier General,
Commanding 120th Infantry Brigade.

9/10/18.

"A" Form.
Army Form C. 2121.
(In pads of 100.)

MESSAGES AND SIGNALS.

No. of Message ....

Prefix .... Code .... m.	Words.	Charge.	This message is on a/c of:	Recd. at .... m.
Office of Origin and Service Instructions.	Sent		.... Service.	Date ....
	At .... m.			From ....
	To			
	By		(Signature of "Franking Officer.")	By ....

TO DAFA JUZI PANI

Sender's Number.	Day of Month.	In reply to Number.	AAA
* G80.	10		

Morning situation AAA

[illegible]

addressed DAFA repeated JUZI and PANI

From JUVO
Place
Time

The above may be forwarded as now corrected. (Z)

.... Censor. Capt .... Signature of Addressor or person authorised to telegraph in his name.

* This line, except **AAA**, should be erased if not required.

Wt. W 3253/P511. 500,000 Pads. 1/18. B. & S. Ltd. **(E2389.)**

"A" Form.

MESSAGES AND SIGNALS.

Army Form C. 2121.
(In pads of 100.)

No. of Message ....

Prefix .... Code .... m.	Words	Charge	This message is on a/c of: .... Service.	Recd. at ...... m.
Office of Origin and Service Instructions.	Sent			Date ....
	At .... m.			From ....
	To			
	By		Signature of "Franking Officer."	By ....

TO DAFA PANI JUZI

Sender's Number.	Day of Month.	In reply to Number.	AAA
	10		

[illegible] ~~[illegible]~~ LINES

NOT [illegible]

[illegible] 14.15

[illegible] between 1400 – 1500 [illegible] AAA

[illegible]

AAA

Addsd DAFA repeated PANI and JUZI

From JUVO

Place

Time

The above may be forwarded as now corrected. (Z)

Censor. Signature of Addressor or person authorised to telegraph in his name

* This line, except **AAA**, should be erased if not required.

Wt. W 3253/P511. 500,000 Pads. 1/18. B. & S. Ltd. **(E2389.)**

Appendix XII.

CONFIDENTIAL.

INTELLIGENCE REPORT - 120th INFANTRY BRIGADE.
RIGHT SECTOR.
06.00 9-10-18 to 06.00 10-10-18.

"A" OUR OPERATIONS.

1. INFANTRY. Patrols were out, but no information of importance obtained.

2. ARTILLERY. During the day activity was normal. Throughout the night 18 pdrs. and 4.5 Hows. carried out harassing fire. Our heavies were active at intervals.

3. AERIAL. Active. Strong formations were observed to cross over enemy lines, meeting with considerable A.A. fire.

4. M. Gs. M.G. positions covering artillery have been established as follows :-

I.1.c.4.4. ... ... 2 guns.
H.12 b.9.5. .. ... 2 guns.

Suspected enemy positions, tracks and light railways were harassed throughout the night.

5. T. Ms. Quiet.

"B" ENEMY OPERATIONS.

1. INFANTRY. Nil.
2. ARTILLERY. Very active throughout the period, I.1.a. and RUE MARLE were shelled by H.V. gun at intervals.
Our forward areas were subjected to scattered shelling from 11.30 to 12.30
The following areas received much attention throughout the period, C.21.b and d, I.1.d., I.2.a.central and I.10.b.
ORVILLE JUNCTION was also shelled during the night.
3. AERIAL. Increased activity during the day. Several single enemy aeroplanes flew over our lines. At 15.00 a strong formation of 11 E.A. flew over our lines at a great height.
4. M. Gs. Our positions were subjected to light harassing fire during the night.
5. T. Ms. Nil.
6. GAS SHELLS. About 50 gas shells are reported to have fallen in Area I.3.d. between 14.30 and 15.30. I.1.b. received 8 gas shells at 05.15

[signature] Barker
Major
for Brigadier General,
Commanding, 120th Infantry Brigade.

10-10-18.

120TH INFANTRY BRIGADE SHELLING REPORT.

.. ..

TIME.	AREA SHELLED.	CALIBRE.	NO. of ROUNDS.	DIRECTION or BEARING.	REMARKS.
08.00 to 10.00.	RUE MARLE.	H.V.Gun.	40	E.S.E.	Continuous & scattered.
11.00	Farm at I.10.b.5.6.	4.2.s.	8	E.	
11.30 to 12.30	Forward areas subjected to scattered shelling.				
13.00 to 13.15.	C. 21.b. & d.	77mm.	30	S.E.	
16.00	I.1.d.cenl.	H.V.Gun.	8	E.S.E.	
21.00 to 04.00	ORVILLE JUNCTION	5.9.s.	12	E.	
~~01.00 to 05.00~~	~~I.1d.Centrl.~~	~~H.V.Gun~~	~~60~~	~~E.S.E.~~	~~Bursts of three & continuous.~~
04.00	I.2.a. Centrl.	5.9s.	8	E.S.E.	

.... 1918.

Brigadier General,
Commanding 120th Infantry Brigade.

SECRET. COPY NO

120TH INFANTRY BRIGADE ORDER NO. 227.

11-10-18.

1. OBJECTIVE. On the 12th instant a Minor Operation will be carried out by the 120th Infantry Brigade to gain an identification and the objective shown on the attached map.

2. TROOPS. The attack will be carried out by one Company of the 10th Bn. K.O.S.B.

3. ASSEMBLY POINT - METHOD OF ATTACK. The Company of the 10th K.O.S.B. will be assembled in INCANDESCENT Support just North of the railway by Zero - 60 minutes.

At Zero this party will advance Northwards along INCANDESCENT SUPPORT under a creeping barrage, while another barrage will comb out the ground to the East of this trench. Details of Artillery barrages are given in para 5.

The Company 10th K.O.S.B. will make good the line of INCANDESCENT SUPPORT as far North as the road in I.5.d. 5.5., and will also send a party to mop up INCANDESCENT Front Line as far North as the road.

4. O.C., 11th Cam. Highrs. will be responsible for gaining touch between the left of this Company on completion of the attack, and the Cameron Post in L'EPINETTE.

5. ARTILLERY. At Zero hour the Field Artillery will open two barrages :-

(a) One on the line of INCANDESCENT SUPPORT from I.11.a.9.5. to I.5.d.6.8., which will move Eastwards lifting 100 yards every two minutes up to Zero plus 20, when it will jump back to the line from I.11.d.6.9. to I.6.c.3.6., where it will remain as a protecting barrage till Zero plus 44.

As much smoke as can be obtained will be fired in this barrage in its early stage.

(b) One on the line from I.11.a.7.9. to I.11.b.3.7. and will move Northwards up the INCANDESCENT TRENCH and SUPPORT, lifting 100 yards every 3 minutes, until it reaches the line from I.5.d.3.9. to I.5.d.6.8 where it will remain as a protecting barrage till Zero plus 44.

From Zero till Zero plus 44 the Heavy Artillery will keep the trenches and strong points in the area I.6.c., I.12.a., I.12.c. under fire, and also the strong point at C.29.central.

6. COMMUNICATIONS.

1. The signal that the objective has been taken will be the firing of 3 Very Lights in quick succession.
2. The Company of the 10th K.O.S.B. will have four pigeons.
3. A runner relay post will be established by Brigade Signals at I.3.d.3.0. at the Level Crossing, where all runner messages for Brigade Headquarters should be sent.

A wire will be laid by Brigade Signals from this relay post to Advanced Brigade Headquarters by Zero - 60 minutes

7 ....

7. GENERAL. (a) Special arrangements for the supply of bombs, rifle grenades and Very Lights to the Company operating must be made.
6 boxes of 'P' bombs are being sent up to H.Qrs. 10th K.O.S.B. to-night.
(b) The co-operation of the Stokes Mortars up by GRAND PORTE EGAL FARM will be arranged direct with O.C., 120th T. M. Battery, if required.
(c) Arrangements for tools for consolidation must be made.

8. SYNCHRONISATION OF WATCHES. An Officer from Brigade Headquarters will be at Headquarters, 10th K.O.S.B. at 19.00 to synchronise watches.

9. BRIGADE HD. QRS. Advanced Brigade Headquarters will open at H.7.b.5.6. at 05.00 12th instant.

10. O.C., 15th K.O.Y.L.I. will send up one Company to-night to replace the Company of the 10th K.O.S.B. All arrangements will be made direct between C.Os.

11. PRISONERS. Any prisoners or identifications obtained will be sent at once to Brigade Headquarters.

12. ZERO HOUR. ZERO hour for the operation will be 05.15.

13. ACKNOWLEDGE.

H. J. Eady

Captain,
Brigade Major,
120th Infantry Brigade.

Issued through Signals
at 1850

Copy No. 1.. G.O.C.
2. Brigade Major.
3.. Staff Captain.
4.. War Diary.
5.. File.
6 to 8 10th K.O.S.B.
9.. 15th K.O.Y.L.I.
10.. 11th Cam. Hrs.
11.. 120th T. M. Battery.
12.. "C" Coy. 39th Bn. M.G.C.
13.. 331st Bde. R.F.A.
14.. 330th Bde. R.F.A.
15.. 64th H.A.Group.
16.. 178th Inf. Bde.
17.. 94th Inf. Bde.
18.. 40th Divn. "G".
19.. Brigade Signals.

"A" Form.

MESSAGES AND SIGNALS.

(In pads of 100.)

No. of Message ....

Prefix .... Code .... m. | Words. | Charge.

Office of Origin and Service Instructions.

Sent

At .... m.

To

By

This message is on a/c of: XIV Service.

Appx (a)

(Signature of "Franking Officer.")

Recd. at .... m.

Date ....

From ....

By ....

TO DAFA JUZI PANI

Sender's Number.	Day of Month.	In reply to Number.	AAA
* B 3	11		

Morning	situation	AAA	Situation
of	right	bay	uncertain
aaa	Hostile	MG	fire
active	on	roads	aaa
Artillery	quiet	aaa	slight
shelling	of	back	areas
aaa			
Addsd	DAFA	reptd	JUZI
and	PANI		

From JUVO

Place

Time

Priority

The above may be forwarded as now corrected. (Z)

Censor. Signature of Addressor or person authorised to telegraph in his name

* This line, except **AAA**, should be erased if not required.

Wt. W 3253/P511. 500,000 Pads. 1/18. B. & S. Ltd. **(E2389.)**

Prefix ...... Code ...... m. | Words. | Charge.

Office of Origin and Service Instructions.

Sent

At ...... m.

To

By

This message is on a/c of:

...... Service

Signature of "Franking Officer."

Recd. at ...... m.

Date

From

By

XIV

TO DAFA JUZI FANI

Sender's Number. 5 | Day of Month. 11th | In reply to Number. | AAA

Evening were AAA Gas reported in D 96 AAA Artillery quiet AAA Wind wild SW AAA Prisoners NIL AAA

Addsd DAFA reptd JUZI and FANI

From JUVU

Place

Time

The above may be forwarded as now corrected. (Z)

Censor. Priority Captain

Signature of Addressor or person authorised to telegraph in his name.

* This line, except AAA, should be erased if not required.

Wt. W 3253/P511. 500,000 Pads. 1/18. B. & S. Ltd. (E2389.)

Appendix XIV

CONFIDENTIAL.

INTELLIGENCE REPORT - 120TH INFANTRY BRIGADE.
RIGHT SECTOR.
06.00 10-10-18 to 06.00 11-10-18.

"A" OUR OPERATIONS.

1. INFANTRY. A fighting patrol of one Officer and 13 O.R. left our post at C.28.b.1.7. at 23.30 with the object of locating enemy posts and to obtain identification.
On reaching C.28.b.6.4. two very lights were fired from C.29.a.2.5. and C.29.c.2.9. M.Gs. then opened fire from C.28.b.9.9., C.29.a.00.35. and C.29.c.8.7., lights being fired continuously.
Ground to flanks and front was searched but no enemy seen. Patrol returned at 03.15.
Enemy appears to be holding old British front and Support Lines in C.28.

2. ARTILLERY. Active throughout the period. Field guns were very active from 21.00 to 23.00. Activity of all calibres was more pronounced throughout the night.
3. AERIAL. Below normal owing to low visibility.
4. M. Gs. Quiet.
5. T. Ms. Quiet.

"B" ENEMY OPERATIONS.

1. INFANTRY. An enemy patrol in front of Right Company was engaged by Lewis Gun fire. Effect of fire not known.
2. ARTILLERY. Active by day, increased activity after dusk. Areas I.2.a. and b., I.4.a., I.5.d., I.11.a. and H.12.b. received much attention after dusk. Areas I.5.d. and I.11.a. were shelled by 24 cm H.V. Naval Gun from 19.15. to 20.30.
3. AERIAL. Active at 09.00 Quiet afterwards.
4. M. Gs. (see our Infantry)
5. T. Ms. Nil.
6. BALLOONS. One balloon was seen up opposite our front from 16.45 to 17.50 on a T.B. of 62° from I.4.a.60.90.
7. Gas Shells. Gas was often mixed with H.E. especially in forward areas.

"C" ENEMY INTELLIGENCE

1. FIRES. A large fire was observed behind enemy lines on a T.B. of 52° from I.4.a.60.90.
2. EXPLOSIONS. A big explosion was heard in the direction of LILLE at 15.30.

[signature] Barker
for Brigadier General,
Commanding, 120th Infantry Brigade.

11-10-18.

LATER:-

PATROLS. A patrol of one Officer and 10 O.Rs. proceeded along SUSSEX AVENUE at 02.30 as far a C.16.d.4.1. without hostile opposition. They then proceeded in a S.E. direction as far as C.22.d.8.8. where patrol was fired on by M.Gs. and snipers. Rifle fire was opened by patrol and enemy was forced to retire. A snipers post was located in tree at approx. C.17.d.8.8. Patrol returned at 06.00.

120TH INFANTRY BRIGADE SHELLING REPORT.

RIGHT SECTOR.

06.00 10-10-18 to 06.00 11-10-18.

Time.	Area Shelled.	Calibre.	No. of Rounds.	Direction or Bearing.	Remarks.
09.50 to 10.00	I.4.a.	77 mm	7	E.N.E.	-
10.30	I.2.b.3.6. & I.2.b.4.0.	77 mm	10	-	-
10.45 to 11.05	I.4.a. & C.28.c.	77 mm	40	E.N.E.	-
19.15.to 20.15	H.12.a. & b. & ARMENTIERES STN.	5.9s & 4.2s	20	E.S.E.	6 gas shells.
19.15 to 20.30	I.5.d. & I.11.a.	24 cm H.V. Navel guns Q.F.	14	Grid bearing of 97° from I.11.a.4.6.	Ground burst & shrapnel
23.00 to 23.45	I.5.d. & I.11.a.	4.2s.	30	E.S.E.	
23.30 to 04.00	H.12.b., I.2.a.& b. and I.7.b.	4.2s.	60	E.S.E.	Many shells were fired during this period containing Lachrymatory Gas.
04.00 05.00 to 06.00	I.8.a. and b.	4.2a.H.E.	6	E.S.E.	

Forward areas subjected to scattered shelling by 77 mm, 4.2s. and 77 mm batteries were very active throuthout the period. Mustard Gas being mixed with H.E.

11-10-.........1918.

Brigadier General,
Commanding 120th Infantry Brigade

Appendix XV

SECRET.

COPY NO. 4

120TH INFANTRY BRIGADE ORDER NO. 228.

==*=*=*=*=*=*=*=*=*=*=*=*=*=*=*=*=

12-10-18.

1. The 120th Infantry Brigade will be relieved in the Advanced Guard Position by the 121st Infantry Brigade on the night 13/14th October, in accordance with the attached relief table.

2. All arrangements for relief will be made direct between C.Os. concerned.

3. All special maps, aeroplane photos, defence instructions, details of work and trench stores will be handed over to incoming Units.

4. Completion of relief will be wired to Brigade Headquarters using following code word :-

"POZZIE"

5. All details of defence of Divisional Main Line of Resistance will be taken over from relieving Units.

6. Brigade Headquarters will close at its present site and re-open at TOUQUET PARMENTIER at 10.00 14th instant, at which hour Command of the Advanced Guard will pass to G.O.C. 121st Infantry Brigade.
Up to 10.00 14th instant all troops in the Advanced Guard Area will be under the tactical control of G.O.C. 120th Infantry Brigade.

7. Particular attention will be paid to handing over the Liaison Posts and Bridge Head Guards on both flanks.

8. ACKNOWLEDGE.

Issued through Signals
at 11-30

[signature]
Captain,
Brigade Major,
120th Infantry Brigade.

DISTRIBUTION :-

Copy No.		Copy No.	
1	G.O.C.	14	176th Inf. Bde.
2	Brigade Major	15	94th Inf. Bde.
3	Staff Captain,	16	331st Bde. R.F.A.
4	War Diary.	17	330th Bde. R.F.A.
5	File.	18	64th H. A. Grp.
6	10th K.O.S.B.	19	"C" Coy. 39th Bn. M.G.C.
7	13th K.O.Y.L.I.	20	137th Field Ambce.
8	11th Cam. Hrs.	21	A.D.S. - do -
9	120th T.M.Bty.	22	224th Field Coy. R.E.
10	40th Divn. "G".	23	"L" Special Coy. R.E.
11	40th Divn. "Q"	24	Brigade Supply Officer.
12	119th Inf. Bde.	25	Brigade Signals.
13	121st Inf. Bde.	26	40th Divnl. Train

RELIEF TABLE TO ACCOMPANY 120TH INFANTRY BRIGADE ORDER NO. 228 dated 12-10-18.

Serial No.	UNIT	FROM.	TO	RELIEVED BY	REMARKS.
1.	15th K.O.Y.L.I.	Reserve in ERQUINGHEM	B.29.a.2.3.	23rd Cheshires.	Relief to be carried out by day in small parties.
2.	10th K.O.S.B.	Support. 2 Coys. N. of ARMENTIERES. 2 Coys. S.E. of do.	B.9.d.7.6.	23rd Lancs.Frs.	
3	11th Cam. Hrs.	Outpost Line.	GOSPEL VILLA	8th R.Irish R.	
4	120th T.M.Bty.	-	B.9.c.2.6.	121st T.M.Bty.	

MESSAGES AND SIGNALS.

No. of Message ......

Prefix .... Code .... m.	Words.	Charge.	This message is on a/c of:	Recd. at ...... m.
Office of Origin and Service Instructions.	Sent		Service.	Date ......
	At ...... m.			From ......
	To			
	By		(Signature of "Franking Officer.")	By ......

Appx XVI

TO	DAFA	JUZI	PANI	
			(a)	

* Sender's Number.	Day of Month.	In reply to Number.	AAA
G 50	12		

Morning situation AAA

Situation quiet [illegible]

nothing to report

Cleared DAFA repeated JUZI and PANI

From	JUVO
Place	
Time	

Priority

The above may be forwarded as now corrected. (Z)

Censor. Signature of Addressor or person authorised to telegraph in his name.

[illegible] Capt.

* This line, except AAA, should be erased if not required.

Wt. W 3253/P511. 500,000 Pads. 1/18. B. & S. Ltd. (E2389.)

No. of Message ....

Prefix ... Code ... m. / Origin and Service Instructions.	Words.	Charge.	This message is on a/c of: .... Service. (Signature of "Franking Officer.")	Recd. at ..... m. Date ..... From ..... By .....
	Sent At ..... m. To ..... By			

TO DAFA JUZI PANI

Sender's Number.	Day of Month.	In reply to Number.	AAA
G 59	12th		

Evening Situation AAA

Addsd DAFA repeated JUZI and PANI

From JUVU

Place

Time

The above may be forwarded as now corrected. (Z)

Censor. Signature of Addressor or person authorised to telegraph in his name.

Captn

* This line, except **AAA**, should be erased if not required.

Wt. W 3253/P511. 500,000 Pads. 1/18. B. & S. Ltd. (E2389.)

Appendix XVI

CONFIDENTIAL.

INTELLIGENCE REPORT - 120TH INFANTRY BRIGADE.
RIGHT SECTOR.
06.00 11-10-18 to 06.00 12-10-18.

'A' OUR OPERATIONS.

1. INFANTRY. A Minor Operation was carried out by 'A' Company 10th Bn. K.O.S.B. at 05.15. Latest information gives the general line as follows :-
North of railway from I.11.a.6.3. - along INCANDESCENT TRENCH - to road at I.5.d.3.6.

Posts have been pushed out in the direction of l'EPINETTE to join up with the 11th Bn. Cam. Highrs. and are being pushed into INCANDESCENT SUPPORT.
No identifications were obtained as the enemy withdrew directly our advance was perceived.

2. ARTILLERY. Fairly active by day with increased activity after dusk.
Two barrages were put down at 05.15 as per Operation Order.
3. AERIAL Below normal owing to weather conditions.
4. M. Gs. Fairly active. 4,000 rounds were fired on INANE ALLEY in I.12.a. between 05.15 and 06.00.
5. T. Ms. T.Ms. co-operatedwith infantry operation.

'B' ENEMY OPERATIONS.

1. INFANTRY. The enemy withdrew from INCANDESCENT TRENCH on the approach of our infantry.
2. ARTILLERY. Heavy calibres inactive. Areas C.21.c. and C.22.a. were shelled intermittently by 77 mm and 4.2s.
A weak barrage was immediately put down on our front line in answer to a red light fired by enemy at 05.15. On a double green light being fired the barrage ceased and our forward areas were subjected to scattered shelling.
4. M. Gs. Normal. Our Infantry met with very little M.G. fire coming from approx. I.5.b.
5. T. Ms. Nil.
6. GAS SHELLS. 12 Gas shells fell in C.14.a. at 09.30.

'C' ENEMY INTELLIGENCE.

1. LIGHTS. A single red loght was fired when our barrage opened at 05.15 about 10 minutes afterwards a double green light was fired.

[signature]
for Brigadier General,
Commanding, 120th Infantry Brigade.

12-10-18.

	Sent	This message is on a/c of	Recd.
0415	At m.	Service	Date
	To		From
	By	(Signature of "Franking Officer.")	By

TO DAFA JUZI ~~PAH~~ MAWA

Sender's Number.	Day of Month.	In reply to Number.	AAA
966	13th		

Morning situation AAA

Addsd DAFA reptd JUZI and ~~PAH~~ MAWA

From JUVO
Place
Time

The above may be forwarded as now corrected. (Z)

Censor. Signature of Addressor or person authorised to telegraph in his name.

* This line, except AAA, should be erased if not required.

Wt. W 3253/P511. 500,000 Pads. 1/18. B. & S. Ltd. (E2389.)

No. of Message ....

Office of Origin and Service Instructions.	Sent At .... m. To .... By	This message is on a/c of: .... Service. (Signature of "Franking Officer.")	Recd. at .... m. Date .... From .... By ....

TO DAFA JUZI MAWA

Sender's Number.	Day of Month.	In reply to Number.	AAA
* G 71			

Evening situation AAA

Situation quiet aaa slight enemy artillery activity aaa pres sues nil

Addsd DAFA reptd JUZI and MAWA

From JUVO

Place

Time

The above may be forwarded as now corrected. (Z)

Censor. Signature of Addressor or person authorised to telegraph in his name.

* This line, except AAA, should be erased if not required.

Wt. W 3253/P511. 500,000 Pads. 1/18. B. & S. Ltd. (E2389.)

CONFIDENTIAL.

Appendix XVII

INTELLIGENCE REPORT - 120TH INFANTRY BRIGADE
RIGHT SECTOR.
06.00 12-10-18 to 06.00 13-10-18.

==*=*=*=*=* =*=*=*=*=*

"A" OUR OPERATIONS.

1. INFANTRY. The line gained yesterday was consolidated and posts established to connect up with the main line on the left. The general line now runs as follows :-
   C.28.a.2.2. - I.5.a.3.7. - I.5.c.0.8. - I.5.c.4.3. - I.5.c.9.3. along INCANDESCENT TRENCH to Railway at I.11.a.6.3. where we are in close liaison with the troops on our right. Area to a depth of 300 yards in front of our line from I.5.a.3.7. to I.5.c.9.3. is a complete bog.

   Active patrolling was carried out during the night but no information of importance gained.
2. ARTILLERY. Normal. Enemy areas were harassed throughout the night, 18 pdrs batteries were very active from 18.45 to 18.55
3. AERIAL. Below normal owing to weather conditions.
4. M.Gs. Fairly quiet. Harassing fire was carried out on suspected enemy posts, tracks and light railways.
5. T.Ms. Nil.

"B" ENEMY OPERATIONS.

1. INFANTRY. Nil.
2. ARTILLERY. Fairly quiet throughout the day but considerable activity during the night.

   A barrage was put down on area I.4.a. from 08.30 to 08.50 of 77 mm and 4.2s. ARMENTIERES and HOUPLINES STATIONS were shelled during the night. The following areas were also shelled:- C.30.c. and d., C.21.d.0.5., C.27.b., C.27.central, I.1.d. and I.2.a., b. and c. Our forward areas were subjected to scattered shelling by 77 mm and 4.2s. throughout the night.
3. AERIAL. Inactive.
4. M. Gs. M.Gs. fired from I.5.b.4.2. and I.5.d.5.8. during the morning. Occasional bursts wre fired from the directing of FRELINGHIEN and from C.17.d.
5. T. Ms. Nil.
6. GAS SHELLS Gas was occasionally mixed with H.E. 3 gas shells fell in I.1.d. at 20.15.
7. BALLOONS. Nil.

"C" ENEMY INTELLIGENCE.

1. LIGHTS. - Green lights were fired by enemy throughout the night no apparent enemy action seen.
2. GENERAL. The wire in front of INCANDESCENT TRENCH was found to be very strong and intact. INCANDESCENT TRENCH was in a very bad state, being nothing more than a chain of shell holes.

[signature] Major
for Brigadier General,
Commanding, 120th Infantry Brigade.

13-10-18.

125TH INFANTRY BRIGADE SHELLING REPORT.

Right Sector.

Period- 06.00 12/10/18 to 06.00 13/10/18.

TIME.	AREA SHELLED.	CALIBRE.	NO.OF ROUNDS&	DIRECTION.	REMARKS.
-	ARMENTIERES STN.	5.9.	16	E.N.E.	Bursts every few minutes during the night.
-	HOUPLINES STN.	5.9.	18	E.N.E.	
06.45.	I.4a.	77mm.& 4.2	60	E.N.E.	
08.30 to 08.50.	I.4a.	77mm.& 4.2	90	E.	Barrage.
11.45	C. 27.b.centl.	5.9.	18	E,S.E.	
12-20	C.20.c.& d.	77mm.	40	E.	
14.20	I.2.a.centl.	5.9.	24	E.	3 minutes intervals
16.10 to 16.50	C.27.centl.	5.9.	20	E.N.E.	
19.30	C.21.d.0.5.	5.9	6	E.N.E.	
19.30 to 20.00	I.2.b.c.&d.	5.9	12	E.N.E.	
20.15	I.1.d.	4.2	6	E,	3 Gas shells
20.15 to 21.15.	C. 27 & 28	5.9	20	E,	
22.30, 21.00 to 05.00.	I.2.a.b.&c.	-	-	-	Considerable number of light shells mixed with gas.

Brigadier

Appendix XVIII

SECRET.

DEFENCE INSTRUCTIONS FOR NIEPPE SYSTEM.

1. The Brigade whilst in Divisional Support, will be disposed as below, and will be responsible, if necessary, for the manning and the defence of the NIEPPE System from the River LYS at H.4.b.8.8. to Northern Divisional Boundary H.4.d.4.2. :-

'A' Battn.	B.19.a.2.3.	T. M. Bty.	B.9.c.2.3.
'B' Battn.	B.9.d.7.3.	Coy., M.G.C.	POSTON FARM.
'C' Battn.	B.27.d.8.0.		

2. In the event of it being necessary to man the NIEPPE SYSTEM, the System will be held as follows :-

(a) Two Battalions in the line, 'A' on the right, 'B' on the left.

(b) One Battalion, 'C', in Brigade Reserve.

The Battalion boundary will be the grid line B.15.c.0.0. - B.17.c.0.0.

3.(a) The two Battalions in the Line will each have one Company in the Outpost Line, two in the NIEPPE System, and one in Support.

(b) The posts of the Outpost Line of the right battalion will be so sited as to cover the crossings over the LYS within the Battalion Sector.

(c) The posts of the Outpost Line of the left battalion will be sited so as to hold the line of the WARNAVE.

(d) The 120th Trench Mortar Battery will have two mortars in each battalion Sector at the disposal of the Battalion Commander, and will keep four in Brigade Reserve at Brigade Headquarters.

(e) The Battalion in Brigade Reserve will be concentrated about the area B.14.d. and B.15.c.

(f) Brigade Headquarters will remain at B.21.b.0.8.

4. On receipt of the Order "MAN NIEPPE SYSTEM" Units will at once move into their battle positions.

5. 1 Company, 39th Bn. M. G. Corps is available for the defence of the NIEPPE System, and will keep its guns in position at all times. Details of these positions will be issued later.

6.(a) All Units will carry out the necessary reconnaissances of the Outpost positions, Main Line of Resistance (i.e. NIEPPE SYSTEM) and the approaches to this system.

(b) Trench Mortar Battery in conjunction with O.Cs. battalions will select positions for Mortars covering the NIEPPE SYSTEM.

7. ACKNOWLEDGE.

W H Endy.
Captain,
Brigade Major,
120th Infantry Brigade.

14-10-18.

Copy to :- 10th Bn. K.O.S.B.
15th Bn. K.O.Y.L.I.
11th Bn. Cam. Highrs.
120th T. M. Battery.
'D' Coy., 39th Bn. M.G.C.
40th Division "G"

S E C R E T. Appendix XIX COPY NO. 4

16-10-18

120TH INFANTRY BRIGADE WARNING ORDER NO. 229.

=

1. All indications point to the enemy carrying out an early withdrawal in front of 40th Division.

2. The 40th Division will be ready to advance in an Easterly direction in conjunction with the advance of 59th and 31st Divisions on both flanks, and will vigorously press the retreating enemy.

3. The objectives allotted to the Division are as follows :-

FORT DE LOMPRET (J.8.b.) - Buildings J.3.c.4.8. - LA TULLERIE FARM (D.27.d.0.7.) - LE COEUR JOYEUX (D.22.b.0.7.) - QUESNOY (exclusive).

4. In the event of the Advanced Guard moving forward, the 120th Infantry Brigade will be prepared to support the 121st Infantry Brigade or to move through the 121st Infantry Brigade if the situation admits of and requires it.

The 120th Infantry Brigade must be prepared to move at short notice on orders being received from Divisional Headquarters.

5. Should the 120th Infantry Brigade move up to support the 121st Infantry Brigade, the former will take up a two battalion frontage, with one Battalion in Support, Units moving as follows :-

(a) 10th Bn. K.O.S.B. will cross the LYS by the bridges North of ARMENTIERES and be prepared to occupy the defences in C.27 and C.22.a. and c.

(b) 15th Bn. K.O.Y.L.I. will cross the LYS by the PONT DE NIEPPE bridge, and moving through ARMENTIERES will be prepared to occupy the defences in I.2.b. and c., I.7.b. with one Company in Support about RUE MARLE.

The Inter-battalion boundary of the above two battalions in the initial stages of the advance will be the grid line through C.26.c.0.0. - C.29.c.0.0.

(c) 11th Bn. Cameron Highrs. will cross the LYS by the ERQUINGHEM bridge in H.4.c. and remain in reserve about ERQUINGHEM, with one Company in the ERQUINGHEM SWITCH between the LYS and Southern Divisional Boundary.

(d) 120th T. M. Battery will move to a position about H.12.b.

(e) 'D' Coy. 39th Bn. M.G.C. now attached to 120th Infantry Bde. will occupy the gun positions allotted in the line of defences immediately East of ARMENTIERES and HOUPLINES and keep the remaining guns in reserve in H.5.d.

(f) Headquarters, 120th Infantry Brigade will move to H.11.b.4.6.

7. ACKNOWLEDGE.

T. Knox-Shaw

Captain,
A/Brigade Major,
120th Infantry Brigade.

Issued through Signals
at 0700.

Copy No. 1..G.O.C.
2..Brigade Major.
3..Staff Captain,
4..War Diary.
5..File.
6..10th K.O.S.B.
7..15th K.O.Y.L.I.
8..11th Cam. Hrs.
9..120th T.M.Bty.
10..40th Divn. "G"
11..119th Inf. Bde.
12..121st Inf. Bde.
13..331st Bde. R.F.A.
14..330th Bde. R.F.A.
15..64th H.A.Grp.
16..'D' Coy. 39th Bn. M.G.C.
17..137th Field Ambce.
18..A.D.S. - do -
19..Brigade Signals.

S E C R E T. COPY NO.1

120TH INFANTRY BRIGADE INSTRUCTIONS NO. 2.

7-10-18.

1. 120th Infantry Brigade Instructions No. 1 of 5-10-18 will be modified as below.

2. The 330th Brigade R.F.A. has been added to the troops of the Advanced Guard, remaining in action about LE BIZET.

3. The Advanced Guard will be disposed as follows :-
   (a) One Battalion holding the Outpost Line.
   (b) One Battalion in Support with two Companies about I.2.b. and c. and I.7.b., and two Companies about C.20.d. which will maintain permanent posts covering the bridges over the LYS.
   (c) One Battalion in Reserve about ERQUINGHEM, with a permanent nucleus garrison of one Company in the ERQUINGHEM SWITCH. This Battalion will be responsible for the defence of the ERQUINGHEM SWITCH from the river LYS to the Divisional Southern Boundary.

4. The two Companies of the Support Battalion North of ARMENTIERES will be tactically under the control of the C. O. of the Battalion in the Outpost Line, but will only be used for guarding the bridge heads and will under no circumstances be moved East of the river LYS without the authority of Brigade Headquarters.

5. The Outpost Line will be held with three Companies, with one Company in Reserve on the left flank, and will be organised in a series of strong posts, each consisting of a force which is a complete fighting Unit, and whose strength should not be less than a platoon.

6. Owing to the wide frontage and the consequent large gaps between posts special patrol precautions must be taken. All patrols must be strong fighting patrols, capable of dealing with any small parties of the enemy encountered.
   For the same reason Officers going round their line from post to post must take a small fighting escort with them capable of dealing with any of the enemy, suddenly encountered, who may have got in between our posts.

7. 8 Machine Guns are allotted to the defence of the Outpost Line, and will be placed in depth; four are left in Support North of ARMENTIERES covering the river crossings, and the battery line, four will be in support on the South of ARMENTIERES covering the Southern Brigade of Artillery.

8. All troops will be responsible for improving the posts they occupy as far as possible.

9. ACKNOWLEDGE.

Captain,
Brigade Major,
120th Infantry Brigade.

Issued to all
recipients of
120th Inf.Bde.
Instructions
No.1. d/5-10-18.

Appendix XX 4.

S E C R E T.

COPY NO

120TH INFANTRY BRIGADE INSTRUCTIONS NO. 3.

The following instructions have been issued to the Advanced Guard and are forwarded for information and compliance when the 120th Infantry Brigade assumes the role of Advanced Guard to the 40th Division :-

"1. When unable to push on, units will state in their reports the position of the troops who have been checked, the position and estimated strength of the enemy opposing them, and how they are dealing with the situation.

2. One Stokes Mortar and 40 rounds of ammunition will accompany each Battalion Headquarters; a proportion of one round of smoke will be carried to every 5 rounds.

3. The above instructions will be made known to all commanders down to Company Commanders."

Reference para 2.
The O.C., 120th Trench Mortar Battery will arrange direct with Battalion Commanders concerned for the carrying parties required for the T. M. ammunition.

T. Knox-Shaw

Captain,
A/Brigade Major,
120th Infantry Brigade.

16-10-18.

Copy No. 1 ... G.O.C.
2 ... Brigade Major.
3 ... Staff Captain.
4 ... War Diary.
5 ... File.
6 - 10 10th Bn. K.O.S.B.
11 - 15 15th Bn. K.O.Y.L.I.
16 - 20 11th Bn. Cam. Highrs.
21 - 24 120th T. M. Battery.
25 ... 'D' Coy. 39th Bn. M.G.C.

S E C R E T.

COPY NO.

120TH INFANTRY BRIGADE ORDER NO. 230.

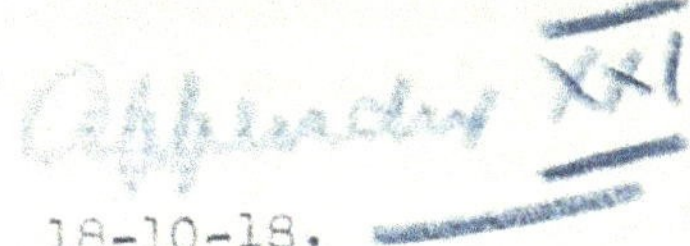

18-10-18.

1. Enemy is withdrawing Eastwards through ROUBAIX and TOURCOING.

2. The 40th Division is to continue to advance to-day.

3. The 120th Infantry Brigade will be about WAMBRECHIES by 12.00 18th instant.

4. Units will march in accordance with attached march table.

5. Units will send representatives to meet Staff Captain at Ponton Bridge across Canal at WAMBRECHIES at 11.00.

6. Working parties are NOT cancelled.
Battalions must arrange for these men to rejoin their Battalions in the new Area.

7. O.C. 10th Bn. K.O.S.B. will throw out a small Advance Guard to preceed the column.

8. Transports will walk with ~~with~~ Units.

9. Brigade Headquarters will close at J.1.central at 09.00 and will re-open at a site to be notified later.

10. ACKNOWLEDGE.

T Knox-Shaw

Captain,
A/Brigade Major,
120th Infantry Brigade.

Issued through Signals
at 01-30

Issued to all recipients of 120th Inf. Bde. Order No. 229.

MARCH TABLE TO ACCOMPANY 120TH INFANTRY BRIGADE ORDER NO. 230.

UNIT.	STARTING POINT.	TIME	ROUTE.	REMARKS.
10th K.O.S.B.	Road junction D.21. c.5.0.	09.00	Route will be notified on arrival at LA CROIX.	
15th K.O.Y.L.I.	Road junction D.27. b.4.0.	09.30	- do -	
Bde. Hd. Qrs.	Road junction J.1. d.5.4.	09.30	- do -	Route to LA CROIX will be notified at Starting Point.
11th Cam. Hrs.	ho - do -	09.35	- do -	
'D' Coy. 39th Bn. M. G. C.	- do -	10.10	- do -	
120th T.M.Bty.	- do -	10.25	- do -	

Appendix XXII

SECRET. COPY NO.

120TH INFANTRY BRIGADE ORDER NO: 231.

Ref: Maps
Sheets 36 and 37.
1/40,000.

27-10-18.

1. The 120th Infantry Brigade will move into billets in the vicinity of LANNOY to-morrow, October 28th, 1918.

2. Units will proceed by route march as under :-

UNIT.	STARTING POINT.	TIME.	ROUTE.
120th Inf.Bde. Headquarters.	Brigade Headquarters	0830	ST ANDRE - LA MADELEINE - Road junction K.18.central - L.13.d.1.5. - L.14.a.5.7. - L.15.c.8.8. - L. 9.d.4.2. - L.16.b.1.9. - L.11.a.5.7. - G.13.a.9.8. - G.8.b.8.5.
120th T.M.B.	K.14.a.7.0.	0831	
15th K.O.Y.L.I.	- do -	0832	
11th Cam. Hrs.	- do -	0835	
10th K.O.S.B.	- do -	0838	
Transport in order of Units as above under Bde. T. O.	- do -	0841	

2. (a) The intervals laid down in F.S.R. will be maintained during the march with the exception that an interval of 100 yards will be maintained between Transport of each Unit.

(b) The usual halts at 10 minutes to each hour will be observed.

(c) Each Battalion will detail 1 Officer and 2 N.C.Os. to act as a rear party and collect any men who are given permission to leave the ranks.

(d) An Ambulance will follow the Column.

4. Billeting parties will meet the Staff Captain at 1100 hours at G.15.b.0.9. where road to LANNOY crosses the Railway.

5. Brigade Headquarters will close at ST ANDRE at 0800 hours, 28th instant and open later on arrival at LANNOY.
Reports to Head of Column.

6. ACKNOWLEDGE.

T Knox-Shaw

Captain,
A/Brigade Major,
120th Infantry Brigade.

Issued through Signals
at 1000 hours.

DISTRIBUTION :-

Copy No 1 ... G.O.C.
2 ... Brigade Major.
3 ... Staff Captain.
4 ... War Diary.
5 ... File.
6 ... 10th Bn. K.O.S.B.
7 ... 15th Bn. K.O.Y.L.I.
8 ... 11th Bn. Cam. Highrs.
9 ... 120th T. M. Battery.
10 ... Brigade Transport Officer.
11 ... 119th Inf. Bde.
12 ... 121st Inf. Bde.
13 ... 40th Divn. "G"
14 ... 40th Divn. "Q"
15 ... D.A.P.M. 40th Divn.
16 ... A.D.M.S. - do -
17 ... 137th Field Ambce.
18 ... No. 3 Coy. Div. Train.
19 ... 40th Divnl. Train.
20 ... Area Commandant, LANNOY.
21 ... Brigade Signals.

(6392) Wt. W6192/P875 1,500,000 4/18 McA & W Ltd (E 2815) Forms W3091/4.

Army Form W.3091.

WO 30

Confidential

Cover for Documents.

Nature of Enclosures.

War Diary.

Headquarters

120th Infantry Brigade.

NOVEMBER 1918.

VOLUME XXX

Notes, or Letters written.

ORIGINAL

Army Form C. 2118.

Instructions regarding War Diaries and Intelligence Summaries are contained in F. S. Regs., Part II. and the Staff Manual respectively. Title pages will be prepared in manuscript.

WAR DIARY
or
~~INTELLIGENCE SUMMARY~~.
(*Erase heading not required.*)

VOLUME XXX.
NOVEMBER, 1918.

Headquarters,
120th Infantry Brigade.

Page 1.

Place	Date	Hour	Summary of Events and Information	Remarks and references to Appendices
LANNOY.	1st		Brigade billeted in LANNOY. Training. Officers of 10th Bn. K.O.S.B. taken by G.O.C. on Tactical Exercise on Outposts.	TRS
	2nd.		Training. Officers of 11th Bn. Cameron Highrs. taken by G.O.C. on same Tactical Exercise. 10th Bn. K.O.S.B precticed Scheme on ground.	TRS
	4th		Training. 11th Bn. Cam. Highrs. precticed Scheme in the morning - G.O.C. took Officers of the 15th Bn. K.O.Y.L.I. in the afternoon.	TRS
	5th		120th Infantry Brigade Order No. 232 issued, ordering move of Brigade on 6th inst. to billets in the Support Area.	appendix I.
			Wet day. G.O.C. delivered lecture on Outposts to Officers at Brigade Headquarters at 14.00 hours.	TRS
	6th		Brigade moved in accordance with 120th Infantry Brigade Order No. 232 dated 5th inst., and were billeted as under :- Brigade Headquarters ... LEERS NORD. 10th Bn. K.O.S.B. ... LEERS NORD. 15th Bn. K.O.Y.L.I. ... NECHIN. 11th Bn. Cam. Highrs. ... ESTAIMPUIS. 120th T. M. Battery ... LEERS NORD.	TRS.
			G.O.C. and Brigade Major attended Conference at Headquarters 119th Infantry Brigade at 14.30 hours at which the Major General Commanding the Division explained a Scheme for the crossing of the SCHELDT.	
	7th		G.O.C. and Brigade Major attended Conference at Headquarters 119th Infantry Brigade at which details of the Scheme for crossing the SCHELDT were arranged. At 16.00 hours the G.O.C. assembled Commanding Officers and Adjutants and explained the Scheme to them	TRS

A6945 Wt. W11422/M1160 350,000 12/16 D. D. & L. Forms/C./2118/14.

Instructions regarding War Diaries and Intelligence Summaries are contained in F. S. Regs., Par. II. and the Staff Manual respectively. Title pages will be prepared in manuscript.

Page 2.

WAR DIARY
or
INTELLIGENCE SUMMARY.
(Erase heading not required.)

VOLUME XXX.
NOVEMBER, 1918.

Army Form C. 2118.

Headquarters,
120th Infantry Brigade.

Place	Date	Hour	Summary of Events and Information	Remarks and references to Appendices
LEERS-NORD.	8th		Unusually quiet. Indications of withdrawal of enemy apparent but patrols of the 119th Infantry Brigade which advanced along causeways at PECQ and WARCOING came under heavy M.G.fire at 11.30 hours. A few shells, fired at extreme range, fell in PECQ about 14.15. Preparations for operations to force passage of SCHELDT continued. Site for Brigade Headquarters selected at Gendarmerie at PECQ. Billeting Area for Battalions in PECQ and WARCOING allotted. G.O.C. attended Conference at Headquarters 119th Infantry Brigade at 15.00 hours.	TKS
	9th		During the night 8/9th 119th Infantry Brigade crossed SCHELDT as the enemy had withdrawn. 120th Infantry Brigade Order No. 233 issued. The Brigade moved into PECQ and WARCOING Area. Brigade Headquarters ...) 10th Bn. K.O.S.B. ...) PECQ. 15th Bn. K.O.Y.L.I. ...) 120th T. M. Battery ...) 11th Bn. Cam. Hrs. ... WARCOING. As both villages had been heavily shelled by the enemy, the houses provided Very poor accommodation in case of wet weather. Permission was obtained to move to HERINNES.	appendix II. TKS TKS
HERINNES.	10th		Brigade Headquarters, 10th Bn. K.O.S.B., 15th Bn. K.O.Y.L.I. and 120th T. M.Battery moved during the afternoon to HERINNES, the 11th Bn. Cam. Highrs. remaining at WARCOING.	
	11th		Armistice declared at 11.00 hours. Brigade ordered to move to TOUFFLERS - NECHIN Area. 120th Infantry Brigade Order No. 234 issued.	TKS appendix III
	12th		Brigade marched to new area : Units were billeted as under :- Brigade Headquarters ... TOUFFLERS. 10th Bn. K.O.S.B. ... -do- 15th Bn. K.O.Y.L.I. ... -do- 11th Bn. Cam. Highrs. ... NECHIN. 120th T.M.Battery ... TOUFFLERS.	TKS.

A6945 Wt. W11422/M1160 35... D. D. & L. Forms/C./2118/14.

Instructions regarding War Diaries and Intelligence Summaries are contained in F. S. Regs., Par. II. and the Staff Manual respectively. Title pages will be prepared in manuscript.

Page 3.

WAR DIARY
or
~~INTELLIGENCE SUMMARY.~~
(*Erase heading not required.*)

VOLUME XXX.
NOVEMBER, 1918.

Army Form C. 2118.

Headquarters,
120th Infantry Brigade.

Place	Date	Hour	Summary of Events and Information	Remarks and references to Appendices
TOUFFLERS.	12th		Conference at which Commanding Officers attended was held at Brigade Headquarters at 17.00 hours. Subjects discussed - Ceremonial Drill - Route March - Football - Recreation - Education Scheme.	TKS
	14th		G.O.C., Brigade Major, Battalion Commanders and Sub.Education Officers attended a Corps Conference at TOURCOING on the subject of "Active Service Army Schools".	TKS
	15th		Brigade exercised in Ceremonial Drill and March Past.	TKS
	16th		Brigade Route March during the morning. Dress - Marching Order with packs.	TKS
	17th		Brigade sent a representative Company to Second Army Thanksgiving Service at ROUBAIX.	TKS
	18th		Brigade exercised in Ceremonial Drill and March Past.	TKS
	19th		Brigade inspected by Corps Commander. The Brigade was highly complimented on the March Past.	TKS
	22nd		Brigadier General The Hon. W.P.HORE-RUTHVEN, C.M.G., D.S.O. assumed command of the 40th Division during the temporary absence of Major General Sir W.E.PEYTON, K.C.B., K.C.V.O. D.S.O., Lieut. Colonel T.W.T.ISAAC, 15th Bn. K.O.Y.L.I. assuming command of the Brigade.	TKS
	25th		120th Infantry Brigade Order No. 235 issued notifying move of Brigade Headquarters on 26th instant.	Appendix IV
			Classes at Brigade Commercial School commenced. Shorthand, & Commercial Arithmetic being taught.	TKS
LANNOY	26th		120th Infantry Brigade Headquarters closed at TOUFFLERS at 11.00 hours and re-opened at LANNOY.	TKS
			Brigadier General The Hon. W.P.HORE-RUTHVEN resumed command of the Brigade.	
	27th		Brigadier inspected one Company of each Battalion on Company Parade grounds in Marching Order with packs.	TKS

A6945 Wt. W11422/M1160 350,000 12/16 D. D. & L. Forms/C./2118/14.

Instructions regarding War Diaries and Intelligence Summaries are contained in F. S. Regs., Par. II. and the Staff Manual respectively. Title pages will be prepared in manuscript.

Army Form C. 2118.

VOLUME XXX
NOVEMBER, 1918.

WAR DIARY
or
INTELLIGENCE SUMMARY.
(Erase heading not required.)

Page 4.

Headquarters,
120th Infantry Brigade.

Place	Date	Hour	Summary of Events and Information	Remarks and references to Appendices
LANNOY.	29th		Brigadier inspected another Company of each Battalion.	T.R.S.

W. Ruthven Brigadier General,
Commanding, 120th Infantry Brigade.

A6945 Wt. W11422/M1160 350,000 12/16 D. D. & L. Forms/C./2118/14.

MARCH TABLE TO ACCOMPANY 120TH INFANTRY BRIGADE ORDER NO. 232 dated 5-11-18.

Serial No.	UNIT	FROM	TO	ROUTE	TAKING OVER BILLETS FROM	REMARKS.
1.	11th Cam. Hrs.	LANNOY	ESTAIMPUIS	FRESNOY - LEERS - cross roads G.6.c.9.5. - road junction A.29.b.4.5. - A.23.d.3.3. - A.18.d.9.0. - B.19.b.6.2.	8th R. Irish R. (Headquarters B.20.a.9.9.)	To be clear of road junction G.10.d.0.1. by 09.30 hours.
2.	10th K.O.S.B.	LANNOY	LEERS-NORD	FRESNOY - LEERS.	23rd Cheshires (Headquarters H.2.b.7.5.)	Head of column to pass road junction G.15.b.6.4. at 09.30 hours.
3.	15th K.O.Y.L.I	LANNOY.	NECHIN	via TOUFFLERS.	23rd Lanc. Frs. (Headquarters H.14.d.2.9.)	Battalion to be clear of cross roads G.16.c.0.7. by 09.30 hours.
4.	120th T.M.Bty.	LANNOY	LEERS-NORD	FRESNOY - LEERS	121st T.M.Bty. (Headquarters H.2.b.2.3.)	To pass road junction G.15.b.6.4. at 10.15 hours.
5.	Headquarters 120th Inf.Bde.	LANNOY.	LEERS-NORD.	FRESNOY - LEERS.	Headquarters 121st Inf.Bde. H.2.a.7.7.	To pass road junction G.15.b.6.4. at 10.10 hours.

Appendix I.

COPY NO.5...

SECRET.

120TH INFANTRY BRIGADE ORDER NO.252.

Ref; Sheet 37
1/40,000

5-11-18.

1. The 120th Infantry Brigade will move on the 6th instant into billets in the Support Brigade Area in accordance with the March Table on the reverse.

2. Units will march accompanied by their Transport and maintain the distances between Companies and vehicles as laid down in S.S. 724.

3. Brigade Headquarters will close at LANNOY at 10.00 hours on 6th instant and will re-open at H.2.a.7.7. (LEERS-NORD) at the same hour.

4. Units will report arrival in billets to Brigade H.Q.

5. ACKNOWLEDGE.

T. Knox-Shaw
Captain,
Brigade Major,
120th Infantry Brigade.

Issued through Signals
at 10.00 hours.

DISTRIBUTION :-

Copy No. 1 ... G.O.C.
2 ... Brigade Major.
3 ... Staff Captain.
4 ... War Diary.
5 ... File.
6 ... 10th Bn. K.O.S.B.
7 ... 15th Bn. K.O.Y.L.I.
8 ... 11th Bn. Cam. Hrs.
9 ... 120th T. M. Bty.
10 ... Bde. Transport Officer.
11 ... 119th Inf. Bde.
12 ... 121st Inf. Bde.
13 ... 40th Divn. "G"
14 ... 40th Divn. "Q"
15 ... C.R.A. 40th Divn.
16 ... C.R.E. 40th Divn.
17 ... A.D.M.S. 40th Divn.
18 ... D.A.P.M. 40th Divn.
19 ... No. 3 Coy. 40th Div.Train.
20 ... 40th Divnl. Train.
21 ... Area Commandant, LANNOY
22 ... Brigade Signals.
23 ... D Coy M.G.C

S E C R E T.

ADMINISTRATIVE INSTRUCTIONS.
MOVE OF 120TH INFANTRY BRIGADE - 6th NOVEMBER, 1918.

1. ACCOMMODATION.
Accommodation of Units of 121st Infantry Brigade will be taken over as follows :-

UNIT.	FROM	LOCATION.
120th Inf.Bde.H.Q.	121st Inf.Bde.H.Q.	LEERS - NORD. (H.2.a.7.7)
10th Bn. K.O.S.B.	23rd Cheshire Rgt.	LEERS - NORD.
15th Bn. K.O Y.L.I.	23rd Lancs. Fusrs.	NECHIN.
11th Bn. Cam. Hrs.	8th R. Irish Rgt.	ESTAIMPUIS.
120th T. M. Bty.	121st T. M. Bty.	LEERS - NORD.

2. TRANSPORT LINES.
Transport lines will be taken over, with the exception of 15th Bn. K.O.Y L.I., from relieved Units at following locations :-

120th Inf. Bde. Hd. Qrs. ... G.6.d.7.3.
10th Battn. K. O. S. B. ... H.2.a.7.9.
15th Battn. K.O.Y.L.I. ... H.13.b. (approx).
11th Battn. Cam. Highrs. ... B.20.a.1.9.

3. QUARTERMASTER'S STORES.
Quartermaster's Stores are in the Battalions Areas.

4. ADVANCE PARTIES
1. Advance arties of all Units will report at Headquarters of Unit which they are relieving at 09.00 hours where guides to all billets will meet them.
2. Units will arrange for guides to all billets at present occupied by them to be at their present Headquarters at 09.00 hours, 6th November to show billets to Advance Parties from Units of 121st Infantry Brigade.

5. TRANSPORT
1. Application has been made for lorries to carry Units blankets, etc.
2. Baggage wagons will report to Battalions on night 5/ 5/6th November, 1918.

6. HANDING OVER.
All Units will obtain certificate of cleanliness of billets from relieving Units and will forward a copy to Brigade Headquarters by last D.R. 6th November, 1918.

7. BATHS.
Details of bathing facilities will be issued later.

8. WATER.
There is a plentiful supply of good water in the Area.

9. SUPPLIES.
No. 3 Coy. A.S.C. Train will remain at its present location (G.8.b.5.1.)

[signature]
Captain,
Staff Captain,
120th Infantry Brigade.

5th November, 1918.

Appendix II.

SECRET.

COPY NO.

120TH INFANTRY BRIGADE ORDER NO. 233.

1. The 119th Infantry Brigade have crossed the River SCHELDT.

2. The 120th Infantry Brigade will move into billets in the PECQ - WARCOING Area to-day in accordance with march table below:-

UNIT	FROM	TO	REMARKS.
Headquarters 120th Inf. Bde.	LEERS-NORD	PECQ	starting at 13.30 hours.
10th K.O.S.B.	- do -	-do-	.. .. 13.00 ..
15th K.O.Y.L.I.	NECHIN	-do-	.. .. 13.30 ..
11th Cam.Hrs.	ESTAIMPUIS	WARCOING	. .. 13.00 ..
120th T. M. Bty.	LEERS-NORD	PECQ.	. .. 13.45 ..

3. "B" Coy. 39th Bn. M.G.C. will leave LEERS-NORD at 13.45 hours and move into billets at ESTAIMBOURG.

4. Transport and Quartermasters Stores will move with Units.
Packs, blankets, etc. will be dumped and collected by Regtl. Transport to-day by doing two journeys.
Baggage wagons will report to Units at 12.00 hours to-day and can be used to do two journeys.

5. Units will report their arrival in billets and give locations of their new Headquarters.

6. Brigade Headquarters close at LEERS-NORD at 13.30 hours and re-open at 14.00 hours at the Gendarmerie at PECQ.

7. ACKNOWLEDGE.

T. Knox-Shaw

Captain,
Brigade Major,
120th Infantry Brigade.

Issued through Signals
at 10.45 hours.

DISTRIBUTION :-

Copy No. . . . G.O.C.
2 . Brigade Major.
3. Staff Captain.
4 . War Diary.
5 . File.
6 . 10th K.O.S.B.
7 . 15th K.O.Y.L.I.
8 . 11th Cam. Hrs.
9 . 120th T.M.Bty.
10 . Bde. Trans. Offr.
11 119th Inf. Bde.
12 . 121st Inf. Bde.
13 . 40th Divn. "G".
14 . 40th Divn. "Q"
15 . C.R.A. 40th Divn.
16 . C.R.E. 40th Divn.
17 . A.D.M.S. 40th Divn.
18 . D.A.P.M. 40th Divn.
19 . No. 3 Coy. Divn. Train.
20 . 40th Divnl. Train.
21 . Brigade Signals.
22 . "B" Coy. 39th Bn. M.G.C.

MARCH TABLE TO ACCOMPANY 120TH INFANTRY BRIGADE ORDER NO.234 dated 11-11-18.

Serial No.	UNIT.	FROM	TO	STARTING POINT PLACE	STARTING POINT TIME	ROUTE.	REMARKS.
1.	Headquarters 120th Inf.Bde.	HERINNES.	TOUFFLERS	Bde.Hd.Qrs.	09.30	LE RIVACE - PECQ - H.11.cent. - NECHIN.	Column to be clear of PECQ by 11.00
2	10th K.O.S.B.	-do-	-do-	cross roads C.27.b.1.3.	09.40	- do -	
3.	15th K.O.Y L.I.	-do-	BUCQUOK	HERINNES Church.	09.34	- do -	
4.	120th T.M.Bty.	-do-	NECHIN.	road junction C.21.d.1.0.	09.44	- do -	
5.	11th Cam.Hrs.	WARCOING	NECHIN	cross roads C.20.a.0.3.	10.00	C.19.d.5.3. - C.25.d.6.9. - C 25.c.8.5. - H.6.b.9.4. - H.11.central - NECHIN.	Bn. joins column in rear of 120th T.M.B. at H.6.b.9.4. "B" & "C" Echelons join rear of whole column at H.6.b.9.4.
6.	Transport Echelons "B" & "C" in order of Units.	HERINNES	TOUFFLERS and NECHIN	Cross roads C.27.b.1.3.	09.45	As for Serial No. 1.	

NOTE :- Distances laid down in F.S.R. will be maintained during the march.
Two Ambulances will join the rear of the column at PECQ.

Appendix III.

S E C R E T. 120TH INFANTRY BRIGADE ORDER NO.254. COPY NO

==*=*=*=*=*=*=*=*=*=*=*=*=*=*=*=*=*=

Ref: Sheet 37
1/40,000

11-11-18.

---

1. The 120th Infantry Brigade will move to-morrow, 12th November, 1918 into billets in the TOUFFLERS - NECHIN Area, in accordance with march table on the reverse.

2. "A" Echelon of Transport will move with Units. The remainder of Transport will be Brigaded and move in the order of march of Units under the Brigade Transport Officer.
The "B" and "C" Echelons of 11th Bn. Cameron Highrs. will join the rear of the column as it passes the road junction H.6.b.9.4.

3. Billeting parties will be detailed to meet the Staff Captain at Church at NECHIN, H.14.c.5.9., at 09.30 hours.
Guides are to meet Battalions at H.14.c.5.9. at 11.30 hours to conduct Companies to their billets.

4. Transport arrangements will be notified later.

5. Units will report their arrival in billets and give the locations of their Headquarters.

6. Brigade Headquarters closes at HERRINNES at 09.00 hours and opens later on arrival at TOUFFLERS.

7. ACKNOWLEDGE.

T. Knox-Shaw
Captain,
Brigade Major,
120th Infantry Brigade.

Issued through Signals
at 20.00 hours.

DISTRIBUTION :-

Copy No.			
1	G.O.C.	12	121st Inf. Bde.
2	Brigade Major.	13	40th Divn. "G"
3	Staff Captain.	14	40th Divn. "Q"
4	War Diary.	15	C.R.A. 40th Divn.
5	File.	16	C.R.E. 40th Divn.
6	10th K.O.S.B.	17	A.D.M.S. 40th Divn.
7	15th K.O.Y.L.I.	18	D.A.P.M. 40th Divn.
8	11th Cam. Hrs.	19	No. 3 Coy. Div. Train.
9	120th T.M.Bty.	20	40th Divnl. Train.
10	Bde. Trans.Offr.	21	Brigade Signals.
11	119th Inf.Bde.	22	"B" Coy. 39th Bn. M.G.C.
23	Town Major TOUFFLERS	24	Billet Warden NECHIN.

==============

Appendix IV.

SECRET. COPY NO. 4

120TH INFANTRY BRIGADE ORDER NO. 235.

Ref. Map Sheet 37 1/40,000 25-11-18.

1. Headquarters 120th Infantry Brigade will close at TOUFFLERS at 11.00 hours on 26th November, 1918 and re-open at LANNOY (G.15.b.3.1.) at the same hour.

2. ACKNOWLEDGE.

T. Knox-Shaw
Captain,
Brigade Major,
120th Infantry Brigade.

DISTRIBUTION:-

Copy No 1 ... G.O.C.
2 ... Brigade Major.
3 ... Staff Captain.
4 ... War Diary.
5 ... File.
6 ... 10th K.O.S.B.
7 ... 15th K.O.Y.L.I.
8 ... 11th Cam. Hrs.
9 ... Bde. Trans. Officer.
10 ... 119th Inf. Bde.
11 ... 121st Inf. Bde.
12 ... 40th Divn. "G"
13 ... 40th Divn. "Q"
14 ... C.R.A. 40th Divn.
15 ... C.R.E. 40th Divn.
16 ... A.D.M.S. 40th Divn.
17 ... D.A.P.M. 40th Divn.
18 ... No. 3 Coy. Divn. Train.
19 ... 40th Divnl. Train.
20 ... Brigade Signals.
21 ... Town Major LANNOY.

Instructions regarding War Diaries and Intelligence Summaries are contained in F. S. Regs., Part II. and the Staff Manual respectively. Title pages will be prepared in manuscript.

WAR DIARY
or
~~INTELLIGENCE SUMMARY.~~

(*Erase heading not required.*)

VOLUME XXX1
DECEMBER, 1918.

Army Form C. 2118.

Headquarters,
120th Infantry Brigade.

Page 1.

Place	Date	Hour	Summary of Events and Information	Remarks and references to Appendices
LANNOY.	3rd.		Brigade billeted in LANNOY. G.O.C. inspected one Company of each Battalion in Matching Order.	
	8th.		Parade held in the Square, LANNOY, at 15.00 hours at which the Divisional Commander presented Medal Ribbons to the undermentioned N.C.Os and men of the Brigade :-	
			CROIXde GUERRE (Division - With Silver Star).	
			No. 64171 Sergt. L. HANSON, 15th Bn. K.O.Y.L.I.	
			CROIX de GUERRE (Brigade or Regiment - With Bronze Star).	
			No. 223825 Sergt. D. BRADFORD, ... Attached, 120th Infy. Bde. Headquarters. " 107009 Sergt. C.P. PETTINGER, D.C.M., 40th Divisional Signal Coy. " 47080 Sergt. E. MEARDON, ... 10th Bn. K.O.S.B. " 47411 Corpl. H. LAMBLEY, ... 10th Bn. K.O.S.B.	
	9th.		Complete Course, comprising the following subjects was started at Brigade Commercial School :- Shorthand - Book-keeping - Business Routine - Commercial Arithmetic - Geography - - French. G.O.C. inspected one Company of each Battalion in Marching Order.	
	10th.		Practice Ceremonial Parade of 3 Infantry Brigades of the 40th Division, held at NECHIN. Brigadier General The Hon. W.P. HORE-RUTHVEN, C.M.G., D.S.O. in Command.	
	11th		G.O.C. inspected billets of 10th Bn. K.O.S.B.	
	12th		G.O.C. inspected billets of 15th Bn. K.O.Y.L.I.	
	13th.		G.O.C. inspected one Company of 15th Bn. K.O.Y.L.I., and 11th Bn. Cameron Highrs. in Marching Order.	

D. D. & L., London, E.C.
(A8001) Wt. W1771/M2031 750,000 5/17 Sch. 52 Forms/C2118/14

Instructions regarding War Diaries and Intelligence Summaries are contained in F. S. Regs., Part II. and the Staff Manual respectively. Title pages will be prepared in manuscript.

WAR DIARY
or
INTELLIGENCE SUMMARY.
(Erase heading not required.)

VOLUME XXXI.
DECEMBER, 1918.

Army Form C. 2118.

Headquarters,
120th Infantry Brigade.

Place	Date	Hour	Summary of Events and Information	Remarks and references to Appendices
LANNOY.	13th.		2/Lieut. A. BARROWCLIFFE, 10th Bn. K.O.S.B. came in first in the Divisional Cross Country Race.	TWS
	14th.		Divnl. Ceremonial Parade cancelled owing to wet weather. Divnl. General held a conference at Brigade Hd. Qrs. at which G.O.Cs and C.Os. of 120th and 121st Infantry Brigades attended. The following subjects were discussed:- (a). Behaviour of Officers and Other Ranks at LILLE. (b). Demobilization Scheme (c). Baths at LANNOY.	TWS
	17th.		XV Corps Commander inspected the 3 Infantry Brigades at NECHIN. He complimented the Troops on their smart appearance and March Past.	TWS
	18th.		Hd. Qrs. and 2 Companies 11th Bn. Cameron Highrs moved from ~~XXXXX~~ NECHIN to LANNOY.	TWS
	19th.		Remaining 2 Companies of 11th Bn. Cam. Highrs. moved to LANNOY. 10th Bn. K.O.S.B. beat R.A.M.C. in Semi-final Of Divisional Association Football.	TWS
	21st.		Conference at Brigade Hd. Qrs, at which C.Os. and Ajutants attended. G.O.C. discussed points raised at a conference which he had attended at Div. Hd. Qrs on 19th. Dec. Copy of notes attached.	TWS Appendix I
	23rd.		Lt-Colonel T.W.T. ISAAC, 15th Bn. K.O.Y.L.I. assumed Command of the Brigade during temporary absence of G.O.C. on leave to Germany.	TWS
	24th.		Personnel of Brigade Agricultural Coy. and detachments away from units rejoined for Christmas.	TWS
	25th, 26th.		Holidays.	
	28th.		Captain T.W. HUCKER, A/Staff Captain. and Captain D. McL. OMAN, B.I.O. mentioned in despatches.	TWS

D. D. & L., London, E.C. (A8001) Wt. W1771/M2031 750,000 5/17 Sch. 52 Forms/C2118/14

Instructions regarding War Diaries and Intelligence Summaries are contained in F. S. Regs., Part II, and the Staff Manual respectively. Title pages will be prepared in manuscript.

WAR DIARY
or
INTELLIGENCE SUMMARY.
(*Erase heading not required.*)

VOLUME XXXI.
DECEMBER, 1919.

Headquarters
120th Infantry Brigade.

Army Form C. 2118.

Page 3.

Place	Date	Hour	Summary of Events and Information	Remarks and references to Appendices
LANNOY.	30th		Divnl. Commander met Battalion Commanders at Brigade Hd.Qrs. as he wished to ask them if they had any question to discuss.	TKS
			Confidential reports on Officers forwarded to Division.	
			10th Bn. K.O.S.B. beat 178th Brigade R.F.A. in Final of Divisional Association Football.	TKS
	31st.		G. O. C. returns from Germany.	

W. Ruttner Brigadier General,
Commanding, 120th Infantry Brigade.

A6945 Wt. W11422/M1160 35,000 12/16 D. D. & L. Forms/C./2118/14.

~~War Diary~~ Appendix I

40th Div. No. 27/7 (G).

CONFIDENTIAL.

HEADQUARTERS, 120th INFANTRY BRIGADE. No. 1M/40V Date

NOTES on CONFERENCE,
HELD at 40th DIVISIONAL HEAD QUARTERS.
19th DECEMBER, 1918.

1. ANNUAL INSPECTION.

Divisional Commander wishes inspections to be carried out in all formations, with a view to ensuring the efficiency of internal economy.

The Divisional Commander expressed the intention of himself inspecting one Brigade of Artillery and one Battalion per Infantry Brigade, on the following dates :-

Artillery ...	January 2nd. 1919.
119th Inf.Bde..	January 3rd. 1919.
120th Inf. Bde.	January 4th. 1919.
121st Inf. Bde.	January 5th. 1919.

Brigadiers to arrange programmes, on the principle that Orderly Room, Books, Billets and Dinners were to be seen, and each Company would be inspected separately, (e.g.) - one to show arms, another to lay out their kits etc.,

2. CONFIDENTIAL REPORTS.

Details of the system of rendering Confidential Reports were explained by the D.A.A.G.,

3. COMPLAINTS.

Divisional Commander instructed Brigadiers when carrying out Annual Inspections to ask on the Battalion Parades if any man has a complaint to make, and expressed the intention of himself doing so when inspecting units. (Vide para 129 K.R.)

4. BILLETS.

Men's comfort in Billets was discussed. Shortage of fuel was stated to be the greatest difficulty, this was generally attributed to transport difficulties, as supply is adequate.

D.A.Q.M.G., was instructed to take steps to provide extra transport, if possible.

5. DAMAGE TO BUILDINGS AT WAMBRECHIES.

The C.R.A., reported that action had been taken to prevent any further damage being done to hutments at WAMBRECHIES.

6. TRAINING.

The question of smartness, saluting and soldierly bearing was discussed. The Divisional Commander is satisfied that there is no falling off in this respect, and that the standard at present is high.

7. EDUCATION.

No new points were raised with regard to Education.

A case was brought up where the Education Officer of the Corps had written to 3 officers of the 120th Infantry Brigade direct offering them posts at Corps Schools. The Divisional Commander stated that the matter had been gone into with Corps.

8. AGRICULTURE.

8. AGRICULTURE.

The question was discussed as to whether Agricultural Companies were doing a full day's work, and decided in the affirmative.

9. RECREATION.

(a) Amusements for the men were reported as running well.

(b) Suggestions were made for the circulation of Divisional and other TROUPES, the Divisional Commander said that there was a strong feeling against this in other Divisions.

(c) Race Meetings are not to be held, but there is no objection to other mounted sports.

(d) The possibility of having a point-to-point race meeting later on over the Course used for the Cross-Country Run was brought up. General Staff were instructed to go into the question.

10. The attitude of Officers was discussed,- a closer personal touch between platoon commanders and their men was suggested.

11. CLIPPING of HORSES.

It was pointed out that though they were under cover now, a considerable number of horses might yet have to be turned out to stand in the open. The question of clipping was left to the discretion of Brigadiers.

12. LOSS of GOVERNMENT BICYCLES.

Divisional Commander pointed out that the loss of Government Bicycles had become a scandal, and that C.Os. must put a stop to it.
A number of suggestions were made, to assist in preventing a continuance of the practice.

13. LEAKAGE of RATIONS.

It was reported that a leakage of rations was suspected. Quartermasters or (in units without one) Q.M.Sergts are to attend every day at Refilling Point to draw rations of their units.

14. BUSSES.

The Busses allotted to take personnel on trips to places of interest were reported as most unreliable.
It was decided to use these Busses within the Divisional Area only in future.

15. PEACE HONOURS LIST.

The small allotment for the Peace Honours List was commented on and the impossibility of any increase noted.

16. BATHS, ETC.,

The question of Baths & Clean Clothing was discussed, and reported to be gradually becoming satisfactory.
The Baths Officer has been instructed to keep constant supervision over the Baths in the Divisional Area.

17. CHRISTMAS DINNERS.

17. CHRISTMAS DINNERS.

The provision of Men's Christmas Dinners was discussed.
It was proposed that the Division should do something in the way of entertaining the children of ROUBAIX. D.A.Q.M.G., was instructed to go into the matter.

18. LEAVE.

The Divisional Commander ruled that leave might be granted to C.Os. provided they were eligible, irrespective of their place on the Battalion Leave Roster as was found convenient at the discretion of Brigadiers.

[signature]

19-12-18.

Major,
General Staff, 40th Division.

O.

17. CHRISTMAS DINNERS.

The provision of Men's Christmas Dinners was discussed.
It was proposed that the Division should do something in the way of entertaining the children of ROUBAIX. D.A.Q.M.G., was instructed to go into the matter.

18. LEAVE.

The Divisional Commander ruled that leave might be granted to C.Os. provided they were eligible, irrespective of their place on the Battalion Leave Roster as was found convenient at the discretion of Brigadiers.

[signature]
Major,
General Staff, 40th Division.

19-12-18.

O.

ORIGINAL

Instructions regarding War Diaries and Intelligence Summaries are contained in F. S. Regs., Part II. and the Staff Manual respectively. Title pages will be prepared in manuscript.

1.

WAR DIARY

~~INTELLIGENCE SUMMARY.~~

(Erase heading not required.)

VOLUME XXXII
JANUARY, 1919.

Army Form C. 2118.

Headquarters,
120th Infantry Brigade.

Vol 32

Place	Date	Hour	Summary of Events and Information	Remarks and references to Appendices
LANNOY.	1st		Holiday.	JMB.
	2nd		G.O.C. inspected billets and books of 15th Bn. K.O.Y.L.I. and discussed Organization with Battalion Commanders.	JMB.
	3rd		G.O.C. inspected billets and books of 11th Bn. Cam. Highrs. and discussed Organization with Battalion Commander.	JMB.
	4th		G.O.C., 40th Division inspected 15th Bn. K.O.Y.L.I.	JMB.
	7th		G.O.C. inspected billets and books of 10th Bn. K.O.S.B. and discussed organization with Battalion Commander.	JMB.
	8th		Conference at Brigade Headquarters at which C.Os. and Adjutants attended. G.O.C. explained Ceremonial of Consecration and Presentation of Colours. Copy of procedure attached	Appx I JMB.
	10th		G.O.C. attends Conference with Corps Commander at Divisional Headquarters when questions of Administration and Organization were discussed. Captain T.KNOX-SHAW M.C. Acting Brigade Major and Captain T.W.HUCKER, Acting Staff Captain awarded CROIX DE GUERRE.	JMB.
	13/18th		Parade held for practice of Ceremonial Drill for Presentation of Colours to Battalions.	JMB.
	20th		Ceremonial Parade held for Consecration and Presentation of Colours to Battalions. Colours presented by Corps Commander, Lieut-General Sir BEAUVOIR de LISLE, K.C.B. D.S.O. Corps Commander addressed the troops after presentation.	JMB.

A6945 Wt. W11422/M1160 350,000 12/16 D. D. & L. Forms/C./2118/14.

Instructions regarding War Diaries and Intelligence Summaries are contained in F. S. Regs., Part II. and the Staff Manual respectively. Title pages will be prepared in manuscript.

Army Form C. 2118.

VOLUME XXXll.
JANUARY, 1919.

2.

WAR DIARY
or
INTELLIGENCE SUMMARY.
(Erase heading not required.)

Headquarters,
120th Infantry Brigade.

Place	Date	Hour	Summary of Events and Information	Remarks and references to Appendices
LANNOY.	24th		Conference of Battalion and Company Commanders at Brigade Headquarters when G.O.C. went into matters concerning Demobilization and especially the needs of the Post-Bellum Army. It was arranged that opportunities should be taken by Company Commanders to impress upon the men the advantages of the Army as a Profession and an endeavour made to get men to re-enlist.	J.W.B.
	29th		Lieut-Colonel T.W.T.ISAAC, 15th Bn. K.O.Y.L.I. assumes Command of 120th Infantry Brigade during the absence of the G.O.C. on leave.	J.W.B.

T.W.T. Isaac Lieut-Colonel,
Commanding, 120th Infantry Brigade.

A6945 Wt. W11422/M1160 350,000 12/16 D. D. & L. Forms/C./2118/14.

Appendix I

CEREMONIAL TO BE ADOPTED AT RECEPTION AND CONSECRATION OF NEW COLOURS BY BATTALIONS OF 120TH INFANTRY BRIGADE.

1. 4 Guards will be formed - 1 from each Battalion.

No. 1 Guard will be a composite Guard divided into 3 Sections composed as follows :-

1 Captain or Major (15th Bn. K.O.Y L.I.)
1 Subaltern (10th Bn. K.O.S.B.)
1 Subaltern (15th Bn. K.O.Y.L.I.)
1 Subaltern (11th Bn. Cam. Highrs).
6 C.S.Ms. or C.Q.M.Ss. - 2 from each Battalion.
6 Sergeants - 2 from each Battalion.
20 ~~32~~ Other Ranks from each Battalion.

No. 2 Guard:-
10th Battn. K.O.S.B.
1 Captain or Major.
2 Subalterns.
2 C.S.Ms. or C.Q.M.Ss.
2 Sergeants.
60 ~~96~~ Other Ranks.

No. 3 Guard:-
15th Battn. K.O.Y.L.I.
1 Captain or Major.
2 Subalterns.
2 C.S.Ms. or C.Q.M.Ss.
2 Sergeants.
60 ~~96~~ Other Ranks.

No. 4 Guard:-
11th Battn. Cam. Highrs.
1 Captain or Major.
2 Subalterns.
2 C.S.Ms. or C.Q.M.Ss.
2 Sergeants.
60 ~~96~~ Other Ranks.

2. Major J.T.GRACIE, 11th Bn. Cameron Highlanders will be in Command of the Parade.

3. The Guards will be formed up on two sides of a square in accordance with attached plan 1.

4. The Captain of No. 1 Guard will be three paces in front of the centre of his Guard, for the position of remainder of Officers of No. 1 Guard see para 8.

5. Positions of Officers of Nos. 2, 3 and 4 Guards :- Captain 3 paces in front of second file from the right, Junior Subaltern 3 paces in front of centre file of Guard, Senior Subaltern 2 paces in front of second file from left of Guard. The C.S.Ms. will act as guides of Nos. 2, 3 and 4 Guards, the markers being found by Sergeants of these Guards.

Guides and markers will fix bayonets and conform to the movements of the men. Guides will be in line on right and left of front rank of each Guard, being covered by markers on right and left of rear rank.

6. Prior to the commencement of the Ceremony bayonets will be fixed and ranks opened by order of the Officer Commanding the Parade.

7. On arrival on the ground of Officer who is to present the Colours a General Salute will be given by order of O.C. Commanding Parade. The Guards will then be ordered to Order Arms and Stand at Ease.

8 ...

8. PRESENTATION AND CONSECRATION OF COLOURS.

A table to take the place of the pile of drums usual on these occasions will be provided under Brigade arrangements, the table will be placed as shown on Plan 1.

3 C.S.Ms. or C.Q.M.Ss. with the 3 Colours (cased) to be presented will be placed as shown on Plan 1. The three Colour parties consisting of the three Subalterns of No. 1 Guard, each with 2 C.S.Ms. from No. 1 Guard will be drawn up in line facing the table, 5 paces distant from it. On arrival of the Chaplain to carry out the Consecration Ceremony the Colours will be uncased by the C.S.Ms. in charge of them and will be placed against the table. The Consecration Ceremony will then be proceeded with and the Colours will, in turn, commencing with the 10th Bn. K.O.S.B. Colour, be handed, by an Officer to be detailed later, to the Officer who is presenting the Colour, this Officer will, in turn, hand the Colour to the Subaltern of the Colour party representing the Battalion, the Subaltern moving up to the table from his place in the Colour party to receive the Colour and stepping backwards to his place after the Colour has been presented to him, the Colour being at "The Carry".

As soon as all three Colours have been presented the Senior Subaltern of Colour party will order Colour parties to "About Turn - By the Right Quick March", the band playing a Quick March. As soon as the Colour parties are opposite position shown on Plan 2 he will give the command "Right Form - Forward by the Right" and when he arrives at position shown on Plan, Halt - About Turn - Right Dress - Order Arms. As soon as the movement from the table commences Guards will be called to Attention and ordered to Present Arms by the Officer Commanding the Parade and as soon as the Colours have arrived in their position and have Ordered Arms, the Guards will be ordered to "Slope Arms - Order Arms - Stand at Ease". The band will cease to play as soon as the Colour Parties have arrived at their position and have been ordered to Halt (i.e. before the Colour parties have turned about).

9. TROOPING THE COLOURS.

As soon as the Guards have been ordered to Stand at Ease the Officer Commanding Parade will give the command "Troop" upon which the Officer Commanding No. 1 Guard will give the command "No. 1 Guard - Attention - Slope Arms - Close Order March - By the Left Quick March", the band playing a Quick March. When the Guard arrives in such a position that when formed to the left the centre of the Guard will be opposite the centre Colour, he will give the command "Left Form - Forward by the Left", when he arrives 10 paces from the Colour parties he will give the command "Halt - Left Dress - Open Order March", the band ceasing to play on the word Halt. As soon as the dressing of No. 1 Guard has been completed the Officer Commanding Colour parties will give the command "Colour Parties - Slope Arms - By the Right Slow March" at the same time Officer Commanding No. 1 Guard will give the command "No. 1 Guard - Present Arms", and the band will play the Salute. Colour parties will move forward until they arrive three paces from the front rank of No. 1 Guard when the Officers carrying the Colours will mark time and turn about in slow time, the C.S.Ms. continuing their march forward in slow time passing through the ranks of No. 1 Guard, and turning about and forming a supernumery rank to No. 1 Guard.

10. As soon as the Colours and the C.S.Ms. have arrived in their places and halted, the Captain of No. 1 Guard will give the command "Slope Arms - By the Right Slow March", the band playing a slow march. When he arrives within 10 paces of No. 4 Guard he will give the command "Right Turn - Left Wheel". When the leading file of No. 1 Guard arrives in line with the left of No. 4 Guard he will again give the command "Left Wheel".

11 ...

11. As soon as the second "Left Wheel" is given the band will cease playing and the Officer Commanding the Parade will give the command "Guards - Attention - Slope Arms - Present Arms". After the Guards have Presented the band will recommence playing a slow march. No. 1 Guard will move in slow time along the line of Guards, the Officers of No. 1 Guard moving three paces in front of line of Officers, the front rank of No. 1 Guard moving between front and rear ranks of line of Guards, the rear rank of No. 1 Guard moving between the rear rank and supernumery rank, and the supernumery rank of No. 1 Guard in rear of supernumery rank of other Guards.

12. As soon as the left file of No. 1 Guard reaches its original position in the line, the band will cease to play and the Captain of No. 1 Guard will give the command "Guard - Halt - Left Turn - Left Dress" the Officers and men will take up their own dressing. The Captain will then give the command "No. 1 Guard - Present Arms", the Officer Commanding the Parade will then give the command "Guards - Slope Arms - Order Arms - Stand at Ease".

13. MARCH PAST.
Guards will then March Past in Quick Time ranks being closed and Close Column of Guards on No. 1 Guard being formed, and the four Guards being moved as a Battalion, to the Saluting Base in the usual manner in Marching Past, the Captain of No. 1 Guard will be four paces in front of centre of his Guard, the three Subalterns with the Colours being three paces in front of centre of their Sections. On the command "Eyes Right" the Colours will be let fly, being caught again on the command "Eyes Front".

14. On completion of March Past, Guards will be formed on their original alignment, No. 4 Guard being halted and turned about, the ranks of this Guard will thus be reversed. As soon as original positions have been reached ranks will be opened and General Salute will be given, Colours being lowered on the command "Present Arms" and raised on the command "Slope Arms".

15. Ranks will then be closed and the Guards will be marched off the ground in fours, bayonets still being fixed. In marching in fours the Colour of each Battalion will be at the head of its Section of No. 1 Guard with the C.S.M. as escort on each side of Officer carrying the Colour.

16. BAND.
The band will be in position as shown on Plan. As soon as No. 1 Guard advances and forms to the left, the band will move forward following up No. 1 Guard and halting when No. 1 Guard halts to receive the Colours and playing the General Salute when No. 1 Guard "Presents Arms". When No. 1 Guard (after receiving the Colours) moves off in slow time the band will follow No. 1 Guard playing a slow march when No. 1 Guard gets the command "Right Turn", the band will wheel in slow time to the left continuing to play. When the wheel is completed it will mark time until the leading file of No. 1 Guard arrives in line with the leading rank of the band when it will move forward in slow time keeping level with the movement of No. 1 Guard until No. 1 Guard arrives at its original place in line. The band will then cease to play, break into Quick Time and wheel into its original place as shown on Plan 1.

When Close Column is formed preparatory to the March Past the band will move out of position ready to play the Guards past, resuming its original position when the last Guard has passed.

Then the Guards march off the ground in fours the Band will play them off from its original position and will follow No. 4 Guard off the ground continuing to play.

=========================

PLAN 1.

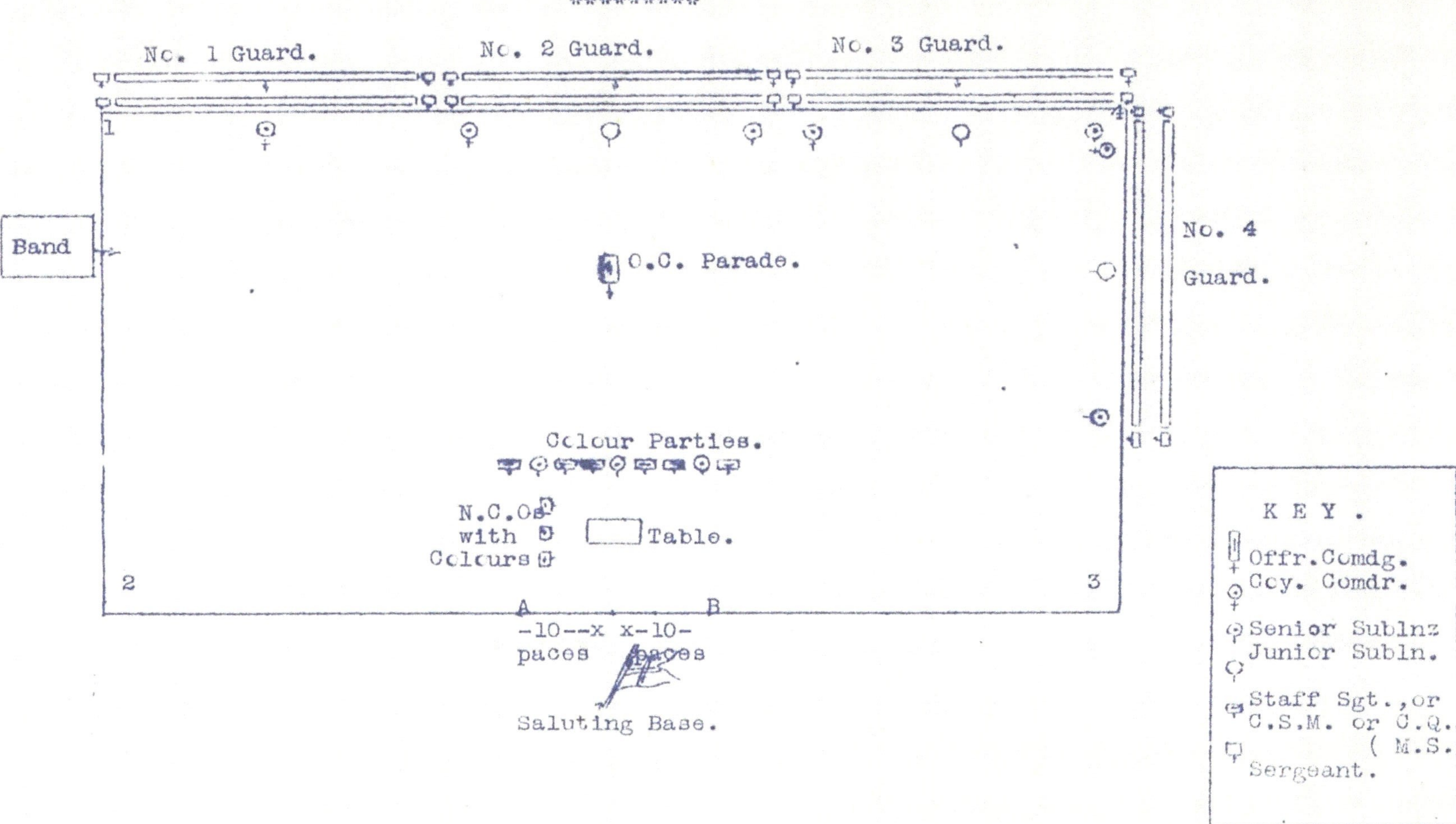
No. 1 Guard.
No. 2 Guard.
No. 3 Guard.
No. 4
Guard.
1
2
3
Band
O.C. Parade.
Colour Parties.
N.C.Os
with
Colours
Table.
A
B
-10--x x-10-
paces paces
Saluting Base.
KEY.
Offr.Comdg.
Coy. Comdr.
Senior Sublnz
Junior Subln.
Staff Sgt.,or
C.S.M. or C.Q.
(M.S.
Sergeant.

P L A N 11

Showing position of Colour parties after Colours have been presented.

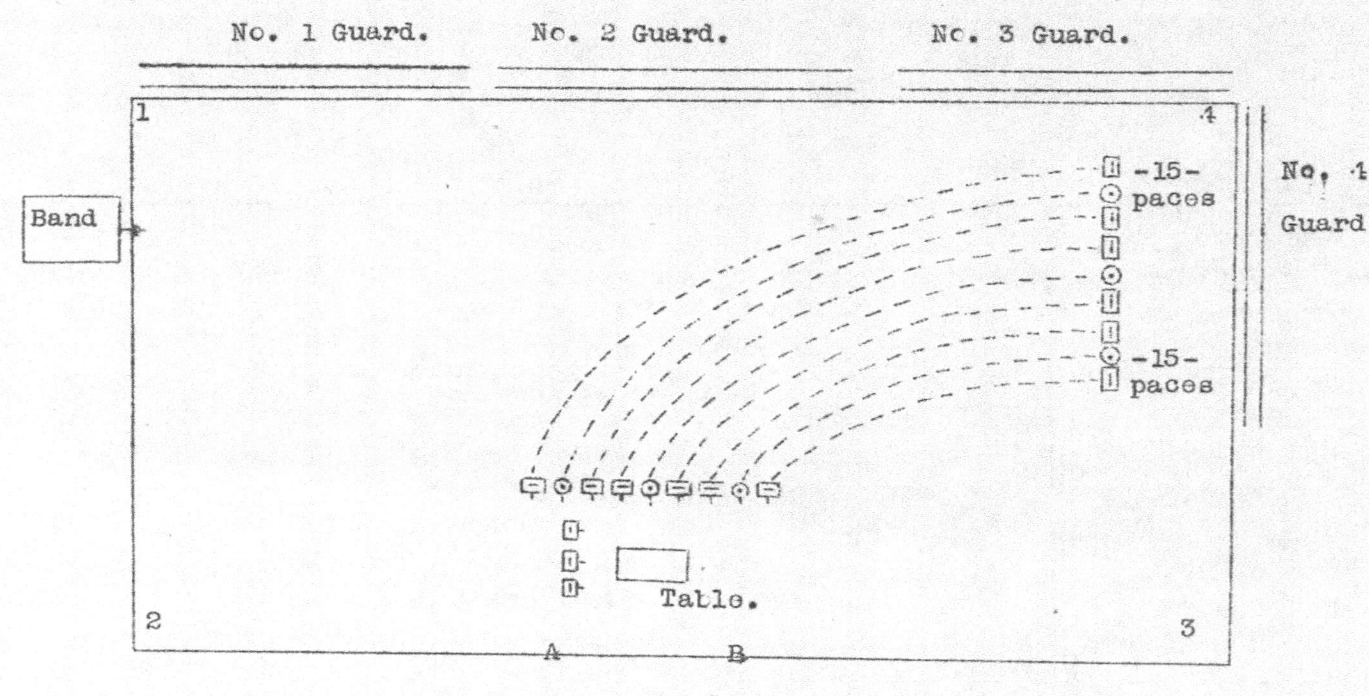

P L A N 111

Showing movement of No.1 Guard to point for receiving Colours.

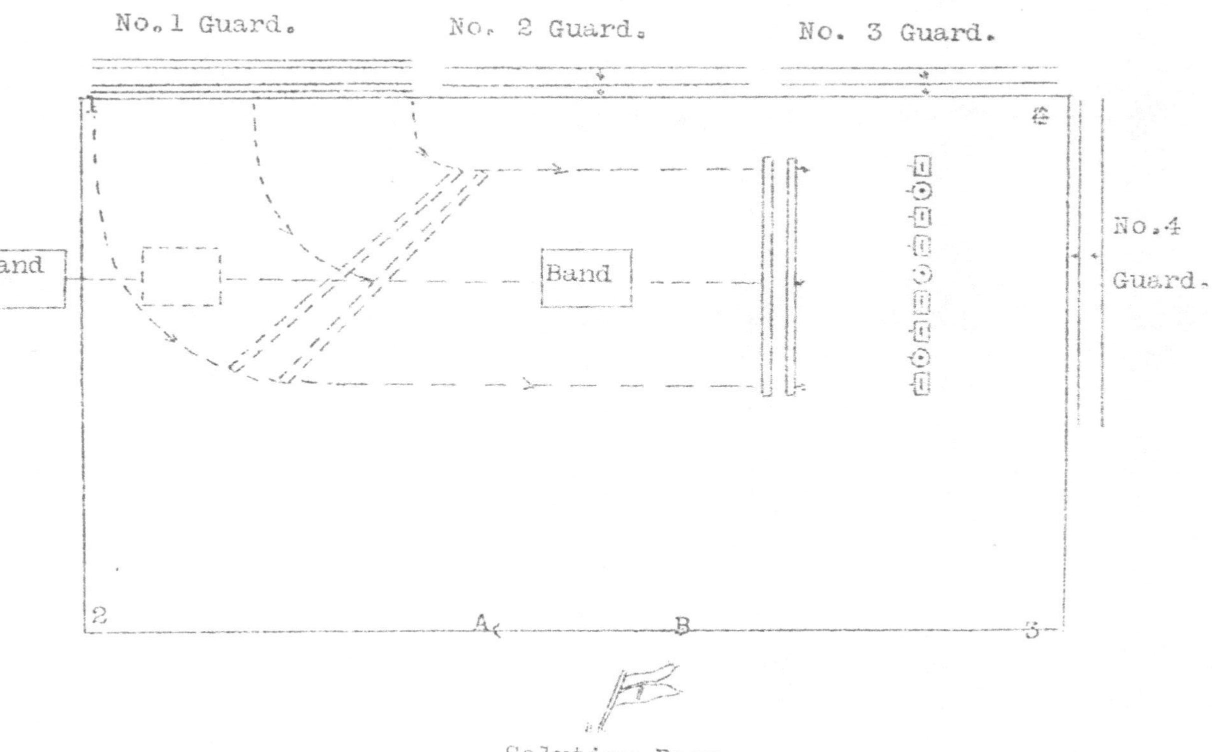

PLAN IV

****

Showing movement of No.3 Guard while
trooping the Colours.

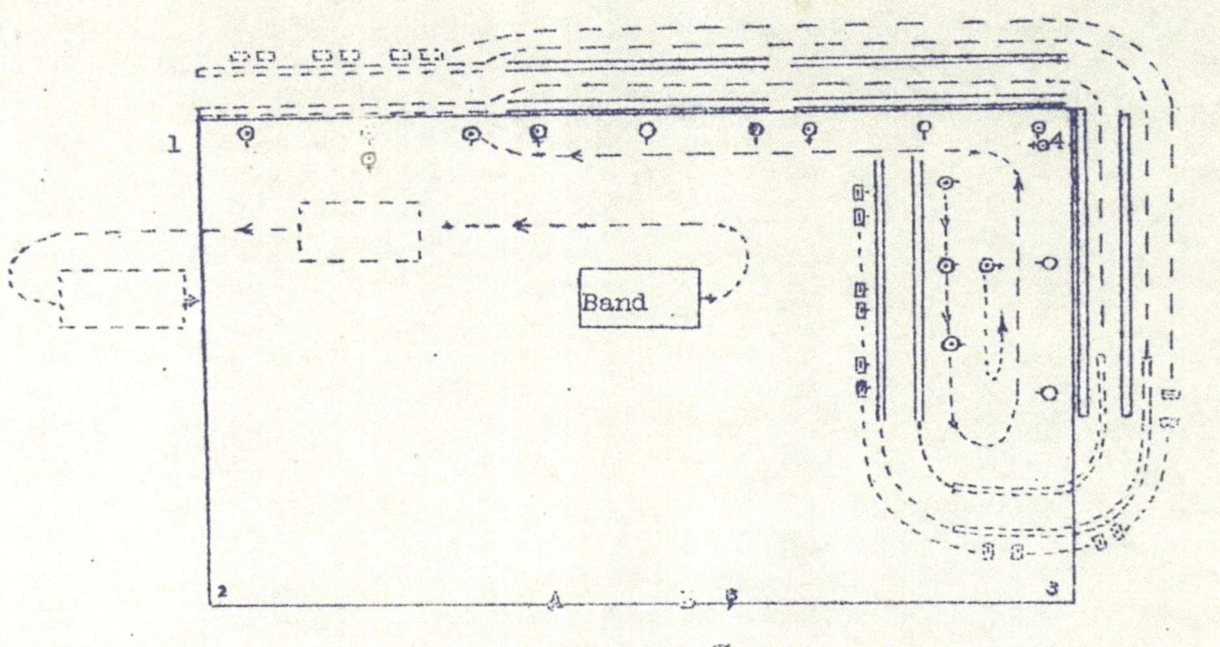

SECRET.

CONFIDENTIAL.

VB 33

WAR DIARY

FOR THE MONTH OF

FEBRUARY, 1919.

OF

HQRS 120th INFANTRY BRIGADE.

VOLUME XXXIII.

Instructions regarding War Diaries and Intelligence Summaries are contained in F. S. Regs., Part II, and the Staff Manual respectively. Title pages will be prepared in manuscript.

1.

WAR DIARY
or
~~INTELLIGENCE SUMMARY~~.
(Erase heading not required.)

VOLUME XXX111
February, 1919.
Headquarters,
120th Infantry Brigade.

Army Form C. 2118.

Place	Date	Hour	Summary of Events and Information	Remarks and references to Appendices
LANNOY	4		Guard sent to relieve guard of 3rd Canadian Division on dump at KAIN.	
	7		Men detailed for Cadre "B" in accordance with Army Order XlV of 29/1/19.	
	9		Wire received from G.H.Q. via 40th Divn. and 10th K.O.S.B. instructed to hold personnel in readiness to proceed to the 2nd Army.	
	11		G.O.C. attended Divisional Headquarters with reference to the case of 2/Lt. J.O.Banks, 10th K.O.S.B.	
	12		Lieut-Colonel Micholls assumed command of 11th Bn. Cam. Highlanders.	
	15		Brigadier General The Hon. W.P.Hore-Ruthven, C.M.G.,D.S.O., resumed command of the Brigade.	
			Major Eady, M.C., returned from Staff Course, Cambridge, and resumed duty as Brigade Major.	
	16		Thaw precautions adopted.	
	18		Lieut.-Colonel T.W.T. Isaac assumed command of the Brigade in the absence of the G.O.C. to U.K. to take command of a Guards Brigade.	
	20		120th Inf. Bde. Post Office amalgamated with 121st Inf. Bde. Post Office at LANNOY.	
			Thaw precautions removed. Major Eady M.C., proceeded to LILLE to take up temporary duty in A.A.G's Office, Fifth Army Headquarters.	
	21		Wire received from G.H.Q. via 40th Division ~~and~~ 11th Bn. Cam. Highrs instructed to hold personnel in readiness to proceed to the 2nd Army.	

A6945 Wt. W11422/M1160 350,000 12/16 D. D. & L. Forms/C./2118/14.

Army Form C. 2118.

Instructions regarding War Diaries and Intelligence Summaries are contained in F. S. Regs., Part II, and the Staff Manual respectively. Title pages will be prepared in manuscript.

WAR DIARY
or
~~INTELLIGENCE SUMMARY.~~
(Erase heading not required.)

2.

VOLUME XXX111
FEBRUARY, 1919.
Headquarters,
120th Infantry Brigade.

Place	Date	Hour	Summary of Events and Information	Remarks and references to Appendices
LANNOY	23		Brigade Cinema closed.	
	25		Lieut. and Q.M. NUNLEY, 15th Bn. K.O.Y.L.I., appointed Brigade Quartermaster in connection with the revised scheme of drawing rations.	
	27		Frontier guard at TOUFFLERS taken over from 15th K.O.Y.L.I. by 10th Bn. K.O.S.B.	
	28		Capt. D.McL, OMAN, B.I.O., and Lieut. Ford M.C.,R.E., B.S.Officer proceeded to U.K. for demobilization.	
		11.00	Capt. T.W.Hucker attended conference on Demobilization at Divisional Headquarters	

T.W.T. Isaac Lieut-Colonel,
Commanding 120th Infantry Brigade.

A6945 Wt. W11422/M1160 350,000 12/16 D. D. & L. Forms/C./2118/14.

www.ingramcontent.com/pod-product-compliance
Lightning Source LLC
Chambersburg PA
CBHW080813010526
44111CB00015B/2550